UNDERSTANDING LABOR LAW

UNDERSTANDING LABOR LAW

FIRST EDITION

RODERICK O. FORD, J.D., SPHR

Copyright © 2018 by Roderick O. Ford.

ISBN: Softcover   978-1-9845-4962-4
           eBook   978-1-9845-4992-1

All rights reserved. No part of this book may be reproduced or transmitted in any form or by any means, electronic or mechanical, including photocopying, recording, or by any information storage and retrieval system, without permission in writing from the copyright owner.

Any people depicted in stock imagery provided by Getty Images are models, and such images are being used for illustrative purposes only.
Certain stock imagery © Getty Images.

Print information available on the last page.

Rev. date: 08/31/2018

To order additional copies of this book, contact:
Xlibris
1-888-795-4274
www.Xlibris.com
Orders@Xlibris.com
784193

Contents

About the Author xi
Acknowledgement xiii
Introduction xv

Chapter 1   Bill Of Rights: The Landrum-Griffin Act Of 1959 1
Chapter 2   Lock-Outs, Strikes, Picketing and Boycotts 61
Chapter 3   Protected Concerted Activity 79
Chapter 4   Negotiating the Collective Bargaining Agreement 103
Chapter 5   Administration of the Collective Bargaining Agreement 121
Chapter 6   Federal Anti-Discrimination Laws and the
            Collective Bargaining Agreement 143
Chapter 7   Union's Duty of Fair Representation 244

Appendix A   Directory of H.R. and Employment Law
             Training Centers 263
Appendix B   Labor Law Digest 267

Author and Editor-in-Chief
Roderick O. Ford, Esq.
Ford & Associates, LLC
Tampa, Florida 33605

A Member of *The Florida Bar*
And
The Human Resources Certification Institute

2018

Special Dedication to

The
University of Illinois College of Law
at Urbana-Champaign

About the Author

Roderick O. Ford is the principal and founder of the employment law firm of Ford & Associates, LLC in Tampa, Florida, and serves as labor and employment Of Counsel to the Porter Law Firm in Stuart Florida. Mr. Ford earned his bachelor of arts (B.A.) degree from Morgan State University and his juris doctor (J.D.) degree from the University of Illinois at Urbana-Champaign. He holds the professional designation of Senior Professional in Human Resources (SPHR) from the Human Resources Certification Institute, as well as a graduate certificate in human resources leadership from Cornell University's School of Industrial and Labor Relations. Mr. Ford represents individual consumers and aggrieved workers before state and federal courts and administrative agencies. His law practice also includes human resources risk management for churches, non-profit organizations, and small businesses. In 2016-17, Mr. Ford was nominated to membership in *Lawyers of Distinction* and in *Best Attorneys of America*.

Acknowledgement

I owe much to various bar leaders, university professors, law practitioners, and human resources professionals from throughout the United States. Many of these men and women were conveniently made accessible to me under the umbrella of four great organizations: the Labor and Employment Law Section of the Florida Bar; the Labor and Employment Relations Association (LERA), which is housed on the campus of the University of Illinois at Urbana-Champaign; the Executive Education Program at Michigan State University's School of Human Resources and Labor Relations; and e-Cornell, which is an on-line division of Cornel University's School of Labor and Industrial Relations. I am also very pleased that two landmark publications within the field of labor law, upon which much of the material in this book was derived, were authored by a former and a current tenured professor at the University of Illinois College of Law: *NLRA Rights in the Nonunion Workplace* by Professor Kenneth T. Lopatka and *Basic Text on Labor Law: Unionization and Collective Bargaining* by Professor Matthew W. Finkin. Finally, I am significantly indebted to the law librarians at the James J. Lunsford Law Library in Tampa, Florida.

Introduction

THE IMPORTANCE OF AMERICAN LABOR LAW

The subject of labor law has been of great interest to me ever since the early 1990s, because it complimented my undergraduate liberal arts training in sociology, economics, history, and political science. Even then, I was early and largely interested in the plight of the working classes. But several years later, after I became a practicing attorney, I drifted away from an interest in organized labor toward traditional American employment law and assisting individual workers—especially civil rights lawsuits that were cognizable under Title VII of the Civil Rights Act of 1964. I then concluded that employment law seemed to have more practical significance for the communities of color which I represented before state and federal administrative agencies and courts. But my overemphasis on traditional American employment law was both a mistake and an unfortunate development in my early career as a labor and employment attorney. For I had relegated the entire field of American labor law to a group of federal statutes that I had misperceived as only applicable to labor unions and to union members. I had no idea that this landmark American labor legislation also significantly regulated non-unionized American workers as well, and that I could utilize this federal labor legislation to significantly assist non-unionized workers who worked in non-unionized workplaces.

Over the years, through trial and error, I learned that the National Labor Relations Board provides to all American workers—and not just labor unions and union members — a potent and powerful weapon to address a large variety of workplace grievances that relate to the terms, conditions, and privileges of employment. Workplace wrongs which may not present a viable charge of discrimination under most state or federal laws, such as Title VII, may nevertheless still pose a very strong labor grievance under the National Labor Relations Act, so long as that labor grievance affects two or more workers who are coordinating their efforts "for other mutual aid and protection" and engaged in "protected concerted activity."

Hence, knowledge of federal labor law certainly made me a more well-rounded and effective employment litigation attorney. This publication is thus designed primarily to help various professionals within the field of employment law and human resources to attain a much better grasp and understanding of the specialized area of American labor law. The popular cliché among American human resources professionals and employment lawyers is that "traditional labor law" is growing less relevant than "traditional employment law," due to the rapid decline in labor unions over the past several decades. But this cliché is a tragic misconception of federal employment and labor legislation, because American "employment law" is really integrally interwoven in on American "labor law." In order to effectively manage employment claims and litigation, one must have a thorough understanding of labor law, and vice versa.

Indeed, federal labor legislation came first, beginning in the early 1930s during the New Deal era. The American labor movement was an outgrowth of economic development since the end of the U.S. Civil War (1861-1865), during the period 1870s-1880s. The United States became less agrarian and more urbanized and industrialized; and millions of American workers became more and more concentrated into urban slums, and left to fend for themselves.

Early efforts at labor organization occurred during the 1870s and 1880s, but both state and federal legislatures routinely crushed these early labor movements, and labeled them to be criminal conspiracies against free trade. In 1890, Congress enacted the Sherman Antitrust Act of 1890 which continued this prevailing trend. This federal legislation was designed to curtail business monopolies and restraints on trade, but the state and federal courts routinely applied the language of the Sherman Antitrust Act to prevent the formation of trade unions.

Beginning in the early 1900s, support for America's labor unions continued to grow, because the plight of American workers in almost every state and in almost every industry was grim and dire. In 1926, Congress enacted the landmark Railway Labor Act, which dealt with many pressing labor problems within the railroad and transportation industries. In 1932, Congress enacted the Norris-LaGuardia Act, which removed the power of state and federal courts to enjoin labor organizing and labor unions. In 1935, Congress enacted the National Labor Relations Act (NLRA), which extended many of the provisions found in the Railway Labor Act of 1926 to every American industry outside of the transportation industry. The NLRA gave workers the right to engage in various union organizing activities and to be free from reprisal. For the next dozen years, the American labor movement grew influential and the plight of the American worker steadily increased up through the end of the World War II period.

At the end of World War II, the problem of internal union corruption became quite obvious, as union power and influence spread. In 1947, Congress enacted the Labor Management Relations Act (the "Taft-Hartley Act of 1947") in order to curtail various abuses with labor unions and to hold the accountable to individual union members. And in 1959, Congress enacted the Labor Management Reporting and Disclosure Act (the "Landrum-Griffin Act of 1959") in order to comprehensively set forth labor's "Bill of Rights."

All of the above-mentioned federal labor laws continue in operation today, and, taken together, they form the foundation of all American labor and employment legislation, including the Fair Labor Standards Act of 1938, Title VII of the Civil Rights Act of 1964, the Americans with Disabilities Act of 1990, the Age Discrimination in Employment Act, the Family and Medical Leave Act of 1993, and a host of other federal employment laws.

For the aforementioned reasons, *Understanding Labor Law* is the book that I wished I had in my hands twenty years ago, when I was launching my career as a labor and employment attorney. This book takes the entire complex field of American labor law and condenses it to seven, easily readable chapters.

The seven chapters in this book are designed so that the reader can become familiar with the most important labor-law terminology, without becoming bogged down into irrelevant details. (Over the years, I have found that most labor-law publications lack this balance in the presentation of labor law subjects.) The seven chapters in this book are also arranged in a logical sequence that I believe will be most suitable for grasping the material. This chapter-sequence should allow anyone, especially those who are relatively new to the field of labor law, to steadily build their labor-law knowledge upon the information presented in the previous chapters.

The first chapter starts off our discussion with a look at labor's "Bill of Rights," and the remaining chapters steadily builds from that very firm foundation. The second chapter looks at lock-outs, strikes, picketing and boycotts; and the second chapter analyzes "protected concerted activity" and activities that constitute "for other mutual aid and protection." In Chapters four, five, and six, we turn our attention to the negotiation phase and the administration phase of the collective bargaining agreement. In these chapters, we look at issues such as the duty of good faith, labor grievance procedures, labor arbitration, unfair-labor- practice (UPL) procedures before the National Labor Relations Board, and unfair employment practices that relate to other federal statutes such as Title VII of the Civil Rights Act of 1964. And finally, in Chapter seven, we close the book with a detailed discussion on the important union duty of fair representation, discussing its historical development in the case of *Steele v. Louisville & N.R. Co.* (1944); and analyzing its current application to federal labor law and policy.

In addition, as this is the companion book to *Understanding Employment Law* (First Edition), this publication is also designed to supplement the various certification review materials which help to prepare men and women for certification examinations in the field of human resources management, labor relations, and employment law. It is multidisciplinary in scope, covering strategic human resources management principles as well as standard American labor and employment jurisprudence. Many human resources practitioners who are studying for one of the several **HRCI** or **SHRM** certification examinations should also find this book to be a very practical and useful supplement to their certification review materials—particularly the **PHR** or **SPHR** review materials. This book thoroughly covers the legal aspects of the **HRCI** and the **SHRM** body of knowledges. Although it is not designed to be a substitute for any of the official certification review materials published by **HRCI** or **SHRM**, the author believes that this book should be read as a very critical and important supplement in preparation for any one of the various **HRCI** or **SHRM** certification examinations. The reason is that those examinations are pragmatic and experiential-based, and the materials presented in this book are written from the perspective of practical experience in the field of labor and employment law and human resources management.

Finally, this book is also designed for rank-and-file employees and workers who need to know what their workplace rights are. Union stewards, labor and industrial chaplains, and worker advocates will find this book to be an indispensable guide as they seek to assist workers. As an experienced labor and employment attorney, the author has presented the material in this book with the common person in mind. The materials are designed for individuals who are not lawyers or experienced human resources practitioners, but who need to attain a working knowledge of labor and employment law within a very short period of time. For example, this book should be very helpful for individuals who are about to face a disciplinary proceeding and need a quick reference guide to understand their rights; or for individuals whose rights under a collective bargaining agreement has been violated and who need to understand what steps to take in order to hold the employer or the labor union accountable.

In closing, I would be remiss if I did not point out that this is the first edition of a self-published work whose general outline and themes were extracted largely from the author's law practice (i.e., news articles, demand letters, appellate briefs, memoranda of law, and motion-hearing notes), I beg all of my readers' forgiveness for any foibles and mistakes contained herein. This book is in essence the author's "white papers" which have been compiled over the course of several years and presented here for the first time to the general public. This publication is an evolving, collaborative, and on-going research project.

Roderick O. Ford
Tampa, FL
August 20, 2018

Chapter One

BILL OF RIGHTS:
THE LANDRUM-GRIFFIN ACT OF 1959

§ 1.01 Introduction 2

§ 1.02 Landrum-Griffin Act of 1959 6

§ 1.03 Title I- Bill of Rights 7

§ 1.04 Title II- Reporting and Disclosure 12

§ 1.05 Title III- Trusteeships 27

§ 1.06 Title IV—Elections 32

§ 1.07 Title V—Limitations on Union Officials 40

§ 1.08 Title VI— Miscellaneous Provisions 52

§ 1.09 Strategic Human Resources and Risk Management 58

§ 1.10 Conclusion 58

§ 1.01 Introduction

Industrial peace and the peaceful settlement of conflict between employees and employers are the goals of federal labor legislation in the United States.[1] Federal labor legislation is not designed to provide favor towards employees or to disadvantage employers. Instead, this legislation is designed to promote industrial peaceful, economic efficiency, and conflict resolution between employees and employers.[2] For this reason, federal labor legislation is enacted pursuant to the Commerce Clause of the United States Constitution.[3]

In addition to federal labor legislation, most of the individual fifty states within the United States have also enacted various forms of state labor legislation, pursuant to their inherent right of "police power." This state labor legislation has similar or the same goals of federal labor legislation.[4] These state laws may not contradict or supplant federal labor legislation.[5] In other words, federal preemption prohibits state laws from regulating subject matter which Congress has intended to regulate without state interference. But state legislation may address broader concerns not found in federal labor legislation. State labor legislation should also be considered to include state common law of contracts, torts, and agency, together with statutory laws such as workers' compensation and unemployment compensation statutes. For example, the common law of trusts has been incorporated into the Labor-Management Reporting and Disclosure Act of 1959 (i.e., the Landrum-Griffin Act of 1959), Title III ("Trusteeships") and Title V ("Safeguards for Labor Organizations"). Even labor unions cannot function properly without ascertaining an adequate working knowledge of state or federal employment laws, such as Title VII of the 1964 Civil Rights Act, 42 U.S.C. §§ 1981 and 1983, the Americans With Disabilities Act of 1990, the Family and Medical Leave Act of 1993, the Employee Retirement Income Security Act, the Age Discrimination in Employment Act, and the Fair Labor Standards Act. Taken together, both state and federal labor policy promote natural law, natural justice, and human

---

[1] 51 *Corpus Juris Secundum*, Labor Relations § 1.

[2] Ibid.

[3] Ibid, § 2.

[4] Ibid, § 3.

[5] Ibid.

rights.[6] The American labor movement began during the late 19th century before any of the above-referenced state or federal employment laws were ever enacted; and thus it is safe to conclude that these laws would not have been enacted without an active and influential American labor movement. Today, the weakening of the American labor movement is due in large measure to its great success in causing both the U.S. Congress and state legislatures to enact health-and-safety laws, workers compensation laws, anti-discrimination laws, and disability laws, all of which provided greater rights to individual workers and thereby somewhat diminished the absolute necessity of forming labor unions in order to protect those interests. On the other hand, experience now teaches that individual workers often encounter tremendous difficulty in enforcing their rights. These workers, who are often rebuffed by the state and federal courts, find even their most basic employment rights nullified through the high expense of legal advocacy and litigation, such that the American labor movement may, in the future, discover that its greatest contribution can be made through the vindication of individual employee rights under federal antidiscrimination legislation. The American labor movement, in the future, may be called upon to shift its focus to addressing the problem of employment law, individual employee rights, and employment litigation as a whole. In other words, the American labor movement of the future may be called upon to re-enter the field of enforcing individual worker rights, in order to maintain its relevancy.

In order for the American labor movement to turn the proverbial corner towards addressing the broader needs of individual workers, who are today more and more unorganized and non-unionized, this movement will need to conceptualize itself as the bulwark against the deprivation of natural law and natural justice within the non-unionized American workplace. That

---

[6] "Legislative enactments dealing with relations between employer and employees and encouraging the peaceful settlement of labor disputes by collective bargaining are remedial in nature and should be broadly and liberally construed; and this rule has been appliwwed in the construction of the National Labor Relations Act and related federal statutes, the Railway Labor Act, and the state statutes of a similar nature. Such statutes are to be construed and applied to effectuate their objectives, such as preventing of industrial strife and to harmonize the procedure with the characteristics of our system of government wherein the law is supreme. The statute should not be interpreted or applied so as to deny to employees the rights provided by the act or to restrict the exercise of those rights, and the right of free speech guaranteed by the First Amendment and by provision of the statute should not be defeated by a narrow or constrained construction." Ibid, § 28.

is to say, the inherent dignity of human beings should remain at the center of every employer-employee relationship, thus guaranteeing industrial due process and the "Seven Principles of Just Cause"[7] for non-unionized, unorganized workers.

> As a general rule, employers and employees have correlative rights, and labor and capital, employer and employee, stand on the same basis before the court with respect to legal and constitutional rights.
>
> The right to labor and the right to carry on [a] business are embraced within the concepts of 'liberty' and 'property,' interference with which is unlawful unless justification is shown; and [an] employer has a property interest in the services of his employee and an employee has a property interest in his employment.
>
> Subject to some exceptions, an employer and employee may contract as they see fit, and the right to sever relations is likewise mutual. Similarly, subject to contractual and statutory provisions, a worker has the right to work for or refuse to work for anyone he sees fit, and an employer has the right to hire and discharge as he sees fit.
>
> An employer has the right to manage his business and to exercise all the prerogatives of management; he has the right to direct employees as to the tasks to be performed and the manner of performance.
>
> The right to work is the foundation on which rests the right to enjoy the blessing of life, liberty, and the pursuit of happiness, and every infringement of that right, by statute, decision, contract, rule or decree, must be carefully scrutinized and construed. However, no one has an unqualified right, inherent, statutory, or constitutional, to enter such employment as he chooses, and the right to work is subject to legislative restrictions.[8]

---

[7] See Chapter Five, "Administration of the Collective Bargaining Agreement."

[8] Ibid, § 6.

It goes without saying that the history of the American labor movement has its share of violence, corruption, crime, and bloodshed, thus resulting in the ultimate loss of labor rights (i.e., natural law, natural justice, and human rights) to the individual worker.[9] As a direct consequence of this history, Congress enacted two landmark, post-World War II labor laws in order to rectify the problem of corruption within labor unions and conspiratorial corruption between employers and union: the Taft-Hartley Act of 1947 and the Labor-Management Reporting and Disclosure Act of 1959 (i.e., the Landrum-Griffin Act of 1959). These statutes were enacted to regulate labor union activity and to proscribe "union unfair labor practices," such as[10]:

- Undue Coercion of employees (whether union members or nonunion members)
- Undue Coercion of employers (e.g., actions taken to force employers to take adverse employment actions against certain employees that the union does not like)
- Featherbedding (i.e., creating non-existent jobs or work for union members)
- Unlawful Secondary Boycotts and Unlawful Picketing
- Hot-Cargo Agreements (i.e., an agreement to cause the employer to cease doing business with a third party, simply because the union does not like that third party)
- Coercive Work-Assignments Disputes (this involves, e.g., the claims of rival unions for particular work within an employer's bargaining unit)
- Refusal to bargain in good faith with employers

For anyone new to American labor law or considering becoming a labor advocate for workers, I would initially refer them to the Landrum-Griffin Act of 1959. This law is "Labor's Bill of Rights," and it provides the student with a general overview of the American labor movement, the nature of worker-union-management conflict, and the issues the comprise labor union corruption and accountability. In addition, this law is also a reflection of problems and challenges of economic democracy. For these

---

[9] "By its plain terms, the NLRA confers rights only on employees, not on unions or their nonemployee organizers." 48 *Am Jur Second*, Labor and Labor Relations § 1.

[10] See, generally, 48A Am Jur Second, Labor and Labor Relations §§ 1689-1910.

reasons, an introduction to the Landrum-Griffin Act allows the student to have a bird's eye-view of what American labor law is all about, together with the very nature of the challenges and problems which it addresses. Various doctrines which we traditionally associate with federal constitutional law are directly applicable-- through the Landrum-Griffin Act of 1959-- to employers and labor unions.[11] Fundamental rights that are guaranteed not only by public law, but also by "natural law and natural justice," are preserved to American workers through the Landrum-Griffin Act of 1959.[12] "A trade union can employ no power as a means of oppression and injustice in respect of its members or deprive any of them, in the form of contractual surrender or otherwise, of their fundamental personal rights when the public interest will not be thereby served...."[13] And, the "labor union's right of self-government carries with it the right of each member thereof to participate in determinations and agreements directly affecting his livelihood and the terms and conditions on which he is bound to labor in the manner prescribed by the union's constitution."[14] Therefore, most labor grievances and conflict should always take into account the union's duties and obligations, together with the individual union member's rights, liberties, and privileges under the Landrum-Griffin Act of 1959.

This chapter thus provides an important overview and summation of each of the six titles within the Landrum-Griffin Act of 1959.[15]

§ 1.02 Landrum-Griffin Act of 1959

Following Congress' enactment of the National Labor Relations Act in 1935, together with other sweeping social legislation that was designed

---

[11] 51 *Corpus Juris Secundum*, Labor Relations § 68.

[12] Ibid.

[13] Ibid.

[14] Ibid.

[15] For additional reference, please also consult the affixed "Law Digest," which contains the following general listing of several United States Supreme Court cases: *Calhoun v. Harvey*, 379 U.S. 134 (1964); *United States v. Brown*, 381 U.S. 437 (1965); *Wirtz v. Local Union No. 125, Laborers' International Union of North America AFL-CIO*,
389 U.S. 477 (1968); *Trbovich v. UMW*, 404 U.S. 528 (1972); *Hall v. Cole*, 412 U.S. 1 (1973); *Local 3489, United Steel Workers v. Usery*, 429 U.S. 305 (1977); and, *Reed v. United Transportation Union*, 488 U.S. 319 (1989).

to protect America's most vulnerable citizens, a conservative, anti-union backlash overtook American politics. Beginning in the late 1940s and early 1950s, there was a powerful movement to curtail labor unions, labor leaders, and their authority, thus leading to the passage of the Labor-Management Relations Act ("Taft-Hartley Act") of 1947 and the Labor Management Reporting and Disclosure Act ("Landrum-Griffin Act") of 1959. Both of these federal statutes focused on curtailing the power of labor unions, and the perceived corruption within these labor unions. The Taft-Hartley Act of 1947 focused on curtailing unfair labor practices on the part of labor unions. Such unfair labor practices are stated in Section 8(5)(b) of the National Labor Relations Act. The Landrum-Griffin Act of 1959 provided specific protections for individual union members and afforded additional remedies against labor-union corruption. This law "was passed in 1959 to protect more fully the rights of union members, to curb abuses of union power, and to promote internal union democracy."[16] Collectively speaking, the various provisions of the Landrum-Griffin Act of 1959 constitute labor's "Bill of Rights."

§ 1.03 Title I- Bill of Rights

Title I of the Landrum-Griffin Act essentially codifies the First Amendment to the U.S. Constitution into federal labor legislation. Section 101(a)(1) provides union members with the right vote; the right to attend meetings; the right to participate in union governance; the right to freedom of speech; the right to fully express their views and opinions; the right to criticize union officials; the right to fair union dues and fair dues-collection procedures; the right to sue either the union or the employer; the right be a witness and to testify against a union; the right to have a copy of the collective bargaining agreement; and the right to due process before being expelled or suspended from union membership.[17] Lawsuits that are filed in court in order to remedy violations of this provision may be brought in the U.S. District Courts inside of the districts where the labor violation(s) occurred.

The text of Title I states:

---

[16] Robert J. Gelhaus and James Oldham, *Labor Law* (Chicago, IL: The Barbri Group, 2002), p. 232.

[17] Ibid., pp. 232-236.

TITLE I -- BILL OF RIGHTS OF MEMBERS OF LABOR ORGANIZATIONS

Bill of Rights

(29 U.S.C. 411)

SEC. 101. (a)(1) EQUAL RIGHTS.-- Every member of a labor organization shall have equal rights and privileges within such organization to nominate candidates, to vote in elections or referendums of the labor organization, to attend membership meetings and to participate in the deliberations and voting upon the business of such meetings, subject to reasonable rules and regulations in such organization's constitution and bylaws.

(2) FREEDOM OF SPEECH AND ASSEMBLY.-- Every member of any labor organization shall have the right to meet and assemble freely with other members; and to express any views, arguments, or opinions; and to express at meetings of the labor organization his views, upon candidates in an election of the labor organization or upon any business properly before the meeting, subject to the organization's established and reasonable rules pertaining to the conduct of meetings: *Provided,* That nothing herein shall be construed to impair the right of a labor organization to adopt and enforce reasonable rules as to the responsibility of every member toward the organization as an institution and to his refraining from conduct that would interfere with its performance of its legal or contractual obligations.

(3) DUES, INITIATION FEES, AND ASSESSMENTS.-- Except in the case of a federation of national or international labor organizations, the rates of dues and initiation fees payable by members of any labor organization in effect on

the date of enactment of this Act shall not be increased, and no general or special assessment shall be levied upon such members, except-

(A) in the case of a local organization, (i) by majority vote by secret ballot of the members in good standing voting at a general or special membership meeting, after reasonable notice of the intention to vote upon such question, or (ii) by majority vote of the members in good standing voting in a membership referendum conducted by secret ballot; or

(B) in the case of a labor organization, other than a local labor organization or a federation of national or international labor organizations, (i) by majority vote of the delegates voting at a regular convention, or at a special convention of such labor organization held upon not less than thirty days' written notice to the principal office of each local or constituent labor organization entitled to such notice, or (ii) by majority vote of the members in good standing of such labor organization voting in a membership referendum conducted by secret ballot, or (iii) by majority vote of the members of the executive board or similar governing body of such labor organization, pursuant to express authority contained in the constitution and bylaws of such labor organization: *Provided,* That such action on the part of the executive board or similar governing body shall be effective only until the next regular convention of such labor organization.

(4) **PROTECTION OF THE RIGHT TO SUE.**-- No labor organization shall limit the right of any member thereof to institute an action in any court, or in a proceeding before any administrative agency, irrespective of whether or not the labor organization or its officers are named as defendants or respondents in such action or proceeding, or the right of any member of a labor organization to appear as a witness

in any judicial, administrative, or legislative proceeding, or to petition any legislature or to communicate with any legislator: *Provided,* That any such member may be required to exhaust reasonable hearing procedures (but not to exceed a four-month lapse of time) within such organization, before instituting legal or administrative proceedings against such organizations or any officer thereof: *And provided further,* That no interested employer or employer association shall directly or indirectly finance, encourage, or participate in, except as a party, any such action, proceeding, appearance, or petition.

(5) SAFEGUARDS AGAINST IMPROPER DISCIPLINARY ACTION.-- No member of any labor organization may be fined, suspended, expelled, or otherwise disciplined except for nonpayment of dues by such organization or by any officer thereof unless such member has been (A) served with written specific charges; (B) given a reasonable time to prepare his defense; (C) afforded a full and fair hearing.

(b) Any provision of the constitution and bylaws of any labor organization which is inconsistent with the provisions of this section shall be of no force or effect.

Civil Enforcement

(29 U.S.C. 412)

SEC. 102. Any person whose rights secured by the provisions of this title have been infringed by any violation of this title may bring a civil action in a district court of the United States for such relief (including injunctions) as may be appropriate. Any such action against a labor organization shall be brought in the district court of the United States for the district where the alleged violation occurred, or where the principal office of such labor organization is located.

Retention of Existing Rights

(29 U.S.C. 413)

SEC. 103. Nothing contained in this title shall limit the rights and remedies of any member of a labor organization under any State or Federal law or before any court or other tribunal, or under the constitution and bylaws of any labor organization.

Right to Copies of Collective Bargaining Agreements

(29 U.S.C. 414)

SEC. 104. It shall be the duty of the secretary or corresponding principal officer of each labor organization, in the case of a local labor organization, to forward a copy of each collective bargaining agreement made by such labor organization with any employer to any employee who requests such a copy and whose rights as such employee are directly affected by such agreement, and in the case of a labor organization other than a local labor organization, to forward a copy of any such agreement to each constituent unit which has members directly affected by such agreement; and such officer shall maintain at the principal office of the labor organization of which he is an officer copies of any such agreement made or received by such labor organization, which copies shall be available for inspection by any member or by any employee whose rights are affected by such agreement. The provisions of section 210 shall be applicable in the enforcement of this section.

Information as to Act

(29 U.S.C. 415)

SEC. 105. Every labor organization shall inform its members concerning the provisions of this Act.

§ 1.04 Title II- Reporting and Disclosure

Title II of the Landrum-Griffin Act requires labor unions to maintain transparency in their dealings with employers and to fully disclose certain basic information to union members, such as:

1. The names of all union officers;
2. Procedures (various types);
3. Accounting statements (i.e., fiscal condition of the union);
4. Fiscal transactions between union officials or labor organizations and employers;
5. Fiscal transactions between union officials or labor organization and other entities with financial ties, joint operations, or affiliations with the employer.

More specifically, Section 202 of Title II requires labor organizations (i.e., labor unions) to adopt a constitution and bylaws for the organization. This means that labor unions cannot operate ad hoc or haphazardly, and must have some organizational form and structure which the general members and the public can look to, so as to ascertain whether its operations and functions are customary and legitimate.

Labor unions must also provide annual financial accounting to the U.S. Department of Labor. They must file "annual financial reports" with the Secretary of Labor. These reports much include items such as (a) assets and liabilities; (b) salaries of all union officers and employees; (b) fringe benefits provided to all union officers and employees; and (c) loans (whether direct or indirect) to union officers and employees). Unions must make this information available to all union members. Hence, a very important right which all union members have is the right to demand that labor unions turn over their annual financial accounting records. If a labor union balks at such requests, and forces the union members to seek legal counsel, then the union members should hire a lawyer, and file a lawsuit in federal court, or file an unfair labor practice charge with the National Labor Relations Board. Sec. 202 provides for the recovery of attorney's fees for the successful prosecution of such actions.

Section 202 also targets "corruption" of union officers. Many rank-and-file union members frequently complain, or express concerns about, union officers who are "in bed with the employer." Such concerns are not without precedent and are historic. For this reason, Congress enacted Section 202 to address corruption among union leaders, union officers, and high-level union executives. This section requires high-level union leadership to discuss with union members any financial transactions (including salaries, wages, stocks, bonds, mutual funds, etc., or anything of financial value) which they receive from every employer that has a collective bargaining agreement with the union, and from every employer from whom the union in engaged in a financial relationship. In addition, the section requires that any such financial transactions on the part of spouses or dependent children of such union leaders, officers, or executives must be similarly disclosed.

Employers also have disclosure obligations under Section 203 of this statute. Employers must annually disclose any payments, loans, money, salary, wages, benefits "or other thing of value" that it makes to any and all labor organizations (including to individual union officers, leaders, employees, officials, etc.).

What this means is that Sec. 202 and Sec. 203 require both labor unions and employers to annually report the same financial information to the U.S. Department of Labor. The rationale behind this policy is that if some financial transactions fall through the "disclosure" cracks, and inadvertently goes undisclosed by either union or employer, then it should more likely than not get disclosed by the party who is opposite of the non-disclosing party. Where both the union and the employer fails to report the exact same financial transaction, then the U.S. Department of Labor might naturally conclude that either there was collusion between the two non-disclosing parties, or there may have been an honest misunderstanding about the nature of what was supposed to be disclosed.

Sec. 202 and Sec. 203 also impose a 5-year document retention requirement, so that the Department of Labor can verify the information which unions and employers report. Finally, 29 U.S.C. Sec. 455 provides that the "contents of the reports and documents filed" with the U.S. Department of Labor "shall be public information." This statute also provides that violations of these provisions in Title II can result on a fine of up to $10,000.00 or imprisonment for not more than one year.

The text of Title II states:

TITLE II -- REPORTING BY LABOR ORGANIZATIONS, OFFICERS AND EMPLOYEES OF LABOR ORGANIZATIONS, AND EMPLOYERS

Report of Labor Organizations

(29 U.S.C. 431)

SEC. 201. (a) Every labor organization shall adopt a constitution and bylaws and shall file a copy thereof with the Secretary, together with a report, signed by its president and secretary or corresponding principal officers, containing the following information-

(1) the name of the labor organization, its mailing address, and any other address at which it maintains its principal office or at which it keeps the records referred to in this title;

(2) the name and title of each of its officers;

(3) the initiation fee or fees required from a new or transferred member and fees for work permits required by the reporting labor organization;

(4) the regular dues or fees or other periodic payments required to remain a member of the reporting labor organization; and

(5) detailed statements, or references to specific provisions of documents filed under this subsection which contain such statements, showing the provisions made and procedures followed with respect to each of the following: (A) qualifications for or restrictions on membership, (B) levying of assessments, (C) participation in insurance or other benefit plans, (D) authorization for disbursement of funds of the labor organization, (E) audit of financial transactions of the labor organization, (F) the calling of regular and special

meetings, (G) the selection of officers and stewards and of any representatives to other bodies composed of labor organizations' representatives, with a specific statement of the manner in which each officer was elected, appointed, or otherwise selected, (H) discipline or removal of officers or agents for breaches of their trust, (I) imposition of fines, suspensions, and expulsions of members, including the grounds for such action and any provision made for notice, hearing, judgment on the evidence, and appeal procedures, (J) authorization for bargaining demands, (K) ratification of contract terms, (L) authorization for strikes, and (M) issuance of work permits. Any change in the information required by this subsection shall be reported to the Secretary at the time the reporting labor organization files with the Secretary the annual financial report required by subsection (b).

(b) Every labor organization shall file annually with the Secretary a financial report signed by its president and treasurer or corresponding principal officers containing the following information in such detail as may be necessary accurately to disclose its financial condition and operations for its preceding fiscal year-

(1) assets and liabilities at the beginning and end of the fiscal year;

(2) receipts of any kind and the sources thereof,

(3) salary, allowances, and other direct or indirect disbursements (including reimbursed expenses) to each officer and also to each employee who, during such fiscal year, received more than $10,000 in the aggregate from such labor organization and any other labor organization affiliated with it or with which it is affiliated, or which is affiliated with the same national or international labor organization;

(4) direct and indirect loans made to any officer, employee, or member, which aggregated more than $250 during the fiscal year, together with a statement of the purpose, security, if any, and arrangements for repayment;

(5) direct and indirect loans to any business enterprise, together with a statement of the purpose, security, if any, and arrangements for repayment; and

(6) other disbursements made by it including the purposes thereof, all in such categories as the Secretary may prescribe.

(c) Every labor organization required to submit a report under this title shall make available the information required to be contained in such report to all of its members, and every such labor organization and its officers shall be under a duty enforceable at the suit of any member of such organization in any State court of competent jurisdiction or in the district court of the United States for the district in which such labor organization maintains its principal office, to permit such member for just cause to examine any books, records, and accounts necessary to verify such report. The court in such action may, in its discretion, in addition to any judgment awarded to the plaintiff or plaintiffs, allow a reasonable attorney's fee to be paid by the defendant, and costs of the action.

(d) Subsections (f), (g), and (h) of section 9 of the National Labor Relations Act, as amended, are hereby repealed.

(e) Clause (i) of section 8(a)(3) of the National Labor Relations Act, as amended, is amended by striking out the following: "and has at the time the agreement was made or within the preceding twelve months received from the Board a notice of compliance with section 9(f), (g), (h)".

Report of Officers and Employees of Labor Organizations

(29 U.S.C. 432)

SEC. 202. (a) Every officer of a labor organization and every employee of a labor organization (other than an employee performing exclusively clerical or custodial services) shall file with the Secretary a signed report listing and describing for his preceding fiscal year-

(1) any stock, bond, security, or other interest, legal or equitable, which he or his spouse or minor child directly or indirectly held in, and any income or any other benefit with monetary value (including reimbursed expenses) which he or his spouse or minor child derived directly or indirectly from, an employer whose employees such labor organization represents or is actively seeking to represent, except payments and other benefits received as a bona fide employee of such employer;

(2) any transaction in which he or his spouse or minor child engaged, directly or indirectly, involving any stock, bond, security, or loan to or from, or other legal or equitable interest in the business of an employer whose employees such labor organization represents or is actively seeking to represent;

(3) any stock, bond, security, or other interest, legal or equitable, which he or his spouse or minor child directly or indirectly held in, and any income or any other benefit with monetary value (including reimbursed expenses) which he or his spouse or minor child directly or indirectly derived from, any business a substantial part of which consists of buying from, selling or leasing to, or otherwise dealing with, the business of an employer whose employees such labor organization represents or is actively seeking to represent;

(4) any stock, bond, security, or other interest, legal or equitable, which he or his spouse or minor child directly or indirectly held in, and any income or any other benefit with monetary value (including reimbursed expenses) which he or his spouse or minor child directly or indirectly derived from, a business any part of which consists of buying from, or selling or leasing directly or indirectly to, or otherwise dealing with such labor organization;

(5) any direct or indirect business transaction or arrangement between him or his spouse or minor child and any employer whose employees his organization represents or is actively seeking to represent, except work performed and payments and benefits received as a bona fide employee of such employer and except purchases and sales of goods or services in the regular course of business at prices generally available to any employee of such employer; and

(6) any payment of money or other thing of value (including reimbursed expenses) which he or his spouse or minor child received directly or indirectly from any employer or any person who acts as a labor relations consultant to an employer, except payments of the kinds referred to in section 302(c) of the Labor Management Relations Act, 1947, as amended.

(b) The provisions of paragraphs (1), (2), (3), (4), and (5) of subsection (a) shall not be construed to require any such officer or employee to report his bona fide investments in securities traded on a securities exchange registered as a national securities exchange under the Securities Exchange Act of 1934, in shares in an investment company registered under the Investment Company Act or in securities of a public utility holding company registered under the Public Utility Holding Company Act of 1935, or to report any income derived therefrom.

(c) Nothing contained in this section shall be construed to require any officer or employee of a labor organization to file a report under subsection (a) unless he or his spouse or minor child holds or has held an interest, has received income or any other benefit with monetary value or a loan, or has engaged in a transaction described therein.

Report of Employers

(29 U.S.C. 433)

SEC. 203. (a) Every employer who in any fiscal year made –

any payment or loan, direct or indirect, of money or other thing of value (including reimbursed expenses), or any promise or agreement therefor, to any labor organization or officer, agent, shop steward, or other representative of a labor organization, or employee of any labor organization, except (A) payments or loans made by any national or State bank, credit union, insurance company, savings and loan association or other credit institution and (B) payments of the kind referred to in section 302(c) of the Labor Management Relations Act, 1947, as amended;

any payment (including reimbursed expenses) to any of his employees, or any group or committee of such employees, for the purpose of causing such employee or group or committee of employees to persuade other employees to exercise or not to exercise, or as the manner of exercising, the right to organize and bargain collectively through representatives of their own choosing unless such payments were contemporaneously or previously disclosed to such other employees;

any expenditure, during the fiscal year, where an object thereof, directly or indirectly, is to interfere with, restrain, or coerce employees in the exercise of the right to organize and bargain collectively through representatives of their own choosing, or is to obtain information concerning the activities of employees or a labor organization in connection with a labor dispute involving such employer, except for use solely in conjunction with an administrative or arbitral proceeding or a criminal or civil judicial proceeding;

any agreement or arrangement with a labor relations consultant or other independent contractor or organization pursuant to which such person undertakes activities where an object thereof, directly or indirectly, is to persuade employees to exercise or not to exercise, or persuade employees as to the manner of exercising, the right to organize and bargain collectively through representatives of their own choosing, or undertakes to supply such employer with information concerning the activities of employees or a labor organization in connection with a labor dispute involving such employer, except information for use solely in conjunction with an administrative or arbitral proceeding or a criminal or civil judicial proceeding; or

any payment (including reimbursed expenses) pursuant to an agreement or arrangement described in subdivision (4);

shall file with the Secretary a report, in a form prescribed by him, signed by its president and treasurer or corresponding principal officers showing in detail the date and amount of each such payment, loan, promise, agreement, or arrangement and the name, address, and position, if any, in any firm or labor organization of the person to whom it was made and a full explanation of the circumstances of all such payments, including the terms of any agreement or understanding pursuant to which they were made.

(b) Every person who pursuant to any agreement or arrangement with an employer undertakes activities where an object thereof is, directly or indirectly-

1. to persuade employees to exercise or not to exercise, or persuade employees as to the manner of exercising, the right

to organize and bargain collectively through representatives of their own choosing; or

2. to supply an employer with information concerning the activities of employees or a labor organization in connection with a labor dispute involving such employer, except information for use solely in conjunction with an administrative or arbitral proceeding or a criminal or civil judicial proceeding;

shall file within thirty days after entering into such agreement or arrangement a report with the Secretary, signed by its president and treasurer or corresponding principal officers, containing the name under which such person is engaged in doing business and the address of its principal office, and a detailed statement of the terms and conditions of such agreement or arrangement. Every such person shall file annually, with respect to each fiscal year during which payments were made as a result of such an agreement or arrangement, a report with the Secretary, signed by its president and treasurer or corresponding principal officers, containing a statement (A) of its receipts of any kind from employers on account of labor relations advice or services, designating the sources thereof, and (B) of its disbursements of any kind, in connection with such services and the purposes thereof. In each such case such information shall be set forth in such categories as the Secretary may prescribe.

(c) Nothing in this section shall be construed to require any employer or other person to file a report covering the services of such person by reason of his giving or agreeing to give advice to such employer or representing or agreeing to represent such employer before any court, administrative agency, or tribunal of arbitration or engaging or agreeing to engage in collective bargaining on behalf of such employer with respect to wages, hours, or other terms or conditions of employment or the negotiation of an agreement or any question arising thereunder.

(d) Nothing contained in this section shall be construed to require an employer to file a report under subsection (a) unless he has made an expenditure, payment, loan, agreement, or arrangement of the kind described therein. Nothing contained in this section shall be construed to require any other person to file a report under subsection (b) unless he was a party to an agreement or arrangement of the kind described therein.

(e) Nothing contained in this section shall be construed to require any regular officer, supervisor, or employee of an employer to file a report in connection with services rendered to such employer nor shall any employer be required to file a report covering expenditures made to any regular officer, supervisor, or employee of an employer as compensation for service as a regular officer, supervisor, or employee of such employer.

(f) Nothing contained in this section shall be construed as an amendment to, or modification of the rights protected by, section 8(c) of the National Labor Relations Act, as amended.

(g) The term "interfere with, restrain, or coerce" as used in this section means interference, restraint, and coercion which, if done with respect to the exercise of rights guaranteed in section 7 of the National Labor Relations Act, as amended, would, under section 8(a) of such Act, constitute an unfair labor practice.

Attorney-Client Communications Exempted

(29 U.S.C. 434)

SEC. 204. Nothing contained in this Act shall be construed to require an attorney who is a member in good standing of the bar of any State, to include in any report required to be filed pursuant to the provisions of this Act any information which was lawfully communicated to such attorney by any of his clients in the course of a legitimate attorney-client relationship.

Reports Made Public Information

(29 U.S.C. 435)

SEC. 205. (a)[3] The contents of the reports and documents filed with the Secretary pursuant to sections 201, 202, **203, and 211** shall be public information, and the Secretary may publish any information and data which he obtains pursuant to the provisions of this title. The Secretary may use the information and data for statistical and research purposes, and compile and publish such studies, analyses, reports, and surveys based thereon as he may deem appropriate.

(b)[4] The Secretary shall by regulation make reasonable provision for the inspection and examination, on the request of any person, of the information and data contained in any report or other document filed with him pursuant to section 201, 202, **203, or 211.**

(c)[5] The Secretary shall by regulation provide for the furnishing by the Department of Labor of copies of reports or other documents filed with the Secretary pursuant to this title, upon payment of a charge based upon the cost of the service. The Secretary shall make available without payment of a charge, or require any person to furnish, to such State agency as is designated by law or by the Governor of the State in which such person has his principal place of business or headquarters, upon request of the Governor of such State, copies of any reports and documents filed by such person with the Secretary pursuant to section 201, 202, **203, or 211,** or of information and data contained therein. No person shall be required by reason of any law of any State to furnish to any officer or agency of such State any information included in a report filed by such person with the Secretary pursuant to the provisions of this title, if a copy of such report, or of the portion thereof containing such information, is furnished to such officer or agency. All moneys received in payment of such charges fixed by the Secretary pursuant to this subsection shall be deposited in the general fund of the Treasury.

Retention of Records

(29 U.S.C. 436)

SEC. 206. Every person required to file any report under this title shall maintain records on the matters required to be reported which will provide in sufficient detail the necessary basic information and data from which the documents filed with the Secretary may be verified, explained or clarified, and checked for accuracy and completeness, and shall include vouchers, worksheets, receipts, and applicable resolutions, and shall keep such records available for examination for a period of not less than five years after the filing of the documents based on the information which they contain.

Effective Date

(29 U.S.C. 437)

SEC. 207. (a) Each labor organization shall file the initial report required under section 201(a) within ninety days after the date on which it first becomes subject to this Act.

(b)[6]Each person required to file a report under section 201(b), 202, 203(a), **the second sentence of section 203(b), or section 211** shall file such report within ninety days after the end of each of its fiscal years; except that where such person is subject to section 201(b), 202, 203(a), **the second sentence of section 203(b), or section 211**, as the case may be, for only a portion of such a fiscal year (because the date of enactment of this Act occurs during such person's fiscal year or such person becomes subject to this Act during its fiscal year) such person may consider that portion as the entire fiscal year in making such report.

Rules and Regulations

(29 U.S.C. 438)

SEC. 208. The Secretary shall have authority to issue, amend, and rescind rules and regulations prescribing the form and publication of reports required to be filed under this title and such other reasonable rules and regulations (including rules prescribing reports concerning trusts in which a labor organization is interested) as he may find necessary to prevent the circumvention or evasion of such reporting requirements. In exercising his power under this section the Secretary shall prescribe by general rule simplified reports for labor organizations or employers for whom he finds that by virtue of their size a detailed report would be unduly burdensome, but the Secretary may revoke such provision for simplified forms of any labor organization or employer if he determines, after such investigation as he deems proper and due notice and opportunity for a hearing, that the purposes of this section would be served thereby.

Criminal Provisions

(29 U.S.C. 439)

SEC. 209. (a) Any person who willfully violates this title shall be fined not more than $10,000 or imprisoned for not more than one year, or both.

(b) Any person who makes a false statement or representation of a material fact, knowing it to be false, or who knowingly fails to disclose a material fact, in any document, report, or other information required under the provisions of this title shall be fined not more than $10,000 or imprisoned for not more than one year, or both.

(c) Any person who willfully makes a false entry in or willfully conceals, withholds, or destroys any books, records, reports, or statements required to be kept by any provision of this title shall be fined not more than $10,000 or imprisoned for not more than one year, or both.

(d) Each individual required to sign reports under sections 201 and 203 shall be personally responsible for the filing of such reports and for any statement contained therein which he knows to be false.

Civil Enforcement

(29 U.S.C. 440)

SEC. 210. Whenever it shall appear that any person has violated or is about to violate any of the provisions of this title, the Secretary may bring a civil action for such relief (including injunctions) as may be appropriate. Any such action may be brought in the district court of the United States where the violation occurred or, at the option of the parties, in the United States District Court for the District of Columbia.

Surety Company Reports[7]

(29 U.S.C. 441)

SEC. 211. Each surety company which issues any bond required by this Act or the Employee Retirement Income Security Act of 1974 shall file annually with the Secretary, with respect to each fiscal year during which any such bond was in force, a report, in such form and detail as he may prescribe by regulation, filed by the president and treasurer or corresponding principal officers of the surety company, describing its bond experience under each such Act, including information as to the premiums received, total claims paid, amounts recovered by way

> of subrogation, administrative and legal expenses and such related data and information as the Secretary shall determine to be necessary in the public interest and to carry out the policy of the Act. Notwithstanding the foregoing, if the Secretary finds that any such specific information cannot be practicably ascertained or would be uninformative, the Secretary may modify or waive the requirement for such information.

§ 1.05 Title III- Trusteeships

Because local labor unions are often mismanaged and fail to discharge their solemn obligations to union members, labor advocates and aggrieved workers should have a basic familiarity with their local labor union's organizational structure, by-laws, and constitution. Most local unions are a part of a larger parent labor organization, usually called the "international" chapter or the "national" chapter. The union's parent organization will also have organizational structure, by-laws, and constitution. Whenever the local union fails to discharge its obligations under its own local by-laws and local constitution, then the local members should contact the parent labor organization in order to get involved, conduct inquires or investigations, and attempt to resolve the problem(s).

Title III of the Landrum-Griffin Act allows parent "national" or "international" labor organizations to take administrative control over from the local union leaders, "for the purpose of correcting corruption, financial malpractice, assuring the performance of the collective bargaining agreement, restoring democratic procedures, and otherwise carrying out the legitimate objects of such labor organizations." When the parent national or international labor organization takes over controls from local labor unions in this matter, it is said to have created a "trusteeship" over the local union.

Sec. 302 of Title III states that trusteeships must be created only in accordance with the constitution and bylaws of the parent national or international labor organization. Whenever a trusteeship is formed, the parent organization must notify the U.S. Department of Labor (Department) within 30 days from when the trusteeship was created. It must provide a written statement that provides the reason(s) for establishing or continuing the trusteeship. Thereafter, semi-annual reports must be submitted to the Department. The trusteeship will be presumed to be valid for 18 months; after this 18-month period, the trusteeship will be presumed to be invalid, as a matter of law.

Violations of the terms and conditions of a valid trusteeship can be reported to the Department, which can prosecute any offending party in the U.S. District Court over the venue where the infractions occurred. The text of Title III states:

TITLE III -- TRUSTEESHIPS

Reports

(29 U.S.C. 461)

SEC. 301. (a) Every labor organization which has or assumes trusteeship over any subordinate labor organization shall file with the Secretary within thirty days after the date of the enactment of this Act or the imposition of any such trusteeship, and semiannually thereafter, a report, signed by its president and treasurer or corresponding principal officers, as well as by the trustees of such subordinate labor organization, containing the following information: (1) the name and address of the subordinate organization; (2) the date of establishing the trusteeship; (3) a detailed statement of the reason or reasons for establishing or continuing the trusteeship; and (4) the nature and extent of participation by the membership of the subordinate organization in the selection of delegates to represent such organization in regular or special conventions or other policy-determining bodies and in the election of officers of the labor organization which has assumed trusteeship over such subordinate organization. The initial report shall also include a full and complete account of the financial condition of such subordinate organization as of the time trusteeship was assumed over it. During the continuance of a trusteeship the labor organization which has assumed trusteeship over a subordinate labor organization shall file on behalf of the subordinate labor organization the annual financial report required by section 201(b) signed by the president and treasurer or corresponding principal officers of the labor organization which has assumed such trusteeship and the trustees of the subordinate labor organization.

(b) The provisions of section 201(c), 205, 206, 208, and 210 shall be applicable to reports filed under this title.

(c) Any person who willfully violates this section shall be fined not more than $10,000 or imprisoned for not more than one year, or both.

(d) Any person who makes a false statement or representation of a material fact, knowing it to be false, or who knowingly fails to disclose a material fact, in any report required under the provisions of this section or willfully makes any false entry in or willfully withholds, conceals, or destroys any documents, books, records, reports, or statements upon which such report is based, shall be fined not more than $10,000 or imprisoned for not more than one year, or both.

(e) Each individual required to sign a report under this section shall be personally responsible for the filing of such report and for any statement contained therein which he knows to be false.

Purposes for Which a Trusteeship May Be Established

(29 U.S.C. 462)

SEC. 302. Trusteeships shall be established and administered by a labor organization over a subordinate body only in accordance with the constitution and bylaws of the organization which has assumed trusteeship over the subordinate body and for the purpose of correcting corruption or financial malpractice, assuring the performance of collective bargaining agreements or other duties of a bargaining representative, restoring democratic procedures, or otherwise carrying out the legitimate objects of such labor organization.

Unlawful Acts Relating to Labor Organization Under Trusteeship

(29 U.S.C. 463)

SEC. 303. (a) During any period when a subordinate body of a labor organization is in trusteeship, it shall be unlawful (1) to count the vote of delegates from such body in any convention or election of officers of the labor organization unless the delegates have been chosen by secret ballot in an election in which all the members in good standing of such subordinate body were eligible to participate or (2) to transfer to such organization any current receipts or other funds of the subordinate body except the normal per capita tax and assessments payable by subordinate bodies not in trusteeship: *Provided,* That nothing herein contained shall prevent the distribution of the assets of a labor organization in accordance with its constitution and bylaws upon the bona fide dissolution thereof.

(b) Any person who willfully violates this section shall be fined not more than $10,000 or imprisoned for not more than one year, or both.

Enforcement

(29 U.S.C. 464)

SEC. 304. (a) Upon the written complaint of any member or subordinate body of a labor organization alleging that such organization has violated the provisions of this title (except section 301) the Secretary shall investigate the complaint and if the Secretary finds probable cause to believe that such violation has occurred and has not been remedied he shall, without disclosing the identity of the complainant, bring a civil action in any district court of the United States having jurisdiction of the labor organization for such relief (including injunctions) as may be appropriate. Any member or subordinate body of a labor organization affected by any violation of this title (except section 301) may bring a civil action in any district court of the United States having jurisdiction of the labor organization for such relief (including injunctions) as may be appropriate.

(b) For the purpose of actions under this section, district courts of the United States shall be deemed to have jurisdiction of a labor organization (1) in the district in which the principal office of such labor organization is located, or (2) in any district in which its duly authorized officers or agents are engaged in conducting the affairs of the trusteeship.

(c) In any proceeding pursuant to this section a trusteeship established by a labor organization in conformity with the procedural requirements of its constitution and bylaws and authorized or ratified after a fair hearing either before the executive board or before such other body as may be provided in accordance with its constitution or bylaws shall be presumed valid for a period of eighteen months from the date of its establishment and shall not be subject to attack during such period except upon clear and convincing proof that the trusteeship was not established or maintained in good faith for a purpose allowable under section 302. After the expiration of eighteen months the trusteeship shall be presumed invalid in any such proceeding and its discontinuance shall be decreed unless the labor organization shall show by clear and convincing proof

> that the continuation of the trusteeship is necessary for a purpose allowable under section 302. In the latter event the court may dismiss the complaint or retain jurisdiction of the cause on such conditions and for such period as it deems appropriate.
>
> **Report to Congress**
>
> (29 U.S.C. 465)
>
> SEC. 305. The Secretary shall submit to the Congress at the expiration of three years from the date of enactment of this Act a report upon the operation of this title.
>
> **Complaint by Secretary**
>
> (29 U.S.C. 466)
>
> SEC. 306. The rights and remedies provided by this title shall be in addition to any and all other rights and remedies at law or in equity: *Provided,* That upon the filing of a complaint by the Secretary the jurisdiction of the district court over such trusteeship shall be exclusive and the final judgment shall be res judicata.

§ 1.06 Title IV—Elections

Economic democracy is one of the touchstones of the American labor system. Union leadership must be democratically elected by the members in good standing. This means that the election of local union leaders and officials must be through fair and lawful processes which afford every general member an opportunity to participate in the process. Title IV sets forth a few mandatory guidelines which unions must follow, in order to ensure the integrity of union elections.

First, elections must be held frequently, so as to ensure perpetual accountability between union members and union leaders. At the national and international level, elections must be held at least once every 5 years. At the intermediate level (i.e., labor units or bodies such as general committees, system boards, deadlock committees, joint appellate boards, joint councils, etc.), elections must be held at least once every 4 years. And at the local labor organization level, elections must be held at least once every 3 years.

Every union member in good standing has the absolute right to run for elective office at all three levels previously mentioned (i.e., national/international; intermediate; and local). Candidates are responsible for financing their own campaigns. No labor union or employer can formally or informally endorse a candidate who is running for a union office. Nor may a union or employer expend any money, or provide any other form of resources to aid or to support, a candidate for a union office. Unions and employers cannot discriminate between candidates, and must provide equal treatment to every candidate. They must also give all candidates free and equal access to union members; they must distribute campaign literature freely and equally to all union members in good standing, without discrimination or endorsement. Within 30 days from the date of the election, unions must give, upon request, each candidate a list of the members in good standing who are eligible to vote in the election.

In "secret ballot" elections, union members must have a reasonable chance to participate and to vote for any candidate of their choosing. Unions must give these members a 15-day written notice of an up-coming union election, mailed to their homes. In addition, union members who are delinquent in the payment of union dues cannot be denied the right to vote solely on the basis of this delinquency.

The union's constitution and by-laws shall be the primary governing documents for elections. However, where these documents fall short or prove to be inadequate, union members can file complaints with the Secretary, U.S. Department of Labor. Prior to filing a complaint with the Department, an individual grievant must first be able to pinpoint a violation of the union's by-laws and constitution; and, secondly, he or she must first petition the union for a remedy. If the union takes no action, or if the union's remedy proves to be inadequate, then an individual grievant can petition the Department, which must determine if there is "probable cause" that a violation has occurred and, if so, whether the union failed to provide a remedy for the violation.

The Secretary must file a complaint in the U.S. District Court within 60 days upon determining that there is probable cause. In general, the

U.S. District Court has general jurisdiction to fashion a wide variety of remedies so as to ensure the integrity of the union election process and to protect the assets of the labor organization. Upon approval and order of the U.S. District Court the Secretary can also fashion temporary safeguards to ensure fair elections. Title IV of the Act states:

TITLE IV - ELECTIONS

Terms of Office; Election Procedures

(29 U.S.C. 481)

SEC. 401. (a) Every national or international labor organization, except a federation of national or international labor organizations, shall elect its officers not less often than once every five years either by secret ballot among the members in good standing or at a convention of delegates chosen by secret ballot.

(b) Every local labor organization shall elect its officers not less often than once every three years by secret ballot among the members in good standing.

(c) Every national or international labor organization, except a federation of national or international labor organizations, and every local labor organization, and its officers, shall be under a duty, enforceable at the suit of any bona fide candidate for office in such labor organization in the district court of the United States in which such labor organization maintains its principal office, to comply with all reasonable requests of any candidate to distribute by mail or otherwise at the candidate's expense campaign literature in aid of such person's candidacy to all members in good standing of such labor organization and to refrain from discrimination in favor of or against any candidate with respect to the use of lists of members, and whenever such labor organizations or its officers authorize the distribution by mail or otherwise to members of campaign literature on behalf of any candidate or of the labor organization itself with reference to such election, similar distribution at the request of any other bona fide candidate shall be made by such labor organization and its officers, with equal treatment as to the expense of such distribution. Every bona fide candidate shall have the right, once within 30 days prior to an election of a labor organization in which he is a candidate, to inspect a list containing the names and last known addresses of all members of the labor organization who are subject to a collective bargaining agreement requiring membership therein as a condition of employment, which list shall be maintained and kept at the principal office of such labor organization by a designated official thereof. Adequate safeguards to insure a fair election shall be provided, including the right of any candidate to have an observer at the polls and at the counting of the ballots.

(d) Officers of intermediate bodies, such as general committees, system boards, joint boards, or joint councils, shall be elected not less often than once every four years by secret ballot among the members in good standing or by labor organization officers representative of such members who have been elected by secret ballot.

(e) In any election required by this section which is to be held by secret ballot a reasonable opportunity shall be given for the nomination of candidates and every member in good standing shall be eligible to be a candidate and to hold office (subject to section 504 and to reasonable qualifications uniformly imposed) and shall have the right to vote for or otherwise support the candidate or candidates of his choice, without being subject to penalty, discipline, or improper interference or reprisal of any kind by such organization or any member thereof. Not less than fifteen days prior to the election notice thereof shall be mailed to each member at his last known home address. Each member in good standing shall be entitled to one vote. No member whose dues have been withheld by his employer for payment to such organization pursuant to his voluntary authorization provided for in a collective bargaining agreement shall be declared ineligible to vote or be a candidate for office in such organization by reason of alleged delay or default in the payment of dues. The votes cast by members of each local labor organization shall be counted, and the results published, separately. The election officials designated in the constitution and bylaws or the secretary, if no other official is designated, shall preserve for one year the ballots and all other records pertaining to the election. The election shall be conducted in accordance with the constitution and bylaws of such organization insofar as they are not inconsistent with the provisions of this title.

(f) When officers are chosen by a convention of delegates elected by secret ballot, the convention shall be conducted in accordance with the constitution and bylaws of the labor organization insofar as they are not inconsistent with the provisions of this title. The officials designated in the constitution and bylaws or the secretary, if no other is designated, shall preserve for one year the credentials of the delegates and all minutes and other records of the convention pertaining to the election of officers.

(g) No moneys received by any labor organization by way of dues, assessment, or similar levy, and no moneys of an employer shall be contributed or applied to promote the candidacy of any person in an election subject to the provisions of this title. Such moneys of a labor organization may be utilized for notices, factual statements of issues not involving candidates, and other expenses necessary for the holding of an election.

(h) If the Secretary, upon application of any member of a local labor organization, finds after hearing in accordance with the Administrative Procedure Act that the constitution and bylaws of such labor organization do not provide an adequate procedure for the removal of an elected officer guilty of serious misconduct, such officer may be removed, for cause shown and after notice and hearing, by the members in good standing voting in a secret ballot conducted by the officers of such labor organization in accordance with its constitution and bylaws insofar as they are not inconsistent with the provisions of this title.

(i) The Secretary shall promulgate rules and regulations prescribing minimum standards and procedures for determining the adequacy of the removal procedures to which reference is made in subsection (h).

Enforcement

(29 U.S.C. 482)

SEC. 402. (a) A member of a labor organization-

1. who has exhausted the remedies available under the constitution and bylaws of such organization and of any parent body, or
2. who has invoked such available remedies without obtaining a final decision within three calendar months after their invocation,

may file a complaint with the Secretary within one calendar month thereafter alleging the violation of any provision of section 401 (including violation of the constitution and bylaws of the labor organization pertaining to the election and removal of officers). The challenged election shall be presumed valid pending a final decision thereon (as hereinafter provided) and in the interim the affairs of the organization shall be conducted by the officers elected or in such other manner as its constitution and bylaws may provide.

(b) The Secretary shall investigate such complaint and, if he finds probable cause to believe that a violation of this title has occurred and has not been remedied, he shall, within sixty days after the filing of such complaint, bring a civil action against the labor organization as an entity in the district court of the United States in which such labor organization maintains its principal office to set aside the invalid election, if any, and to direct the conduct of an election or hearing and vote upon the removal of officers under the supervision of the Secretary and in accordance with the provisions of this title and such rules and regulations as the Secretary may prescribe. The court shall have power to take such action as it deems proper to preserve the assets of the labor organization.

(c) If, upon a preponderance of the evidence after a trial upon the merits, the court finds-

1. that an election has not been held within the time prescribed by section 401, or
2. that the violation of section 401 may have affected the outcome of an election,

the court shall declare the election, if any, to be void and direct the conduct of a new election under supervision of the Secretary and, so far as lawful and practicable, in conformity with the constitution and bylaws of the labor organization. The Secretary shall promptly certify to the court the names of the persons elected, and the court shall thereupon enter a decree declaring such persons to be the officers of the labor organization. If the proceeding is for the removal of officers pursuant to subsection (h) of section 401, the Secretary shall certify the results of the vote and the court shall enter a decree declaring whether such persons have been removed as officers of the labor organization.

(d) An order directing an election, dismissing a complaint, or designating elected officers of a labor organization shall be appealable in the same manner as the final judgment in a civil action, but an order directing an election shall not be stayed pending appeal.

Application of Other Laws

(29 U.S.C. 483)

SEC. 403. No labor organization shall be required by law to conduct elections of officers with greater frequency or in a different form or manner than is required by its own constitution or bylaws, except as otherwise provided by this title. Existing rights and remedies to enforce the constitution and bylaws of a labor organization with respect to elections prior to the conduct thereof shall not be affected by the provisions of this title. The remedy provided by this title for challenging an election already conducted shall be exclusive.

Effective Date

(29 U.S.C. 484)

SEC. 404. The provisions of this title shall become applicable-

1. ninety days after the date of enactment of this Act in the case of a labor organization whose constitution and bylaws can lawfully be modified or amended by action of its constitutional officers or governing body, or
2. where such modification can only be made by a constitutional convention of the labor organization, not later than the next constitutional convention of such labor organization after the date of enactment of this Act, or one year after such date, whichever is sooner. If no such convention is held within such one-year period, the executive board or similar governing body empowered to act for such labor organization between conventions is empowered to make such interim constitutional changes as are necessary to carry out the provisions of this title.

§ 1.07 Title V—Limitations on Union Officials

The Landrum-Griffin Act also incorporates the common law of trusts into the official duties of union officials in Section 501 of the act. This law states that all union officials, including agents, shop stewards, and other representatives "occupy positions of trust" vis-à-vis the labor organization and union members as a group.

This means that union officials must hold and manage all union monies and properties for the benefit of the labor organization. Any union official who "embezzles, steals, or unlawfully and willfully abstracts or converts to his own use" property of the union shall be liable up to $10,000.00 or imprisonment of not more than five (5) years. Union officials must also refrain from dealing or acting with an inappropriate party that could pose a conflict of interest to their labor organization. Nor can they act as an adverse party to the labor union, or assist a party that has an adverse interest to the labor union. They also have a duty to account for all monies and property belonging to the labor union. And no by-laws and (or) constitutions of labor organizations can override or abridge these legal requirements governing the fiduciary and trust responsibilities of union officials.

Due to the seriousness of Sec. 504, all union officials who handle union monies or valuable property must be bonded. Persons without bonds "shall not be permitted to receive, handle, disburse, or otherwise exercise custody" of monies, funds, property belonging to labor organizations. Penalties for violating these bonding requirements are fines of up to $5,000.00 or one (1) year of imprisonment. No labor organization shall be permitted to pay any fines on behalf of a union official.

Closely tied to the provision governing the bonding requirements is Sec. 504's prohibition of certain persons who cannot serve any official or advisory (e.g., labor consultant) position with a union or labor organization. This section states that:

> No person who is or has been a member of the Communist Party or who has been convicted of, or served any part of a prison term resulting from his conviction of, robbery, bribery, extortion, embezzlement, grand larceny, burglary, arson, violation of narcotics laws, murder, rape, assault with intent to kill, assault which inflicts grievous bodily injury, or a violation of title II or III of this Act, any felony involving abuse or misuse of such person's

position or employment in a labor organization or employee benefit plan to seek or obtain an illegal gain at the expense of the members of the labor organization or the beneficiaries of the employee benefit plan, or conspiracy to commit any such crimes or attempt to commit any such crimes, or a crime in which any of the foregoing crimes is an element [shall be permitted to serve as an officer or consult to a labor organization].[18]

Significantly, every individual union member has standing to enforce Section 504. They can file a grievance directly with the labor union, citing any violations of Sec. 504 or other provisions. If the labor union fails to adequately address or resolve the grievance, then the individual union member can file a lawsuit in the U.S. District Court, in the venue where the labor union is located.

Employers are also prohibited from violating the fiduciary and trust relationships between labor organizations and union members. This generally means that employers cannot bribe union leaders or union officials with jobs, cash-payments, loans, benefits, favors, or gifts to their family members. Employers can, however, pay the normal salaries to union officials *who are also* employees of the employer. Employers can also participate in, and make available to their employees, employee-benefit programs, such as, e.g., hospital, medical, pension, disability, injury, illness, and unemployment benefits. Employers can also participate in other forms for group benefits such as day care services, scholarship funds, housing assistance, and legal services plans for the benefit of all union members. Furthermore, the text of Title V states:

---

[18] But see, e.g., *United States v. Brown*, 381 U.S. 437 (1965)("Term 'member of the Communist Party,' in statute making it crime for member to serve as officer or employee of labor union, was not merely convenient permissible shorthand term for list of characteristics of persons likely to incite political strikes, but was prohibited empirical judgment of particular group of men. Labor-Management Reporting and Disclosure Act of 1959, § 504....").

TITLE V-SAFEGUARDS FOR LABOR ORGANIZATIONS

Fiduciary Responsibility of Officers of Labor Organizations

(29 U.S.C. 501)

SEC. 501. (a) The officers, agents, shop stewards, and other representatives of a labor organization occupy positions of trust in relation to such organization and its members as a group. It is, therefore, the duty of each such person, taking into account the special problems and functions of a labor organization, to hold its money and property solely for the benefit of the organization and its members and to manage, invest, and expend the same in accordance with its constitution and bylaws and any resolutions of the governing bodies adopted thereunder, to refrain from dealing with such organization as an adverse party or in behalf of an adverse party in any matter connected with his duties and from holding or acquiring any pecuniary or personal interest which conflicts with the interests of such organization, and to account to the organization for any profit received by him in whatever capacity in connection with transactions conducted by him or under his direction on behalf of the organization. A general exculpatory provision in the constitution and bylaws of such a labor organization or a general exculpatory resolution of a governing body purporting to relieve any such person of liability for breach of the duties declared by this section shall be void as against public policy.

(b) When any officer, agent, shop steward, or representative of any labor organization is alleged to have violated the duties declared in subsection (a) and the labor organization or its governing board or officers refuse or fail to sue or recover damages or secure an accounting or other appropriate relief within a reasonable time after being requested to do so by any member of the labor organization, such member may sue such officer, agent, shop steward, or representative in any district court of the United States or in any State court of competent jurisdiction to recover damages or secure an accounting or other appropriate relief for the benefit of the labor organization. No such proceeding shall be brought except upon leave of the court obtained upon verified application and for good cause shown which application may be made ex parte. The trial judge may allot a reasonable part of the recovery in any action under this subsection to pay the fees of counsel prosecuting the suit at the instance of the member of the labor organization and to compensate such member for any expenses necessarily paid or incurred by him in connection with the litigation.

(c) Any person who embezzles, steals, or unlawfully and willfully abstracts or converts to his own use, or the use of another, any of the moneys, funds, securities, property, or other assets of a labor organization of which he is an officer, or by which he is employed, directly or indirectly, shall be fined not more than $10,000 or imprisoned for not more than five years, or both.

Bonding

(29 U.S.C. 502)

SEC. 502. (a)[8] Every officer, agent, shop steward, or other representative or employee of any labor organization (other than a labor organization whose property and annual financial receipts do not exceed $5,000 in value), or of a trust in which a labor organization is interested, who handles funds or other property thereof shall be bonded **to provide protection against loss by reason of acts of fraud or dishonesty on his part directly or through connivance with others.** The bond of each such person shall be fixed at the beginning of the organization's fiscal year and shall be in an amount not less than 10 per centum of the funds handled by him and his predecessor or predecessors, if any, during the preceding fiscal year, but in no case more than $500,000. If the labor organization or the trust in which a labor organization is interested does not have a preceding fiscal year, the amount of the bond shall be, in the case of a local labor organization, not less than $1,000, and in the case of any other labor organization or of a trust in which a labor organization is interested, not less than $10,000. Such bonds shall be individual or schedule in form, and shall have a corporate surety company as surety thereon. Any person who is not covered by such bonds shall not be permitted to receive, handle, disburse, or otherwise exercise custody or control of the funds or other property of a labor organization or of a trust in which a labor organization is interested. No such bond shall be placed through an agent or broker or with a surety company in which any labor organization or any officer, agent, shop steward, or other representative of a labor organization has any direct or indirect interest. Such surety company shall be a corporate surety which holds a grant of authority from the Secretary of the Treasury under the Act of July 30, 1947 (6 U.S.C. 6-13), as an acceptable surety on Federal bonds: ***Provided,*** **That when in the opinion of the Secretary a labor organization has made other bonding arrangements which would provide the protection required by this section at comparable cost or less, he may exempt such labor organization from placing a bond through a surety company holding such grant of authority.**

(b) Any person who willfully violates this section shall be fined not more than $10,000 or imprisoned for not more than one year, or both.

Making of Loans; Payment of Fines

(29 U.S.C. 503)

SEC. 503. (a) No labor organization shall make directly or indirectly any loan or loans to any officer or employee of such organization which results in a total indebtedness on the part of such officer or employee to the labor organization in excess of $2,000.

(b) No labor organization or employer shall directly or indirectly pay the fine of any officer or employee convicted of any willful violation of this Act.

(c) Any person who willfully violates this section shall be fined not more than $5,000 or imprisoned for not more than one year, or both.

Prohibition Against Certain Persons Holding Office

(29 U.S.C. 504)

SEC. 504. (a) No person who is or has been a member of the Communist Party [2] or who has been convicted of, or served any part of a prison term resulting from his conviction of, robbery, bribery, extortion, embezzlement, grand larceny, burglary, arson, violation of narcotics laws, murder, rape, assault with intent to kill, assault which inflicts grievous bodily injury, or a violation of title II or III of this Act,[10] **any felony involving abuse or misuse of such person's position or employment in a labor organization or employee benefit plan to seek or obtain an illegal gain at the expense of the members of the labor organization or the beneficiaries of the employee benefit plan, or conspiracy to commit any such crimes or attempt to commit any such crimes, or a crime in which any of the foregoing crimes is an element, shall serve or be permitted to serve -**

1. as a consultant or adviser to any labor organization,
2. as an officer, director, trustee, member of any executive board or similar governing body, business agent, manager, organizer, employee, or representative in any capacity of any labor organization,

3. as a labor relations consultant or adviser to a person engaged in an industry or activity affecting commerce, or as an officer, director, agent, or employee of any group or association of employers dealing with any labor organization, or in a position having specific collective bargaining authority or direct responsibility in the area of labor-management relations in any corporation or association engaged in an industry or activity affecting commerce, or
4. in a position which entitles its occupant to a share of the proceeds of, or as an officer or executive or administrative employee of, any entity whose activities are in whole or substantial part devoted to providing goods or services to any labor organization, or
5. in any capacity, other than in his capacity as a member of such labor organization, that involves decisionmaking authority concerning, or decisionmaking authority over, or custody of, or control of the moneys, funds, assets, or property of any labor organization,

during or for the period of thirteen years after such conviction or after the end of such imprisonment, whichever is later, unless the sentencing court on the motion of the person convicted sets a lesser period of at least three years after such conviction or after the end of such imprisonment, whichever is later, or unless prior to the end of such period, in the case of a person so convicted or imprisoned,

his citizenship rights, having been revoked as a result of such conviction, have been fully restored, or if the offense is a Federal offense, the sentencing judge or, if the offense is a State or local offense, the United States district court for the district in which the offense was committed, pursuant to sentencing guidelines and policy statements under section 994(a) of title 28, United States Code, determines that such person's service in any capacity referred to in clauses (1) through (5) would not be contrary to the purposes of this Act. Prior to making any such determination the court shall hold a hearing and shall give notice of such proceeding by certified mail to the Secretary of Labor and to State, county, and Federal prosecuting officials in the jurisdiction or jurisdictions in which such person was convicted. The court's determination in any such proceeding shall be final. No person shall knowingly hire, retain, employ, or otherwise place any other person to serve in any capacity in violation of this subsection.

(b) Any person who willfully violates this section shall be fined not more than $10,000 or imprisoned for not more than five years, or both.

(c) For the purpose of this section-

1. A person shall be deemed to have been "convicted" and under the disability of "conviction" from the date of the judgment of the trial court, regardless of whether that judgment remains under appeal.
2. A period of parole shall not be considered as part of a period of imprisonment.

(d) Whenever any person-

1. by operation of this section, has been barred from office or other position in a labor organization as a result of a conviction, and
2. has filed an appeal of that conviction,

any salary which would be otherwise due such person by virtue of such office or position, shall be placed in escrow by the individual employer or organization responsible for payment of such salary. Payment of such salary into escrow shall continue for the duration of the appeal or for the period of time during which such salary would be otherwise due, whichever period is shorter. Upon the final reversal of such person's conviction on appeal, the amounts in escrow shall be paid to such person.

Upon the final sustaining of such person's conviction on appeal, the amounts in escrow shall be returned to the individual employer or organization responsible for payments of those amounts. Upon final reversal of such person's conviction, such person shall no longer be barred by this statute from assuming any position from which such person was previously barred.

Amendment to Section 302, Labor Management Relations Act, 1947

SEC. 505. Subsections (a), (b), and (c) of section 302 of the Labor Management Relations Act, 1947, as amended, are amended to read as follows:

[1]SEC. 302. (a) It shall be unlawful for any employer or association of employers or any person who acts as a labor relations expert, adviser, or consultant to an employer or who acts in the interest of an employer to pay, lend, or deliver, or agree to pay, lend, or deliver, any money or other thing of value-

1. to any representative of any of his employees who are employed in an industry affecting commerce; or
2. to any labor organization, or any officer or employee thereof, which represents, seeks to represent, or would admit to membership, any of the employees of such employer who are employed in an industry affecting commerce; or
3. to any employee or group or committee of employees of such employer employed in an industry affecting commerce in excess of their normal compensation for the purpose of causing such employee or group or committee directly or indirectly to influence any other employees in the exercise of the right to organize and bargain collectively through representatives of their own choosing; or

4. to any officer or employee of a labor organization engaged in an industry affecting commerce with intent to influence him in respect to any of his actions, decisions, or duties as a representative of employees or as such officer or employee of such labor organization.

(b)(1) It shall be unlawful for any person to request, demand, receive, or accept, or agree to receive or accept, any payment, loan, or delivery of any money or other thing of value prohibited by subsection (a).

(2) It shall be unlawful for any labor organization, or for any person acting as an officer, agent, representative, or employee of such labor organization, to demand or accept from the operator of any motor vehicle (as defined in section 10101 of Title 49)[12] employed in the transportation of property in commerce, or the employer of any such operator, any money or other thing of value payable to such organization or to an officer, agent, representative or employee thereof as a fee or charge for the unloading, or in connection with the unloading, of the cargo of such vehicle: *Provided,* That nothing in this paragraph shall be construed to make unlawful any payment by an employer to any of his employees as compensation for their services as employees.

(c) The provisions of this section shall not be applicable

1. in respect to any money or other thing of value payable by an employer to any of his employees whose established duties include acting openly for such employer in matters of labor relations or personnel administration or to any representative of his employees, or to any officer or employee of a labor organization, who is also an employee or former employee of such employer, as compensation for, or by reason of, his service as an employee of such employer;
2. with respect to the payment or delivery of any money or other thing of value in satisfaction of a judgment of any court or a

decision or award of an arbitrator or impartial chairman or in compromise, adjustment, settlement, or release of any claim, complaint, grievance, or dispute in the absence of fraud or duress;

3. with respect to the sale or purchase of an article or commodity at the prevailing market price in the regular course of business;
4. with respect to money deducted from the wages of employees in payment of membership dues in a labor organization: *Provided,* That the employer has received from each employee, on whose account such deductions are made, a written assignment which shall not be irrevocable for a period of more than one year, or beyond the termination date of the applicable collective agreement, whichever occurs sooner;
5. with respect to money or other thing of value paid to a trust fund established by such representative, for the sole and exclusive benefit of the employees of such employer, and their families and dependents (or of such employees, families, and dependents jointly with the employees of other employers making similar payments, and their families and dependents): *Provided,* That

- such payments are held in trust for the purpose of paying, either from principal or income or both, for the benefit of employees, their families and dependents, for medical or hospital care, pensions on retirement or death of employees, compensation for injuries or illness resulting from occupational activity or insurance to provide any of the foregoing, or unemployment benefits or life insurance, disability and sickness insurance, or accident insurance;
- the detailed basis on which such payments are to be made is specified in a written agreement with the employer, and employees and employers are equally represented in the administration of such fund, together with such neutral persons as the representatives of the employers and the representatives of employees may agree upon and in the event the employer and employee groups deadlock on the administration of such fund and there are no neutral persons empowered to break such deadlock, such agreement provides that the two groups shall agree on an impartial umpire to decide such dispute, or in event

of their failure to agree within a reasonable length of time, an impartial umpire to decide such dispute shall, on petition of either group, be appointed by the district court of the United States for the district where the trust fund has its principal office, and shall also contain provisions for an annual audit of the trust fund, a statement of the results of which shall be available for inspection by interested persons at the principal office of the trust fund and at such other places as may be designated in such written agreement; and

o such payments as are intended to be used for the purpose of providing pensions or annuities for employees are made to a separate trust which provides that the funds held therein cannot be used for any purpose other than paying such pensions or annuities;

6. with respect to money or other thing of value paid by any employer to a trust fund established by such representative for the purpose of pooled vacation, holiday, severance or similar benefits, or defraying costs of apprenticeship or other training programs: *Provided,* That the requirements of clause (B) of the proviso to clause (5) of this subsection shall apply to such trust funds;

7. with respect to money or other thing of value paid by any employer to a pooled or individual trust fund established by such representative for the purpose of

o scholarships for the benefit of employees, their families, and dependents for study at educational institutions,

o child care centers for preschool and school age dependents of employees, or

o financial assistance for employee housing:[13] *Provided,* That no labor organization or employer shall be required to bargain on the establishment of any such trust fund, and refusal to do so shall not constitute an unfair labor practice: *Provided further,* That the requirements of clause (B) of the proviso to clause (5) of this subsection shall apply to such trust funds;

8. with respect to money or any other thing of value paid by any employer to a trust fund established by such representative for the purpose of defraying the costs of legal services for employees, their families, and dependents for counsel or plan of their choice: *Provided*, That the requirements of clause (B) of the proviso to clause (5) of this subsection shall apply to such trust funds: *Provided further*, That no such legal services shall be furnished:

- to initiate any proceeding directed (i) against any such employer or its officers or agents except in workman's compensation cases, or (ii) against such labor organization, or its parent or subordinate bodies, or their officers or agents, or (iii) against any other employer or labor organization, or their officers or agents, in any matter arising under the National Labor Relations Act, as amended, or this Act; and
- in any proceeding where a labor organization would be prohibited from defraying the costs of legal services by the provisions of the Labor-Management Reporting and Disclosure Act of 1959; or

9. with respect to money or other things of value paid by an employer to a plant, area or industrywide labor management committee established for one or more of the purposes set forth in section 5(b) [14] of the Labor Management Cooperation Act of 1978.[15]

[The remaining subsections, (d) through (g), of section 302 of the Labor Management Relations Act, 1947, are found at 29 U.S.C. 186(d) through (g).]

§ 1.08 Title VI— Miscellaneous Provisions

Title VI of the Landrum-Griffin Act is an omnibus provision that deals with a variety of unrelated topics. It guarantees, for example, the right to a jury trial in the United States District Court for all charges of "criminal contempt" under this Act. Title VI prohibits violence and the threat of violence against anyone who exercises their rights under this Act; it also prohibits labor unions from retaliating against (e.g., levying fines, suspensions, to expel union members, or other forms of discipline against union members) its members who exercise any rights under this Act. Title VI prohibits extortionate picketing of employers, thus providing a penalty of up to $10,000.00 and (or) not more than 20 years imprisonment.

Title VI also gives state prosecutors the right to bring and prosecute criminal charges in state courts. In addition, all rights, duties, responsibilities and privileges of labor union officers, agents, shop stewards, or other representatives, which are preserved "under any other federal law or under the laws of any state," are not abridged by this Act. Finally, the Secretary, U.S. Department of Labor, has authority to conduct investigations into any acts where there is reason to believe that a violation has occurred.

TITLE VI -- MISCELLANEOUS PROVISIONS

Investigations

(29 U.S.C. 521)

SEC. 601. (a) The Secretary shall have power when he believes it necessary in order to determine whether any person has violated or is about to violate any provision of this Act (except title I or amendments made by this Act to other statutes) to make an investigation and in connection therewith he may enter such places and inspect such records and accounts and question such persons as he may deem necessary to enable him to determine the facts relative thereto. The Secretary may report to interested persons or officials concerning the facts required to be shown in any report required by this Act and concerning the reasons for failure or refusal to file such a report or any other matter which he deems to be appropriate as a result of such an investigation.

(b) For the purpose of any investigation provided for in this Act, the provisions of sections 9 and 10 (relating to the attendance of witnesses and the production of books, papers, and documents) of the Federal Trade Commission Act of

September 16, 1914, as amended (15 U.S.C. 49, 50), are hereby made applicable to the jurisdiction, powers, and duties of the Secretary or any officers designated by him.

Extortionate Picketing

(29 U.S.C. 522)

SEC. 602. (a) It shall be unlawful to carry on picketing on or about the premises of any employer for the purpose of, or as part of any conspiracy or in furtherance of any plan or purpose for, the personal profit or enrichment of any individual (except a bona fide increase in wages or other employee benefits) by taking or obtaining any money or other thing of value from such employer against his will or with his consent.

(b) Any person who willfully violates this section shall be fined not more than $10,000 or imprisoned not more than twenty years, or both.

Retention of Rights Under Other Federal and State Laws

(29 U.S.C. 523)

SEC. 603. (a) Except as explicitly provided to the contrary, nothing in this Act shall reduce or limit the responsibilities of any labor organization or any officer, agent, shop steward, or other representative of a labor organization, or of any trust in which a labor organization is interested, under any other Federal law or under the laws of any State, and, except as explicitly provided to the contrary, nothing in this Act shall take away any right or bar any remedy to which members of a labor organization are entitled under such other Federal law or law of any State.

(b) Nothing contained in titles I, II, III, IV, V, or VI of this Act shall be construed to supersede or impair or otherwise affect the provisions of the Railway Labor Act, as amended, or any of the obligations, rights, benefits, privileges, or immunities of any carrier, employee, organization, representative, or person subject thereto; nor shall anything contained in said titles (except section *505*) of this Act be construed to confer any rights, privileges, immunities, or defenses upon employers, or to impair or otherwise affect the rights of any person under the National Labor Relations Act, as amended.

Effect on State Laws

(29 U.S.C. 524)

SEC. 604. Nothing in this Act shall be construed to impair or diminish the authority of any State to enact and enforce general criminal laws with respect to robbery, bribery, extortion, embezzlement, grand larceny, burglary, arson, violation of narcotics laws, murder, rape, assault with intent to kill, or assault which inflicts grievous bodily injury, or conspiracy to commit any of such crimes.

Service of Process

29 U.S.C. 525)

SEC. 605. For the purposes of this Act, service of summons, subpena, or other legal process of a court of the United States upon an officer or agent of a labor organization in his capacity as such shall constitute service upon the labor organization.

Administrative Procedure Act

(29 U.S.C. 526)

SEC. 606. The provisions of the Administrative Procedure Act shall be applicable to the issuance, amendment, orrescission of any rules or regulations or any adjudication, authorized or required pursuant to the provisions of this Act.

Other Agencies and Departments

(29 U.S.C. 527)

SEC. 607. In order to avoid unnecessary expense and duplication of functions among Government agencies, the Secretary may make such arrangements or agreements for cooperation or mutual assistance in the performance of his functions under this Act and the functions of any such agency as he may find to be practicable and consistent with law. The Secretary may utilize the facilities or services of any department, agency, or establishment of the United States or of any State or political subdivision of a State, including the services of any of its employees, with the lawful consent of such department, agency, or establishment; and each department, agency, or establishment of the United States is authorized and directed to cooperate with the Secretary and, to the extent permitted by law, to provide such information and facilities as he may request for his assistance in the performance of his functions under this Act. The Attorney General or his representative shall receive from the Secretary for appropriate action such evidence developed in the performance of his functions under this Act as may be found to warrant consideration for criminal prosecution under the provisions of this Act or other Federal law.

Criminal Contempt

(29 U.S.C. 528)

SEC. 608. No person shall be punished for any criminal contempt allegedly committed outside the immediate presence of the court in connection with any civil action prosecuted by the Secretary or any other person in any court of the United States under the provisions of this Act unless the facts constituting such criminal contempt are established by the verdict of the jury in a proceeding in the district court of the United States, which jury shall be chosen and empaneled in the manner prescribed by the law governing trial juries in criminal prosecutions in the district courts of the United States.

Prohibition on Certain Discipline by Labor Organization

(29 U.S.C. 529)

SEC. 609. It shall be unlawful for any labor organization, or any officer, agent, shop steward, or other representative of a labor organization, or any employee thereof to fine, suspend, expel, or otherwise discipline any of its members for exercising any right to which he is entitled under the provisions of this Act. The provisions of section 102 shall be applicable in the enforcement of this section.

Deprivation of Rights Under Act by Violence

(29 U.S.C. 530)

SEC. 610. It shall be unlawful for any person through the use of force or violence, or threat of the use of force or violence, to restrain, coerce, or intimidate, or attempt to restrain, coerce, or intimidate any member of a labor organization for the purpose of interfering with or preventing the exercise of any right to which he is entitled under the provisions of this Act. Any person who willfully violates this section shall be fined not more than $1,000 or imprisoned for not more than one year, or both.

Separability Provisions

(29 U.S.C. 531)

SEC. 611. If any provision of this Act, or the application of such provision to any person or circumstances, shall be held

> invalid, the remainder of this Act or the application of such provision to persons or circumstances other than those as to which it is held invalid, shall not be affected thereby.

§ 1.09 Strategic Human Resources and Risk Management

For human resources managers and senior executives, the knowledge of the Landrum-Griffin Act of 1959 may provide valuable insight into union operations and functions, as well as the relationships between union members, local labor unions, and parent national or international labor organizations. These relationships are fraught with the difficulty of managing fiduciary and trusteeship responsibilities. Human resources professionals should thoroughly understand these internal union relationships, when negotiating with union members and union officials. For instance, with knowledge of the Landrum-Griffin Act, a human resources officer, who receives a complaint against the employer from an individual employee, might also recognize that the real culprit is not the employer, but the labor union's leadership. In addition, knowledge of the Landrum-Griffin Act can help educate human resources management as to how to combat unionization of non-unionized workplaces and how to educate non-unionized workers regarding the potential downside to having a union. The history of labor-union corruption thus allows human resources professionals to honestly inform their non-unionized workers that labor unions can become corrupt, and that bringing in a labor union might cause more harm than good. Employers may also cite relevant examples and prior cases, where federal courts haves cited labor unions with one or more violations under the Landrum-Griffin Act, in order to explain to their non-unionized workers that bringing in a labor union is not the best course of action to take.

§ 1.10 Conclusion

The Labor Management Reporting and Disclosure Act of 1959 (i.e., the Landrum-Griffin Act of 1959) is not the first national labor law enacted in the United States, but I suggest that any course or initial overview of federal labor law begin with an introduction and summary of this important law. The reason is because this federal law goes to the very heart of why individual workers desire to join labor unions: economic security and fair representation. If the labor union cannot guarantee fair treatment, then individual workers simply would have no need for labor unions. And when, through false pretenses, corruption, or incompetence, a labor union fails to provide fair treatment, the Landrum-Griffin Act steps in to guarantee that individual union members retain various fundamental, inalienable rights. These rights are extremely important to know: *union members* need to know these rights, for their own self-interest and protection; *union officials* need to know these rights, in order to faithfully discharge their obligations to their union constituency; and, *management officials* need to know these rights, in order to defend themselves against the effects of labor-union inefficiencies. Perhaps most importantly, employment attorneys and union stewards need to know these rights, in order to know how best to assist individual union members.

For each of these reasons, individual union grievances should always initially begin through a quick review of the Landrum-Griffin Act of 1959, in order to determine whether the source of the labor problem lay with management or with the union. Sometimes, and perhaps more often than normally understood to be the case, the labor union's own inefficiencies and corruption are the primary causes of local union-member grievances. But unfortunately, without any knowledge of the Landrum-Griffin Act, a union steward or an individual union member would not know just what to do or how to proceed against their local labor union. The result of this lack of knowledge is that many union grievances go unresolved and unsolved. And, even when new local union elections result in new local officers, the culture of corruption and inefficiencies within local union leadership persist unabated. If these inefficiencies do not impair the interests of management or the employer, then most managers and employers will either be ignorant of the problem of union corruption, or they will simply ignore the problem. The burden thus shifts to rest upon the shoulders of individual union members, many of whom are ignorant of the Landrum-Griffin Act and its prohibitions and remedies. For this reason, I have dedicated the first chapter of this book to this most important of federal labor laws. Union members, union stewards, and labor advocates should attain a working knowledge of the general provisions of this Act.

BIBLIOGRAPHY

Books:

Gelhaus, Robert J. and James Oldham. *Labor Law.* Chicago, IL: The BarBri Group, 2002.

References:

48 American Jurisprudence (Second), Labor and Labor Relations, §§ 1-4

48A American Jurisprudence (Second), Labor and Labor Relations, §§ 1113-1272

51 Corpus Jurisprudence Secundum, Labor Relations, §§ 1-42

51B Corpus Jurisprudence Secundum, Labor Relations, §§ 48-147

Case Law:

U.S. Supreme Court

Calhoun v. Harvey, 379 U.S. 134 (1964)

United States v. Brown, 381 U.S. 437 (1965)

Wirtz v. Local Union No. 125, Laborers' International Union of North America AFL-CIO, 389 U.S. 477 (1968)

Trbovich v. UMW, 404 U.S. 528 (1972)

Hall v. Cole, 412 U.S. 1 (1973)

Local 3489, United Steel Workers v. Usery, 429 U.S. 305 (1977)

Reed v. United Transportation Union, 488 U.S. 319 (1989)

Chapter Two

LOCK-OUTS, STRIKES, PICKETING AND BOYCOTTS

§ 2.01 Introduction 62

§ 2.02 Employer Lock-Outs 63

§ 2.03 Strikes 66

§ 2.04 Picketing 68

§ 2.05 Boycotts 71

§ 2.06 Remedies for Illegal Strikes, Picketing or Boycotts 73

§ 2.07 Human Resources and Strategic Risk Management 74

§ 2.08 Conclusion 75

§ 2.01 Introduction

The goal of federal labor legislation in the United States is industrial peace and the peaceful settlement of conflict between employees and employers.[19] Therefore, the National Labor Relations Act and the Railway Labor Act mandate that labor arbitration is the preferred method for resolving labor-management disputes.[20] Most collective-bargaining agreements contain mandatory "arbitration clauses." These arbitration clauses require labor unions to submit their grievances to labor arbitration. Consequently, the National Labor Relations Board (NLRB) will deem any strikes, picketing or boycott activities to be illegal, whenever these activities' underlying grievances had not first been submitted to mandatory labor arbitration.[21] Significantly, federal labor policy requires good-faith arbitration even where the collective bargaining agreement *does not* have an arbitration clause.[22] Hence, an employer who is the victim of an illegal strike, picket, boycott, or other coercive actions, where arbitration has been ignored, may:

- File an Unfair Labor Practice Charge before the National Labor Relations Board. These Section 8(b)(4) charges take priority over other pending charges and are expedited. If the NLRB determines that there is "reasonable cause," then it must seek an immediate injunction against the Union or other third party found to be in violation of Section 8(b)(4).
- File a Lawsuit for Injunctive Relief in either State or Federal Court. Such lawsuits are based upon common law, and are generally designed to prevent acts of violence and coercion. Such suits may also be filed in order to enforce any "no-strike" provisions found in an operative collective bargaining agreement. If there has been "economic" loss, then such suits may also assert a claim for compensatory damages as per Section 303 of the Taft-Hartley Act.

---

[19] 51 *Corpus Juris Secundum*, Labor Relations § 1.

[20] 48 Am Jur Second, Labor and Labor Relations §§ 354-356.

[21] Ibid.

[22] Ibid.

Remedies against illegal employer lock-outs are more difficult to analyze, because the general rule of thumb is that a business organization can simply shut down its entire operation, even if union bias or animas is the chief reason for doing so. Of course, as discussed below, there are exceptions to this general rule of thumb, but those exceptions are extremely rare and difficult to prove.

§ 2.02 Employer Lock-Outs[23]

Industrial strife can deteriorate into open antipathy between management and labor, especially when there are a group of determined workers who have an out-spoken leader— particularly an articulate, well-respected, and knowledgeable labor advocate. Oftentimes, however, individual workers (or groups of workers) will take matters into their own hands and engage in illegal "wild-cat" strikes. A "wild-cat" strike is one that occurs outside the scope of normal channels, such as where a group of individual workers decide to go on a strike without first receiving prior approval from their union leaders; or when a union approves a strike that does not follow the proper procedures as set forth in an established collective bargaining agreement (CBA). In other circumstances, workers decide to "sabotage" the production, work-flow, or other employer administrative processes, thus creating a steady or sharp drop in the employer's efficiency, out-put, and profits. In other words, these "wild-cat" strikers report to work, but they actually sabotage their employer's workflow, or they only pretend to do productive work, while loafing off on the timeclock. In addition, sometimes various unscrupulous workers' make violent threats against management—threats which management must, of course, take very seriously. And when an employer receives such threats, it is natural that it might also feel unsure about employee-sabotage. Even heated negotiations during collective bargaining could lead to the same insecurities, leading employers to the conclusion that it needs to shore up its bargaining position.[24] For any of these reasons, the employer may decide to launch a "lock-out," in order to prevent on-going hostilities, or to prevent damage to property, persons, or profits. Accordingly:

---

[23] 48B Am Jur 2d, Labor and Labor Relations §§ 2652-2668.

[24] Ibid., pp. 233-234.

[A] lockout is an employer's legitimate economic weapon; a lockout occurs when an employer discontinues all or a portion of its operations or refuses to allow employees to work for the purpose of bringing pressure upon the union, and it may be either lawful or unlawful, depending upon its justification. A lockout is a legitimate move by an employer in the face of a strike, and this legitimate economic tactic will turn into an unfair labor practice only if, in the use of the tactic, the employer violates the NLRA by discriminating against its employees for exercising their right to bargain collectively and to act together in mutual support, or by discriminating in regards to hiring in order to discourage membership in a union. An employer commits an unfair labor practice when its actions interfere with employee organizing rights to the extent that the damage imposed outweighs the business justification, thus, a lockout may be unlawful without a discriminatory motive. An employer lockout that is inherently destructive of the employees' rights constitutes an unfair labor practice whether or not the lockout is based on important business considerations, and even where the lockout has only a relatively slight impact on the rights of the employees, it may constitute an unfair labor practice unless the employer can demonstrate that there are legitimate and substantial reasons to justify its conduct.[25]

An employer may not lawfully terminate an operation and contract out that work in order to prevent unionization or to evade

---

[25] Ibid., p. 323; see, also, 48A *Am Jur Second*, Labor and Labor Relations § 1477 ("An employer may lawfully lock out employees to prevent losses in the face of repeated 'quickie' strikes or to pressure the union to accept the employer's legitimate bargaining position, as long as the employer conducts the lockout in a manner reasonably adapted to achieve legitimate business ends or to deal with business exigencies. To be reasonably adapted to achieve legitimate business ends, the employer's conduct throughout the lockout must be consistent with the advancement of its legitimate bargaining position so that the employees are able to knowingly reevaluate their position. An employer will violate the NLRA's prohibition against illegal lockouts if it fails to reinstate striking workers without showing a legitimate and substantial business justification. Moreover, an illegal lockout will be found where an employer fails to respond to a union's offer to return to work and fails to provide the union with information about how it can end the lockout.")

the collective-bargaining process....[26] An employer's diversion of work from the unionized portion of a double-breasted operation to the nonunion part in order to avoid the terms of the existing labor agreement or its duty to bargain with the union constitutes unlawful discrimination.[27]

In the absence of a statute so declaring, a lockout is not unlawful per se. The right to lock out has been considered correlative with the right of employees to strike, and, during the course of bargaining, the employer may use a lockout as a legitimate weapon to protect himself from economic hardship. In determining whether or not a lockout was justified, each case must be carefully measured in its own setting, and justification is not limited to economic hardship.... Where an employer's association bargains collectively with a union, it has a right as a group to resort to a temporary economic lockout of their employees.[28]

In sum, the National Labor Relations Act (NLRA), Sections 8(a)(1) or 8(a)(3) govern employer lock-outs. "A lockout is not unlawful where it results from economic conditions necessitating a decrease in the work force and not from an intent to interfere with, restrain, or coerce employees."[29] A lock-out will be deemed to be valid and legal if (a) during collective bargaining the parties have reached an "impasse" or (b) any of the "special circumstances," as previously mentioned above, occurs. Conversely, if an employer cannot credibly articulate any valid reasons for the lock-out of its workers, then it will be deemed to have committed an unfair labor practice and to have violated the NLRA. See, e.g., *American Ship Building Co. v. NLRB*, 330 U.S. 330 (1965). Significantly, an employer can shut down its entire operation for any reason, including anti-union bias. See, e.g., *Textile Workers Union of America v. Darlington Manufacturing Co.*, 380 U.S. 263 (1965). However, without any "special circumstances" in support of initiating the

---

[26] 48A *Am Jur Second*, Labor and Labor Relations § 1646.

[27] 48A *Am Jur Second*, Labor and Labor Relations § 1647.

[28] 51A *Corpus Juris Secundum*, Labor Relations § 274.

[29] 48B *Am Jur* 2d, Labor and Labor Relations § 2653.

lock-out, examples of which are stated above, an employer generally cannot strategically shut down specific plants, departments or operations *solely to target pro-union employees* or *solely to discourage unionization*. See, e.g., *Textile Workers Union of America v. Darlington Manufacturing Co*, supra. Under normal circumstances, the shut-down must proceed a real and present economic threat from unlawful union or organizing activities, or there must be a legitimate business reason or other economic justification.

Of significant importance to the legal issue of a valid lock-out is whether an employer can replace the uncooperative workers. The National Labor Relations Board has ruled that an employer *may not permanently replace* workers during a valid lock-out. *Johns-Manville Products Corp.*, 223 NLRB 1317 (1976). But employers may temporarily replace uncooperative, permanent workers, see, e.g., *Inter-Collegiate Press v. NLRB*, 486 F.2d 837 (8th Cir. 1973); and even subcontract out the work during the valid, lawful lockout, see, e.g., *International Paper Co. v. NLRB*, 115 F.3d 1045 (D.C. Cir. 1997).

§ 2.03 Strikes[30]

As previously mentioned, a strike is the refusal to perform work in protest of employer policies or other terms, conditions, privileges of employment. In general, "the object of a strike, the means used in its conduct must not be unlawful or contrary to public policy."[31] A strike is unlawful if it involves, for example:

- Showing up to work, but not actually performing any work (so-called partial or intermittent strikes);
- Threats or violence;
- Violations of the grievance procedures and other terms of a valid Collective Bargaining Agreement;
- Strikes based upon an employer's implementation of civil rights laws in order to protect minority group workers (i.e., race, sex, religion, color, national origin, disability, age, military or veteran status, sexual orientation, etc.);

---

[30] 51A *Corpus Juris Secundum*, Labor Relations §§ 276-277.

[31] Ibid., p. 49.

- Strikes to control workflow or production processes that keeps or restricts certain desirable jobs within a bargaining unit (i.e., creating jobs which do not really exist; illegal "featherbedding" agreements);
- Strikes to coerce an employer to refrain from purchasing services or products from another employer that is engaged in labor dispute with a sister union (i.e., "hot cargo" agreements);
- Strikes to coerce an employer to recognize a union that has not been certified by the NLRB;
- Strikes to coerce an employer to assign certain jobs to union members; or,
- Strikes to enforce collective bargaining over provisions within a Collective Bargaining Agreement must first afford 60-day notice to employers; strikes that violate this 60-day notice provision violate the NLRA.

The right to strike is based largely upon state common law and federal laws which protect workers against unsafe, unhealthy, and threatening working conditions. The right to strike is also protected under the Section 7 of National Labor Relations Act, since it constitutes "protected, concerted activity." Employers may not interfere with employees who decide to go on strike. When the employer has committed an unfair labor practice, as defined by the NLRB and the courts, the employer must also guarantee the job tenure of the strikers and they may not be permanently replaced. When there are no unfair labor practices or "ULPs," and no credible evidence of unsafe, unhealthy, or threatening working conditions, then employees take a greater risk of permanently losing their jobs whenever they engage in a strike. See, e.g., *NLRB v. MacKay Radio & Telegraph Co.*, 304 U.S. 333 (1938). When no unfair labor practices have been committed, and the strikers are arguing only over "economic" terms and conditions, then their jobs will not be protected under Section 7 of NLRA. This is the so-called "economic strikers" rule. See, e.g. *Trans World Airlines v. Flight Attendants*, 489 U.S. 426 (1989). Economic strikers can be permanently replaced.

There are many other variables involving whether an employer has a legal obligation to return a "striking" worker to their former job. An employer does not have a legal obligation to create a job. In other words, where a job has been validly eliminated, then the employer is under no obligation to return the striking worker to a prior or similar job. And where there are "seniority rules" in place, whether stemming from a collective bargaining agreement or from another valid employer provision, then an employer may also abide by its seniority-status return-to-work policies, when refusing to return particular "junior-status" workers to their former positions.

Savvy union officials are well-versed in handling strikes and know how to get around all of these various limitations by negotiating "return-to-work strike agreements" with employers. Therefore, while there are black-and-white legal restrictions on the law books, with respect to strikers and strikes in general, anything is possible where union officials and employers are at the bargaining table. Union leaders and employers are certainly free to negotiate "return-to-work" strike agreements which afford great protections to strikers than what are provided in the National Labor Relations Act.

Interestingly, "[t]here is no legal time limit on strikes. Ordinarily a strike is ended by an agreement between the parties and the return of the strikers to work. However, a strike may be terminated in other ways, as where the business of the employer is no longer materially affected by it or where the employer goes out of business."[32] "The right to strike does not carry with it the exclusive right to determine the timing and duration of all work stoppages and does not give employees the right to strike over a matter that is within the sole discretion of the management, such as a decision to fire non-unit employees."[33] If the subject matter of the strike is already covered in a collective bargaining agreement, then the strike will generally violate the National Labor Relations Act as an unfair labor practice, because typically such matters will be subject to mandatory arbitration in lieu of a strike.[34]

§ 2.04 Picketing

Picketing is a form of "protest" speech that workers may rely upon to communicate their dissatisfaction to the general public. As a general

---

[32] Ibid., p. 50.

[33] 48B *Am Jur* 2d, Labor and Labor Relations § 2597.

[34] Ibid. See also 48A Am Jur 2d, Labor and Labor Relations §1283 ("An employer may recover damages resulting from the violation of a non-strike provision in a collective-bargaining agreement.")

rule, "[p]icketing as an aid to strike is not necessarily unlawful provided it does not consist of coercive or otherwise unlawful acts, or amount to an invasion of the rights of others, and provided it is not done for an unlawful purpose."[35] Picketing typically involves the display of signs that include protest language and that are held by numerous protesters who either stand or march together in unison either on or near an employer's place of business.

Picketing activities are analyzed by civil courts, which generally ask two basic questions:

- Is the picketing lawful?
- Is the picketing being carried out in a peaceful manner?

In order to answer the first question (i.e., "Is the picketing lawful?"), courts analyze both state and federal law. "The view has been taken that a valid labor dispute is a prerequisite to the right to picket."[36] "Striking employees have the right to establish a picket line, to use arguments in support of their position, and to attempt by proper means to induce other persons not to work at jobs which they have vacated by striking or to patronize the establishments."[37] "Picketing that may be protected includes area standards picketing, that is, picketing by a union to protest the fact that the employer is not a union and that it pays below-the-wage rates established in the area...; and picketing by an employee in front of a company other than his or her employer, in protest of an alleged racially discriminatory personnel practice."[38] Both the NLRB and the courts have determined the following activities to be unlawful forms of picketing:

- Picketing that is likely to induce violence due in large measure to its peculiar set of circumstances and peculiar setting, e.g., the presence of threats, or other circumstances that take into account the entire setting of where the picketing is taking place. See, e.g., *Thornhill v. Alabama*, 310 U.S. 88 (1940).

---

[35] 51A *Corpus Juris Secundum*, Labor Relations § 281.

[36] Ibid.

[37] Ibid.

[38] 48B *Am Jur* 2d, Labor and Labor Relations § 2644.

- Picketing that obstructs the entrance of persons into the picketed employer's place of business operations. In other words, any acts that prevents persons from entering or leaving the employer's place of business operations. *International Woodworkers, Local Union 303*, 144 NLRB 912 (1963).
- Picketing by "uncertified" unions for recognition or organizational purposes. NLRA, Section 8(b)(7). "To constitute a violation Section 8(b)(7), the picketing in question must have recognition or organization as one of its immediate objectives. [*Department & Specialty Store Employees' Union, Local 1265 v. Brown*, 284 F.2d 619 (9th Cir. 1960), cert. denied, 366 U.S. 934 (1961)—fact that picketing was also for 'informational and advisory' purposes did not make it lawful, since one of its objects was unlawful]."[39]
- Picketing by a labor organization that violates any of the special provisions of Section 8(b) of the National Labor Relations Act (i.e., "unfair labor practices" by labor organizations).
- Picketing a third-party in order to induce it to take action against an employer with whom the union or employees have a grievance. This is known as unlawful "secondary" picketing.
- "Picketing that is not protected…includes: picketing by an unlawfully discharged former employee without the support of fellow workers or union approval, and without having used the grievance procedure; picketing by union members in an attempt to persuade their employer to hire black employees where they did not seek action by the union that represented the employees; and 'mass' picketing aimed at blocking access to a worksite."[40]

There are other very specific rules that regulate picketing, such as rules governing when and where a picket may take place. For this reason, prior to commencing any picketing activity, the protesters should contact the National Labor Relations Board or a labor attorney for specific guidance and instruction.

---

[39] Robert J. Gelhaus and James Oldham, *Labor Law* (Chicago, IL: BarBri, 2002), p. 181.

[40] 48B *Am Jur* 2d, Labor and Labor Relations § 2644.

§ 2.05 Boycotts

Boycotts are a form of strike-activity and picketing-activity. The general rule of thumb is that boycotts are legal for as long as they are peaceful and do not involve the "coercion" of third- party, neutral businesses in order to compel them to stop doing business with an employer with whom the union is protesting. If no "coercion" of the third-party neutral business is involved, and the nature of the boycott simply focuses on the employer's "goods, products, or services" that are being distributed or sold by the third-party neutral business, then the boycott will be deemed to be legal under the NLRA. If the third-party, neutral business has been contacted by the employer and *specifically asked to perform work on behalf of that employer*, then the third-party neutral business will be deemed to be an "ally" of the employer, and thereby it can be boycotted through "coercion," etc. This same rule applies under the "alter-ego" doctrine, where the third-party neutral business is really, in fact, a subsidiary or legal agent of the employer.

Hence, a difference can be made between (a) primary boycotts and (b) secondary boycotts. With respect to primary boycotts, "in general…, a primary boycott, by a union has been held to be a lawful combination which will not be enjoined, even though the execution of its object may tend to diminish the profits of the party against whom such act is aimed, in the absence of the adoption of illegal means and methods to effect it, as by coercion, threat, or fear of violence; and it is immaterial that the employer is unable to grant the demands made on him. However, where for any reason a boycott is, under the circumstances, regarded as unlawful, it will be enjoined."[41]

Secondary boycotts, that is, boycotts of "innocent third parties" who are caught in the middle of a labor dispute, are per se illegal, with limited exceptions.[42] For instance, secondary boycotts of third-party businesses often focus on the handling, purchase, and sale of the struck employer's goods. These boycotts typically focus on informing consumers, who are standing on the premises at the third-party business, not to purchase the struck employer's goods, products or services being sold there. This activity is also known as "consumer" picketing.[43] Thus, "consumer" boycotts are

---

[41] 51B *Corpus Juris Secundum*, Labor Relations § 818.

[42] 51B *Corpus Juris Secundum*, Labor Relations §§ 847, 881.

[43] Another twist is when the boycott of a secondary, neutral business is "non-coercive"

economic in nature and naturally involve innocent third-party businesses, such as the struck employer's customers and vendors. These boycotts are "secondary" in nature, since they occur on or near the premises of a third-party business. These boycotts have also been deemed to be valid, legal boycotts under the NLRA.

Once, however, the consumer picketing activity shifts from boycotting the struck employer's good or products, to actually boycotting other *general economic activities* of the innocent third-party business, then that picketing activity is almost always illegal, as per Section 8(b)(4) of the NLRA. In other words, placing pressure on consumers to cease doing any business whatsoever with an innocent third-party business is illegal under the NLRA. Additionally, placing pressure on innocent third-party businesses, in order to compel them to stop doing any business whatsoever with the struck employer, violates Section 8(b)(4). This provision also prohibits putting pressure on the employees of innocent, third-party businesses, and inducing them to take adverse actions against their own supervisors and managers.

When, however, an innocent thirty-business "enhances the economic value of the product ultimately sold or consumed," then a labor union may lawfully picket and boycott entire business operation of that innocent third-party business. The theory here is based upon the fact that, by actually enhancing the struck-employer's products, that innocent third-party is actually within the chain of production and thus acts as a "secondary" employer of the struck employer. As a secondary employer, the innocent third-party business is said to operate "within the marketing chain" of the struck employer. Therefore, a union may lawfully picket such a "secondary" employer. See, e.g., *Great Western Broadcasting Corp., v. NLRB*, 356 F.2d 434 (9th Cir.).

Finally, another issue is whether or not an employee from a secondary neutral business, who refuses to cross the picket line, is legally protected under the National Labor Relations Act. In general, the refusal to cross the picket line is considered to be legal boycott activity, as per Section 8(b)(4)

---

and is focused only on customers. Since such activity is not designed to coerce a secondary, neutral business to cease doing business with the employer, but instead is designed specifically to encourage customers to stop purchasing the employer's products, which are being sold at the secondary, neutral business, then there is no violation of Section 8(b)(4) of the NLRA. See, e.g., NLRB V. Fruit & Vegetable Packers & Warehousemen Local 760, 377 U.S. 58 (1964).

of the NLRA. Moreover, an employee who refuses to cross a picket line of another third-party business is also engaged in legally-protected activity, as per Section 7, NLRA.

§ 2.06 Remedies for Illegal Strikes, Picketing or Boycotts

One of the most important skills that labor lawyers and human resources professionals must possess is knowledge of how to properly respond to unlawful strikes, picketing, and boycotts. In fact, employers with unionized working environments should develop emergency response plans in order to deal effectively with such a crisis. Since neutral, innocent and third-party businesses may encounter an illegal third-party boycott, employers with non-unionized working environments should also maintain emergency response action plans that address strikes, picketing and boycotts.

In general, an employer who is the victim of an illegal strike, picket, boycott, or other coercive union actions may:

- File an Unfair Labor Practice Charge before the National Labor Relations Board. These Section 8(b)(4) charges *take priority* over other pending charges and *are expedited*. If the NLRB determines that there is "reasonable cause," then it must seek an immediate injunction against the Union or other third party.
- File a Lawsuit for Injunctive Relief in either State or Federal Court. Such lawsuits are based upon common law, and are generally designed to prevent acts of violence and coercion. Such suits may also be filed in order to enforce any "no-strike" provisions found in an operative Collective Bargaining Agreement. If there has been "economic" loss, then such suits may also assert a claim for compensatory damages as per Section 303 of the Taft-Hartley Act.

The employer can sue a labor union, together with its international affiliate that is a party to the collective bargaining agreement, for breach of a "no-strike" provision within the collective bargaining agreement.[44]

---

[44] 45A Am Jur Second, Labor and Labor Relations § 1277.

§ 2.07 Human Resources and Strategic Risk Management

Human resources professionals need a working knowledge of the National Labor Relations Act and the National Labor Relations Board in order to effectively manage labor activities in the unionized workplace. Indeed, every human resources professional, including those who work for non-unionized employers, should maintain this same working knowledge, because strikes, picketing, and boycott activities often spill over into workspaces that are non-unionized. HR professionals should know how to recognize an unfair labor practice, in order to effectively negotiate with union officials and to properly manage the collective bargaining agreement. As strategic business partners of senior management, human resources professionals should know how to coordinate timely and relevant labor training for front-line supervisors, mid-level managers, and senior executives. And, whenever labor conflict is imminent, human resources professionals need to have sufficient labor-law knowledge in order to communicate meaningfully and effectively with a company's general counsel or defense law firm.

Of course, as risk managers, human resources professionals should develop an expertise in surveying employee morale and concerns in order to prevent adversarial employee actions, such as sabotage, wildcat strikes, and the like. Keeping the pulse of employee morale may be done either formally, such as through written questionnaires or focus groups; or, it may be done informally, through keeping tabs on the "water-cooler" gossip around the workplace. Any information regarding employee grievances—especially concerns that affect more than one employee, or concerns that can lead to strikes, wildcat strikes, boycotts, picketing, or other forms of concerted activity—should be taken very seriously and proactively addressed. Also, the "human resources business partner" should be competent at ensuring that:

- The working environment is open and inclusive;
- There is clear and open communication with employees;
- That there is an established and effective conflict-resolution and complaint procedure in place;
- That there are disciplinary procedures that include an impartial, complete review of facts prior to taking disciplinary actions;

- That any non-union statements are clearly disseminated to employees;
- That there are education programs as to the real limitations of labor unions in the workplace; and
- That there are effective climate assessments that identify and respond to labor/ management deficiencies before they deteriorate.

In an industry that is susceptible to unionization, human resources professionals should encourage periodic management training on how to prevent strikes, picketing and boycotts; how to determine between legal and illegal activities; and how to secure injunctions and other remedies through the National Labor Relations Board or the state or federal courts. Management training should stress:

- Enforcement of open door policies;
- Fair and proper treatment of employees;
- Effective grievance procedures and thorough investigations;
- Effective responsiveness to complaints; and,
- Proper steps to prevent unionization.

Lastly, human resources professionals should pay careful attention to important metrics such as turnover, absenteeism, customer satisfaction surveys, statistics regarding the number of claims filed with the EEOC, the number of employee lawsuits filed against the employer, the cost of litigating and settling those lawsuits, and the number of pending or ongoing disciplinary actions.

§ 2.08 Conclusion

An employer and labor union (including groups of non-unionized workers) have the general duty, at all times, to bargain in good faith—and this duty to bargain in good faith actually extends to the actual administration of the collective bargaining agreement (CBA). A breakdown in communications during formal and informal negotiations of the CBA, or disputes that arise after the ratification of the CBA, together with poor human resources leadership, may result in lock-outs, strikes, picketing, and boycotts. Employer lock-outs generally occur after management has determined that industrial relations have reached a nadir; and, in order to protect property, business assets, and profits, the best approach is to prevent employees from returning to work (i.e., the lock-out). Conversely, employees may choose not to return to work (i.e., go on "strike."). There are legal and illegal strikes, and therefore both management and labor unions should be well-versed in this area of the law (or have ready access to experienced labor counsel and maintain direct liaison with professionals at the National Labor Relations Board). The same holds true with respect to picketing and boycotts. Labor law in these areas can be quite complex, depending upon any number of factors, such as the location of the protected activity and the relationship of a third-party neutral business to the employer. For this reason, periodic training in labor law and human resources risk management are highly encouraged.

Chapter Two Bibliography

Books:

Ford, Roderick O. *Understanding Employment Law*. Tampa, FL: Xlibris Pub., 2017.

Gelhaus, Robert J. and James Oldham. *Labor Law*. Chicago, IL: The BarBri Group, 2002.

References:

48 American Jurisprudence (Second), Labor and Labor Relations, §§ 1-1112

48A American Jurisprudence (Second), Labor and Labor Relations, §§ 1477, 1673-2401

48B American Jurisprudence (Second), Labor and Labor Relations, §§ 2402-3569

51 Corpus Jurisprudence Secundum, Labor Relations, §§ 1-262

51A Corpus Jurisprudence Secundum, Labor Relations, §§ 263-780

51B Corpus Jurisprudence Secundum, Labor Relations, §§ 781-1354

Case Law:

U.S. Supreme Court

NLRB v. MacKay Radio & Telegraph Co., 304 U.S. 333 (1938)

Thornhill v. Alabama, 310 U.S. 88 (1940)

NLRB V. Fruit & Vegetable Packers & Warehousemen Local 760, 377 U.S. 58 (1964)

American Ship Building Co. v. NLRB, 330 U.S. 330 (1965)

Textile Workers Union of America v. Darlington Manufacturing Co., 380 U.S. 263 (1965)

Trans World Airlines v. Flight Attendants, 489 U.S. 426 (1989).

U.S. Circuit Courts

Department & Specialty Store Employees' Union, Local 1265 v. Brown, 284 F.2d 619 (9th Cir. 1960), cert. denied, 366 U.S. 934 (1961)

Inter-Collegiate Press v. NLRB, 486 F.2d 837 (8th Cir. 1973)

International Paper Co. v. NLRB, 115 F.3d 1045 (D.C. Cir. 1997)

Great Western Broadcasting Corp., v. NLRB, 356 F.2d 434 (9th Cir.)

National Labor Relations Board

International Woodworkers, Local Union 303, 144 NLRB 912 (1963)

Johns-Manville Products Corp., 223 NLRB 1317 (1976)

Chapter Three

PROTECTED CONCERTED ACTIVITY

§ 3.01 Introduction 80
    § 3.01 (a) History and Purpose of the NLRA
    § 3.01 (b) Non-Unionized Workers and the NLRA

§ 3.02 Protected Concerted Activity: Individual Complaints ("Personal Protests") 87

§ 3.03 Protected Concerted Activity: Individual Spokespersons ("Group Protests") 87

§ 3.04 Protected Concerted Activity: "For Other Mutual Aid and Protection" 89

§ 3.05 Protected Concerted Activity: Right to Participate or Not Participate 90

§ 3.06 Protected Concerted Activity: Protest of Class-wide Race Discrimination 91

§ 3.07 Protected Concerted Activity:
Appeals for Public Support/ Political Protests 92

§ 3.08 Protected Concerted Activity:
Free Speech and the First Amendment 92

§ 3.09 Protected Concerted Activity: Illegal Company Unions 94

§ 3.10 Protected Concerted Activity: Group Action or Class
Action Lawsuits 95

§ 3.11 Protected Concerted Activity: Union Organizing Activities 95

§ 3.12 Human Resources and Strategic Risk Management 99

§ 3.13 Conclusion 100

§ 3.01 Introduction

One of the great tragedies of the modern economic era is the lack of knowledge among non-unionized American workers regarding their collective rights under the National Labor Relations Act of 1935 (NLRA).[45] This lack of knowledge is the cause of much harm to the modern-day American labor movement. Unorganized, non-unionized workers have much more power than most of them realize. In general, if two or more workers meet together to address their problems and concerns, regarding the terms, conditions, and privileges of their employment, they may summon the aid of the National Labor Relations Board, whenever, if ever, they encounter retaliation or discrimination from their employer. American workers can avail themselves of these rights, even if they are not members of a labor union. Unfortunately, the general lack of understanding among today's workforce regarding fundamental rights under the NLRA results in much avoidable workplace agony and abuse. For this reason, this chapter is devoted to the dissemination of basic, important labor-law knowledge on "protected concerted activities" in the workplace.

---

[45] This chapter is especially dedicated to the non-unionized American workforce.

The NLRA was enacted to protect all American workers—and not just union members—from unfair labor practices ("UPL's") from both employers and unions alike. Fundamentally, all American workers—and not just union members-- have the right to meet with each other; to consult and converse among themselves to discuss their terms, conditions, and privileges of employment; and to organize joint and concerted action in order to redress workplace problems and grievances.[46] And they are protected in their efforts to work together in order to address their concerns—these efforts are called "protected concerted activity" under the NLRA. This protected concerted activity must, by definition, involve at least two workers, and not simply one employee acting alone on his or her own behalf:

> Concerted activity protected under the NLRA does not include individual action taken by a worker without contacting fellow employees, even though the worker has a desire to help all the workers; rather, it encompasses only those circumstances in which an individual worker seeks to initiate or induce or to prepare for group action, as well as where an individual worker brings truly group complaints to the attention of management. Actions are concerted if, from all of the circumstances, a reasonable inference can be drawn that the persons involved considered that they had a grievance and decided among themselves that they would take it up with management. Conduct of an individual employee may be considered 'concerted activity' for purposes of the NLRA if the employee's actions are made on behalf of other employees or at least made with the objective of inducing or preparing for group action.[47]

---

[46] Sec. 7. [§ 157.] "Employees shall have the right to self-organization, to form, join, or assist labor organizations, to bargain collectively through representatives of their own choosing, and to engage in other concerted activities for the purpose of collective bargaining or other mutual aid or protection, and shall also have the right to refrain from any or all of such activities except to the extent that such right may be affected by an agreement requiring membership in a labor organization as a condition of employment as authorized in section 8(a)(3) [section 158(a)(3) of this title]."

[47] 48A *Am Jur Second*, Labor and Labor Relations § 1317.

No employer may retaliate against a worker simply because he or she has engaged in such protected concerted activity.[48] The same rule also holds for labor organizations and unions. These labor organizations or labor unions may not retaliate against individual workers for exercising their rights under the NLRA.[49] This is very important information for

---

[48] Sec. 8. [§ 158.] "(a) [**Unfair labor practices by employer**] It shall be an unfair labor practice for an employer-- (1) to interfere with, restrain, or coerce employees in the exercise of the rights guaranteed in section 7 [section 157 of this title]; (2) to dominate or interfere with the formation or administration of any labor organization or contribute financial or other support to it: Provided, That subject to rules and regulations made and published by the Board pursuant to section 6 [section 156 of this title], an employer shall not be prohibited from permitting employees to confer with him during working hours without loss of time or pay; (3) by discrimination in regard to hire or tenure of employment or any term or condition of employment to encourage or discourage membership in any labor organization: Provided, That nothing in this Act [subchapter], or in any other statute of the United States, shall preclude an employer from making an agreement with a labor organization (not established, maintained, or assisted by any action defined in section 8(a) of this Act [in this subsection] as an unfair labor practice) to require as a condition of employment membership therein on or after the thirtieth day following the beginning of such employment or the effective date of such agreement, whichever is the later, (i) if such labor organization is the representative of the employees as provided in section 9(a) [section 159(a) of this title], in the appropriate collective-bargaining unit covered by such agreement when made, and (ii) unless following an election held as provided in section 9(e) [section 159(e) of this title] within one year preceding the effective date of such agreement, the Board shall have certified that at least a majority of the employees eligible to vote in such election have voted to rescind the authority of such labor organization to make such an agreement: Provided further, That no employer shall justify any discrimination against an employee for non-membership in a labor organization (A) if he has reasonable grounds for believing that such membership was not available to the employee on the same terms and conditions generally applicable to other members, or (B) if he has reasonable grounds for believing that membership was denied or terminated for reasons other than the failure of the employee to tender the periodic dues and the initiation fees uniformly required as a condition of acquiring or retaining membership; (4) to discharge or otherwise discriminate against an employee because he has filed charges or given testimony under this Act [subchapter]; (5) to refuse to bargain collectively with the representatives of his employees, subject to the provisions of section 9(a) [section 159(a) of this title]." See, also, *Hugh H. Wilson Corp.*, 171 N.L.R.B. 1040 (1968)("By interfering with, restraining, or coercing its employees in the exercise of rights guaranteed in Section 7 of the Act, Respondent has engaged in and is engaging in unfair labor practices within the meaning of Section 8(a)(1) of the Act.... Said unfair labor practices affect commerce within the meaning of Section 2(6) and (7) of the Act.")

[49] Sec. 8. [§ 158.] "(b)[**Unfair labor practices by labor organization**] It shall be

American workers to know, because in order to be considered "concerted protected activity" under the NLRA, there needs to be only two or more employees who are engaging in communications or joint efforts to improve their working conditions. The nature of these working conditions cover, in general, every aspect of the employer-employee relationship, particularly all of the terms, conditions, and privileges of employment, including:

- Wages
- Hours of work
- Employee Benefits
- Shifts and Shift Differentials
- Health and Safety
- Civil Rights/ Employment Discrimination
- Unions and union organizing (boycotts, strikes, picketing)
- Time-off from work/ work-life issues
- Discipline, suspension, and discharge
- Other terms, conditions, or privileges of employment

What this means is that, underneath the protective arm of the National Labor Relations Act, any two or more American workers can come together

---

an unfair labor practice for a labor organization or its agents--(1) to restrain or coerce (A) employees in the exercise of the rights guaranteed in section 7 [section 157 of this title]: Provided, That this paragraph shall not impair the right of a labor organization to prescribe its own rules with respect to the acquisition or retention of membership therein; or (B) an employer in the selection of his representatives for the purposes of collective bargaining or the adjustment of grievances; (2) to cause or attempt to cause an employer to discriminate against an employee in violation of subsection (a) (3) [of subsection (a)(3) of this section] or to discriminate against an employee with respect to whom membership in such organization has been denied or terminated on some ground other than his failure to tender the periodic dues and the initiation fees uniformly required as a condition of acquiring or retaining membership; (3) to refuse to bargain collectively with an employer, provided it is the representative of his employees subject to the provisions of section 9(a) [section 159(a) of this title]; (4) (i) to engage in, or to induce or encourage any individual employed by any person engaged in commerce or in an industry affecting commerce to engage in, a strike or a refusal in the course of his employment to use, manufacture, process, transport, or otherwise handle or work on any goods, articles, materials, or commodities or to perform any services; or (ii) to threaten, coerce, or restrain any person engaged in commerce or in an industry affecting commerce, where in either case an object thereof is- -

to organize, to lodge grievances and concerns; and to address a wide range of workplace problems.

§ 3.01 (a) History and Purpose of the NLRA

Importantly, the NLRA affords American workers the right to protected concerted activity, not simply for the benefit of workers, but rather for the general welfare of the American economy. The NLRA states that "experience" has taught us that unless workers are given a meaningful voice in the workplace, disruptions to industrial peace will be the inevitable result, thus causing further damage to the American economy. In other words, the NLRA states that it behooves employers, labor unions, and workers to civilly address workplace grievances and problems through collective bargaining (particularly, labor arbitration). The actual text of the NLRA states:

> FINDINGS AND POLICIES
>
> Section 1.[§151.] The denial by some employers of the right of employees to organize and the refusal by some employers to accept the procedure of collective bargaining lead to strikes and other forms of industrial strife or unrest, which have the intent or the necessary effect of burdening or obstructing commerce by (a) impairing the efficiency, safety, or operation of the instrumentalities of commerce; (b) occurring in the current of commerce; (c) materially affecting, restraining, or controlling the flow of raw materials or manufactured or processed goods from or into the channels of commerce, or the prices of such materials or goods in commerce; or (d) causing diminution of employment and wages in such volume as substantially to impair or disrupt the market for goods flowing from or into the channels of commerce.
>
> The inequality of bargaining power between employees who do not possess full freedom of association or actual liberty of contract and employers who are organized in the corporate or other forms of ownership association substantially burdens and affects the flow of commerce, and tends to aggravate recurrent business

depressions, by depressing wage rates and the purchasing power of wage earners in industry and by preventing the stabilization of competitive wage rates and working conditions within and between industries.

Experience has proved that protection by law of the right of employees to organize and bargain collectively safeguards commerce from injury, impairment, or interruption, and promotes the flow of commerce by removing certain recognized sources of industrial strife and unrest, by encouraging practices fundamental to the friendly adjustment of industrial disputes arising out of differences as to wages, hours, or other working conditions, and by restoring equality of bargaining power between employers and employees.

Experience has further demonstrated that certain practices by some labor organizations, their officers, and members have the intent or the necessary effect of burdening or obstructing commerce by preventing the free flow of goods in such commerce through strikes and other forms of industrial unrest or through concerted activities which impair the interest of the public in the free flow of such commerce. The elimination of such practices is a necessary condition to the assurance of the rights herein guaranteed

It is declared to be the policy of the United States to eliminate the causes of certain substantial obstructions to the free flow of commerce and to mitigate and eliminate these obstructions when they have occurred by encouraging the practice and procedure of collective bargaining and by protecting the exercise by workers of full freedom of association, self- organization, and designation of representatives of their own choosing, for the purpose of negotiating the terms and conditions of their employment or other mutual aid or protection.

I have included this brief introduction to the NLRA, because it alleviates much confusion regarding its legislative purpose and objectives. The NLRA was enacted to encourage both employers and employees to "meet and confer" in order to discuss workplace problems and to engage in collective bargaining. This means that employers have a legal obligation to meet with two or more employees who have workplace problems and grievances. Employers must not simply acknowledge employees' grievances and concerns, but they must make a good faith effort to address and resolve those grievances and concerns. Failure to do so might lead to an "unfair labor practice" charge and prosecution for a "refusal to bargain" before the National Labor Relations Board. The NLRA affords these rights to both unionized and non-unionized American workers.

§ 3.01 (b) Non-Unionized Workers and the NLRA

As previously mentioned, too many non-unionized American workers falsely believe that the NLRA does not apply to them, because they are not members of labor unions. As a consequence, these workers often feel powerless and unable to address collectively their workplace concerns and issues, due in large measure to their own ignorance of the NLRA. Many of these workers have never heard of the NLRA, and are not familiar with the National Labor Relations Board. They do not know that they have the right to meet collectively with fellow co-workers and to discuss with their collective grievances with their employers; and that these collective grievances may include all manners of employment concerns regarding their collective terms, conditions, and privileges of employment. In sum, non-unionized workers have the right to present their collective grievances and concerns to their employers. And this statutory right is known as "protected concerted activity" under the NLRA. Thus, the NLRA protects non-unionized workers while pursuing their collective efforts; and, specifically, non-unionized workers are protected against discrimination, reprisal, disciplinary action, and termination that occur as a result of having engaged in concerted protected activity. Again, there must be at least two employees who decide to address collective workplace issues in order to trigger NLRA protections.

§ 3.02 Protected Concerted Activity: Individual Complaints ("Personal Protests")

As previously mentioned, an employee will not be deemed to have engaged in "protected concerted activity" where he or she is acting purely for personal benefit. Both the National Labor Relations Board (NLRB) and the courts apply a "totality of circumstances test," to determine if an individual employee is really protesting for his own behalf or on behalf of himself and other workers. This particular area of labor law can be a minefield for employees, non-experienced union stewards, labor advocates, and lawyers, because the NLRB frequently changes its rulings on which conduct will meet the definition of "protected concerted activity" and which conduct falls outside of that definition. For example, "[i]ndividual action is not protected concerted activity when, in a personal protest, an employee temporarily refuses to operate a bulldozer in order to try to obtain a wage increase, or when, during a discussion with a manager, an individual employee makes a purely personal complaint about a change in his compensation, and only as an afterthought raises several issues that other employees had complained about."[50]

For additional examples of how the NLRB and the courts have ruled on cases involving this particular issue, please also consult Kenneth T. Lopatka's *NLRA Rights in the Nonunion Workplace*.[51]

§ 3.03 Protected Concerted Activity: Individual Spokespersons ("Group Protests")

In the non-unionized working environment, two or more workers may very well organize to function much similar to a local union. The NLRA gives these workers the right to formally authorize one of their fellow co-workers to function as their spokesperson. Such *authorization gives the spokesperson legal authority* under the NLRA to act and speak on behalf of other workers who share the same concern.

---

[50] 48A *Am Jur Second*, Labor and Labor Relations § 1319.

[51] Kenneth T. Lopatka, *NLRA Rights in the Nonunion Workplace* (Arlington, VA: BNA Books, 2010).

In prior decisions of the National Labor Relations Board (NLRB), it has long been settled that when an individual employee has been authorized to speak on behalf of another employee or group of employees, the individual's action is deemed to be "protected concerted activity."[52] In the case of *Walter Brucker & Co.*,[53] the NLRB stated that "[w]e agree with the judge that Wright's discussion with his fellow employees at lunch on 6 November about the applicable wage rate for performing corrective punch list work at the project was an effort to initiate and promote concerted action. As the judge noted, when Wright spoke to the Respondent and later to the Authority, he voiced a complaint about wages that Culbreath and he both shared. Wright was clearly acting 'on the authority of other employees.' Because the record shows that Culbreath refrained from making his own wage complaint, relying instead on Wright to resolve the matter."[54]

And in the case of *Cone Bros. Contracting Co.*,[55] the NLRB stated that "[t]he only issue here is whether the Company discriminatorily discharged Exum by reason of his union affiliation or because he engaged in concerted activities with other employees.… By discriminating in regard to the hire and tenure of employment of Gerald W. Exum, the Company has engaged in and is engaging in unfair labor practices within the meaning of Section 8(a)(3) and (1) of the Act."[56]

Finally, in the case of *Smith Victory Co.*,[57] the NLRB stated, "[b]y discriminating in regard to the hire of employment of Florence McMaster because she engaged in concerted activities with and on behalf of other employees for the purpose of collective bargaining and other mutual aid and protection, Respondent interfered with, coerced, and restrained its employees in the exercise of rights guaranteed by Section 7 of the Act, and Respondent has thereby engaged and is engaging in unfair labor practices within the meaning of Section 8(a)(3) of the Act."[58]

---

[52] Ibid., p. 102

[53] *Walter Brucker & Co.*, 273 N.L.R.B. 1306 (1984).

[54] Id.

[55] *Cone Bros. Contracting Co.*, 125 N.L.R.B. 843 (1959).

[56] Id.

[57] *Smith Victory Co.*, 90 N.L.R.B. 2089 (1950).

[58] Id.

§ 3.04 Protected Concerted Activity: "For Other Mutual Aid and Protection"

Importantly, a worker who speaks up for himself concerning the terms, conditions, or privileges of employment, *which are also of concern to other co-workers*, may be deemed to have engaged in an activity that is "for other mutual aid and protection" of fellow co-workers. Section 7 of the National Labor Relations Act deems this activity to be "protected concerted activity."

According to previous NLRB decisions, all that seems to be necessary to infer authorization in the person who is doing the speaking is that more than one employee exhibit *a concern about a particular aspect of their employment* and *decide that they want it changed.* This is a liberal interpretation of the rule, and the NLRB has over the years changed or restricted the position that: *when a single employee articulates a protest on behalf of himself, and that protest can reasonably relate to a group of other co-workers, then he or she may be found to have been implicitly authorized by his or her coworkers and thus to be acting concertedly.*[59] As per this more liberal position, the NLRB will look to see if there is any chance that the individual protest may constitute "mutual aid and protection."

In the case of *Eastex, Inc. v. NLRB*[60], the U.S. Supreme Court held that such protection should be given broad construction, because the "National Labor Relations Act's definition of 'employee' was intended to protect employees when they engage in otherwise proper concerted activities in support of employees of employers other than their own, and it has long been held that 'mutual aid and protection' encompasses such activity.... Employees do not lose their protection under the 'mutual aid or protection' clause of the National Labor Relations Act when they seek to improve terms and conditions of employment or otherwise improve their lot as employees through channels outside the immediate employee-employer relationship National Labor Relations Act, §§ 2(3)."[61]

In the case of *Barnsider, Inc.*,[62] the Board ruled that since the individual employee's protest was related to "working conditions" that the said protest must constitute "mutual aid and protection" under the NLRA. The Board

---

[59] Ibid.

[60] *Eastex, Inc. v. NLRB*, 437 U.S. 556 (1978).

[61] Ibid.

[62] *Barnsider, Inc.*, 195 N.L.R.B. 754 (1972).

stated that "[b]y discharging James P. Walsh on April 27, 1971, because of his concerted activities in protesting certain policies of the Respondent relating to working conditions, the Respondent engaged in unfair labor practices within the meaning of Section 8(a)(1) of the Act.... By failing and refusing on April 29, 1971, and thereafter until May 6, 1971, to honor the unconditional request of its employees named in footnote 1, above, to return to work, thereby locking out and discriminating against said employees because they had engaged in concerted activities for the purpose of collective bargaining and other mutual aid and protection, the Respondent engaged in unfair labor practices within the meaning of Section 8(a)(1) and (3) of the Act."[63]

Similarly, in the case of *Guernsey-Muskingum Elec. Co-op.*,[64] the Board ruled that "[b]y discharging James Richard (Dick) Boyer, thus discriminating in regard to his hire and tenure of employment because he had engaged in protected concerted activities for the purposes of collective bargaining or other mutual aid and protection, the Respondent had engaged in and is engaging in unfair labor practices within the meaning of Section 8(a)(3) and (1) of the Act.... By interfering with, restraining, and coercing its employees in the exercise of the rights guaranteed in Section 7 of the Act, the Respondent has committed unfair labor practices within the meaning of Section 8(a)(1) of the Act."[65]

§ 3.05 Protected Concerted Activity: Right to Participate or Not Participate

It is important for union leaders and organizers to understand that the National Labor Relations Act affords workers *the right not to participate* in any unionizing or organizing activities.[66] This right to refrain from engaging in union activities is, however, limited by the NLRA's allowance of "union security agreements" (i.e., union shop and agency shop clauses) within collective bargaining agreements. See, e.g., Chapter Four, § 4.6. "Thus, employees need not affiliate themselves with any particular labor

---

[63] Ibid.

[64] *Guernsey-Muskingum Elec. Co-op.*, 124 N.L.R.B. 618 (1959).

[65] Id.

[66] 48A *Am Jur Second*, Labor and Labor Relations § 1309.

organization, may choose not to participate in union activities, and may choose to refrain from strike activities."[67]

§ 3.06 Protected Concerted Activity: Protest of Class-wide Race Discrimination

The National Labor Relations Act also shares jurisdiction with Title VII of the 1964 Civil Rights Act over "class-wide" racial discrimination grievances and over grievances alleging that there are employer policies, practices, and patterns of systematic racial discrimination. As a general rule:

> Discrimination based on race or national origin violates the National Labor Relations Act only if it directly interferes with the National Labor Relation Board's role of fostering collective bargaining and protecting employees' rights to act concertedly. However, an employer violates the NLRA by maintaining a policy and practice of invidious discrimination against its employees on account of race or national origin, as such a policy creates an unjustified clash of interest between groups of workers, thus frustrating the possibility of concerted action. In addition, an employee's conduct is protected activity under the NLRA when the employee voices, on behalf of other employees, concerns and complaints about alleged race discrimination.[68]

As a practical matter, employees and labor advocates who are addressing class-wide racial discrimination, or situations involving retaliation for complaining about patterns and practices of racial discrimination, should consider filing charges of discrimination before the National Labor Relations Board (NLRB) in lieu of the U.S. Equal Employment Opportunity Commission, for a variety of reasons: the NLRB has enforcement authority; moves with much more efficiency and rapidity;

---

[67] Ibid.

[68] 48A *Am Jur Second*, Labor and Labor Relations §1311.

and provides their own lawyers (i.e., the General Counsel) who are paid by the taxpayers rather than individual workers.[69]

§ 3.07 Protected Concerted Activity: Appeals for Public Support/ Political Protests

When one or more employees opt to contact a newspaper, local television station, or public agency or elected official for support in redressing their workplace grievances (i.e., terms, conditions, and privileges of employment), on behalf of themselves and others, then they will likely be deemed to have engaged in "protected concerted activity," as per the NLRA. Employers therefore may not restrict or prohibit this activity; nor may they retaliate against their employees who opt to take such actions.[70]

§ 3.08 Protected Concerted Activity: Free Speech and the First Amendment

During union organizing activities, employees are generally free to express themselves, including using vulgar language. Such vulgar language might be profanity and it may even constitute obscenity; but it may not be abusive, threatening, or disturb the efficient operation of the employer's business. Nor may such language be willfully false, or asserted with flagrant disregard for truth.[71]

Furthermore, employers "may not restrict employees' statements through the use of a collective bargaining provision that authorizes discharge or discipline" for statements that are otherwise permissible under the National Labor Relations Act.[72] However, the First Amendment of the United States Constitution protects an employer "in expressing its opinions, preferences, and prejudices relative to labor relations. The right to discuss and inform people concerning the advantages and disadvantages

---

[69] See, generally, Kenneth T. Lopatka, *NLRA Rights in the Nonunion Workplace* (Arlington, VA: BNA Books, 2010).

[70] 48A *Am Jur Second*, Labor and Labor Relations § 1312.

[71] Ibid, §§ 1315-1316.

[72] Ibid.

of unions and joining them is protected not only as part of free speech, but as part of free assembly."[73]

It is therefore obvious that both employers and unions (and individual employees) have free speech rights under the National Labor Relations Act that can come into conflict with each other; and, therefore, these "free speech" rights require delicate weighing and balancing, especially during campaigns to organize a labor union. This weighing and balancing process is a highly detailed and specialized area of labor law. For this reason, employees, union stewards, and labor advocates should refer their questions to the National Labor Relations Board (NLRB) for processing and review. As a general rule of thumb, the NLRB will take into account a number of factors in determining whether an employer has violated the NLRA, including:

- The timing of the speech;
- The words used in the speech;
- Whether the speech targeted union supporters; and
- Whether the speech was directed toward employees who were being threatened.[74]

The common rule is that an employer may not engage in "T.I.P.S,"— that is to say, an employer may not *"threaten"* its employees; it may not *"interrogate"* its employees; it may not *"promise"* benefits to dissuade union organizing; and it may not *"spy"* upon employees who are engaging in union organizing.[75]

For more examples of how the NLRB and the courts have ruled on cases involving "free speech" and the workplace, please also consult the National Labor Relations Board's website or contact this agency directly for additional material.

---

[73] Ibid, § 1341.

[74] Ibid, § 1345.

[75] Ibid, §§ 1362-1453.

§ 3.09 Protected Concerted Activity: Illegal Company Unions

As per various unfair labor practices rules of the NLRA, the employer may not pose as a wolf in sheep's clothing in order to dominate the local union or to put undue pressure upon local union leaders. Such friendly support and gestures from employers, toward their local union leaders and organizers, defeat the objectives of the National Labor Relations Act and are illegal. Indicia of employer dominance can occur in a variety of ways. For example, employers might try to improperly participate in union elections, union meetings, union committees, and decisions determining whether an employee's grievance should advance to the next stage in the grievance procedures, or go to arbitration. Illegal employer interference and dominance have also occurred where the employer colludes with the union to operate a "closed shop" or other form of illegal "union security clause," regardless of whether that clause is written or unwritten.

Additionally, "[a]n employer's domination of a labor organization will be inferred in the following circumstances:

- From the manner in which union meetings are conducted where meetings are called by the employer, held on company time, and with full management participation;
- Where employee committees operate on a consensus decision-making basis and have management committee members that retain veto power over any committee action;
- Where meetings of an employee committee are held at the employer's convenience, on its premises, and never in management's absence;
- Where an employee committee holds no meetings apart from its discussions with management, discusses only those subjects on the employer's agenda, conducts the meetings on company premises, and management writes and circulates communications concerning the committee's work; and
- Where a personnel committee's permanent chairperson, appointed by the employer, changes the voting procedures for membership on the committee, unilaterally abrogates two elective positions, and dictates the agenda."[76]

---

[76] Ibid, § 1487.

Union stewards, labor advocates, and employees should therefore remain watchful as to the nature of the actual working relationships and interactions between union leadership and management. Are there any conflicts of interest?

If there are any red flags whatsoever, and the union members feel that their labor rights are jeopardized as a result of their employer's undue influence upon the labor union, then these concerned union members should notify the National Labor Relations Board, express their grievances and concerns, and request further assistance. Here, it is also helpful to refer the reader back to Chapter One, "Labor's Bill of Rights."

§ 3.10 Protected Concerted Activity: Group Action or Class Action Lawsuits

When one or more employees decide to participate in a lawsuit against their employer, for any reason, but especially lawsuits involving the terms, conditions, or privileges of employment, then they will be deemed to have engaged in protected concerted activity pursuant to Section 7 of the National Labor Relations Act. Employers may not take retaliatory or discriminatory actions against them. Here, we should take into account employees who are asked to serve as witnesses in support of their fellow co-workers, even in cases involving litigation involving other forms of workplace violations, such as racial discrimination and sexual harassment, which are both cognizable under Title VII of the 1964 Civil Rights Act.

§ 3.11 Protected Concerted Activity: Union Organizing Activities

Section 7 of the National Labor Relations Act gives individual workers the right to seek out help from labor unions; to bring in a new labor union into the workplace; to engage in organizing efforts; to reach out to fellow co-workers to discuss working conditions; to distribute union literature; to discuss wages or other conditions of employment with fellow co-workers; and to otherwise engage in union organizing activities. An employer may not threaten, spy upon, interrogate, or dissuade these workers from engaging in such labor organizing activities.[77]

It is important here to remember that there are three basic rights under the NLRA: (a) the right to self-organize; (b) the right to bargain collectively; and (c) the right to act together for "mutual aid and protection." An "unfair labor practice" occurs whenever the employer or a union prevents workers from exercising these rights.

Workers have the right to decide that bringing in a formal labor union is also in their best interests. When this occurs, both workers and managers should be mindful of the four-stage process of bringing in and formalizing a collective bargaining agreement between an employer and union: (a) union organizing campaign; (b) authorization card signatures; (c) final determination of the bargaining unit; and (d) election and certification results.

Unions have the right, also, to influence and to educate workers about the benefits of having a labor union. Unions may send "undercover" union agents to apply for a job at a prospective employer, in order to influence and organize the workforce. This process is called "salting."

Organizing efforts generally take the form of informal meetings and discussions between union officials and workers. This initial stage of union organizing often includes getting the workers to sign "authorization cards." At least 30% of the workers who fall within the similarly-situated group of workers must sign the authorization cards, in order for the National Labor Relations Board (NLRB) to schedule an election.

Human resources professionals and labor attorneys must educate front-line managers to avoid handling the authorization cards. This is because the NLRB has ruled in previous cases, that when an employer's representative takes physical possession of the authorization cards, the employer tacitly acknowledges the union as the official representative of the bargaining unit. In order to avoid this result, employers should ask union organizers to forward the authorization cards directly to the NLRB. Otherwise, an employer's physical handling of these authorization cards could lead to automatic recognition of the union.

There are three other methods whereby a union can win "automatic recognition": (a) when the union convinces the employer to accept and witness the majority status of employees who are in favor of the union,

---

[77] Ibid, §§ 1326-1329.

such as an authorization card with signatures from more than 50% of the prospective bargaining unit; (b) when the union convinces the employer to grant recognition, due to a number of other reasons; and (c) the union wins recognition through an unfair labor practices charge that results in a bargaining order from the NLRB.

Under certain circumstances, a good labor attorney may present a successful argument to the NLRB, on behalf of the employer-client, in order to prevent an election from taking place. These are *"election bar" defenses*. For example, where the NLRB has already issued a certification of representation to another labor organization, then no election can take place within twelve months from the date of that certification. This is called the *"certification bar."* Another defense to allowing a certification election is called the *"contract bar,"* which prevents a certification election from taking place for so long as another valid collective bargaining agreement is already in existence. A caveat to the "contract bar" is that a special election may be held within a period that is the 180th day to the 150th day [or 120th day to 90th day, depending upon the industry] from the end of a three-year collective bargaining agreement. This is, in other words, a 30-day window in order to conduct an election. This 30-day window opens and closes between 4-6 months before the expiration of an existing collective bargaining agreement. (NOTE: the NLRA prohibits a collective bargaining agreement from being longer than three years). A third defense is the *"prior-petition bar."* An election petition cannot be filed until after six months from the date of a previous petition. And, finally, the *"election year bar"* defense prohibits an election from taking place, when a prior valid election has occurred within one year from the date of the proposed election.

Assuming that the union is able to attain an authorization card with at least 30% of signatures from workers within a prospective bargaining unit, the NLRB will then conduct a "pre-election" meeting between the NLRB official, the union officials, and the employer's representatives. The NLRB officials set the ground rules for conducting the election; they also forewarn both employers and labor unions against committing unfair labor practices during the election; and they set a schedule and time-frame for election campaigning. These NLRB officials also determine which employees fall within the "bargaining unit." After a formal petition for an election is filed, after this meeting, the NLRB will then schedule the election. The union will need to secure 50% of the vote from the bargaining unit, plus 1 additional vote, in order to win the election.

The workers who are eligible to vote in the election are, of course, all of those workers whom the NLRB will have determined to be within the bargaining unit. The workers must be on payroll during both the payroll period immediately before the date of the election and following the election. Employees who have been permanently laid off, even if subject to recall, cannot vote; employees who are on a long-term leave of absence and who must apply for reinstatement in order to return to work, also cannot vote in the election. However, employees who are on strike might be able to vote; the rule of thumb is that if the election is held within twelve months of the strike, then the striking workers will be able to vote.

Both employees and employers should remain mindful of the types of unfair labor practices that occur frequently during these elections. In general, an employer may not (a) threaten, (b) interrogate, (c) promise benefits or monetary compensation, or (d) spy on the workers. The acronym used collectively to describe these unfair labor practices is called "T.I.P.S."

After a successful election, and after the NLRB has ruled that a particular labor union is the recognized bargaining agent, the formal negotiations between an employer and a labor organization may begin. This is called "collective bargaining." What workers should know is that this "collective bargaining" is a statutory duty that is imposed upon employers by the National Labor Relations Act. Collective bargaining is an on-going process throughout the entire life of the collective bargaining agreement; filing grievances is a part of this process; union representation is a part of this process; and, likewise, the employer's duty to address and resolve grievances are a part of this same process. Thus, whenever any party fails to discharge its statutory duties under the collective bargaining agreement, they will have committed an unfair labor practice or either breached the collective bargaining agreement. Although breaching the collective bargaining agreement is not always the same as the commission of an unfair labor practice, these two concepts more often overlap; and, sometimes, they are simultaneously remedied through ULP charges before the NLRB.

Employers, union officials, labor advocates, labor attorneys and senior managers need to understand that after the NLRB orders collective bargaining, there are no hard-and-fast rules that govern this process. (For this reason, I spent two days at Harvard Law School's Program on Negotiation in order to learn more about the theory, method, and practice of collective bargaining.)[78] In general, there are four broad types of collective bargaining:

(a). *Integrative bargaining* or Integrative Interests-Based (IIB) bargaining: this bargaining approach occurs when more than one issue needs to be resolved, and both parties attempt to reconcile and create solutions that are of great benefit for both parties' interests.

(b). *Distributive bargaining*: this is an approach to bargaining that is used when the parties are in conflict over an issue, and the outcome represents a gain for one party, and a loss for the other party. This is also called "zero-sum" bargaining.

(c). *Concessionary bargaining*: this is a bargaining approach that demands concessions from the unions in return for job security.

(d). *Continuous bargaining*: this approach to bargaining occurs when both labor unions and management meet continuously, over a period of time, to resolve problems that are of common interest. This form of bargaining is similar to integrative bargaining.

In addition to these four basic approaches to collective bargaining, many national unions, such as the International Brotherhood of Teamsters and the United Automobile Workers (U.A.W.) engage *in tactical bargaining* (i.e., the *"whipsaw"* or *"parallel bargaining"*) whereby they negotiate with multiple employers within the same industry either successively or simultaneously, in order to leverage their bargaining power and positions.

§ 3.12 Human Resources and Strategic Risk Management

Over the past few decades, the human resources profession has evolved into the "business" partner for front-line, mid-level, and senior-level management. Its function has become more complex, requiring a greater level of strategic management skill-sets. One of the major skill-sets

---

[78] See, e.g., Richard E. Walton and Robert B. McKersie, *A Behavioral Theory of Labor Negotiations: An Analysis of a Social Interaction System* (Ithaca, N.Y.: Cornell ILR Press, 1991); Michael L. Moffit and Robert C. Bordone, *The Handbook of Dispute Resolution* (San Francisco, CA: Jossey-Bass, 2005).

now required from human resources leaders is that of the prevention of unionization of the non-unionized workplace. In other words, human resources professionals must be able to recognize when the workforce is becoming so demoralized that it might seek assistance from outside sources, such as a labor union. These human resources professionals must know when and how to speak to disgruntled workers about the disadvantages of bringing in a labor union. At the same time, they must be able to steer clear of violating any other provisions under the NLRA, such as threatening, interrogating, promising pay or other benefits, or spying upon the workers.

Therefore, the human resources profession must take inventory of the nature of the complaints and grievances that are being lodged from within the workforce; and they must assist both workers and supervisors with finding methods to resolve workplace problems. Sometimes this may require restructuring jobs, teams, and the flow of work (e.g., techno-structural changes such as total quality management (TQM) and Six-Sigma implementations). Sometimes this may mean establishing a "high performance" organization (HI PO), which gives lower-level workers more input into the decision-making aspects of the work, as well as pay-for-performance schemes. Sometimes this might mean restructuring the compensation packages, in order give workers a greater share of the profits. Sometimes this may mean revisiting the organization's values, culture, and ethics policies. Sometimes this might mean building a brand new "conflict resolution" management program. Sometimes, this might mean implementing a cultural diversity program. Therefore, it behooves workers to understand what to bargain for and what to actually demand from human resources leaders. Likewise, it behooves human resources leaders to know, understand, and resolve workplace problems before they ripen into more serious workplace conflicts, such as strikes, picketing, boycotts, EEOC charges, lawsuits, and the like.

§ 3.13 Conclusion

The National Labor Relations Act (NLRA) is the most important federal labor law for non-unionized American workers. It is the only federal law that allows non-unionized workers to address and to protest every aspect of their working conditions. It is the only federal law that requires employers to meet with employees in order to discuss the terms, conditions, and privileges of their employment. Unfortunately, most American workers are unaware of their NLRA privileges and rights. And many workers, who know about the NLRA, are unaware that it applies to workers who are not members of labor unions. This misconception among most non-unionized American workers has created a "chilling effect" upon workers' willingness to address workplace injustices. They are unaware that it only takes two employees to form "protected concerted activity," which carries protected legal status under the NLRA. These American workers are tragically unaware that, in order for them to avail themselves of many important rights afforded under the NLRA, they need not be active members of labor unions. One individual employee, who addresses workplace issues that relate to general working conditions, may be engaging in "protected concerted activity" under the NLRA, if his or her grievances are of important concern to other co-employees. Hence, the NLRA provides workers with very powerful tools which they may rely upon in order to address workplace problems. For this reason, this chapter has been dedicated especially to the non-unionized American workforce.

Chapter Three Bibliography

Books:

Ford, Roderick O. *Understanding Employment Law*. Tampa, FL: Xlibris Pub., 2017.

Gelhaus, Robert J. and James Oldham. *Labor Law*. Chicago, IL: The BarBri Group, 2002.

Gormon, Richard A. and Matthew W. Finkin. *Basic Text on Labor Law: Unionization and Collective Bargaining*. St. Paul, MN: West Publishing Co., 2004.

Lopatka, Kenneth T. *NLRA Rights in the Nonunion Workplace*. Arlington, VA: BNA Books, 2010.

References:

48A *Am Jur Second*, Labor and Labor Relations §§ 1335-1736.

Case Law:

Walter Brucker & Co., 273 N.L.R.B. 1306 (1984)

Cone Bros. Contracting Co., 125 N.L.R.B. 843 (1959)

Smith Victory Co., 90 N.L.R.B. 2089 (1950)

Eastex, Inc. v. NLRB, 437 U.S. 556 (1978)

Barnsider, Inc., 195 N.L.R.B. 754 (1972)

Hugh H. Wilson Corp., 171 N.L.R.B. 1040 (1968)

Guernsey-Muskingum Elec. Co-op., 124 N.L.R.B. 618 (1959)

Chapter Four

NEGOTIATING THE COLLECTIVE BARGAINING AGREEMENT

§ 4.01 What is Collective Bargaining?... 104

§ 4.02 Employer's Duty to Recognize the Union 105

§ 4.03 Union's Exclusive Authority to Represent Bargaining Unit 107

§ 4.04 Duty to Bargain in Good Faith.. 109

§ 4.05 Successor Employer's Duty to Bargain 113

§ 4.06 Mandatory, Permissive, and Illegal Subjects of Collective Bargaining 113

§ 4.07 Union Security Clauses... 115

§ 4.08 Human Resources and Strategic Risk Management.................. 116

§ 4.09 Conclusion.. 117

§ 4.01 What is Collective Bargaining?

In a very narrow, legal, and technical sense, the National Labor Relations Act (NLRA) considers "collective bargaining" to include those moments when a single individual speaks up on behalf of himself and at least one other person, regarding a term, condition, or privilege of employment. This is true regardless of whether or not a labor union is involved in the discussion.[79] However, under most circumstances, "collective bargaining" generally involves on-going negotiations and transactions between a labor union and an employer. Hence, whenever labor unions are involved in customary "collective bargaining," we typically classify such involvement as falling into two categories: (a) the *formation phase* of creating the collective bargaining agreement (CBA); and (or), (b) the *administrative phase* of carrying out the terms of the CBA (e.g., the processing of individual employee grievances[80]; see, also, Chapter Five).

This chapter, however, focuses on collective bargaining during the "formation phase" of creating the collective bargaining agreement. The "administrative phase" shall be covered in Chapter Five. According to *Corpus Juris Secundum,* collective bargaining is defined as "a procedure looking toward the making of a collective agreement between the employer and the accredited representative of his employees concerning wages, hours, and other conditions of employment."[81] Additionally, and equally important, "[e]mployees have the right to bargain collectively with their employer, and the right to organize is essential to the right to bargain collectively. The right of employees to bargain collectively and to engage in concerted activities for the purpose of collective bargaining, or for other mutual aid and protection, has long been recognized by the courts and public opinion as lawful and in the public interest...."[82] Thus, when employees make demands regarding the terms, conditions, and privileges of their employment, the NLRA mandates that employers meet and confer with individual employees, groups of employees, or labor unions, in good faith.[83]

---

[79] See, e.g., Chapter Three, "Protected Concerted Activity."

[80] 48A Am Jur Second, Labor and Labor Relations § 2211.

[81] 51 *Corpus Juris Secundum,* § 148.

[82] 51 *Corpus Juris Secundum,* § 150.

[83] "Collective bargaining presupposes that the employees shall have an opportunity in

Traditionally, the NLRA especially regulates the duty of employers to negotiate and to bargain with labor unions. The NLRA makes it an unfair labor practice for an employer to refuse to bargain collectively with the representatives of its employees. "The employer's obligation to bargain arises on the date a majority of the appropriate bargaining-unit employees select the union as their representative. However, there is no obligation to bargain with union locals absent either a certified union election or voluntary recognition based upon a contemporaneous showing of majority support."[84]

As previously mentioned, the duty to bargain in good faith extends to wages, hours, and other terms and conditions of employment. "Thus, in order to establish a prima facie case of an employer's refusal to bargain collectively with labor union representatives, a petitioner must show that an obligation to bargain existed, and that the employer refused to bargain either directly," [85] or that it failed to bargain by unilaterally effecting a change in working conditions. When determining whether an employer failed to bargain in good faith, the reviewing court will examine the employer's conduct in the totality of circumstances in which the bargaining took place.[86]

§ 4.02 Employer's Duty to Recognize the Union

When must collective bargaining actually commence? Interestingly enough, the process may begin almost immediately, even whenever a group of workers (i.e., the bargaining unit) is not represented by an established

---

the absence of their employer to canvass their grievances, formulate their demands, and instruct an advocate who they believe will best press their claims. It involves the right of members of a labor organization, either through a committee or through a representative, to confer with the employer, and to present their claims or grievances as to hours, wages, and general conditions incident to their employment, with the end in view of arriving at a reasonable and amicable adjustment of such matters. Collective bargaining is a continuing process which, among other things, involves day-to-day adjustments in the contract and other working rules, resolution of new problems not covered by existing agreements, and the protection of employee rights already secured by contract." 51 *Corpus Juris Secundum,* § 148.

[84] 48A Am Jur. 2d, § 1673.
[85] Ibid.
[86] Ibid.

labor union.[87] In other words, any group of non-unionized workers may select a fellow co-worker to speak up on their behalf "for other mutual aid and protection," and the employer has a legal obligation to listen to that representative, and to redress the grievances of the entire group of workers.[88] In other words, the National Labor Relations Act, Section 7, protects non-unionized workers and affords them the opportunity to petition their employers for the redress of collective grievances involving the terms, conditions, and privileges of their employment.[89] Specifically, Section 7 of the NLRA guarantees employees "the right to self-organization, to form, join, or assist labor organizations, to bargain collectively through representatives of their own choosing, and to engage in other concerted activities for the purpose of collective bargaining or other mutual aid or protection," as well as the right "to refrain from any or all such activities."[90] In addition, Section 8 prohibits either employers or labor unions from retaliating against or discriminating against workers who chose to organize and to redress their workplace grievances pursuant to Section 7.[91] Specifically, Section 8(a)(1) of the Act makes it an unfair labor practice for an employer "to interfere with, restrain, or coerce employees in the exercise of the rights guaranteed in Section 7" of the Act.[92] For this reason, workers who are non-unionized should establish a very close liaison with a representative from the National Labor Relations Board whenever, if ever, they chose to take action or to redress their workplace grievances.[93]

At some point, a labor union may get involved in order to provide technical assistance to the unorganized, non-unionized group of workers. If the workers select a representative from a labor union to speak up on their behalf, an employer *is not required* to bargain with the labor union's representative *unless* the NLRB has first "certified" the labor union, following a certification election, or there has been voluntary recognition of that labor union, based upon a contemporaneous showing of majority support. Once the labor union is "certified," following an election, it

---

[87] See, e.g., Chapter Three, "Protected Concerted Activity."
[88] Ibid.
[89] Ibid.
[90] Ibid.
[91] Ibid.
[92] Ibid.
[93] Ibid.

must "request bargaining" in order to trigger "an employer's duty to bargain."[94] At that point, the employer must "bargain" or negotiate a collective bargaining agreement for at least a reasonable period of time (typically one year) following the NLRB's "certification." See, e.g., *Brooks v. NLRB*, 348 U.S. 96 (1954). This one-year provision applies to brand-new labor organizations that have been newly-introduced to the workplace. In this situation, the new labor organization needs time to get established. Therefore, the Supreme Court has ruled that the employer must allow the new labor union to have a minimum period of at least one year, following a certification election. This one-year period request the employer to negotiate in good faith with the new labor union. This one-year provision is designed to prevent disgruntled employees from colluding with employers to destabilize a newly-elected labor union, thus eroding the NLRA's goal of establishing industrial peace in the workplace.

§ 4.03 Union's Exclusive Authority to Represent Bargaining Unit

Labor and employment lawyers, who represent individual workers, should recognize the fact that whenever the NLRB has certified a labor union, that labor union has the "exclusive authority to represent all employees within the bargaining unit" on matters that fall within the purview of the collective bargaining agreement. Typically, individual workers may seek an attorney to represent them before a grievance proceeding, but attorney-representation of individual union members are normally improper. In most cases, union officials must consent to allowing an attorney to represent an individual union member before a regular labor grievance proceeding. Otherwise, the labor union has the exclusive right to adjust grievances on behalf of union members pursuant to the collective bargaining agreement, and to engage in continuing negotiations with the employer. See, NLRA, Sec. 9(a). In other words, an individual union member will not normally be able to simultaneously avail himself of both labor union representation and the assistance of a private attorney. He must choose one or the other, but not both.

---

[94] 48A Am Jur Second, Labor and Labor Relations § 2208.

Individual workers may choose, however, to go directly to the employer, and to bypass the labor union, and to adjust his or her own individual grievances that fall within the purview of the collective bargaining agreement (CBA). In other words, an individual worker does not need to rely upon a union official in order to address his or her grievances under a CBA. The individual worker may choose to go it alone. If an individual worker decides to go it alone, he or she may, of course, hire a private attorney. In the end, this course of action may be unwise, since no private attorney or individual union member can force the employer into an arbitration proceeding—only the local labor union can do that. Therefore, if the case is still unresolved at the very last grievance step, it may very well warrant proceeding to "labor arbitration." But without union approval and involvement, the case could not proceed to arbitration. That individual worker (whether he or she hired a private attorney or not) would have no other remedies, except perhaps to file a lawsuit in court. In addition, even though an individual worker may choose to bypass the union, and to adjust his or her grievances individually without the union's assistance, *the labor union must still be notified* of the individual worker's decision to go it alone. In addition, the labor union *also retains the right to be present during all grievance hearings*, even though an individual union member does not want union representation.

Individual workers do not have the right to negotiate an individual contract that is separate and apart from the CBA, unless they are not members of the bargaining unit for which the CBA applies. See, e.g., *Order of Railroad Telegraphers v. Railway Express Agency, Inc.*, 321 U.S. 342 (1944). In certain circumstances, however, a group of workers who are within a bargaining unit, may have *special skills* that necessitate that they also have special provisions governing the terms, conditions, and privileges of their employment. These "special provisions" may be delineated either within the established CBA, or separated from the CBA in a different contractual agreement between the employer and these workers with special skills. See, e.g., *Caterpillar, Inc. v. Williams*, 482 U.S. 386 (1987). In other words, workers' with special skills may be able to negotiate individual employments with an employer, even though they are also members of a labor union that has a standing CBA with that same employer.

§ 4.04 Duty to Bargain in Good Faith

Importantly, the "duty to bargain in good faith" includes not simply the process of discussing and negotiating the terms and provisions of the collective bargaining agreement (CBA), but this duty also includes the processing of employee grievances and labor arbitration as well. At all times, the employer must "bargain" in good faith. See NLRA, Section 8(d). This duty requires the employer to "meet and confer" with union officials at reasonable times and to negotiate "in good faith."[95] Specifically, the duty to negotiate in good faith includes the obligations:

(1) To approach negotiations with a sincere resolve to reach a collective-bargaining agreement;
(2) To be represented at negotiations by duly authorized representatives prepared to discuss and negotiate any condition of employment;
(3) To meet at reasonable times and convenient places as frequently as may be necessary and to avoid unnecessary delays; and
(4) If an agreement is reached, to execute upon the request of any party to the negotiations a written document that includes all of the agreed upon terms, and to take such steps that are necessary to implement the agreement.[96]

What is the substantive meaning of "good faith?" "Good faith requires a serious intent to adjust differences and to reach an acceptable common ground."[97] In sum, there must be credible evidence of a genuine desire to reach an agreement. The case law and the NLRB decision on this subject matter are voluminous, and examples of "bad faith" negotiations have been cited as[98]:

- Dilatory tactics and "surface bargaining"
- Demand that Union drop pending NLRB charges
- "Take It or Leave It" proposals
- Refusal to Bargain about pending race discrimination claims

---

[95] See, generally, 48 Am Jur Second, Labor and Labor Relations §§ 313-318.
[96] Ibid.
[97] 48A. Am Jur Second, Labor and Labor Relations § 2220.
[98] See, generally, 48A Am Jur Second, Labor and Labor Relations §§ 1673-1688.

- Refusal to turn over documents or information necessary to have a meaningful and informed discussion
- Sending an incompetent employer negotiator with lack of adequate authority
- Delays in starting or completing negotiations
- Refusal to meet at reasonable times, or for sufficient time to bargain effectively
- Refusal to meet at reasonable places, or to engage in face-to-face bargaining
- Refusal to supply necessary information
- Refusal to change bargaining position, despite receiving clear evidence
- Refusal to submit proposal or counterproposal, as evidence of reasonable proof of good-faith effort to reach an agreement
- Placing unreasonable conditions on negotiating terms, such as requiring an end to a strike

But as a practical matter, non-lawyers who engage in collective bargaining may greatly benefit from the experience of labor and employment attorneys who engage in pre-trial, pre-litigation discovery on a continuing basis. The various state and federal rules of discovery of documents, may serve as helpful guides, because these civil rules of procedure often deal with disclosure issues regarding the "reasonable scope" of discoverable materials and the "relevancy" of evidence that are necessary to make a fair and reasonable determination of disclosure issues.

Hence, the parties should start off negotiations with (a) specific objectives in mind, and (b) a time-table for reaching those objectives and concluding the negotiations. Hopefully, if parties have these two criteria in mind, from the very beginning of their negotiations, the potential for future misunderstandings, miscommunications and confusion will be lessened. To be sure, "good faith" is a very difficult concept to define and grasp, when dealing with individual facts. Parties invent bad excuses for their dilatory actions; reasons for delays and miscommunications often change. Such "dilatory tactics" are often difficult to define and to enforce. But the parties and their agents must insist on reasonable time-tables to get the CBA negotiated and finalized. This time-table should include (a) issues to be discussed and resolved during negotiations; (b) the documents which each side will exchange and turn-over in order to permit the opposing party to make an informed decision and to engage in a meaningful discussion; and (c) a target date to ratify a new CBA. Any unnecessary and untoward deviations from this time-table may be construed to be "bad faith" negotiations, and thus punishable by the NLRB as an unfair labor practice.

What is an "impasse?" This is also a very important, loaded question which non-union officials should present for consultation and guidance to labor and employment attorneys. At a mediation conference, an issue has not reached an impasse, until it has been thoroughly and meaningfully discussed at mediation. Each side should have an opportunity to hear the other side's point of view, to make counter-points and counter-demands, and to evaluate alternative solutions. Until this negotiation process takes place, then no true "impasse" has been reached. Similarly, in collective bargaining, neither party will be allowed to claim that an "impasse" has been reached, without having meaningfully engaged in a thorough discussion—i.e., a "back-and forth" dialogue—as to the critical matters, regarding the material issues. Otherwise, the only way to describe an issue that has not been thoroughly debated is to call it a "take-it or leave-it" presentation, which constitutes "bad faith" under NLRA, Section 8(d).

Employers, union officials, labor advocates, labor attorneys and senior managers need to understand that after the NLRB orders collective bargaining, there are no hard-and-fast laws or rules to govern this process. (For this reason, I spent two days at Harvard Law School's Program on Negotiation to learn more about the theory, method, and practice of collective bargaining.)[99] In general, there are four broad types of collective bargaining:

(a). *Integrative bargaining* or Integrative Interests-Based (IIB): this method of bargaining occurs when more than one issue needs to be resolved and both parties attempt to reconcile and create solutions that are of great benefit for both parties' interests.
(b). *Distributive bargaining*: this method is an approach to bargaining or negotiating that is used when the parties are in conflict over an issue, and the outcome represents a gain for one party and a loss for the other party. This is also called "zero-sum" bargaining.

---

[99] See, e.g., Richard E. Walton and Robert B. McKersie, *A Behavioral Theory of Labor Negotiations: An Analysis of a Social Interaction System* (Ithaca, N.Y.: Cornell ILR Press, 1991); Michael L. Moffit and Robert C. Bordone, *The Handbook of Dispute Resolution* (San Francisco, CA: Jossey-Bass, 2005).

(c). *Concessionary bargaining*: this method of negotiating occurs when a labor union to make concessions to employers, in return for job security.

(d). *Continuous bargaining*: this method of negotiating occurs when both labor and management meet continuously to solve problems that are of common interest. This form of bargaining is similar to integrative bargaining.

In addition to these four basic approaches to collective bargaining, many national labor unions, such as the International Brotherhood of Teamsters and the United Automobile Workers (U.A.W.) engage in tactical bargaining—i.e., "*parallel bargaining*" or "*whipsaw*" negotiations--- whereby they negotiate with multiple employers within the same industry, either successively or simultaneously, in order to leverage their bargaining power and positions.

Labor advocates should remain mindful that the National Labor Relations Board (NLRB) exists to enforce the duty to negotiate in good faith.[100] "[I]n order to establish a prima facie case of an employer's refusal to bargain collectively with labor union representatives, a petitioner must show that an obligation to bargain existed, and that the employer refused to bargain either or did not bargain by unilaterally effecting a change in working conditions."[101]

Remedies for the failure to bargain in good faith are found in NLRA Section 10(c). The NLRB cannot order a party to "accept" a term or to accept a proposal, but it can order continuing bargaining between the parties, and it can compel the disclosure of discovery documents previously withheld, and—in extreme cases of abuse-- to award attorney's fees and compensatory damages. See, e.g., *Alwin Manufacturing Co.*, 326 NLRB No. 63 (1998).

---

[100] "Under the National Labor Relations Act (NLRA), it is an unfair labor practice for an employer to refuse to bargain collectively with the representatives of its employees." 48A Am Jur Second, Labor and Labor Relations § 1673.

[101] Ibid.

§ 4.05 Successor Employer's Duty to Bargain

A new employer taking over an old business has a duty to bargain in good faith with any existing labor unions then in existence in the workplace. However, it does not need to ratify any existing collective bargaining agreements. It may unilaterally revoke or unilaterally adopt existing collective bargaining agreements. When the new employer rejects an existing collective bargaining agreement that was previously ratified by an old employer, the new employer must bargain in good faith with any existing labor organizations which had an existing, unexpired collective bargaining agreement with the old employer.

Often times, where there has been a merger or acquisition, the new employer might object to negotiating a new collective bargaining agreement with an existing labor union and defend its actions with the argument that *the labor union no longer represents the new workforce.* This argument is essentially that "there is no substantial continuity between the pre- and post-affiliation (or merger) union."[102] When this occurs, employees and labor unions will often file unfair labor practices charges, and the National Labor Relations Board (NLRB) will be summoned to assist during this process.[103] The NLRB can (a) order an election or (b) issue a collective bargaining order, under appropriate circumstances.

§ 4.06 Mandatory, Permissive, and Illegal Subjects of Collective Bargaining

Significantly, practitioners should be familiar with the differences between the subject-matter of collective bargaining. These are classified as "mandatory," "permissive," or "illegal." Mandatory subjects of collective bargaining are required by the NLRA, Section 8(d), including "wages, hours and other terms and conditions of employment," such as:

- Health and Safety standards
- Wages, hours, bonuses, vacation, sick leave, insurance plans, etc.
- Retirement plans

---

[102] 48A *Am Jur Second*, Labor and Labor Relations § 2245.

[103] Ibid, § 2223.

- Work assignments
- Grievance processes and procedures; employee discipline
- Labor arbitration
- Ethics codes
- Job security; seniority
- Workplace privacy and employee surveillance
- Unit work performed by supervisors that deprive overtime work to bargaining members
- Employer plans to change nature of business operations
- Note: this list is not exclusive, and you should consult legal counsel regarding specific questions.

Non-mandatory, permissive subjects of collective bargaining include the following:

- "Other terms and conditions of employment," such as employee benefits
- Management's right to unilaterally change other terms or employment (i.e., "management prerogatives)
- Subcontracting of work out of the bargaining unit
- Unit work by supervisors
- Sale, transfer, and Closure of Business (Union participation rights)
- Provisions regarding Lock-Outs and Strikes (i.e., Replacement Workers)
- Note: this list is not exclusive, and you should consult legal counsel regarding specific questions.

Non-permissive, illegal subjects of collective bargaining include the following:

- Duty to recognize a union, as stated in the NLRA
- Right of Union to establish a "Closed Shop"
- Right of the Union to establish preferential hiring of union members
- Right to waive statutory requirements of "Check Off" (i.e., when an employer deducts union dues from employee pay checks and distributes to the union)

- Right to waive the distribution of union-related literature (since this could violate the Section 7 rights of individual workers)
- Note: this list is not exclusive, and you should consult legal counsel regarding specific questions.

§ 4.07 Union Security Clauses[104]

One of the most important issues in collective bargaining is whether a union may establish a closed shop, a union shop, or an agency shop within a collective bargaining agreement. A "closed shop" provision allows the labor union to mandate that the employer can hire only workers who are members of that particular labor union. Closed-shop provisions were rendered illegal through the Taft-Hartley Act of 1947. Thus, formal closed-shop provisions have ceased to exist. However, some unions may try to impose "informal, discreet, and unwritten" closed-shop agreements through other means; and the NLRB has likewise found such informal efforts to constitute illegal closed-shop provisions.

The "union shop" provision allows the employer to hire both union and non-union members; however, the non-union member, upon initial hire and an initial grace period (e.g., a 30 day grace period), will have a limited time period to officially join the union or otherwise risk mandatory termination. Union shop agreements are still valid in several states which have not adopted "right-to-work" laws.

An "agency shop" provision is a slight modification of the "union shop" provision. With regards to an "agency shop," employers are allowed to hire non-union members who will not be later required to official join the labor union. However, after being hired as a regular employee, the employer will be required to deduct what is comparable to "union dues" from their scheduled paychecks. These dues are official known as "agency shop" fees, and these are designed to prevent the "free-rider" problem of allowing non-union members to benefit from labor-union representation, without having to pay any union dues. Instead, these members will be required to pay "agency shop" fees, which are the equivalent to the union dues.

Both the "union shop" and the "agency shop" clauses are known as "union security agreements" or "union security clauses." However, these clauses are not made to be mandatory requirements within the

---

[104] See, generally, 48 Am Jur Second, Labor and Labor Arbitration §§ 84-87; 1066-1079.

National Labor Relations Act. Nor are these provisions subject to federal preemption. Therefore, state legislatures have the constitutional authority to render "agency shop" or "union shop" clauses to be "unconstitutional" according to their state constitutional amendments or state legislation. Such state constitutional laws and provision are known as "right to work laws." Under these "right to work" laws, a labor union cannot require an employer to hire only union members; nor can it require non-union workers to pay "agency shop fees" or "union dues." For this reason, "right to work" laws remain highly political and controversial, because they have been widely characterized as causing great damage to the American labor movement.

§ 4.08 Human Resources and Strategic Risk Management

Human resources business partners and leaders must ensure that managers and senior executives understand their obligations and duties under the National Labor Relations Act, both before and after the National Labor Relations Board certifies a union. Non-unionized workers have important rights to collectively redress their grievances and to bargain collectively with their employers. And all bargaining, whether in the form of addressing grievances or negotiating a Collective Bargaining Agreement (CBA), must be done in good faith. For this reason, human resources professionals should treat "groups" of employees nearly the same as they treat regular labor organizations.

Human resources professionals should also develop an expertise in collective bargaining strategies. Joint labor-management training for mid-level management and senior leaders should be arranged periodically. Where there are unionized workplaces, the collective bargaining agreement needs to be thoroughly reviewed and administered in accordance with federal labor laws. These laws generally consider "collective bargaining" to include both *the formation phase of negotiating* the collective bargaining agreement, as well as *the administration phase* of adjusting labor grievances and implementing the day-to-day provisions of the collective bargaining agreement. This means that the duty to bargain in good faith extends throughout the entire life of the collective bargaining agreement. Strategic human resources should thus focus on making sure that managers and senior executives thoroughly understand the definition of "good faith," and how to properly negotiate and administer the collective bargaining agreement.

§ 4.09 Conclusion

An employer and labor union have the general duty, at all times, to bargain in good faith. This duty to bargain in good faith includes both negotiating the collective bargaining agreement and administrating the collective bargaining agreement. But the duty to bargain directly with employees in good faith arises even before the National Labor Relations Board (NLRB) has certified a labor union. That is to say, non-unionized employees have the same right to engage in "protected concerted activity" as do labor unions, within the express parameters of Section 7 of the National Labor Relations Act. These non-unionized employees may collectively petition their employers for the redress of workplace grievances. If non-unionized employees bring in a labor union, and that labor union attains certification from the NLRB, then employers must negotiate in good faith with that labor union. This duty to negotiate with the certified labor union *extends for one year* following the certification. During this one-year period, good-faith negotiation is mandatory; and to cut down on confusion and future unfair labor practices claims, the parties should start off negotiations with a "negotiation plan" that includes a time-table to complete negotiating the labor agreement. It would perhaps behoove both the labor union and the employer to involve experienced labor counsel at the inception of the negotiations, in order to clearly delineate what documents should be turned over to the opposing party, and which documents shall be kept confidential. This should help the labor union and the employer to determine whether NLRB involvement will be needed, and also to determine their chances of reaching a final labor agreement without an impasse.

Chapter Four Bibliography

Books:

Ford, Roderick O. *Understanding Employment Law.* Tampa, Fl: Xlibris Pub., 2017.

Gelhaus, Robert J. and James Oldham, *Labor Law.* Chicago, IL: The BarBri Group, 2002.

References:

48 American Jurisprudence (Second), Labor and Labor Relations, §§ 1-1112

48A American Jurisprudence (Second), Labor and Labor Relations, §§ 1673-2401

48B American Jurisprudence (Second), Labor and Labor Relations, §§ 84-87; 2402-3569

51 Corpus Jurisprudence Secundum, Labor Relations, §§ 1-262

51A Corpus Jurisprudence Secundum, Labor Relations, §§ 263-780

51B Corpus Jurisprudence Secundum, Labor Relations, §§ 781-1354

Case Law:

U.S. Supreme Court

J.I. Case Co. v. NLRB, 321 U.S. 332 (1944)

Order of Railroad Telegraphers v. Railway Express Agency, Inc., 321 U.S. 342 (1944)

Brooks v. NLRB, 348 U.S. 96 (1954).

NLRB v. Truitt Manufacturing Co., 351 U.S. 149 (1956)

John Wiley & Sons, Inc. v. Livingston, 376 U.S. 543 (1964)

NLRB v. Gissel Packing Co., 395 U.S. 575 (1969)

H.K. Porter Co. v. NLRB, 397 U.S. 99 (1970)

NLRB v. Burns International Security Services, Inc., 406 U.S. 272 (1972)

Golden State Bottling Co. v. NLRB, 414 U.S. 168 (1973)

Emporium Capwell Co. v. Western Addition Community Organization, 420 U.S. 50 (1975)

Nolde Bros., Inc. v. Local No. 358, Bakery & Confectionary Workers Union, 430 U.S. 243 (1977)

Detroit Edison Co. v. NLRB, 440 U.S. 301 (1979)

NLRB v. Bildisco & Bildisco, 465 U.S. 513 (1984)

Fall River Dyeing & Finishing Corp. v. NLRB, 482 U.S. 27 (1987)

National Labor Relations Board

Mar-Jac Poultry Co., 136 N.L.R.B. 785 (1962)

Perfect Service Gas Co., 146 N.L.R.B. 1686 (1964)

Gopher Aviation, Inc., 160 N.L.R.B. 1698 (1966)

American Sink Top & Cabinet Co., 242 N.L.R.B. 408 (1979)

Columbus Products, 259 N.L.R.B. 220 (1981)

Colgate-Palmolive Co., 261 N.L.R.B. 90 (1982)

Borden Chemical Co., 261 N.L.R.B. 64 (1982)

Gourmet Foods, Inc., 270 N.L.R.B. 1105 (1984)

Service Electric Co., 281 N.L.R.B. 633 (1986)

Alwin Manufacturing Co., 326 NLRB No. 63 (1998).

Detroit Newspaper Agency, 327 N.L.R.B. No. 164 (1999)

Tree-Free Fiber Co., 328 N.L.R.B. No. 51 (1999)

Chapter Five

ADMINISTRATION OF THE COLLECTIVE BARGAINING AGREEMENT

§ 5.01 Introduction 122

§ 5.02 Unfair Labor Practices and the NLRB 122

§ 5.03 Labor Grievances and Labor Arbitration 128

§ 5.04 Taft-Hartley Act, Hybrid Section 301 Breach of Contract Claims 136

§ 5.05 Appeals of Arbitration Rulings (the Civil Courts) 138

§ 5.06 Human Resources and Strategic Risk Management 139

§ 5.07 Conclusion 140

§ 5.01 Introduction

The employer and the labor union, which are parties to a validly-executed collective bargaining agreement ("labor agreement"), have a duty to perform and administer that labor agreement "according to its terms, and a failure to perform the obligations so undertaken constitutes a breach of the contract without demand for performance."[105] Therefore, the duty to administer the labor agreement applies to both the employer and the labor union; and the failure to properly administer the labor agreement in accordance with its terms and conditions constitutes a "breach of contract." When a breach of the labor agreement occurs, two primary legal questions arise: first, who can enforce the labor agreement's terms upon the breaching party? And, second, what remedies are available to the non-breaching party or the victim (i.e., the individual worker)?

It should be noted that individual employees (i.e., union members) are often the most potent weapon for the enforcement of the terms and conditions of the collective bargaining agreement. This means that under most circumstances, only individual union members can initiate the grievance procedures whereby the terms of the collective bargaining agreement can be enforced. For example, individual union members might file grievances through the regular grievance process; or they might file lawsuits in state or federal court; or they might file unfair labor practices charges before the National Labor Relations Board. Such grievances, charges, or complaints can be lodged against the employer, the union, or both the employer and union.[106] And through these processes, the terms of the collective bargaining agreement are brought to life and actively enforced.

§ 5.02 Unfair Labor Practices and the NLRB

A not well-known but powerful weapon which individual employees may utilize to fight a variety of forms of employment discrimination is the unfair labor practices (ULP) charge before National Labor Relations Board (NLRB). Many employees mistakenly believe that the NLRB

---

[105] 51 *Corpus Juris Secundum*, Labor Relations § 262.

[106] Ibid.

processes only ULPs from labor unions or union members—but this is incorrect misinformation. The NLRB also process ULP charges that impact individual employees who are not members of labor unions.[107] To begin with, an employer can commit an unfair labor practice under the NLRA for improperly discharging a non-unionized worker for engaging in protected concerted activities.[108] This means that, under some circumstances, a discharged worker, who is not a member of a labor union, might nevertheless appeal to the NLRB for relief. Often times, these workers will have engaged in a "protected concerted activity," but the employer retaliates against them for some falsified reason, such as allegations of violating company policy, insubordination, and other similar trumped-up, unfounded charges. The NLRB hears and resolves these types of cases as "unfair labor practices" charges involving reprisal for having engaged in protected concerted activities.[109] (NOTE: for additional information regarding the rights of non-unionized individual workers under the National Labor Relations Act, see Chapter Three, Protected Concerted Activity).

According to the official website for the National Labor Relations Board, non-unionized and unionized workers my process claims before the National Labor Relations Board (NLRB), pursuant to Sections 7 and 8 of the NLRA, stating, inter alia, the following:

> Employees have the right to unionize, to join together to advance their interests as employees, and to refrain from such activity. It is unlawful for an employer to interfere with, restrain, or coerce employees in the exercise of their rights. For example, employers may not respond to a union organizing drive by threatening, interrogating, or spying on pro-union employees, or by promising benefits if they forget about the union.
>
> Section 7 of the National Labor Relations Act (the Act) guarantees employees "the right to self-organization, to form, join, or assist labor organizations, to bargain collectively through representatives of their own choosing, and to engage in other concerted activities

---

[107] See, e.g., Chapter Three, "Protected Concerted Activity."

[108] 48A *Am Jur Second*, Labor and Labor Relations §§ 1454-1464.

[109] Ibid.

for the purpose of collective bargaining or other mutual aid or protection," as well as the right "to refrain from any or all such activities."

Section 8(a)(1) of the Act makes it an unfair labor practice for an employer "to interfere with, restrain, or coerce employees in the exercise of the rights guaranteed in Section 7" of the Act. For example, <u>you may not</u>

- Threaten employees with adverse consequences, such as closing the workplace, loss of benefits, or more onerous working conditions, if they support a union, engage in union activity, or select a union to represent them.
- Threaten employees with adverse consequences if they engage in protected, concerted activity. (Activity is "concerted" if it is engaged in with or on the authority of other employees, not solely by and on behalf of the employee himself. It includes circumstances where a single employee seeks to initiate, induce, or prepare for group action, as well as where an employee brings a group complaint to the attention of management. Activity is "protected" if it concerns employees' interests as employees. An employee engaged in otherwise protected, concerted activity may lose the Act's protection through misconduct.)
- Promise employees benefits if they reject the union.
- Imply a promise of benefits by soliciting grievances from employees during a union organizing campaign. (However, if you regularly solicited employee grievances before the campaign began, you may continue that practice unchanged.)
- Confer benefits on employees during a union organizing campaign to induce employees to vote against the union.
- Withhold changes in wages or benefits during a union organizing campaign that would have been made had the union not been on the scene, unless you make clear to employees that the change will occur whether or not they select the union, and that your sole purpose in postponing the change is to avoid any appearance of trying to influence the outcome of the election.

- Coercively question employees about their own or coworkers' union activities or sympathies. (Whether questioning is coercive and therefore unlawful depends on the relevant circumstances, including who asks the questions, where, and how; what information is sought; whether the questioned employee is an open and active union supporter; and whether the questioning occurs in a context of other unfair labor practices.)
- Prohibit employees from talking about the union during working time, if you permit them to talk about other non-work-related subjects.
- Poll your employees to determine the extent of their support for a union, unless you comply with certain safeguards. You must not have engaged in unfair labor practices or otherwise created a coercive atmosphere. In addition, you must (1) communicate to employees that the purpose of the poll is to determine whether the union enjoys majority support (and that must, in truth, be your purpose); (2) give employees assurances against reprisal; and (3) conduct the poll by secret ballot.
- Spy on employees' union activities. ("Spying" means doing something out of the ordinary to observe the activity. Seeing open union activity in workplace areas frequented by supervisors is not "spying.")
- Create the impression that you are spying on employees' union activities.
- Photograph or videotape employees engaged in peaceful union or other protected activities.
- Solicit individual employees to appear in a campaign video.
- Promulgate, maintain, or enforce work rules that reasonably tend to inhibit employees from exercising their rights under the Act.
- Deny off-duty employees access to outside nonworking areas of your property, unless business reasons justify it.
- Prohibit employees from wearing union buttons, t-shirts, and other union insignia unless special circumstances warrant.
- Convey the message that selecting a union would be futile.
- Discipline or discharge a union-represented employee for refusing to submit, without a representative, to an investigatory

interview the employee reasonably believes may result in discipline.
- Interview employees to prepare your defense in an unfair labor practice case, unless you provide certain assurances. You must communicate to the employee the purpose of the questioning, assure him against reprisals, and obtain his voluntary participation. Questioning must occur in a context free from employer hostility to union organization and must not itself be coercive. And questioning must not go beyond what is needful to achieve its legitimate purpose. That is, you may not pry into other union matters, elicit information concerning the employee's subjective state of mind, or otherwise interfere with employee rights under the Act.
- Initiate, solicit employees to sign, or lend more than minimal support to or approval of a decertification or union-disaffection petition.
- Discharge, constructively discharge, suspend, layoff, fail to recall from layoff, demote, discipline, or take any other adverse action against employees because of their protected, concerted activities.

Individual ULP claims may be initiated by completing a charge form (i.e., a "Charge of Discrimination/ Violation"), either on-line or in person, and filing it at the National Labor Relations Board's regional office, which is headed by a Regional Director. The Regional Director's assistants will accept, review, and evaluate whether there is any merit to the ULP charge. If there is at least a "prima facie case" of a violation of the NLRA, then a "complaint will be issued," and the National Labor Relations Board's General Counsel will evaluate the complaint to determine whether further prosecution of the [ULP charge] will effectuate the policies of the Act." During the meanwhile, the NLRB's representatives will contact the employer and attempt to effectuate a pre-investigation or pre-hearing solution and settlement.

Most NLRB charges get resolved between the respective parties, but a few do not. In the event a ULP charge does not get resolved, then it is are docketed for hearing before an Administrative Law Judge. As with most situations involving labor disputes, two of the most common remedies afforded by the NLRB are (a) an *injunction* (i.e., preventing the employer or union from taking specific actions to prevent wrongdoing), and (b) *specific performance* (i.e., ordering the employer or the union to take specific actions or steps to correct wrongdoing). The payment of money damages, such as the back-payment of lost wages, administrative costs, and attorney's fees may also form part of a UPL remedy.

Administrative hearings before an Administrative Law Judge (ALJ) are trial-like, evidentiary proceedings. The ALJ will issue an "intermediate report," either "with exceptions" or "without exceptions." A "without exceptions" report constitutes a final decision of the NLRB, unless an appeal is filed within 20 days of the docketing of that report. If an appeal is filed, the NLRB will review the ALJ's report. A "with exceptions" report does not constitute a final decision; and the NLRB will automatically review a "with exceptions" ALJ report. Upon review of the "with exceptions" ALJ report, the NLRB may substitute its own findings and issue its own, independent final order.

The NLRB's final order is reviewable through an appeal to a U.S. Court of Appeals for the federal circuit where the regional NLRB office is located.[110] The U.S. Court of Appeals will review the NLRB's finding of facts based upon a "preponderance of the evidence standard," which means that the NLRB's decision must be based upon substantial competent evidence in the record as a whole. In addition, a U.S. Court of Appeals will conduct a *de novo* review of the NLRB's interpretation and application of the law (i.e., federal labor laws). "A federal circuit court decision which has not been overturned by the Supreme Court represents the highest law or statutory interpretation available in that circuit, and is binding on administrative agencies such as the NLRB, which do not have the same authority as these courts."[111]

To conclude this section, it is important to present the reader with the following disclaimer: the *myriad forms of unfair labor practices* cover a far broader and vaster area of legal analysis than can be included within the narrow limits of this book.[112] Although other chapters within this book discuss situations that constitute unfair labor practices, the reader should

---

[110] 51A *Corpus Juris Secundum,* Labor Relations §§ 650-723.

[111] 48 *Am Jur Second,* Labor and Labor Relations § 8.

[112] See, e.g., 51 *Corpus Juris Secundum,* Labor Relations §§ 177-262; 51A *Corpus Juris Secundum,* Labor Relations §§ 328-401; and 48 Am Jur Second, Labor and Labor Relations §§ 300-318.

understand that employers and (or) unions have been found to have violated either Sections 7 or 8 of the NLRA by committing *a vast array of violations*, which are too numerous and cumbersome to list in this book. Therefore, specific questions as to whether *a specific set of circumstances* constitutes an "unfair labor practice" should be directed to a competent union steward, labor advocate, labor attorney, or to the National Labor Relations Board. NLRB officers are very proactive and helpful in providing technical assistance especially to employers and human resources officers.

§ 5.03 Labor Grievances and Labor Arbitration

Perhaps the very best source or reference guide on practical "nuts-and-bolts" for preparing for labor arbitration is Charles S. Loughran's *How to Prepare and Present a Labor Arbitration Case: Strategy and Tactics for Advocates.*[113] This text provides in-depth strategies and suggestions on how to prepare for labor arbitration. Of course, a through and detailed analysis of the labor-arbitration process is beyond the scope of this book. The reader should thus consider Loughran's great book, *How to Prepare and Present a Labor Arbitration Case*, to be virtually incorporated by reference into this section, as the author's endorsement as the authoritative reference on labor arbitration.

Otherwise, suffice it to say, the following concise summary of the labor-arbitration process is appropriate:

In summary, a labor arbitration case is the culmination of two or three failed attempts to resolve a labor dispute during the grievance process. The grievance process consists of standard procedures that are set forth within a collective bargaining agreement ("labor agreement"). The labor agreement typically includes a two-, three-, or four-step grievance procedure, such as the following:

First-Step Grievance: the disgruntled employee presents his or her grievance to an immediate supervisor or manager;

Second-Step Grievance: when the grievance is not resolved at the First-Step, a more formal hearing is generally held before a Department Director, which sometimes will have the supervisor, manager, and human

---

[113] Charles S. Loughran, *How to Prepare and Present a Labor Arbitration Case: Strategy and Tactics for Advocates* (Washington, D.C.: The Bureau of National Affairs, Inc., 1996).

resources manager present. Meanwhile, the employee will usually have a union official present;

Third-Step Grievance: when the grievance is not resolved at the Second-Step, an appeal may be made to a Chief Executive Officer or other Executive Director who typically reviews the lower proceedings and acts like an appellate judged to determine if the Second-Step decision should be up-held or overturned.

NOTE: The United States Supreme Court has held that a union member is required to have a union official present if the said union member is questioned by a supervisor or manager, with the objective of determining whether a rule violation has occurred, whereby the said union member might be disciplined. See, e.g., *NLRB v. Weingarten, Inc.*, 420 U.S. 251 (1975).

If the grievance is not resolved at the Third-Step Grievance hearing, then the final step is labor arbitration, which is presided over by a single, neutral person who is given the authority to open a hearing, take testimony, receive documentary evidence, cross-examine witnesses, hear opening statements and closing statements, and review memoranda of law concerning various matters governing labor and employment law. Arbitration hearings generally consist of from between 1 and 5 days of hearing testimony. And because most labor unions have to invest a substantial amount of time and money in taking a case to arbitration, many cases that are not satisfactorily resolved at the third-step grievance are not selected for arbitration by the Union.

Union grievances and labor arbitration hearings are governed largely by the important evidentiary standard known as the "Seven Principles of Just Cause." In other words, no adverse action should be taken against an employee, or upheld during a grievance or arbitration proceeding, unless there is sufficient evidence to prove that the charges brought against the individual employee. Employees, union stewards, and labor advocates should thoroughly investigate the facts of their cases, so that they can make strong, credible arguments that the employer's disciplinary actions (e.g., demotion, suspension, write-up, termination, etc.) failed to meet the legal standard known as "Just Cause."[114] To determine whether there was

---

[114] Arbitrator Carroll Daugherty developed the Seven Principles of Just Cause in the landmark case of *Enterprise Wire Co. and Enterprise Independent Union* (46 LA 359, 1966):

"The standard of just cause provides important protections against arbitrary or unfair termination and other forms of inappropriate workplace discipline. Just

"just cause," the hearing officer (or arbitrator) must apply the following seven standards:

---

cause has become a common standard in labor arbitration, and is included in labor union contracts as a form of job security. Typically, an employer must prove just cause before an arbitrator in order to sustain an employee's termination, suspension, or other discipline. Usually, the employer has the burden of proof in discharge cases or if the employee is in the wrong.

In the workplace, just cause is a burden of proof or standard that an employer must meet to justify discipline or discharge. Just cause usually refers to a violation of a company policy or rule. In some cases, an employee may commit an act that is not specifically addressed within the employers' policies but one of which the employer believes warrants discipline or discharge. In such instances, the employer must be confident that they can defend their decision.

"When an arbitrator looks at a discipline dispute, the arbitrator first asks whether the employee's wrongdoing has been proven by the employer, and then asks whether the method of discipline should be upheld or modified. In 1966, an arbitrator, Professor Carroll Daugherty, expanded these principles into seven tests for just cause. The concepts encompassed within his seven tests are still frequently used by arbitrators when deciding discipline cases.

"Daugherty's seven tests are as follows:

Was the employee forewarned of the consequences of his or her actions?

Are the employer's rules reasonably related to business efficiency and performance the employer might reasonably expect from the employee?

Was an effort made before discipline or discharge to determine whether the employee was guilty as charged?

Was the investigation conducted fairly and objectively?

Did the employer obtain substantial evidence of the employee's guilt?

Were the rules applied fairly and without discrimination?

Was the degree of discipline reasonably related to the seriousness of the employee's offense and the employee's past record?

"The last test, the degree of discipline, is important because arbitrators want to ensure that the "punishment fits the crime." An employer's use of progressive discipline often gives the employer an advantage in arbitration.

The culture of the community or community standards sometimes play an important role in how just cause is defined, especially if there are issues of immorality. What is accepted in an urban and liberal community may not be accepted in a rural and religiously conservative community. The courts or arbitrator who will rule on a challenge to the discipline may be a product of those communities. Just cause can become controversial in instances when the employers personnel policies do not address a specific act but the employer believes that just cause exists. For example, if an employee is arrested and charged with a misdemeanor, the employer may deem that sufficient cause for dismissal, even if the employee is not incarcerated or is not convicted." Citation:

"Just Cause" https://en.wikipedia.org/wiki/Just_cause.

(1) Adequate warning;
(2) Reasonableness;
(3) Completeness of investigation;
(4) Objectivity of investigation;
(5) Proof of infraction;
(6) Uniformity of the Rules application; and,
(7) Reasonableness of discipline.

Labor advocates should also become familiar with a legal encyclopedia called "Labor Arbitration Reports," which reports and publishes arbitration decisions from throughout the United States and Canada. Nearly all of the cases published in these labor arbitration reports include a general application and discussion of the above-mentioned "Seven Principles of Just Cause." These published arbitration decisions can become very important when initially assessing whether a labor grievance has merit, and whether it is likely that a labor grievance can succeed at arbitration. In addition, these published arbitration decisions should be used to educate shop stewards, union members, and front-line managers on how to interpret and apply specific language and articles that are published within the collective bargaining agreement and how to apply general labor standards, such as "past practices" and "just cause."

Finally, these published arbitration decisions should be cited and quoted in any written legal arguments that are presented during the grievance or arbitration stages. These decisions might also be included in formal letters between union officials and senior-level management, or between union officials and the labor arbitrator. As an example of the value and importance of these published arbitration decisions, consider the following list of samples:

> Douglas *Aircraft Co., Inc.*, 1 LA 350 (June 30, 1945)("Issues: I Discharge of Ode Luckett... which union claimed was unjust and asks reinstatement without loss of seniority and payment for fine lost....II Discharge of Kenneth Gardner... which union claimed was unjust and ask reinstatement without loss of seniority and payment...." Summary of Awards: Reinstatement of both Luckett and Garner, with full seniority).

Douglas Aircraft Co., Inc., 3 LA 598 (June 7, 1946)(Issue "— Discharge for repeated violations of plan rule.... Award. John V. Manning shall be reinstated as an employee of the Douglas Aircraft Company, Inc., with full seniority as of March 1, 1946, the date of his discharge, and shall be paid for time lost in the period between March 18 and March 28, 1946, less any monies earned or received from California state unemployment insurance during that period.").

Joy MFG Co., 6 LA 430 (July 31, 1946)("It ruled that the subject employee was improperly discharged, that he shall 'be reinstated without 'loss of seniority; and that he shall be reimbursed for all monies lost as a result of the discharge."');

United States Spring & Bumper Co., 5 LA 109 (October 4, 1946) ("Employees who were discharged for alleged participation in dice •game in violation of rule forbidding gambling on premises should be reinstated with back pay and restoration of all employment rights. Employees should. however, receive written reprimand which shall be entered into their personnel records. Discharge penalty was too severe under circumstances since (I) there is no evidence that all employees who were discharged actually participated in gambling, (2) other participants were not disciplined, (3) rule had not previously been enforced, (4) there is no substantial evidence that employees were familiar with plant rule though it was posted and is part of employee manual, (5) discharge was not known to be penalty for violation of ride, (6) employees were not warned before discharge, and (7) employees were skilled workers with considerable seniority who never received previous warning for violation of any plant rule.")

Chrysler Corp., 5 LA 420 (October 17, 1946)("Employees who obeyed spirit of recently announced company rule against abuse of wash-up period privilege but technically violated one detail of rule may not be punished for such violation where evidence indicates that violation was result of their not having been adequately informed of details of rule.")

Norwich Pharmacal Co., 5 LA 536 (December 10, 1946)("Employer may hot levy discipline against an employee for committing an act which is not wrong per se and which has been previously condoned unless it has been made known to the employees in unequivocal language ...that such shall be regarded as contrary to company rules");

WLEU Broadcasting Co., 7 LA 150 (March 6, 1947)("Under contract which permits employer to discharge for just cause but requires employer to give employees reasonable warning before discharge, discharge is excessive penalty for first rule violation or first insubordinate act of an employee since discharge is not normally imposed for first offense of such character and contract reference to "warning" clearly implies that offenses should be followed by Warning or by disciplinary measure, which is less severe than discharge. Appropriate penalty for employee who was first offender on both counts is two-week suspension.")

Alan Wood Steel Co., 3 LA 557 (June 15, 1947)("Five-day layoff should not have been imposed where employee, although he repeatedly violated plant rule, had never been warned or reprimanded: therefore and (2) repeated breach of same rule by other employees had established a practice which employees may have been justified in believing proper inasmuch as employer had in past failed to enforce rule. Employee is awarded back pay for time off.")

Allis-Chalmers MFG Co., 8 LA 177 (June 24, 1947)("Employee who was given disciplinary layoff for violating plant rule prohibiting employees from selecting. their own work materials without foreman's permission was disciplined without "cause" in violation of contract, despite fact that employee picked wrong material by mistake and caused spoilage, since employer condoned violation of rule over long period of time and never warned employee against selection of his own work materials. Employer may not condone practice for long time and impose discipline only when some loss results to company.")

Again, published labor arbitration decisions can be extremely helpful in guiding the steps and actions of disgruntled employees, union stewards, and labor advocates throughout the process of any grievance or arbitration proceedings.

If labor union officials determine not to take a disgruntled employee's grievance to arbitration, then that disgruntled employee will need to consider other options. He or she will not have independent authority to take the grievance to arbitration. Only the labor union has the authority to proceed to labor arbitration. For this reason, conflict between labor unions and their disgruntled, aggrieved union members are not uncommon. At that point, the only recourse for the disgruntled, aggrieved employee would be to thoroughly evaluate the union's actions in order to determine if it breached its duty of fair representation; and, secondly, to thoroughly evaluate whether he or she may sue the employer in state or federal court under a different legal theory, such as, for example, discrimination under Title VII of the 1964 Civil Rights Act or the Americas with Disabilities Act of 1990 (ADA).

At some point, a disgruntled, aggrieved employee may very well determine that the labor union's decision not to proceed to arbitration was a gross violation of their rights under the labor agreement. They will thus conclude that the employer breached the labor agreement, and, secondly, that the union recklessly allowed the employer to get off the hook. At that point, the aggrieved employee would need to evaluate his options: typically, (a) to sue the employer for breach of contract in state or federal court; (b) to sue both the employer and the labor union, either in state court or in federal court under Section 301 of the Taft-Hartley Act, pursuant to a theory that the primary reason that the employer breached the collective bargaining agreement is because the union failed to discharge its duty to provide fair representation; or, (c) file an unfair labor practices charge against the labor union before the NLRB. A six-month statute of limitations governs these legal actions, and so the aggrieved employee must at all times act diligently when dealing with labor grievances. The general rule of thumb is that an individual employee must elect which route he or she will take; although it is possible to pursue both an unfair labor practice charge before the NLRB, while either a grievance or a lawsuit is still pending.

Here it is important to stress the fact that individual workers have a right to sue in state or federal court, under the collective bargaining agreement:

An employee may sue on a collective bargaining agreement only for violation of, or to enforce, provisions of the agreement made for his benefit, that is, for infringement of individual rights. Thus an employee may sue on a collective bargaining agreement for violation of provisions as to compensation or wages, and individual employees may maintain a common-law action in a state court to recover unpaid wages due them on contracts of hire made under, or by virtue of, a collective bargaining agreement executed under the provisions of the National Labor Relations Act. An employee may also sue on a collective bargaining agreement for violation of provisions as to seniority, and as to dismissal, layoff, or discharge; but a claim for damages for wrongful discharge may not be coupled with a claim for reinstatement and back pay, since relinquishment for the latter claim would be a prerequisite to the exercise of the right to maintain an action for wrongful discharge.

An employee may not be entitled to maintain an action for breach of a provision which was not intended to be for his individual benefit, as where the breach was as to a matter affecting all union members, and such things as union security, recognition, and deduction of dues are matters of general union interest, and are not individual rights for which suit may be brought by individual employees.

An action for wrongful discharge in violation of a collective bargaining agreement may be the alternative to administrative procedure provided for in the collective bargaining agreement, but only if the administrative remedies are pursued to a conclusion, or not pursued at all, and where a discharged employee has invoked such procedures, but has abandoned them prior to conclusion, he is precluded from maintaining an action in the court for wrongful discharge.

While a representative of class action may be maintained to enforce a collective bargaining agreement, employees may not be entitled to maintain an action at law where they are not united in interest, and there is no question of common or general interest among them which could be established by the same evidence, and where a joint trial of their several causes of action is not possible.[115]

In other words, employees and labor advocates should consider the collective bargaining agreement ("labor agreement") to be an employment contract just as it would consider any other type of employment contract, such as an independent contractor's agreement. The general rule of thumb is that, if the employer breached the labor agreement, it can be sued for damages in state or federal court.[116]

§ 5.04 Taft-Hartley Act, Hybrid Section 301 Breach of Contract Claims

Whenever a labor union decides not to take a case to arbitration, the disgruntled, aggrieved employee will often seek separate legal counsel in order to sue the labor union under a theory called the breach of the "duty of fair representation." In other words, the aggrieved union member's argument will be that the labor union's refusal to take the employee's grievance to labor arbitration constituted gross negligence, recklessness, and (or) bad faith. Such claims constitute the law of breach of the "duty of fair representation."[117] A breach of the "duty of fair representation" is a very difficult legal standard to understand, and non-lawyers should seek legal advice from a competent, experienced labor attorney. In general, a union breaches its duty of fair representation whenever, if ever, its conduct is "arbitrary, discriminatory, or in bad faith." See, e.g, *Vaca v. Sipes*, 386 U.S. 171 (1967).

> If the union 'arbitrarily' refuses to press an employee's grievance under the procedures outlined in the agreement, or otherwise fails to represent her fairly, the employee may then bring suit against the employer to enforce the collective bargaining agreement—on the theory that, as a member of the bargaining unit, she is a third-party beneficiary of the agreement [Jenkins v. W.M. Schluderberg-T.J.

---

[115] 51A *Corpus Juris Secundum*, Labor Relations § 763.

[116] Ibid.

[117] See, also, Chapter Seven, "Union's Duty of Fair Representation."

Kurdle Co., 144 A.2d 88 (Md. 1958)—individual employee could sue because union had 'arbitrarily' failed to take the case to arbitration; and see *Vaca v. Sipes*...; *Hines v. Anchor Motor Freight, Inc.*, [424 U.S. 554 (1976)]....

If the union's failure to act on an employee's behalf amounts to a breach of its duty of fair representation (i.e., if its refusal was **'arbitrary, discriminatory or in bad faith'**), the aggrieved employee can (i) file an unfair union labor practice charge with the NLRB, (ii) file a private damages action against the union under Taft-Hartley section 301, or (iii) initiate procedures under Title VII, where applicable... [i.e., where has been discrimination because of race, sex, color, religion, or national origin]....[118]

(For additional information regarding "fair representation" involving Title VII claims (i.e., claims based race, sex, color, religion, or national origin) against either a labor union or employer, see, also, Chapter Six, "Collective Bargaining Agreement and Federal Antidiscrimination Laws."[119])

Breach of the duty of fair representation claims, which result from "unfair labor practices" that are based upon Sections 7 and 8 of the National Labor Relations Act, may also be filed as charges of discrimination before the National Labor Relations Board. Otherwise, "fair representation" claims can be filed in state or federal court as a "breach of contract claim," whereby both *the union* and *the employer* will be held jointly and severally liable for all of the damages awarded, as per Section 301 of the Taft-Hartley Act.

These are called "hybrid-Section 301" lawsuits because both labor unions and employers are implicated as co-defendants. These lawsuits are generally filed in the U.S. District Court. Even if the employee only wishes to sue the union, and only names the union in the lawsuit, the court will require that the employer be impleaded or interpleaded into the action as a party-in-interest. Thus adding the employer to the litigation, as a necessary party-litigant, is a mandatory requirement under Section 301

---

[118] Robert J. Gelhaus and James Oldham, *Labor Law* (Chicago, IL: The Barbri Group, 2002), p. 219.

[119] See, also, Roderick O. Ford, *Understanding Employment Law* (Tampa, FL.: Xlibris Pub., 2017).

of the Taft-Hartley-Act, since both the employer and the union can be held jointly and severally liable for any breach of the collective bargaining agreement.

§ 5.05 Appeals of Arbitration Rulings (the Civil Courts)

If the labor union takes an employee's grievance to arbitration, and the arbitrator rules in favor of the employer, the inevitable question becomes: what next? Can the aggrieved employee appeal to a court of law for redress? Yes.[120] A state or federal court cannot retry the case, but it can sit as an appellate tribunal in order to determine two fundamental questions:

- Did the labor arbitrator limit his decision to the terms of the collective bargaining agreement; and,
- Was the labor arbitrator's decision based upon improper sources, other than "the unwritten sources that shape the 'common law of the shop.'"[121]

In other words, whenever a labor arbitrator renders his or her decision, the only legal question for review is whether that decision is based upon (1) customary, standard labor law principles and (2) the collective bargaining agreement (CBA).[122] Interestingly, the expressed language of the CBA often refers to Title VII of the 1964 Civil Rights Act, such that any issues involving Title VII discrimination (i.e., race, color, sex, religion, or national origin) might become the proper subject matter of the labor arbitration forum, whereby a labor arbitrator could be allowed to apply standard federal case law regarding Title VII matters. And, by analogy, any other similar federal or state laws that have been incorporated by reference into the labor agreement might similarly become the subject matter of a labor arbitration forum.

In any event, the reviewing state or federal court can only review an arbitration award to ensure that it met the minimal standards of applying the terms of the labor agreement and the minimal standards of customary

---

[120] 51A *Corpus Juris Secundum*, Labor Relations §§ 481-500.

[121] Richard A. Gormon and Matthew W. Finkin, *Basic Text on Labor Law: Unionization and Collective Bargaining* (St. Paul, MN: West Publishing Co., 2004), pp. 814-815.

[122] Ibid.

labor law (e.g., the "Seven Principles of Just Cause"). A reviewing appellate court cannot overturn an arbitration award on the basis that the grievance was incorrectly decided. "The Supreme Court's mandate that great deference be given to arbitration awards, and that courts refrain from reexamining the merits, was strongly reinforced in the Court's decision in *United Paperworkers International Union v. Misco*, [484 U.S. 29 (1987)]."[123] In other words, state and federal courts simply cannot re-examine the merits of a labor arbitration award, but they are restricted to determining only whether the labor arbitration applied the correct labor law (i.e., the terms of the labor agreement and standard, customary labor law).

§ 5.06 Human Resources and Strategic Risk Management

In working environments where there are labor unions and collective bargaining agreements ("labor agreements"), human resources professionals should develop an expertise in the day-to-day administration and management of the labor agreement. This will certainly involve developing an expertise in the area of "employee relations." Employee relations comprise the art and science of conflict resolution, human relations, human resources management, and alternative dispute resolution. These managerial skills are also necessary in strategic human resources management, which includes monitoring the workforce climate, collecting attitude surveys, conducting diversity panels, focus groups, and morale-and-welfare activities. Although these additional H.R. functions are not directly related to the handling and processing of labor grievances and arbitration, they do much to foment and sustain good labor-management relations (i.e., "employee relations"), which can be extremely important when administering and managing the collective bargaining agreement.

In addition, human resources business partners and leaders must cultivate an expertise and practical working knowledge of employees' rights under Sections 7 and 8 of the National Labor Relations Act (NLRA). Without this knowledge, they cannot hope to effectively prevent unnecessary grievances, or to successfully resolve these grievances during the earliest possible stages of the grievance procedures. Human resources

---

[123] Ibid., p. 815.

officers should be able to recognize activities and grievances that constitute "protected concerted activities" under the NLRA. And they should develop a competence in preventing grievances, resolving grievances, and preparing supervisors and managers in defending against employee grievances. Human resources professionals should also develop a working knowledge of NLRB-complaint procedures and how to defend against NLRB grievances. Lastly, human resources professionals should attain expert knowledge on the operative labor agreement, as well as the "past practices" of employment operations, since they will frequently be asked to testify as "expert" witnesses both at arbitration and in state or federal court.

§ 5.07 Conclusion

An employer's duty to bargain in good faith includes the duty to process employee grievances under the collective bargaining agreement ("labor agreement") as well as the duty to not interfere with employees' rights to organize for mutual aid, benefit and protection, pursuant to Sections 7 and 8 of the National Labor Relations Act. Accordingly, employees in unionized workplaces may generally file three forms of complaints: grievances under the labor agreement which may lead to arbitration hearings; unfair labor practices claims before the National Labor Relations Board (NLRB); and lawsuits in state or federal court for the breach of the collective bargaining agreement. Sometimes, aggrieved employees may file two forms of these complaints simultaneously; however, if this is done, the NLRB may defer to the grievance process under the labor agreement, or it may defer to the state or federal court where a case is pending. In other words, the NLRB may wait to take official action, until after a pending labor grievance or lawsuit is resolved. Complaints under both the labor agreement and made at the NLRB are reviewable in state or federal court.

Chapter Five Bibliography

Books:

Ford, Roderick O. *Understanding Employment Law*. Tampa, FL: Xlibris Pub., 2017.

Gelhaus, Robert J. and James Oldham. *Labor Law*. Chicago, IL: The BarBri Group, 2002.

Gormon, Richard A. and Matthew W. Finkin. *Basic Text on Labor Law: Unionization and*

Collective Bargaining. St. Paul, MN: West Publishing Co., 2004.

Loughran, Charles S. *How to Prepare and Present a Labor Arbitration Case: Strategy and*

Tactics for Advocates. Washington, D.C.: The Bureau of National Affairs, Inc., 1996.

Reed, Sandra M. and Anne M. Bogardus. *PHR/ SPHR Professional in Human Resources*

Certification Study Guide. 4th Edition. New York, N.Y.: John Wiley & Sons, Inc., 2012.

References:

48 *Am Jur Second*, Labor and Labor Relations §§ 8; 300-318

51 *Corpus Juris Secundum*, Labor Relations §§ 177-262

51A *Corpus Juris Secundum*, Labor Relations §§ 328-401; 481-500; 763-780

Case Law:

U.S. Supreme Court

Vaca v. Sipes, 386 U.S. 171 (1967)

NLRB v. Weingarten, Inc., 420 U.S. 251 (1975)

Hines v. Anchor Motor Freight, Inc., 424 U.S. 554 (1976)

United Paperworkers International Union v. Misco, 484 U.S. 29 (1987)

American Labor Arbitration Reports

Douglas Aircraft Co., Inc., 1 LA 350 (June 30, 1945)

Douglas Aircraft Co., Inc., 3 LA 598 (June 7, 1946)

Joy MFG Co., 6 LA 430 (July 31, 1946)

United States Spring & Bumper Co., 5 LA 109 (October 4, 1946)

Chrysler Corp., 5 LA 420 (October 17, 1946)

Norwich Pharmacal Co., 5 LA 536 (December 10, 1946)

WLEU Broadcasting Co., 7 LA 150 (March 6, 1947)

Alan Wood Steel Co., 3 LA 557 (June 15, 1947)

Allis-Chalmers MFG Co., 8 LA 177 (June 24, 1947)

Enterprise Wire Co., (46 LA 359, 1966)

Chapter Six

FEDERAL ANTI-DISCRIMINATION LAWS AND THE COLLECTIVE BARGAINING AGREEMENT

§ 6.01 Introduction 144

§ 6.02 Federal Employment Law Causes of Action 151
    [1] Failure To Promote
    [2] Race Discrimination
    [3] Color Discrimination ("Colorism")
    [4] National Origin Discrimination
    [5] Sex Discrimination
    [6] Religion Discrimination
    [7] Hostile Working Environment/ Harassment
    [8] Failure To Train
    [9] Disability: Discrimination/ Harassment
    [10] Age Discrimination
    [11] Lay-off/ Recall Rights/ Discrimination
    [12] Retaliation/ Reprisal

§ 6.03 Federal Prima Facie Case Standards... 230
    [1] Failure To Promote
    [2] Race Discrimination
    [3] Color Discrimination
    [4] National Origin Discrimination
    [5] Sex Discrimination
    [6] Religious Discrimination
    [7] Hostile Work Environment (Under Title VII)
    [8] Failure to Train
    [9] Failure to Promote/Hire
    [10] Disability Discrimination
    [11] Disability -- Failure to Accommodate
    [12] Age Discrimination
    [13] Discriminatory Lay-Off
    [14] Discriminatory Recall Rights
    [15] Retaliation
    [16] Reprisal Under Sec. 8(3)(a) of National Labor Relations Act

§ 6.04 Human Resources and Strategic Risk Management 241

§ 6.05 Conclusion..242

§ 6.01 Introduction

Title VII of the 1964 Civil Rights Act, 42 U.S.C. § 1981, and other federal antidiscrimination laws regulate every sphere of activities and actions of labor unions in the United States.[124] This means that labor

---

[124] "Discrimination based on race or national origin violates the National Labor Relations Act only if it directly interferes with the National Labor Relation Board's role of fostering collective bargaining and protecting employees' rights to act concertedly. However, an employer violates the NLRA by maintaining a policy and practice of invidious discrimination against its employees on account of race or national origin, as such a policy creates an unjustified clash of interest between groups of workers, thus frustrating the possibility of concerted action. In addition, an employee's conduct is protected activity under the NLRA when the employee voices, on behalf of other employees, concerns and complaints about alleged race discrimination." 48A *Am Jur Second*, Labor and Labor Relations §1311.

unions cannot discriminate against individual union members because of their protected status, such as race, color, sex, religion, disability, age, or national origin. If a labor union violates Title VII in any way, a charge of discrimination may be brought against it before the U.S. Equal Employment Opportunity Commission, and it can be sued in state or federal court. And, to the extent that a labor union fails or refuses to represent an individual because of his or her race, sex, religion, color, age, disability, or national origin, it may be sued under a legal theory known as the "breach of the duty of fair representation."[125] Thus, Title VII and other federal antidiscrimination laws also impose upon labor unions the duty of fair representation, to wit:

> To establish a prima facie Title VII claim against a union for *breach of its duty of fair representation*, the plaintiff must show that:
>
> - The *employer* violated the collective bargaining agreement with respect to the plaintiff;
> - The *union* permitted the violation to go unrepaired, thereby breaching the union's duty of fair representation; and
> - There was some indication that the union's actions were motivated by a discriminatory animus.[126]

For example, under Title VII of the 1964 Civil Rights Act, an employee must prove that the union breached its duty of fair representation *because of* his or her race, color, sex, religion, or national origin. Presumably, similar claims may be made under the Age Discrimination in Employment Act (ADA) and the Americans with Disabilities Act (ADA).

In addition, nearly every collective bargaining agreement ("labor agreement") incorporates state and federal anti-discrimination laws into the expressed language of the labor agreement. For example, somewhere in the labor agreement, one will usually find language such as:

---

[125] 45B Am Jur Second, Job Discrimination §§ 1048-1053.
[126] Ibid., §1048.

> **"Article 23. Nondiscrimination**
>
> 23.1 The parties specifically agree that all provisions of this Agreement shall be applied in accordance with applicable law to all employees in the bargaining unit without regard to **race, color, religion, national origin, sex, sexual orientation, gender identity** or **expression, age, disability, familial status** or **marital status,** or **membership/non-membership in any labor organization**; except that the certified employee organization shall not be required to process grievances or provide services for employees who are not members of the organization.
>
> 23.2 It is agreed that no employee shall be required as a condition of employment or promotion within **the bargaining unit to join or refrain from joining the Union.** Furthermore, it is agreed that neither Union officers or representatives nor the Employer shall **discriminate, interfere, or coerce any employees into joining or not joining the Union**.
>
> 23.3 Employee allegations of discrimination may be filed through the grievance procedure (Article 4), the Federal Equal Employment Opportunity Commission, the State's Fair Employment Practices Commission on Human Rights, the City's Department of Community Affairs (Office of Human Rights/Community Services) and/or any other procedure provided by law.
>
> 23.4 A copy of B1.2, Discriminatory Conduct, Personnel Manual, shall be reprinted in the appendix of this Agreement.

What this means is that federal and state anti-discrimination laws can, or must, be read into the daily administration of the collective bargaining agreement. An individual employee who might express his or her grievance as an "unfair labor practice" under Section 8 of the National Labor Relations Act, might also express that very same grievance as a violation of the collective bargaining agreement's as anti-discrimination provision. At the same time, the same individual could file a valid charge of discrimination before the U.S. Equal Opportunity Commission.

For this reason, human resources officials, union stewards and union members need to cultivate a working knowledge of how various local, state, and federal agencies can work in tandem with their local union stewards in order to vindicate the rights of individual union members. Claims under a collective bargaining agreement may sometimes be filed directly with the union steward or employer; but, at the same time, these claims could also be filed with the National Labor Relations Board (i.e., unfair labor practices); and (or) the U.S. Equal Employment Opportunity Commission (i.e., unfair employment practices involving race, color, sex, national origin, religion, and disability claims); U.S. Department of Labor- Wage and Hour Division (i.e. unfair employment practices involving wage, hour, Family and Medical Leave Act); U.S. Department of Labor—Employee Benefit Security Administration (i.e., unfair employment practices involving insurance, health, and disability benefits). State and local-government agencies might also have comparable fair employment practices agencies (FEPAs) where these individual might also dual-file charges of discrimination.

****

This chapter is thus designed to provide an overview for legal practitioners as to the various legal elements of most causes of action, or claims for relief, that arise under Title VII of the Civil Rights Act of 1964, the Americans with Disabilities Act, the Age Discrimination in Employment Act, and the National Labor Relations Act. Although "legal elements" tend to come into sharp focus during court litigation, they are also extremely helpful when grievances are being investigated and discussed during investigations into initial complaints or grievances, during the process of labor grievance administration, and throughout labor arbitration proceedings.

Because this chapter is presented in a simplified format, it is also designed to help employees, human resources professionals, and managers to attain a working knowledge of the legal elements of various labor and employment-law causes of action.

The two major parts of this chapter are (a) "causes of action" or "claim for relief" and (b) "prima facie case standards." It is important to understand that these two concepts are similar, but they are not the same. A "cause of action" or "claim for relief" is much broader in scope than the "prima facie case" standard. A "cause of action" or "claim for relief" deals with *pleading standards*, and asks the fundamental question of whether sufficient information has been correctly alleged within a written complaint. On the other hand, the "prima facie case" standard addresses *standards of proof* which, arise during a later stage of litigation, or at a later stage of the discovery process (e.g., a motion for summary judgment proceeding) or trial (e.g., a motion for directed verdict). See Table 1.

Table 1. Employment Law Pleading/ Evidence Standards

LEGAL STANDARD (COURT)	TYPE	EMPLOYER-DEFENSE MOTION
Cause of Action (Federal Court)	Pleading Standard	Motion to Dismiss
Claim For Relief (State Court)	Pleading Standard	Motion to Dismiss
Prima Facie Case (State or Federal Court)	Evidentiary Standard	Motion for Summary Judgment; Motion For Directed Verdict

Unlike the "cause of action" or "claim for relief," the "prima facie case" standard is not a pleading standard. Instead, the prima facie case standard asks, typically at the close of pre-trial discovery, whether the plaintiff can produce sufficient evidence to withstand a motion for summary judgment, or a motion for a directed verdict at trial. Obviously, both concepts include the same sort of facts and legal analysis. However, employees, human resources professionals, and other non-lawyers should be careful when trying to analyze these matters without legal advice from an attorney. For this reason, I have included a few case citations at the end of each section in order to assist the reader with further research and review. Hopefully, these case citations will help to further explain each legal principle within each section.

The law of employment discrimination is fundamentally the natural law of inherent equality among and between human beings—that is to say, *two employees who are similarly-situated ought to be treated the same, regardless of a protected characteristic which the law acknowledges.* Hence, I strongly believe that the federal law of employment discrimination is fundamentally a law of common sense; and it relies heavily upon the facts and circumstances of each case. It is therefore of critical importance to remember that the "cause of action," "claim for relief," and "prima facie case" standards, which have been articulated by the courts, are *merely a starting point.* These standards were never meant to be inflexible, strict rules of evidence or procedure.[127] Instead, they are simply tools for articulating the basic elements or factors regarding employment discrimination. To be sure, there may conceivably be circumstances that give rise to an inference of discrimination which do not neatly fit into one of the court-established prima facie case standards; and, in that instance, it is the stern duty of the employee advocate to enunciate a new prima face case standard that takes into account the unique set of discriminatory circumstances not previously brought before the bar in any other case.[128] This is true because human behavior (and especially employment discrimination) is kaleidoscopic and multifaceted.

Several federal laws prohibit discrimination on the basis of age, disability, race, color, ethnic origin, religion, sex, participation in labor union activities, etc. This chapter includes a few of the most common prima facie case criteria for proving employment discrimination under federal statutes such as Title VII of the Civil Rights Act of 1964, the Age Discrimination in Employment Act (ADEA), the Americans with Disabilities Act (ADA), and the National Labor Relations Act (NLRA).

---

[127] *McDonnell Douglas Corp. v. Green*, 411 U.S. 792, 93 S.Ct. 1817 36 L.Ed.2d 302 (1973).

[128] In this regards, the employee advocate may very well consider invoking the court's equity jurisdiction. It is a general rule of thumb that "equity follows law" and that "equity will not permit the deprivation of right without affording a remedy."

§ 6.02 FEDERAL EMPLOYMENT LAW CAUSES OF ACTION

(PLEADING STAGE)

§ 6.02 Federal Employment Law Causes of Action

In federal court, a "cause of action" is not to be confused with a "claim for relief," even though both concepts address pleading standards. The "claim for relief" predated the "cause of action," and it originates with state law courts. The state-law "claim for relief" pleading standard is typically much narrower and stricter in scope than the federal court "cause of action" pleading standard. In general, a "cause of action" under Rule 8 of the Federal Rules of Civil Procedure is much broader in scope than corresponding state law rules which adopt the "claim for relief" pleading standard. The federal cause of action standard deals with the general wrong(s) alleged in accordance with the corresponding law or statute that will be applied to a particular case. In federal court, this does not matter if the law or statute is a state law or a federal law; the "cause of action" pleading standard will always be used in accordance with Rule 8 of the Federal Rules of Civil Procedure.

A cause of action in federal court need only allege or infer all of the component parts of the prima facie case, but in general pleading a prima facie claim or even a stricter claim for relief this is not necessary in federal court. What is needed in federal court to present a cause of action is a general allegation setting for the basic facts which allege a violation of a law or statute, together with a basic description of the facts which support that claim for relief. The facts, of course, should be as detailed as possible; and the litigant should go ahead and include all known, relevant facts within the original complaint. The cause of action in federal court is actually the underlying story—the facts stated in clear, concise, and chronological order. For the sake of convenience, the courts have separated employment law into various categories or types of "causes of action," which I have listed below.

[1] Failure To Promote

In employment law, there is a cause of action called "failure to promote." Again, what the court wants to see is the entire story that underlies this case: basically, what happened? What is the time sequence of events? Who, what, when, where and how? All of this information needs to be included in the complaint in order to set forth a "cause of action." Although the federal "cause of action" need not include or articulate every single element listed within the "prima facie" case standard, the best course of action is to draft the federal "cause of action" so that each and every element of the "prima facie" case standard is included within the original complaint.

Individuals who work hard and have a substantial record of good or superb performance are often passed over for promotions which they believe that they should have received. It is important to remember that state and federal courts will not second-guess employer or managerial discretionary decisions. Even if the decision to promote another candidate is a bad one, it may not necessarily violate any state or federal laws. In general, a plaintiff must be able to present competent evidence that the he or she is far more qualified than the successful candidate. If two candidates were fairly similar in work experience and education, then the courts typically will not reverse an employment promotion or adjudge the promotion to be unlawful. The following cases provide examples of the legal elements involved with proving various components of "failure to promote" claims.

Annotated Notes to § [1] Failure to Promote

U.S. Eleventh Circuit Court of Appeals (Alabama, Florida, Georgia)

1. *Wilson v. B/E Aerospace, Inc*, 376 F.3d 1079 (11th Cir. 2004)("Under the McDonnell Douglas framework, to prevail on a Title VII **failure to promote claim**, an employee may establish a prima facie case of sex discrimination by showing that: (1) she is a member of a protected class, (2) she was qualified and applied for the promotion, (3) she was rejected despite her qualifications, and (4) other equally or less qualified employees who were not members of the protected class were promoted.")

2. *Combs v. Plantation Patterns*, 106 F.3d 1519 (11th Cir. 1997)("To establish prima facie case of discriminatory **failure to promote**, plaintiff must prove that he is a member of protected class, that he was qualified for and applied for promotion, that he was rejected, and that other equally or less qualified employees who were not members of protected class were promoted.... By meeting its burden of producing legitimate reasons for

its decision to promote another candidate rather than black employee to welding supervisor position, former employer successfully eliminated presumption of discrimination that initially accomplished black employee's prima facie case under Title VII, where employer proffered evidence in support of three legitimate, nondiscriminatory reasons for its promotion decision, including other candidate's superior welding experience and superior supervisory experience, and recommendations of supervisors.")

3. *Denney v. City of Albany*, 247 F.3d 1172 (11th Cir. 2001)("Under the rubric of McDonnell Douglas, to establish a prima facie case of discriminatory **failure to promote**, Title VII plaintiff must prove: (1) that plaintiff is a member of a protected class, (2) that plaintiff was qualified for and applied for the promotion, (3) that plaintiff was rejected, and (4) that other equally or less qualified employees who were not members of the protected class were promoted."

4. *Stuart v. Jefferson County Dept. of Human Resources*, 152 Fed.Appx. 798 (11th Cir. 2005)("Employee failed to establish that employer's reason for **not selecting** him for a **promotional position**, that the female chosen for the position had more experience for the position, was a pretext for gender discrimination under Title VII; he failed to offer any evidence that he was more qualified than the female."

5. *Walker v. Mortham*, 158 F.3d 1177 (11th Cir. 1998)(**failure to promote**)("In order to establish prima facie case of discrimination under Title VII using the McDonnell Douglas framework, an employee or job applicant need not identify the successful applicant for his or her coveted position, but need only establish that such applicant is not within her protected class.")

6. *Brown v. Alabama Dept. of Transp.* 597 F.3d 1160 (11th Cir. 2010) ("The plaintiff bears the burden of establishing a prima facie case of discrimination in Title VII cases that are supported by circumstantial evidence.... In the **failure-to-promote** context, a prima facie Title VII case consists of showing these elements: (1) that the plaintiff belongs to a protected class; (2) that she applied for and was qualified for a promotion;

(3) that she was rejected despite her qualifications; and (4) that other equally or less-qualified employees outside her class were promoted.")

7. *Price v. M & H Valve Co.*, 177 Fed.Appx. 1 (11th Cir. 2006)("Employee establishes prima facie case of discriminatory **failure to promote** by showing that (1) he is a member of a protected class, (2) he was qualified and applied for the promotion, (3) he was rejected despite his qualifications, and (4) other equally or less qualified employees who were not members of the protected class were promoted."

8. *Vessels v. Atlanta Independent School System*, 408 F.3d 763 (11th Cir. 2005)("Where an employer does not formally announce a position, but rather uses informal and subjective procedures to identify a candidate, a plaintiff, in order to establish a prima facie case of discrimination under McDonnell Douglas framework, need not show that he applied for the position, only that the employer had some reason to consider him for the post…. To demonstrate that he was qualified for the position, a Title VII plaintiff seeking to establish prima facie **failure to promote** claim need only show that he or she satisfied an employer's objectively verifiable qualifications; employer may then introduce its subjective evaluations of the plaintiff at the later stages of the *McDonnell Douglas* framework.")

9. *Williams v. Waste Management, Inc.*, 411 Fed.Appx. 226 (11th Cir. 2011)("African-American employee's failure to apply for open position precluded recovery on his **failure to promote** claim, given absence of any evidence that employer had engaged in systematic discrimination that had successfully deterred job applications from members of minority groups…. Two-month gap between African-American employee's complaints about racially derogatory comments and employer's failure to promote him was not enough to establish a prima face case of retaliation under Title VII or § 1981.")

10. *Connor v. Lafarge North America, Inc.*, 343 Fed.Appx. 537 (11th Cir. 2009)("Employer's legitimate, nondiscriminatory reason for **failure to promote** African-American employee, that he performed poorly in interviews for that position, specifically in portions of interview dealing with crucial areas of leadership, decision-making, safety, and computer skills, was not pretext for race discrimination in violation of Title VII,

although person hired for position did not have listed qualifications for 'minimum of 2 years cement plant or terminal operating experience' and 'supervisory experience' and employee did; employer declared all internal candidates qualified by virtue of their being internal candidates and based promotion decision on interviews alone, there was no evidence that employer had ever filled supervisory positions using any method other than exclusive reliance on interviews, and employee admitted that 4 of 5 panel members did not harbor racial animus toward him.")

11. *Summerlin v. M & H Valve Co.*, 167 Fed.Appx. 93 (11th Cir. 2006) ("African-American male employee [did] not need to show that he was more qualified than the non-minority individual who received the promotion, in order to establish prima facie claim for racial **failure-to-promote** discrimination under Title VII.... Employer's proffered legitimate reason for promoting non-minority individual rather than African-American male employee to supervisory position, that the non-minority individual was more qualified and had more experience, was not pretext for race discrimination, as required to prove a Title VII racial failure-to-promote discrimination claim; non-minority individual had over 10 years experience, in contrast to employer's two months of experience, and non-minority individual had three years of supervisory experience in the business, and employee's only supervisory experience was outside of the business.")

U.S. Fifth Circuit Court of Appeals (Louisiana, Mississippi, Texas)

1. *Davis v. Dallas Area Rapid Transit*, 383 F.3d 309 (5th Cir. 2004)("Prima facie case of discrimination in Title VII **failure-to-promote** case requires showing that: (1) employee is member of protected class; (2) he sought and was qualified for position; (3) he was rejected for position; and (4) employer continued to seek, or promoted, applicants with plaintiff's qualifications.")

2. *Shackelford v. Deloitte & Touche, LLP*, 190 F.3d 398 (5th Cir. 1999) ("A prima facie case is established under Title VII once the employee has proved that he or she: (1) is a member of a protected class; (2) was qualified

for his or her position; (3) was subjected to an adverse employment action; and 4) was replaced by someone outside the protected class.")

3. *Trevino v. Celanese Corp.*, 701 F.2d 397 (5th Cir. 1983)("Discriminatory **failure to promote** represents an actionable, continuing violation of Title VII.... For purposes of Title VII employment discrimination, an employee may be promoted, or denied promotion, from one to another nominally independent entity provided the two entities' activities, operations, ownership or management are sufficiently interrelated, and whether transfer from one work force to another constitutes a 'promotion' or a 'hiring' depends on the facts of each case.")

[2] Race Discrimination

In employment law, there is a cause of action called "disparate treatment- race" or "race discrimination." Again, what the court wants to see is the entire story that underlies this case: basically, what happened? What is the time sequence of events? Who, what, when, where and how? All of this information needs to be included in the complaint in order to set forth a "cause of action." Although the federal "cause of action" need not include or articulate every single element listed within the "prima facie" case standard, the best course of action is to draft the federal "cause of action" so that each and every element of the "prima facie" case standard is included within the original complaint.

Race discrimination against African American workers is the most prevalent form of racial discrimination, according to the U.S. Equal Employment Opportunity Commission.

There are a multitude of Title VII causes of action that may fall with the category of "race discrimination," and so the list of cases which follow is not exhaustive. Instead, this list simply provides a sample of the various types of legal elements that are involved with racial discrimination cases that arise under Title VII of the 1964 Civil Rights Act.

Annotated Notes to § [2] Race Discrimination

U.S. Eleventh Circuit Court of Appeals (Alabama, Florida, Georgia)

1. *Equal Employment Opportunity Commission v. Catastrophe Management Solutions*, 2016 WL 7210059 (11th Cir. 2016)("To prevail on **disparate treatment claim**, Title VII plaintiff must demonstrate that employer intentionally discriminated against her on basis of protected characteristic.... **Disparate impact claim** under Title VII does not require proof of discriminatory intent, but rather targets employment practice that has actual, though not necessarily deliberate, adverse impact on protected groups..... Title VII plaintiff can prove disparate treatment by direct evidence that workplace policy, practice, or decision relies expressly on protected characteristic, or by circumstantial evidence.... Meaning of word 'race' in Title VII is, like any other question of statutory interpretation, question of law for court.... When words are not defined in statute, they are interpreted as taking their ordinary, contemporary, common meaning.")

2. *Crawford v. Carroll*, 529 F.3d 961 (11th Cir. 2008)("To make out prima facie case of **racial discrimination** under Title VII or in § 1983 equal protection claim, plaintiff must show that: (1) she belongs to protected class; (2) she was qualified to do job; (3) she was subjected to adverse employment action; and (4) her employer treated similarly situated employees outside her class more favorably.... Prima facie case of retaliation under Title VII requires showing that: (1) employee engaged in activity protected under Title VII: (2) she suffered adverse employment action; and (3) there was causal connection between protected activity and adverse employment action.... In order to satisfy '**adverse employment action**' element of Title VII discrimination action, employee must show either ultimate employment decision, i.e. termination, failure to hire, or demotion, or, for conduct falling short of ultimate employment decision, serious and material change in terms, conditions or privileges of employment.... **Poor performance evaluation** that directly results in denial of pay raise of any significance clearly affects employee's compensation and thus constitutes **adverse employment action** under Title VII.")

3. *In re Birmingham Reverse Discrimination Employment Litigation*, 20 F.3d 1525 (11th Cir. 1994)("Employers may develop **affirmative action plans** designed to further Title VII's purpose of eliminating effects of discrimination in workplace…. In determining whether affirmative action plan was implemented consistent with Title VII's purpose and without unduly infringing interests of nonblacks, Court of Appeals was required to first determine whether employer's consideration of race of promotional candidates was justified by manifest racial imbalance that reflected underrepresentation of blacks in traditionally segregated job categories, and, if such justification was present when plan was developed, to determine whether plan itself provided proper remedy for that imbalance…. For purposes of challenge under Title VII to affirmative action plan, when job requires no special expertise, determining whether market imbalance exists that would justify race-conscious decision making by employer involves comparison of percentage of minority employees in that job with percentage of minorities in general labor market; however, when job requires special skills or training, appropriate comparison is to those in labor market who possess that special skill or training… For trial court to conclude that remedial action under Title VII is warranted, there must be sufficient evidence to allow it to make factual determination that employer had strong basis in evidence for its conclusion that remedial action was necessary…. Before city may settle Title VII litigation by consent decree, it is necessary that trial court make some finding that city engaged in past discrimination, in order to allow for proper judicial review of city's use of race in its affirmative action plan.")

4. *Equal Employment Opportunity Commission v. Catastrophe Management Solutions*, 2016 WL 7210059 (11th Cir. 2016)("To prevail on **disparate treatment claim**, Title VII plaintiff must demonstrate that employer intentionally discriminated against her on basis of protected characteristic…. Disparate impact claim under Title VII does not require proof of discriminatory intent, but rather targets employment practice that has actual, though not necessarily deliberate, adverse impact on protected groups…. Title VII plaintiff can prove disparate treatment by direct evidence that workplace policy, practice, or decision relies expressly on protected characteristic, or by circumstantial evidence…. One way to figure out meaning of word that is not defined in statute is by looking at dictionaries in existence around time of enactment.")

5. *Standard v. A.B.E.L. Services, Inc.*, 161 F.3d 1318 (11th Cir. 1998)("To establish a prima facie case of **retaliation** under the ADA, employee must show (1) that he engaged in statutorily protected activity, (2) that he suffered an adverse employment action, and (3) a causal link between the protected activity and the adverse action.... To engage in protected activity for purposes of ADA retaliation claim, it is sufficient that an employee have a good faith, objectively reasonable belief that his activity is protected by the statute.... Employee's requests for accommodation of his back injury did not constitute statutorily protected activity, for purposes of ADA retaliation claim, absent showing that he had good faith, objectively reasonable belief that he was disabled under the **ADA** at time he made the requests.... In determining whether an injury **substantially limits a major life activity**, so as to constitute disability under ADA, court considers (1) the nature and severity of the impairment, (2) the duration or expected duration of the impairment, and (3) the permanent or long term impact, or the expected permanent or long term impact of or resulting from the impairment.... To make out a prima facie case of age discrimination for a reduction-in-force termination, former employee must prove that (1) he was a member of the age group protected by the ADEA at the time of his termination, (2) he was qualified at the time of his termination, and (3) there is evidence from which a reasonable fact finder could conclude that the employer intended to discriminate on the basis of age in making the decision.... To establish a case under Title VII, a plaintiff may use three different kinds of evidence of discriminatory intent: direct evidence, circumstantial evidence or statistical evidence; the analytical framework and burden of production varies depending on the method of proof chosen.... Under McDonnell Douglass burden-shifting framework for establishing employment discrimination claims, once plaintiff establishes prima facie case of discrimination, the employer must offer legitimate, nondiscriminatory reasons for the employment action to rebut the presumption of discrimination; if the employer successfully rebuts the presumption, the burden shifts back to the plaintiff to discredit the proffered nondiscriminatory reasons by showing that they are pretextual.... Former employee who was discharged as part of **reduction-in-force** could establish a prima facie case of discrimination under Title VII by (1) showing that he was a member of protected group and was adversely affected by an employment decision, (2) proving that he was qualified for his own position or to assume another position at the time of the discharge,

and (3) producing sufficient evidence from which a rational fact finder could conclude that his employer intended to discriminate against him in making the discharge decision.... Title VII plaintiff may show that employer's proffered reasons for challenged employment decision are pretext (1) by showing that the legitimate nondiscriminatory reasons should not be believed, or (2) by showing that, in light of all the evidence, discriminatory reasons more likely motivated the decision than the proffered reasons.... To directly attack employer's proffered nondiscriminatory reasons for employment decision, Title VII plaintiff must demonstrate such weaknesses, implausibilities, inconsistencies, incoherencies or contradictions in the employer's proffered legitimate reasons for its action that a reasonable fact finder could find all of those reasons unworthy of credence.... To establish prima facie case of discriminatory **failure to promote**, plaintiff in § 1981 case must show that (1) he was in a protected group, (2) he was not given the promotion, (3) he was qualified for the position and (4) someone outside of the protected group was given the position.")

6. *Smith v. CH2M Hill Inc.*, 521 Fed.Appx. 773 (11th Cir. 2013) ("Employee's allegations were sufficient to state plausible claim for **race discrimination** under Title VII; employee alleged that he was black, that he had experience and was qualified for his work, that his termination was substantially motivated by race, that he was replaced by non-African-American person, and that less-qualified non-African-American persons in his job classification retained their employment when he was discharged, that he was pressured by city officials to selectively enforce applicable codes in racially discriminatory manner, in effect enforcing some codes against black citizen under circumstances substantially similar to a situation in which he had been directed not to enforce those codes against white citizen, and that, after he objected to discriminatory enforcement, city demanded that employers remove him from his job and employers complied and terminated him with full knowledge of discriminatory motive.")

7. *Paye v. Secretary of Defense*, 157 Fed.Appx. 234 (11th Cir. 2005)("Asian-American former employee had to offer evidence on summary judgment about race of her replacement, if any, evidence about any other Asian-American employees and whether they also were subject to discriminatory actions, or evidence about any employees who were not fired after failing to meet performance improvement plan (**PIP**) requirements, in order to

establish prima facie case of **race discrimination** under Title VII against Department of Defense, as employer, under test that required her to show that someone outside her protected class was treated differently than she was or under her theory that she should have been required to show only that she was replaced by someone outside her class.")

8. *Hill v. Emory University*, 346 Fed.Appx. 390 (11th Cir. 2009) ("Employee failed to show that private university employer's stated reasons for terminating him, that the funds from which employee was paid were running budget deficits and the program that employee was hired to develop was handled primarily by an outside vendor, where pretext for **race discrimination**, as required to prevail in § 1981 termination claim.... Employee of private university employer failed to establish prima facie claim of wage discrimination on account of race, as would support Title VII claim; although coworkers who were not members of racial minority received salary increases, and employee did not, the coworkers were not similarly situated to employee, since they presented the employer with evidence of a competing job offer, while employee did not.... Employee of private university was not subjected to severe and pervasive harassment as required to establish Title VII hostile work environment claim; although employee alleged that his workgroup was referenced to a counseling session, that employee was demoted, that his requests for supporting office staff were denied, one of his hiring decision was denied, that his request to attend educational conference was denied, that his request to reclassify himself was denied, that employee was never assigned any direct reports, that he was never assigned any office space, that he was not awarded pay raises comparable to his coworkers, and that employer failed to reabsorb him after his job was terminated or provide him with a list of available job openings, such actions were not so severe or pervasive as to alter the terms and conditions of employment.")

9. *Vessels v. Atlanta Independent School System*, 408 F.3d 763 (11th Cir. 2005)("Where an employer does not formally announce a position, but rather uses informal and subjective procedures to identify a candidate, a plaintiff, in order to establish a **prima facie case of discrimination** under McDonnell Douglas framework, need not show that he applied for the position, only that the employer had some reason to consider him for the post.... To demonstrate that he was qualified for the positon, a Title

VII plaintiff seeking to establish prima facie failure to promote claim need only show that he or she satisfied an employer's objectively verifiable qualifications; employer may then introduce its subjective evaluations of the plaintiff at the later stages of the McDonnell Douglas framework.... Where an employee seeks to prove through qualifications alone that race-neutral reasons for failure to promote were pretextual, the difference in qualifications must be so glaring that no reasonable impartial person could have chosen the candidate selected for the promotion in question over the employee; however, where the qualifications disparity is not the sole basis for arguing pretext, the disparity need not be so dramatic to support an inference of pretext.")

10. *Holifield v. Reno*, 115 F.3d 1555 (11th Cir. 1997)("Employer presented legitimate, non-discriminatory reason for transferring and later terminating black doctor, as required to rebut doctor's prima facie case of **race discrimination** in violation of Title VII, by showing that evaluations indicated schism between doctor and his colleagues, supervisors, and support staff, and that reviewers recommended doctor be removed for delaying treatment and evaluation of patients, displaying unprofessional behavior toward staff and physicians, and causing conflict within department and with administration.... Black doctor's unsubstantiated assertion that his supervisors began documenting untrue assessment of his performance to terminate him because of his race was insufficient to show that employer's articulated reason for transfer and termination was pretext for race discrimination in violation of Title VII.... Peer review, performance appraisals, and testimony of supervisors, colleagues, and medical staff showing that work for which black doctor was responsible was not performed properly was fatal to doctor's claim he was transferred and terminated in violation of Title VII, in retaliation for filing equal employment opportunity complaint and expressing concerns about racism to his supervisor.")

U.S. Fifth Circuit Court of Appeals (Louisiana, Mississippi, Texas)

1. *McCoy v. City of Shreveport*, 492 F.3d 551 (5th Cir. 2007)("Assuming a Title VII plaintiff has exhausted his administrative remedies, he may prove a claim of **intentional discrimination** or **retaliation** either by

direct or circumstantial evidence.... Under the framework for establishing a Title VII discrimination claim based upon circumstantial evidence, the plaintiff must first establish a prima facie case of discrimination, which requires a showing that the plaintiff: (1) is a member of a protected group; (2) was qualified for the position at issue; (3) was discharged or suffered some adverse employment action by the employer; and (4) was replaced by someone outside his protected group or was treated less favorably than other similarly situated employees outside the protected group.... Under the framework for establishing a Title VII retaliation claim based upon circumstantial evidence, a Title VII plaintiff must establish that: (1) he participated in an activity protected by Title VII; (2) his employer took an adverse employment action against him; and (3) a causal connection exists between the protected activity and the adverse employment action.... If a Title VII plaintiff makes a prima facie showing, the burden then shifts to the employer to articulate a legitimate, nondiscriminatory or nonretaliatory reason for its employment action.... In a Title VII action, the employer's burden of articulating a legitimate, nondiscriminatory or nonretaliatory reason for its employment action is only one of production, not persuasion, and involves no credibility assessment.... If the employer meets its burden of production by articulating a legitimate, nondiscriminatory or nonretaliatory reason for its employment action, the Title VII plaintiff then bears the ultimate burden of proving that the employer's proffered reason is not true but instead is a pretext for the real discriminatory or retaliatory purpose.... To carry the burden of proving that an employer's proffered reason is not true but instead is a pretext for the real discriminatory or retaliatory purpose, a Title VII plaintiff must rebut each nondiscriminatory or nonretaliatory reason articulated by the employer.... In determining whether an employer's actions toward a Title VII plaintiff constitute a constructive discharge, the Court of Appeals examines the following relevant factors: (1) demotion; (2) reduction in salary; (3) reduction in job responsibilities; (4) reassignment to menial or degrading work; (5) badgering, harassment, or humiliation by the employer calculated to encourage the employee's resignation; or (6) offers of early retirement that would make the employee worse off whether the offer were accepted or not.... The inquiry into whether an employer's actions toward a Title VII plaintiff constitute a constructive discharge is an objective one, 'reasonable employee,' test under which the Court of Appeals ask whether a reasonable person in the plaintiff's shoes would have felt compelled to resign.")

2. *Okoye v. University of Texas Houston Health Science Center*, 245 F.3d 507 (5th Cir. 2001)("In order to survive summary judgment in Title VII case, former employee was required to raise a genuine issue as to a material fact that employer **discriminated** against her, and to do so, was required to satisfy burden shifting test annunciated in *McDonnell Douglas Corp.*"

3. *Simmons-Myers v. Caesars Entertainment Corp.*, 515 Fed.Appx. 269 (5th Cir. 2013)("Termination of white employee was not **racial discrimination** that would violate § 1981, where employee's position was completely eliminated, all co-workers in same position, all of whom, other than employee, were black, were all fired, and employee was not replaced.")

4. *Laxton v. Gap Inc.*, 333 F.3d 572 (5th Cir. 2003)("In Title VII **employment discrimination** action, evidence demonstrating that employer's explanation for adverse employment action is false or unworthy of credence taken together with employee's prima facie case is likely to support inference of discrimination even without further evidence of defendant's true motive.... Employee's prima facie case of discrimination under Title VII combined with showing of pretext in employer's proffered nondiscriminatory reason for adverse employment action is insufficient to establish discrimination only when: (1) record conclusively reveals some other, nondiscriminatory reason for employer's decision, or (2) plaintiff creates only weak issue of fact as to whether employer's reason was untrue, and there is abundant and uncontroverted evidence that no discrimination occurred.")

5. *Byers v. Dallas Morning News, Inc.*, 209 F.3d 419 (5th Cir. 2000)("In order to establish prima facie case of **discriminatory discharge** based on **race** in violation of Title VII, employee must establish: (1) that he/she is member of protected group; (2) that he/she was qualified for the position held; (3) that he/she was discharged from position; and (4) that he/she was replaced by someone outside of the protected group.... White newspaper employee who was discharged from management position shortly after his supervisor was replaced by another employee, who happened to be black, did not establish prima facie case of **reverse racial discrimination**

in violation of Title VII, where each of the two employees who took over his duties was also white, and employee failed to produce any evidence that supervisor acted with discriminatory intent, but relied solely on his subjective belief that supervisor had discriminated against him because he was white.")

[3] Color Discrimination ("Colorism")

In employment law, there is a cause of action called "disparate treatment—color" or "color discrimination." Again, what the court wants to see is the entire story that underlies this case: basically, what happened? What is the time sequence of events? Who, what, when, where and how? All of this information needs to be included in the complaint in order to set forth a "cause of action." Although the federal "cause of action" need not include or articulate every single element listed within the "prima facie" case standard, the best course of action is to draft the federal "cause of action" so that each and every element of the "prima facie" case standard is included within the original complaint.

Color discrimination is real but less prevalent that race, sex and other forms of discrimination. When considering cases where the "harasser" or "perpetrator" is black, and the "victim" is also black, "color discrimination" may very well be the cause, although the practice has fallen into disfavor and is no longer widespread. The following list of cases provide samples of color discrimination which human resources and legal practitioners may find useful.

Annotated Notes to § [3] Color Discrimination

U.S. Eleventh Circuit Court of Appeals (Alabama, Florida, Georgia)

1. *Word v. AT & T*, 576 Fed.Appx. 908 (11th Cir. 2014)("Employer's terminating African American employee for five consecutive unexcused absences after employee had been previously suspended was not pretext for **retaliation** for employee's filing administrative discrimination charge,

as would violate Title VII and § 1981; employee was not only employee to advance to next level of discipline after only one occurrence, occurrence was five consecutive absences, employer's attendance guidelines did not dictate number of occurrences as sole measuring stick for determining discipline, and employee did not fill out paperwork to request vacation.... Two Caucasian and **two lighter-skinned African American co-workers** who were reinstated after termination and subsequently discharged as second time after multiple absences or tardies were not similarly situated to African American employee terminated after one occurrence that followed reinstatement, as required for employee's Title VII and § 1983 race and color discrimination claims; employee's occurrence was being absent for five consecutive days, which was more total time missed than co-workers'.")

2. *Walker v. Secretary of the Treasury, Internal Revenue Service*, 713 F.Supp. 403 (U.S. N.D. Ga. 1989)("Allegation by black former employee that she was discharged by black supervisor because she was **a light-skinned black person**, while supervisor was a dark-skinned black person, stated a cause of action for discrimination under Title VII.... In the employment context, § 1981 is not available to federal employees; Title VII establishes the exclusive remedy for federal employment discrimination.... Actions of federal officials under color of federal law rather than state law are not subject to suit under § 1983.")

U.S. Fifth Circuit Court of Appeals (Louisiana, Mississippi, Texas)

1. *Khalfani v. Balfour Beatty Communities, LLC*, 595 Fed.Appx. 363 (5th Cir. 2014)("We analyze this case pursuant to our Title VII jurisprudence. In general, that analysis follows in three parts: (1) the employee-plaintiff must make a prima facie case of unlawful retaliation or **race/color discrimination**, (2) the burden of production shifts to the employer-defendant, who must articulate a legitimate, non-discriminatory reason for the challenged action, and (3) if it does, the plaintiff can show that the defendant's stated reason is pretextual.")

Other U.S. Circuit Courts of Appeal and Lower-level District Courts

2. *Bryant v. Bell Atlantic Maryland, Inc.*, 288 F.3d 124 (4th Cir. 2002)(4th Cir. 2002)("**Color discrimination** in violation of Title VII arises when the particular hue of the employee's skin is the cause of the discrimination, such as in the case where a **dark-colored African-American** individual is discriminated against in favor of a **light-colored African-American** individual…. ")

3. *Williams v. Wendler*, 530 F.3d 584 (7th Cir. 2008)("The university authorities were not choosing between black and white in punishing the hazers, but between black and black, which is like choosing between white and white. There can, it is true, be 'racial' discrimination within the same race, broadly defined, because 'race' is a fuzzy term…. Title VI, like Title VII, forbids discrimination on the basis of color as well as on the basis of race; since **light-skinned blacks** sometimes discriminate against **dark-skinned blacks**, and vice versa, and either form of discrimination is literally 'color discrimination.'… ").

4. *Cooper v. Jackson-Madison County General Hospital District*, 742 F.Supp. 2d 941 (U.S. W.D. Tenn. 2010)("Although the terms race and color were not defined by Congress in Title VII, the two terms are not synonymous; 'color' refers to pigmentation, complexion, or skin shade or tone, and **'color discrimination'** occurs when a person is discriminated against based on the lightness, darkness, or other color characteristic of the person.

5. *Richardson v. HRHH Gaming Senior Mezz, LLC*, 99 F.Supp.3d 1267 (U.S. D.Nev. 2015)(**Color discrimination** and race discrimination are similar but they are not the same. Therefore, an individual may not rely upon his "race" EEOC charge of discrimination to bring a "color" discrimination complaint in federal court. "The Cooper court, relying in part on an EEOC compliance manual, explained the difference between race and color discrimination, stating that color discrimination 'arises when the particular hue of the plaintiff's skin is the cause of the discrimination, such as in the case where a **dark-colored African-American** individual is discriminated against in favor of a **light-colored African-American** individual.'")

[4] National Origin Discrimination

In employment law, there is a cause of action called "disparate treatment—national origin discrimination" or "national origin discrimination." Again, what the court wants to see is the entire story that underlies this case: basically, what happened? What is the time sequence of events? Who, what, when, where and how? All of this information needs to be included in the complaint in order to set forth a "cause of action." Although the federal "cause of action" need not include or articulate every single element listed within the "prima facie" case standard, the best course of action is to draft the federal "cause of action" so that each and every element of the "prima facie" case standard is included within the original complaint.

National origin discrimination has always existed in the United States as a result of it being a "land of immigrants." Labor market competition among various ethnic groups in America's large cities began to intensify with the coming of the industrial revolution. In modern times, Mexicans, Central Americans, Muslims and Americans with Islamic-sounding surnames have often faced unfair ethnic-origin discrimination.

Annotated Notes to §[4] National Origin Discrimination

U.S. Supreme Court

1. *Espinoza v. Farah Mfg. Co.*, 414 U.S. 86 (1973)(NOTE: citation taken from Zascha Blanco Abbott, "Equal Employment Opportunity Laws: Substantive Claims, Defenses and Related Matters"© 15th Florida Bar Labor and Employment Law Annual Update and Certification Review, Vol. II (2015)("Although non-citizens may be subject to discrimination based on their national origin, discrimination on the basis of citizenship is not per se **national origin discrimination**. After Espinoza, the EEOC revised its guidelines concerning national origin. The revised guidelines state that Title VII is violated if an employer's citizenship requirement has the purpose or effect of discrimination against persons of a particular national origin. 29 C.F.R. § 1606.5.")

U.S. Eleventh Circuit Court of Appeals (Alabama, Florida, Georgia)

1. *Jianxin Fong v. Sch. Bd.*, 2014 U.S. App. LEXIS 21224 * 6-7 (11th Cir. 2014) (NOTE: citation taken from Zascha Blanco Abbott, "Equal Employment Opportunity Laws: Substantive Claims, Defenses and Related Matters"© 15th Florida Bar Labor and Employment Law Annual Update and Certification Review, Vol. II (2015)("Discrimination based on an employee's accent can be **national origin discrimination**. However, an employee's heavy accent or difficulty with spoken English can be a legitimate basis for adverse employment action where effective communication skills are reasonably related to job performance.")

2. *Albert-Aluya v. Burlington Coat Factory Warehouse Corp.*, 470 Fed.Appx. 847 (11th Cir. 2012)("Nigerian-born employee established prima facie case that she was wrongfully terminated because of her **national origin** in violation of Title VII; her supervisor often made derogatory comments to her about her African ethnicity and accent and employee testified that at meeting where she was told of firing, regional manager stated that termination was because of her 'thick African accent' and 'being too brash with people' and regional human resource generalist criticized her for 'failing to speak more like an American.'")

3. *Abbes v. Embraer Services, Inc.*, 195 Fed.Appx. 898 (11th Cir. 2006) ("Terminated employee, a Canadian and Tunisian citizen, failed to present a prima facie case of **national origin discrimination** under Title VII; employee presented no evidence that employer treated similarly situated engineers outside of his protected class more favorably than him.... Terminated employee... failed to prove that any alleged harassment was so severe that if altered the terms and conditions of his employment, as required to prove claim of national origin harassment under Title VII; even if the acts employee complained of qualified as unwelcome harassment, he presented no evidence that employer's management took these actions because of his Tunisian background.")

4. *Alvarez v. Royal Atlantic Developers, Inc.*, 610 F.3d 1253 (11th Cir. 2010) ("Cuban American employee's testimony that other employees told her they heard discriminatory remarks about Cubans was inadmissible

hearsay, which could not be used to defeat summary judgment on her Title VII **national-origin discrimination** claim, where employee did not offer any affidavits or deposition testimony from these other employees.... Although employer planned to fire employee by the time employee sent letter to employer's chief executive officer (CEO) asserting that employer's chief financial officer (CFO) was planning to fire employee and a co-worker because they were of Cuban origin, the letter did cause employee to be fired the day after she e-mailed it, which was sooner than she otherwise would have been, and thus employee suffered an adverse action, as element of her Title VII retaliation claim.... Employer's proffered reason for firing employee sooner than it was planning to, that letter she sent to employer's chief executive officer (CEO) after decision to terminate had been made, which letter asserted that employer's chief financial officer (CFO) was planning to fire employee and a co-worker because they were of Cuban origin, demonstrated that employee was unhappy working for the company and thus it would be 'awkward and counterproductive' to keep her around, was not a legitimate, non-retaliatory reason under Title VII to fire employee.")

5. *Aristyld v. City of Lauderhill*, 543 Fed.Appx. 905 (11th Cir. 2013)("City employee failed to identify any similarly situated individual outside of his protected class who was treated more favorably, as required to establish prima facie case of discriminatory failure-to-promote on the basis of his **national origin**.... City employee failed to show that city's proffered legitimate, nondiscriminatory reasons for his termination, that is, multiple complaints about the conditions in the bathrooms and park recreation areas he was required to clean, were pretextual, as would support his retaliatory hostile work environment claim under Title VII.")

6. *Standard v. A.B.E.L. Services, Inc.*, 161 F.3d 1318 (11th Cir. 1998)("Alleged statements of management members that company's president wanted only Hispanics to be hired and that one of the reasons why Caucasian employee was not considered for certain promotion was because he was not Hispanic did not constitute direct evidence of race or **national origin discrimination** with regard to employee's termination; such management members did not make decision to terminate employee, and statements referred to hiring practices for department other than employee's.... [and] did not constitute direct evidence of race or national origin discrimination

with regard to employee's termination; any direct link between the statement and discriminatory intent against employee was broken when employee was hired on the management member's recommendation, and employee had not worked in production department.")

7. *Enwonwu v. Fulton-Dekalb Hosp. Authority*, 286 Fed.Appx. 586 (11th Cir. 2008)("Black female former employee of Nigerian **national origin** had to establish that policy of county employer of requiring all help desk employees to work in data center was serious and material change in terms, conditions, or privileges of her employment and that transfer from help desk office to data center involved reduction in pay, prestige, or responsibility to show that she suffered adverse employment action when employer required her to work in data center when other employees had been allowed to work in office, on her Title VII claim that policy to work in data center had been applied disparately.... Terms and conditions of employment of black female employee of Nigerian national origin had not been altered, and discriminatorily abusive working environment had not been created, in violation of Title VII, on supervisor's statement that 'people not like [that employee], have tried [to complain] but that the point is you have to do what [the other supervisor] says,' even if statement was based upon protected characteristic.")

8. *Tippie v. Spacelabs Medical, Inc.*, 180 Fed.Appx. 51 (11th Cir. 2006) ("Female, American employee failed to prove by a preponderance of evidence that failure to promote her was based on discriminatory animus for her **national origin** or gender, in violation of Title VII; employee was unable to show her qualifications were so much better than those of candidate who was not American or female that no reasonable person could have chosen candidate for the position, and employer's reasons for selecting candidate were consistent throughout the entire hiring process.")

9. *Cazeau v. Wells Fargo Bank, N.A.*, 614 Fed.Appx. 972 (11th Cir. 2015) ("Employee, a male of Haitian origin who worked as bank teller, failed to demonstrate that employer's proffered reasons for not promoting him to service manager were pretext for discrimination based on **national origin** in violation of Title VII; employer cited, as bases for its actions, other applicant's superior qualification, as well as internal company policy

limiting eligibility to employees who had been in their current position for at least 12 months unless that requirement was waived by a manager or by human resources, and though employee, who had been in his lead teller position for 12 months, contended that he had received permission from his supervisor and store manager to apply for the service manager position, there was no evidence to rebut recruiter's testimony that he had not been contacted by a manager giving employee permission to apply, nor did employee offer evidence to rebut employer's contention that other applicant was more qualified.")

U.S. Fifth Circuit Court of Appeals (Louisiana, Mississippi, Texas)

1. *E.E.O.C. v. WC&M Enterprises, Inc.*, 496 F.3d 393 (5th Cir. 2007) ("Party may be able to establish Title VII discrimination claim based on **national origin**, even though the party committing the alleged discriminatory acts does not correctly identify the first party's actual country of origin…. To state hostile work environment claim under Title VII, plaintiff must show: (1) that victim belongs to protected group; (2) that victim was subjected to unwelcome harassment; (3) that this harassment was based on protected characteristic; (4) that harassment affected a term, condition or privilege of employment; and (5) that victim's employer knew or should have known of harassment and failed to take prompt remedial action…. To determine whether victim's work environment was objectively offensive, as required for employer to be liable on 'hostile work environment' theory under Title VII, courts consider totality of circumstances, including: (1) frequency of discriminatory conduct; (2) its severity; (3) whether it is physically threatening or humiliating, or merely an offensive utterance; and (4) whether it interferes with employee's work performance; however, no single factor is determinative."

2. *Pickens v. Shell Technoliogy Ventures*, 118 Fed.Appx. 842 (5th Cir. 2004) ("Multinational employer's proffered reason for terminating American employee was not pretext for discrimination based on **national origin**; director, who was American, exclusively made decision to terminate employee, and fact that Scottish executive who had made anti-American comments, e-mailed director recommending that employee be fired, did

not reflect that executive leverage or control over director's decisionmaking, as required to impute his discriminatory attitude to director.")

[5] Sex Discrimination

Sex discrimination is the most frequently disputed and litigated cause of action, according the U.S. Equal Opportunity Commission. This is true for a number of reasons. Sex discrimination primarily involves women as victims of discrimination, and women have surpassed men in terms of the number of workers in the American economy. Secondly, sex discrimination involves every subject-matter of the employee-employer relations; it covers all of the terms, conditions and privileges of employment, such as equal pay, maternity leave, quid pro quo sexual harassment, and anti-womanist harassment or retaliation. The following list of cases provide only a few examples of the multitude of sexual harassment lawsuits that impact the American workplace.

Annotated Notes to § [5] Sex Discrimination

U.S. Supreme Court

1. *Price Waterhouse v. Hopkins*, 490 U.S. 228, 235 (1989))(NOTE: citation taken from Zascha Blanco Abbott, "Equal Employment Opportunity Laws: Substantive Claims, Defenses and Related Matters"© 15th Florida Bar Labor and Employment Law Annual Update and Certification Review, Vol. II (2015)("Title VII's prohibition against **gender discrimination** includes discrimination based on sexual stereotypes, such as an expectation that women should dress in a certain way, or should not be aggressive or use profanity.... Recently, 'sex stereotyping' has provided the basis for a number of claims involving employees who are undergoing reassignment, either with or without surgery.")

2. *Burlington Industries, Inc. v. Ellerth*, 524 U.S. 742 (1998)("*Held:* Under Title VII, an employee who refuses **the unwelcome and threatening sexual advances of a supervisor**, yet suffers no adverse, tangible job

consequences, may recover against the employer without showing the employer is negligent or otherwise at fault for the supervisor's actions, but the employer may interpose an affirmative defense. Pp. 6–21... In deciding whether an employer has vicarious liability in a case such as this, the Court turns to agency law principles, for Title VII defines the term "employer" to include "agents." §2000e(b). Given this express direction, the Court concludes a uniform and predictable standard must be established as a matter of federal law. The Court relies on the general common law of agency, rather than on the law of any particular State. *Community for Creative Non-Violence* v. *Reid,* 490 U. S. 730. The Restatement (Second) of Agency (hereinafter Restatement) is a useful beginning point, although common-law principles may not be wholly transferable to Title VII. See *Meritor, supra,* at 72. Pp. 9–10.... (c) A master is subject to liability for the torts of his servants committed while acting in the scope of their employment. Restatement §219(1). Although such torts generally may be either negligent or intentional, sexual harassment under Title VII presupposes intentional conduct. An intentional tort is within the scope of employment when actuated, at least in part, by a purpose to serve the employer. *Id.,* §§228(1)(c), 230. Courts of Appeals have held, however, a supervisor acting out of gender-based animus or a desire to fulfill sexual urges may be actuated by personal motives unrelated and even antithetical to the employer's objectives. Thus, the general rule is that sexual harassment by a supervisor is not conduct within the scope of employment. Pp. 10–12.... Thus, in order to accommodate the agency principle of vicarious liability for harm caused by misuse of supervisory authority, as well as Title VII's equally basic policies of encouraging forethought by employers and saving action by objecting employees, the Court adopts, in this case and in *Faragher* v. *Boca Raton, post,* p. ___, the following holding: An employer is subject to vicarious liability to a victimized employee for an actionable hostile environment created by a supervisor with immediate (or successively higher) authority over the employee. When no tangible employment action is taken, a defending employer may raise an affirmative defense to liability or damages, subject to proof by a preponderance of the evidence, see Fed. Rule. Civ. Proc. 8(c). The defense comprises two necessary elements: (a) that the employer exercised reasonable care to prevent and correct promptly any sexually harassing behavior, and (b) that the plaintiff employee unreasonably failed to take advantage of any preventive or corrective opportunities provided by the employer or to avoid harm otherwise. While proof that an employer had promulgated an antiharassment policy with a complaint procedure is not necessary in every instance as a matter of law, the need for a stated policy suitable to the employment circumstances may appropriately be addressed in any case when litigating the first element of the defense. And while proof that an employee failed to fulfill the corresponding obligation of reasonable care to avoid harm is not limited to showing any unreasonable failure to use any complaint procedure provided by the employer, a demonstration of such failure will normally suffice to satisfy the employer's burden under the second element of the defense. No affirmative defense is available, however, when the supervisor's harassment culminates in a tangible employment action.")

U.S. Eleventh Circuit Court of Appeals (Alabama, Florida, Georgia)

1. *Jeffries v. Harris County Community Action Ass'n*, 615 F.2d 1025 (11th Cir. 1980)("Where claims of race discrimination, **sex discrimination**, and discrimination based on both race and sex were properly raised in the pleadings and at trial and former employee contended that district court erred in its consideration of each of her claims of discrimination in promotion, all the claims were properly before the reviewing court.")

2. *Willingham v. Macon Tel. Pub. Co.*, 507 F.2d 1084 (5th Cir. 1975)[binding 11th Cir. opinion]("Inclusion of **'sex plus' discrimination** within the proscription of the Civil Rights Act has legitimate legislative and judicial underpinning.... Distinctions in employment practices between men and women on the basis of something other than immutable characteristics or legally protected rights do not inhibit employment opportunities in violation of the Civil Rights Act.")

3. *Glenn v. Brumby, 663 F.3d 1312 (11th Cir. 2011)*)(NOTE: citation taken from Zascha Blanco Abbott, "Equal Employment Opportunity Laws: Substantive Claims, Defenses and Related Matters"© 15th Florida Bar Labor and Employment Law Annual Update and Certification Review, Vol. II (2015)("In December 2011... the Eleventh Circuit held that a public employer's firing of a male employee, who was transitioning to female, because of the transition was a constitutional violation (equal protection). The court noted that a person is transgender 'precisely because of the perception that his or her behavior transgresses gender stereotypes.'...

Therefore, discrimination against transsexuals or transgendered people was necessarily unlawful **sex discrimination**.... Although the decision was reached on constitutional grounds, it also applies to Title VII. See also *Barnes v. City of Cincinnati*, 401 F.3d 729 (6th Cir. 2005); *Smith v. City of Salem*, 378 F.3d 566 (6th Cir. 2004)(suspension of male transsexual firefighter based on failure to conform to sex stereotypes violated Title VII and equal protection). However, an employer must be aware that the person is transgendered, or perceived him as such. *Hunter v. UPS, Inc.*, 697 F.3d 697 (8th Cir. 2012).")

4. *Toney v. Montgomery Jobs Corps*, 211 Fed.Appx. 816 (11th Cir. 2006) ("Supervisor's statements to black male employee that she was a strong independent black woman and male employee could not handle it merely suggested that she may have fired male employee because of his sex but was not direct evidence that firing was discriminatory.... Black male former employee failed to establish that he was similarly situated to female employees whom he identified as receiving favorable treatment, and thus, he failed to establish a prima face case of **sex discrimination**; although former employee pointed to evidence of several instances where females were only reprimanded for engaging in a similar practice that violated workplace policy, that evidence ignored three other instances of misconduct that he was involved in or accused of that female employees were not.")

5. *Weeks v. Southern Bell Tel. & Tel. Co.*, 408 F.2d 228 (5th Cir. 1969) [binding 11th Cir. opinion]("Telephone and telegraph company which denied switchman's job because applicant was a woman had burden of proof to demonstrate that such position fit within the **'bona fide occupational qualification'** exception to Civil Rights Act prohibiting discrimination in employment on account of **sex**.")

6. *Diaz v. Pan Am. World Airways, Inc.*, 442 F.2d 385 (5th Cir. 1971) [binding 11th Cir. opinion]("Being a female was not a bona fide occupational qualification for job of flight cabin attendant and employer's refusal to hire males solely because of their **sex** constituted violation of 1964 Civil Rights Act.")

7. *Miranda v. B & B Cash Grocery Store, Inc.*, 975 F.2d 1518 (11th Cir. 1992) ("Employee's failure to establish prima facie case under Equal Pay Act

does not preclude employee from bringing claim for **sex-based wage discrimination** under Civil Rights Act.")

8. *Langley v. State Farm Fire & Cas. Co.*, 644 F.2d 1124 (5th Cir. 1981)[binding 11th Cir. opinion]("To establish a violation for **sex discrimination** under Title VII of the Civil Rights Act of 1964, a plaintiff must initially prove that challenged policy has a discriminatory effect on women by establishing that the policy, although neutral on its face, imposes on female employees a substantial burden that men need not suffer; if this prima facie case is established, then burden shifts to employer to justify a challenged practice and, if employer meets this burden, plaintiff, to recover, must then show that employer could use alternative practices to accomplish same purpose without discriminatory effects.")

9. *Hardin v. Stychcomb*, 691 F.2d 1364 (11th Cir. 1982)("In action alleging **employment discrimination** in sheriff's department based on **sex**, defendants failed to prove that it was essential to functioning of sheriff's department that all new deputy sheriffs be initially assigned to county jail and also failed to prove that they could not rearrange job responsibility so that female deputies assigned to male section of jail would not have to perform duties that impinged upon inmate privacy rights; thus, bona fide occupational qualification exception to Title VII did not justify defendants' arbitrary practice of funneling deputy sheriffs into positions reserved almost exclusively for males.")

10. *E.E.O.C. v. Joe's Stone Crab, Inc.*, 220 F.3d 1263 (11th Cir. 2000)("In **sex discrimination** case against restaurant, finding of disparate treatment would require no more than a finding that women were intentionally treated differently by restaurant because of or on account of their gender, and, if restaurant deliberately and systematically excluded women from food server positions based on a sexual stereotype which simply associated 'fine-dining ambience' with all-male food service, it then could be found liable under Title VII for intentional discrimination regardless of whether it also was motivated by ill-will or malice toward women.")

11. *Causey v. Ford Motor Co.*, 516 F.2d 416 (5th Cir. 1975)[binding 11th Cir. opinion]("Plaintiff had burden of establishing a **prima face case of discrimination** in civil rights employment discrimination case; once

prima facie case was established, burden to articulate some legitimate, nondiscriminatory reasons for action shifted to defendants; upon rebuttal evidence being offered, ultimate burden of persuasion by preponderance of evidence that discrimination had taken place fell upon plaintiff.")

12. *Orr v. Frank R. MacNeill & Son, Inc.*, 511 F.2d 166 (5th Cir. 1975) [binding 11th Cir. opinion]("In equal employment opportunity case, evidence that employer paid female worker's male successor almost same salary as she had been receiving although he was less experienced was not probative of **sex discrimination** in absence of evidence that successor's work was not done as well.... Evidence as a whole, in equal employment opportunity case, failed to sustain district court's determination that job of plaintiff female worker was 'substantially equal' to other jobs, performed by men, or that there had been any discrimination by reason of sex.")

13. *Womack v. Runyon*, 147 F.3d 1298 (11th Cir. 1998)("Male employee could not maintain **sex discrimination** claim based on contention that he was denied promotion due to favoritism shown to supervisor's alleged paramour, who was selected for the position; preferential treatment based on consensual relationship between supervisor and female employee did not constitute cognizable sex discrimination cause of action under Title VII.")

U.S. Fifth Circuit Court of Appeals (Louisiana, Mississippi, Texas)

1. *E.E.O.C. v. Boh Bros. Const. Co., L.L.C.*, 731 F.3d 444 (5th Cir. 2013) ("Under Title VII, an employer's liability for **workplace harassment** depends on the status of the harasser: if the harassing employee is the victim's co-worker, the employer is liable only if it was negligent in controlling working conditions; if the harasser is a 'supervisor,' and the harassment culminates in a tangible employment action, the employer is strictly liable; and if the harasser is a 'supervisor,' and no tangible employment action is taken, the employer may escape liability by establishing, as an affirmative defense, that the employer exercised reasonable care to prevent and correct any harassing behavior and that the victim unreasonably failed to take advantage of the preventive or corrective opportunities that the employer provided.... An employer can satisfy the first prong of the Ellerth/Faragher defense to Title VII claims of vicarious liability for sexual harassment

carried out by supervisors in their employ, that the employer exercised reasonable care to prevent and correct promptly any sexually harassing behavior, by implementing suitable institutional policies and educational programs regarding **sexual harassment**.") See, also, Zascha Blanco Abbott, "Equal Employment Opportunity Laws: Substantive Claims, Defenses and Related Matters"© 15th Florida Bar Labor and Employment Law Annual Update and Certification Review, Vol. II (2015)("In *EEOC v. Boh Bros. Const. Co.*, 731 F.3d 444 (5th Cir. 2013), the Fifth Circuit examined whether gender stereotyping could support a same sex sexual harassment claim where the plaintiff alleged he was harassed by his male supervisor on a construction crew not for not being 'manly' enough. Reasoning that 'because of sex' includes failure to conform to gender stereotypes, the court focused on the harasser's subjective perception of his victim to conclude that a jury properly found same sex sexual harassment. Whether the plaintiff was or was not actually 'manly' was beside the point.")

2. *Smith v. Liberty Mut. Ins. Co.*, 569 F.2d 325 (5th Cir. 1978)("Congress, by its proscription of **sex discrimination** in Title VII of Civil Rights Act of 1964, intended only to guarantee equal job opportunities for males and females.... Evidence supported trial court's finding that black job applicant was not refused employment because of his race, and that refusal was, instead, grounded on permissible basis that applicant appeared effeminate.")

3. *Willingham v. Macon Tel. Pub. Co.*, 507 F.2d 1084 (5th Cir. 1975) ("Employer's grooming code, requiring different hair lengths for male and female employees, constituted discrimination on the basis of grooming standards, not **on the basis of sex**, and was thus outside the proscription of the Civil Rights Act.")

4. *Jefferies v. Harris County Community Action Ass'n*, 615 F.2d 1025 (5th Cir. 1980)("Where claims of race discrimination, **sex discrimination**, and discrimination based on **both race and sex** were properly raised in the pleadings and at trial and former employee contended that district court erred in its consideration of each of her claims of discrimination in promotion, all the claims were properly before the reviewing court.")

5. *Plemer v. Parsons-Gilbane*, 713 F.2d 1127 (5th Cir. 1983)("Where female former employee's evidence, apart from statistics showing that women were generally on the bottom rung of pay ladder, made a prima facie case under the **Equal Pay Act** and Title VII by demonstrating that she was paid less than her male successor for identical position, the statistics were relevant and should have been considered in determining whether asserted justifications for the pay differential was pretextual.")

[6] Religion Discrimination

In employment law, there is a cause of action called "disparate treatment—religion" or "religion discrimination." Again, what the court wants to see is the entire story that underlies this case: basically, what happened? What is the time sequence of events? Who, what, when, where and how? All of this information needs to be included in the complaint in order to set forth a "cause of action." Although the federal "cause of action" need not include or articulate every single element listed within the "prima facie" case standard, the best course of action is to draft the federal "cause of action" so that each and every element of the "prima facie" case standard is included within the original complaint.

More and more, sincere and deeply-religious workers are encountering workplace discrimination from inflexible, secular-minded employers who are only motivated by profits. On the other hand, some deeply-religious workers are also unreasonable what they request as reasonable accommodations as well. This often creates a clash of cultures. What that law seeks to provide is a balance. The follow list of cases provide examples of how the law has struck that balance.

Annotated Notes to § [6] Religion Discrimination

U.S. Eleventh Circuit Court of Appeals (Alabama, Florida, Georgia)

1. *Morrissette-Brown v. Mobile Infirmary Medical Center*, 506 F.3d 1317 (11th Cir. 2007)("An employee asserting **religious discrimination** under

Title VII must first establish a prima facie case of religious discrimination by presenting evidence sufficient to prove that (1) he had a bona fide religious belief that conflicted with an employment requirement, (2) he informed his employer of his belief, and (3) he was discharged for failing for failing to comply with the conflicting employment required.")

2. *Beadle v. Hillsborough County Sheriff's Dept.*, 29 F.3d 589 (11th Cir. 1994) ("For purposes of section of Title VII provision prohibiting employer from discriminating against employee on **basis of religion** unless employer demonstrates that he is unable to reasonably accommodate employee's religious beliefs without 'undue hardship' on conduct of business, phrase 'undue hardship' refers to any act that would require an employer to bear great than a de minimis cost in accounting employee's beliefs.")

3. *Dixon v. The Hallmark Companies, Inc.*, 627 F.3d 849 (11th Cir. 2010) ("To prevail on Title VII claim of failure to **accommodate religious beliefs**, plaintiffs must establish that (1) they held a bona fide religious belief that conflicted with an employment requirement; (2) they informed employer or that belief; and (3) they were discharged for failing to comply with the conflicting employment requirement.")

4. *Lubestsky v. Applied Card Systems, Inc.*, 296 F.3d 1301 (11th Cir. 2002) ("Decision-maker who ordered rescission of employment offer did not know that applicant was Orthodox Jew, and applicant thus failed to establish prima facie Title VII case, where recruiter testified she never told decision-maker about plaintiff's **religion**, decision-maker testified he didn't know applicant was Orthodox Jew, and decision-maker testified he ordered rescission based on his recollection of applicant's personality and demeanor during previous encounter.")

5. *Mack Muhammad v. Cagle's Inc.*, 379 Fed.Appx. 801 (11th Cir. 2010) ("Former employee failed to establish prima facie case of **religious discrimination** in violation of Title VII where former employee did not show that he was qualified for superintendent position from which he was terminated or show that similarly situated employees who were not Muslim were treated more favorably or that he was replaced by non-Muslim employee.")

6. *Postell v. Green County Hosp. Authority*, 265 Fed.Appx. 856 (11th Cir. 2008)("Employee alleging **religious discrimination** against employer in violation of Title VII was required to show that she was terminated or permanently removed from work schedule, constructively discharged, or suffered any other adverse employment action in contrast with similarly situated employees.... Hospital's failure to return employee to schedule, after her complaints of discrimination, did not constitute a materially adverse employment action, as required to establish a prima facie case of retaliation in violation of Title VII.")

7. *Beadle v. City of Tampa*, 42 F.3d 633 (11th Cir. 1995)("Once employer demonstrates that it reasonably accommodated employee's **religious** needs, statutory inquiry in connection with religious discrimination claim ends.")

8. *Richardson v. Dougherty County, Ga.*, 185 Fed.Appx. 785 (11th Cir. 2006) ("Seven Day Adventist deputy did not present evidence that employees outside of his protected class were treated more favorably than him, as was required to establish a **prima facie case** of **religious discrimination**, based on disparate treatment; other deputies accused of sexual misconduct, all of whom were outside of deputy's protected class, were, like him, given the option of resigning or termination.")

9. *Walden v. Centers for Disease Control and Prevention*, 669 F.3d 1277 (11th Cir. 2012)("In **religious accommodation** cases, court applies a burden-shifting framework akin to that articulated in *McDonnell Douglas*; under that framework, the plaintiff must first establish a prima facie claim by presenting evidence sufficient to prove that (1) she had a bona fide religious belief that conflicted with an employment requirement, (2) she informed her employer of her belief, and (3) she was discharged for failing to comply with the conflicting employment requirement.")

10. *Jordan v. Conway*, 441 Fed.Appx. 761 (11th Cir. 2011)("Georgia deputy sheriff who was terminated after appearing at his ex-wife's church after having been told by pastor on previous occasions not to return, despite having been acquitted of criminal trespass charge, failed to establish prima facie case of **religious discrimination** under Title VII based on circumstantial evidence; no one from sheriff's department ordered him

to stay away from the church until after incident in question, so he could not have been terminated for failing to comply with sheriff's department requirement that he avoid the church.")

11. *Bush v. Regis Corp.* 257 Fed.Appx. 219 (11th Cir. 2007)("Employer offered employee, who was a Jehovah's Witness, a reasonable accommodation other religious beliefs, thus defeating her discrimination claim under Title VII, despite her claim that a Sunday shift prevented her from doing field service with her family, which constituted **a bona fide religious belief**; field service was not required to be performed on Sundays, but rather, that was the day the employee and her family wished to perform field service.")

12. *Dixon v. Palm Beach County Parks and Recreation Dept.*, 343 Fed.Appx. 500 (11th Cir. 2009)("County parks and recreation department's conduct in giving African-American **Christian employee** a written record of counseling, initially denying employee's requests for Sundays off, and transferring him from the bicycle patrol unit were not 'adverse employment actions,' as required to establish prima facie discrimination claims, and retaliation claim under Title VII; the employee's actions did not result in a serious and material change in the terms, conditions, and privileges of employment.")

13. *Cooper v. General Dynamics, Convair Aerospace Division, Ft. Worth Operation*, 533 F.2d 163 (5th Cir. 1976)[11th Cir. Opinion]("Civil Rights Act requirement that employer tolerate all **religious conduct** except that which cannot be reconciled with business-like operations extended to beliefs of certain employees that any support of a labor union, including payment of dues under agency shop provisions, is a godless act and inconsistent with the commandment to love one's neighbor, i.e., the employer, and that support of the union places a person's soul in jeopardy; Act mandates that all **reasonable accommodations** of employees' beliefs be considered, including permitting continuation of regular work assignment while not paying union dues or equivalent.")

14. *Dixon v. The Hallmark Companies, Inc.*, 627 F.3d 849 (11th Cir. 2010) ("To prevail on Title VII claim of **failure to accommodate religious beliefs**, plaintiff must establish that: (1) they held a bona fide religious belief that conflicted with an employment requirement; (2) they informed

employer of that belief; and (3) they were discharged for failing to comply with the conflicting employment requirement.")

U.S. Fifth Circuit Court of Appeals (Louisiana, Mississippi, Texas)

1. *Equal Employment Opportunity Commission v. Mississippi College*, 626 F.2d 477 (5th Cir. 1980)("Only the relationship between a church and its minister is exempt from coverage of Title VII; relationship between a **religious educational institution** and its faculty is not exempt from such coverage.")

2. *Mousa v. Capital Area Human Services Dist.*, 463 Fed.Appx. 253 (5th Cir. 2012)("State employer's reasons for terminating employment of internal auditor who was of **Egyptian ethnicity**, that he had failed to make progress during probationary period on his single work assignment and had continuously complained about almost every aspect of his job and the workplace, were legitimate and non-discriminatory, rather than pretext for **racial discrimination** in violation of Title VII.")

3. *Dediol v. Best Chevrolet, Inc.*, 655 F.3d 435 (5th Cir. 2011)("To establish a prima facie case of harassment based on **religion** under Title VII, a plaintiff must produce evidence that (1) he belongs to a protected class; (2) he was subject to unwelcome harassment; (3) the harassment was based on religion; (4) the harassment affected a term, condition, or privilege of employment; and (5) the employer knew or should have known of the harassment and failed to take prompt remedial action.")

4. *Cooper v. General Dynamics, Convair Aerospace Division, Ft. Worth Operation*, 533 F.2d 163 (5th Cir. 1976)("All forms and aspects of an **employee's religion**, however eccentric, and not merely Sabbath observance, are protected under the Civil Rights Act except those which cannot be, in practice and with honest effort, reconciled with a business-like operation.... Under provision of Civil Rights Act requiring union and employer to tolerate religious practices unless doing so would create an undue hardship, court must consider hardship imposed on the union as well as on the employer.")

5. *Aryain v. Wal-Mart Stores Texas LP*, 534 F.3d 473 (5th Cir. 2008)("A retaliation claim under Title VII may rest on an action that a reasonable employee would have found to be materially adverse, which in this context means it well might have dissuaded a reasonable worker from making or supporting a charge of discrimination.... Alleged poor treatment of employee by her supervisors did not rise to level of material adversity required to establish *prima facie* case of **retaliation** under Title VII, but instead, treatment fell into category of petty slights, minor annoyances, and simple lack of good manners regularly encountered in workplace; alleged poor treatment included transferring employee to infant department, requiring employee to break down clothing racks on hot day, undesirable break schedule, looking at employee angrily, and making employee wait outside manager's office for a long time.")

6. *Weber v. Roadway Exp., Inc.*, 199 F.3d 270 (5th Cir. 2000)("To establish a prima facie case of **religious discrimination** under Title VII, an employee must establish that he or she had a bona fide religious belief that conflicted with an employment requirement, informed the employer of the belief, and was discharged for failing to comply with the conflicting employment requirement.... Employer did not violate Title VII when it failed to accommodate truck driver's religious beliefs which required him to refrain from making overnight runs with a female partner, inasmuch as 'skipping over' truck driver when scheduling such runs might adversely affect other drivers, and thus would impose undue hardship, notwithstanding that affected drivers had no contract entitling them to a particular run or job preference.")

7. *Butler v. MBNA Technology, Inc.*, 111 Fed.Appx. 230 (5th Cir. 2004) ("Single alleged incident in which coworker posted picture and quote was neither pervasive nor severe, as was required to establish hostile work environment claim under Title VII; essence of alleged harassment was employee's disapproval of quotation that she felt took a tenet of her **religion** out of context, there was no evidence that coworker intended the posting to serve as a commentary on the Muslim religion, and, when employee complained that picture offended her, employer's personnel department promptly investigated and had picture removed.")

8. *Daniels v. City of Alrington, Tex.*, 246 F.3d 500 (5th Cir. 2001)("Police officer terminated for wearing cross pin on his uniform, in violation of police department policy which prohibited wearing pins on uniform unless approved by police chief, could not establish **religious discrimination** claim under Title VII; officer failed to respond to police chief's reasonable offers of accommodation, which included allowing officer to wear cross ring or bracelet instead of pin.")

9. *Tagore v. U.S.*, 735 F.3d 324 (5th Cir. 2013)("Title VII does not require **religious accommodations** that impose more than de minimis costs on an employer.")

10. *Turpen v. Missouri-Kansas-Texas R.Co.*, 736 F.2d 1022 (5th Cir. 1984) ("**Religious discrimination** prohibition of Title VII does not require an employer to bypass duly elected bargaining representatives to negotiate directly with individual employees to determine whether the employee would be willing to swap work days with an employee whose work schedule called for him to work on his Sabbath.")

11. *Nobach v. Woodland Village Nursing Center, Inc.*, 799 F.3d 374 (5th Cir. 2015)("When evaluating causation in a Title VII case, the question is not what the employer knew about the employee's **religious beliefs**, nor is the question whether the employer knew that there would be a conflict between the employee's religious belief and some job duty; instead, the critical question is what motivated the employer's employment decision.")

[7] Hostile Working Environment/ Harassment

In employment law, there is a cause of action called "hostile working environment" or "workplace harassment." Again, what the court wants to see is the entire story that underlies this case: basically, what happened? What is the time sequence of events? Who, what, when, where and how? All of this information needs to be included in the complaint in order to set forth a "cause of action." Although the federal "cause of action" need not include or articulate every single element listed within the "prima facie" case standard, the best course of action is to draft the federal "cause of action" so that each and every element of the "prima facie" case standard is included within the original complaint.

The law of hostile working environment is a very fact-specific, case-by-case, and daunting area of labor and employment law. The nature of the harassment can be "retaliatory" or it can be based upon a person's "protected characteristic" or "protected activity."

However, employees and employee-advocates should take into account the legal definition of "harassment" or "hostile working environment," before proceeding with a grievance, claim, or complaint. These legal elements must be proven, or else a claim of harassment/ hostile work environment will fail. For this reason, the following list of cases provides examples of these important legal elements.

Annotated Notes to § [7] Hostile Working Environment/ Harassment

U.S. Eleventh Circuit Court of Appeals (Alabama, Florida, Georgia)

1. *Miller v. Kenworth of Dothan, Inc.*, 277 F.3d 1269 (11th Cir. 2002)("A hostile work environment claim under Title VII is established upon proof that the workplace is permeated with discriminatory intimidation, ridicule, and insult, that is sufficiently severe or pervasive to alter the conditions of the victim's employment and create an abusive working environment.... To establish a **hostile work environment** claim under Title VII, an employee must show: (1) that he belongs to a protected group; (2) the he has been subject to unwelcome harassment; (3) that the harassment must have been based on a protected characteristic of the employee, such as national origin; (4) that the harassment was sufficiently severe or pervasive to alter the terms and conditions of employment and create a discriminatory abusive working environment; and (5) that the employer is responsible for such environment under either a theory of vicarious or of direct liability.")

2. *Gowski v. Peake*, 682 F.3d 1299 (11th Cir. 2012)("To establish a **hostile work environment claim** under Title VII, a plaintiff must show that the workplace is permeated with discriminatory intimidation, ridicule, and

insult, that is sufficiently severe or pervasive to alter the conditions of the victim's employment and create an abusive working environment…. To be actionable in a retaliatory hostile work environment claim under Title VII, an employer's behavior must result in both an environment that a reasonable person would find hostile or abusive and an environment that the victim subjectively perceives to be abusive.")

3. *Reeves v. C.H. Robinson Worldwide, Inc.*, 594 F.3d 798 (11th Cir. 2010) ("To prove a **hostile work environment** under Title VII, a plaintiff must show that her employer discriminated because of her membership in a protected group, and that the offensive conduct was either severe or pervasive enough to alter the terms or conditions of employment…. Title VII is not a civility code, and not all profane or sexual language or conduct will constitute discrimination in the terms and conditions of employment.")

4. *Adams v. Austal, U.S.A., L.L.C.*, 754 F.3 1240 (11th Cir. 2014)("An employee alleging a Title VII **hostile work environment** claim must prove five elements if he bases his harassment claim on race: (1) that he is a member of a protected class; (2) that he was subjected to unwelcome racial harassment; (3) that the harassment was based on his race; (4) that the harassment was severe or pervasive enough to alter the terms and conditions of his employment and create a discriminatorily abusive working environment; and (5) that the employer is responsible for the environment under a theory of either vicarious or direct liability.")

5. *Jones v. UPS Ground Freight*, 683 F.3d 1283 (11th Cir. 2012)("An employer is liable to an employee for racially **hostile work environment** under both Title VII and § 1981 if employee proves that: (1) he belongs to protected group, (2) he was subjected to unwelcome harassment, (3) harassment was based on his membership in protected group, (4) it was severe or pervasive enough to alter terms and conditions of employment and create hostile or abusive working environment, and (5) employer is responsible for that environment under theory of either vicarious or direct liability.")

6. *Mendoza v. Borden, Inc.*, 195 F.3d 1238 (11th Cir. 1999)("To establish **hostile-environment** sexual-harassment claim under Title VII based on harassment by a supervisor, employee must show: (1) that he or she belongs

to a protected group; (2) that employee has been subject to unwelcome sexual harassment, such as sexual advances, requests for sexual favors, and other conduct of a sexual nature; (3) that harassment was based on the sex of the employee; (4) that harassment was sufficiently severe or pervasive to alter terms and conditions of employment and create a discriminatorily abusive working environment; and (5) a basis for holding employer liable.")

7. *Chambless v. Louisiana-Pacific Corp.*, 481 F.3d 1345 (11th Cir. 2007) ("A Title VII **hostile work environment claim** depends on a series of separate acts that collectively constitute one unlawful employment practice.... The entire time period of the alleged hostile work environment may be considered by a court for the purposes of determining liability, if an act relating to the claim occurred within the limitations period.")

8. *McCann v. Tillman*, 526 F.3d 1370 (11th Cir. 2008)("To establish a prima facie showing of **retaliation** under Title VII, the plaintiff must show (1) that she engaged in statutorily protected expression; (2) that she suffered an adverse employment action; and (3) that there is some causal relation between the two events.... To establish a hostile work environment claim under Title VII, an employee must show: (1) that she belongs to a protected group; (2) that she has been subject to unwelcome harassment; (3) that the harassment must have been based on a protected characteristic of the employee; (4) that the harassment was sufficiently severe or pervasive to alter the terms and conditions of employment and create a discriminatorily abusive working environment; and (5) that the employer is responsible for such environment under either theory of vicarious or of direct liability.")

9. *Perry v. Rogers,* 627 Fed.Appx. 823 (11th Cir. 2015)("African-American agent of state alcoholic beverage control board established prima facie case of **retaliation** under Title VII through evidence that agent's placement under supervision of another employee the month after she filed discrimination complaint, and his subsequent close monitoring of her, constituted materially adverse action that was causally related to her protected activity.")

10. *McKitt v. Alabama Alcoholic Beverage Control Bd.*, 571 Fed.Appx. 867 (11th Cir. 2014)("State employer's alleged disparate treatment of employee was not objectively severe or pervasive, and thus employer did not create

racially **hostile work environment** in violation of Title VII, where alleged harassment was not physically threatening or frequent, and employee only heard one overtly racially derogatory remark over the course of 19 years of employment.")

11. *Bryant v. Jones*, 575 F.3d 1281 (11th Cir. 2009)("[Qualified Immunity under § 1983]: To prove that government official is not entitled to **qualified immunity, § 1983** plaintiff must first show that official violated a constitutional right and then demonstrate that the constitutional right was clearly established at the time of the alleged wrongful act; if court, after viewing all evidence in light most favorable to plaintiff and drawing all inferences in his favor, determines that plaintiff has satisfied these two requirements, then defendant may not obtain qualified immunity.")

12. *Freeman v. City of Riverdale*, 330 Fed.Appx. 863 (11th Cir. 2009) ("Former city employee did not make prima facie case of **hostile work environment** under Title VII, discrete acts of alleged race discrimination that occurred more than 180 days prior to filing of charge with Equal Employment Opportunity Commission (EEOC) had to be charged separately and could not be considered, and in any case, 11 incidents involving use of racially derogatory language over period of 13 years were too sporadic and isolated, and therefore, did not demonstrate that discrimination was so severe or pervasive as to create hostile work environment.")

13. *Smith v. Naples Community Hosp., Inc.*, 433 Fed.Appx. 797 (11th Cir. 2011) ("Alleged instances involving female hospital employee's male supervisor, in which he allegedly acted in manner that was aggressive, angry, and physically threatening, were not sufficiently severe to alter conditions of employee's employment and create **hostile work environment**, thus precluding employee's hostile work environment claim based on gender under Title VII and Florida Civil Rights Act (FCRA).")

14. *Hulsey v. Pride Restaurants, LLC*, 367 F.3d 1238 (11th Cir. 2004) ("An employer is liable under Title VII if it, even unknowingly, permits

a supervisor to take a tangible employment action against an employee because she refused to give in to his sexual overtures; liability exists regardless of whether the employee took advantage of any employer-provided system for reporting **harassment**.")

15. *Barrow v. Georgia Pacific Corp.*, 144 Fed.Appx. 54 (11th Cir. 2005) ("Employee failed to establish that alleged racial **harassment**, including symbols and slurs, was sufficiently severe or pervasive to alter his working conditions, as required to prevail on hostile work environment claims under § 1981; he presented evidence of isolated, sporadic instances of racial harassment over his more than 14 years of employment.")

16. *Dar Dar v. Associated Outdoor Club, Inc.*, 201 Fed.Appx. 718 (11th Cir. 2006)("In determining whether female employee's claims that male co-worker had asked her whether she had even seen 'built-in butt' depicted in magazine ad, and that another male co-worker had told her he had seen an individual's 'whale of a dick' while in men's restroom, were sufficiently severe and pervasive to create **hostile working environment**, trial court was required to consider incidents as a whole under totality of circumstances, and not in isolation.")

17. *Walton v. Johnson & Johnson Services, Inc.*, 347 F.3d 1272 (11th Cir. 2003)("Under 'aided by agency' theory, employer is subject to vicarious liability to victimized employee under Title VII for actionable **hostile environment** created by supervisor with immediate or successively higher authority over employee.... To succeed on Title VII sexual harassment claim based on *constructive discharge*, employee must show that her working conditions were so difficult that reasonable person would have felt compelled to resign, standard is higher than that for proving hostile work environment.")

18. *Kelly v. Dun & Bradstreet, Inc.*, 557 Fed.Appx. 896 (11th Cir. 2014) ("Employee alleged in Equal Employment Opportunity Commission (EEOC) charge that he suffered a **hostile work environment**, and thus, provided sufficient facts for the EEOC to investigate the claim.")

U.S. Fifth Circuit Court of Appeals (Louisiana, Mississippi, Texas)

1. *Huckabay v. Moore*, 142 F.3d 233 (5th Cir. 1998)(**Hostile working environment**. "In determining whether 'continuing violation' exists under Title VII, inquiry may involve several factors, including (1) subject matter, (2) frequency, and (3) perhaps most importantly, degree of permanence; these factors inquire whether alleged acts involve same type of discrimination, tending to connect them in continuing violation, whether alleged acts are recurring or are more in nature of isolated assignment or employment decision, and whether act has degree of permanence which should trigger employee's awareness of and duty to assert his or her expected without being dependent on continuing intent to discriminate.")

2. *Sheperd v. Comptroller of Public Accounts of State of Texas*, 168 F.3d 871 (5th Cir. 1999)("There are five elements necessary to set forth a sexually **hostile work environment** claim under Title VII: (1) that the employee belongs to a protected class, (2) that the employee was subject to unwelcome sexual harassment, (3) that the harassment was based on sex, (4) that the harassment affected a term, condition or privilege of employment, and (5) that the employer knew or should have known of the harassment and failed to take prompt remedial action.")

3. *Hernandez v. Yellow Transp., Inc.*, 670 F.3d 644 (5th Cir. 2012) ("Harassment 'affects a term, condition, or privilege of employment,' as required to support **hostile work environment** claim under Title VII, if it is sufficiently severe or pervasive to alter conditions of victim's employment and create an abusive working environment…. In deciding whether workplace harassment is sufficiently severe or pervasive to alter conditions of victim's employment, and to support hostile work environment claim, courts consider: frequency of the discriminatory conduct; its severity; whether it is physically threatening or humiliating, or a mere offensive utterance; and whether it unreasonably interferes with employee's work performance.")

4. *Brooks v. Firestone Polymers, LLC*, 640 Fed.Appx. 393 (5th Cir. 2016) ("Alleged incident in which African-American employee was asked not to use a restroom, which he perceived as a racially discriminatory request,

did not support **hostile work environment** claim under § 1981, where employee used the restroom anyway, did not report the incident despite being asked about it by management, and stated that he viewed it as settled and that it did not recur.... Alleged incident in which employer's video monitors showed offensive images was not sufficiently severe or pervasive to create a hostile work environment under § 1981; alleged incident was isolated and, upon learning of the displays, management took prompt remedial action that ended the display of the images.... Alleged incidents in which racial slurs were used, 'black faces' were drawn in bathroom stalls in the workplace, and manager commented that as long as he was in charge of a certain unit, 'there would be no blacks in the control room' were not sufficiently severe or pervasive to create a hostile work environment under § 1981; while alleged incidents were reprehensible, they established only isolated incidents and offhand remarks, did not involve physical threats, were not apparently addressed to African-American employee, and did not appear to have interfered with his work....Alleged incident in which African-American employee found a miniature hangman's noose placed inside his hard hat at work did not create a hostile work environment that was actionable under § 1981; employee did not show how incident affected the terms and conditions of his employment, it appeared to have been an isolated incident, and there was no indication that employer knew or should have known about the incident.")

5. *E.E.O.C. v. WC&M Enterprises, Inc.*, 496 F.3d 393 (5th Cir. 2007) ("Title VII is violated, on **'hostile work environment'** theory, when workplace is permeated with discriminatory intimidation, ridicule and insult that is sufficiently severe or pervasive to alter conditions of victim's employment and create abusive working environment.")

6. *Harvill v. Westward Communications, L.L.C.*, 433 F.3d 428 (5th Cir. 2005)("In determining whether a **work environment is hostile or abusive** within the meaning of Title VII, courts look at the totality of the circumstances including the frequency of the discriminatory conduct, its severity, whether it is physically threatening or humiliating, or a mere offensive utterance, and whether it unreasonably interferes with an employee's work performance.... To be actionable as sexual harassment under Title VII, based on a hostile work environment, the challenged conduct must be both objectively offensive, meaning that a reasonable

person would find it hostile and abusive, and subjectively offensive, meaning that the victim perceived it to be so.")

7. *Lauderdale v. Texas Dept. of Criminal Justice, Institutional Div.*, 512 F.3d 157 (5th Cir. 2007)("Where the claim of **harassment** is against a supervisor, there are four elements of a Title VII hostile working environment claim: (1) that the employee belongs to a protected class, (2) that the employee was subject to unwelcome sexual harassment, (3) that the harassment was based on sex, and (4) that the harassment affected a 'term, condition, or privilege' of employment.")

8. *Farpella-Crosby v. Horizon Health Care*, 97 F.3d 803 (5th Cir. 1996)("To be actionable, conduct being challenged in **hostile work environment** sexual harassment claim must create environment that reasonable person would find hostile or abusive…. Mere utterance of epithet which engenders offensive feelings in employee is not alone sufficient to support Title VII liability.")

9. *Hockman v. Westward Communictions, LLC*, 407 F.3d 317 (5th Cir. 2004) ("Male coworker's alleged **harassment** of female employee, in purportedly making offhand remark to her about another female employee's body and asking her to come into work early so that they could be alone together, in allegedly once slapping her 'behind' with newspaper and once attempting to kiss her, in once speaking to her as she washed her hands through open door of restroom, and in brushing up against her breasts and backside on multiple occasions, was not so severe and pervasive as to 'affect term, condition, or privilege of employment,' as required to support her hostile-work-environment claim; incidents were generally isolated and non-serious in nature or, in case of 'brushings,' originally perceived as being accidental and not sufficiently severe to support hostile-work-environment claim.")

10. *Ramsey v. Henderson*, 286 F.3d 264 (5th Cir. 2002)("In determining whether workplace constitutes **hostile work environment**, for purpose of Title VII claim, court considers: frequency of discriminatory conduct; its severity; whether it is physically threatening or humiliating, or mere offensive utterance; and whether it unreasonably interferes with employee's work performance.")

11. *Weller v. Citation Oil & Cas Corp.*, 84 F.3d 191 (5th Cir. 1996)("Title VII is only meant to bar **conduct** that is so **severe and pervasive** that it destroys protected class member's opportunity to succeed in the workplace.")

[8] Failure To Train

In employment law, there is a cause of action called "failure to train," meaning that the employer failed to provide adequate training to an employee because his or her age, disability, race, color, sex, national origin, religion, etc.

Again, what the court wants to see is the entire story that underlies this case: basically, what happened? What is the time sequence of events? Who, what, when, where and how? All of this information needs to be included in the complaint in order to set forth a "cause of action." Although the federal "cause of action" need not include or articulate every single element listed within the "prima facie" case standard, the best course of action is to draft the federal "cause of action" so that each and every element of the "prima facie" case standard is included within the original complaint.

One of the most historic forms of economic discrimination since the end of the Civil War is the "failure to train" men and women because of their race, ethnic origin, or union affiliation.

The reasons are obvious: to prevent certain men and women from learning how to perform competitive tasks and duties; becoming competent in certain aspects of jobs; and to prevent promotions, transfers, or other remunerative opportunities.

The "failure to train" claim may also be used as a defense against adverse employment actions, such as write-ups, suspensions, and terminations. The list of cases below provides examples of how various courts within the 5th and 11th U.S. Circuit Courts of Appeals have addressed "failure-to-train" claims.

Annotated Notes to § [9] Failure to Train

U.S. Eleventh Circuit Court of Appeals (Alabama, Florida, Georgia)

1. *Gold v. City of Miami*, 151 F.3d 1346 (11th Cir. 1998)("Allegation of **failure to train** or supervise can be basis for municipal liability under § 1983 only where municipality inadequately trains or supervises its employees, this failure to train or supervise is a city policy, and that policy causes employees to violate citizen's constitutional rights.... Since municipality rarely will have express written or oral policy of inadequately training or supervising its employees, **§ 1983** plaintiff may prove city policy by showing that municipality's failure to train evidenced a 'deliberate indifference' to rights of its inhabitants, and, to establish a 'deliberate or conscious choice' or such 'deliberate indifference,' plaintiff must present some evidence that municipality knew of need to train and/or supervise in particular area and the municipality made deliberate choice not to take any action. 42 U.S.C.A. § 1983")

2. *Price v. M & M Valve Co.*, 177 Fed.Appx. 1 (11th Cir. 2006)("Employee establishes prima face case of discriminatory **failure to promote** by showing that (1) he is a member of a protected class, (2) he was qualified and applied for the promotion, (3) he was rejected despite his qualifications, and (4) other equally or less qualified employees who were not members of the protected class were promoted.... Before employee may pursue Title VII discrimination claim, he first must exhaust his administrative remedies by filing timely charge of discrimination with Equal Employment Opportunity Commission (EEOC); to be timely within a nondefendant state, such as Alabama, charge must be filed within 180 days of the last discriminatory act.... To extent he was relying on Title VII, African-American employee failed to timely exhaust his administrative remedies before bringing claims of discriminatory failure to promote, as he did not file Equal Employment Opportunity Commission (EEOC) charge until 184 days after one employee's promotion to supervisory position and more than 20 months after another's promotion.")

3. *Grech v. Clayton County, Ga.*, 335 F.3d 1326 (11th Cir. 2003)("County's liability under **§ 1983** may not be based on **doctrine of respondeat**

superior.... County is liable under § 1983 only when county's official policy causes constitutional violation.... Plaintiff may establish that county's official policy caused constitutional violation, as required to hold county liable under § 1983, by identifying either (1) officially promulgated county policy, or (2) unofficial custom or practice of county shown through repeated acts of final policymaker for county.... Plaintiff alleging that county's official policy caused constitutional violation, as required to hold county liable under §1983, (1) must show that county has authority and responsibility over governmental function in issue, and (2) must identify those officials who speak with final policymaking authority for county concerning act alleged to have caused particular constitutional violation in issue.... County sheriff was not county policymaker for his law enforcement conduct and policies regarding warrant information on state computer systems of training and supervision of his employees in that regard, as require to hold county liable under § 1983 for alleged false arrest and violation of due process arising from arrest of arrestee on expired bench warrant which had not been withdrawn from computer systems.")

4. *Holder v. Nicholson*, 287 Fed.Appx. 784 (11th Cir. 2008)("Federal employee's termination was separate act from other prior allegedly discriminatory and **retaliatory actions** against her, such as purported assault by co-worker and failure to promote, and thus employee was required to contact EEO counselor within 45 days of her firing in order to preserve her claims under Title VII and ADEA. Age Discrimination in Employment Act of 1967.")

5. *DaCosta v. Birmingham Water Works & Sewer Bd.*, 256 Fed.Appx. 283 (11th Cir. 2007)("Employer's reason for **failing to promote** Indian employee, that he had not completed classes and certification tests necessary for the positions involved and outlined in company policy, was legitimate non-discriminatory reason for employment decision, for purposes of employee's discrimination action against employer alleging violations of Title VII and **§§ 1981** and **1983**....")

6. *Sewell v. Town of Lake Hamilton*, 117 F.3d 488 (11th Cir. 1997)("To hold municipality liable under **§ 1983 for failure to train** and supervise police officer, it is not enough to show that situation will arise and that taking wrong course in that situation will result in injuries to citizens;

rather, there must be likelihood that failure to train or supervise will result in officer making wrong decision…. Where proper response is obvious to all without training or supervision, then failure to train or supervise is generally not 'so likely' to produce wrong decision as to support inference of deliberate indifference by city policymakers to need to train or supervise; thus, failure to train or supervise in such circumstances will not lead to municipal liability under § 1983.")

7. *American Federation of Labor and Congress of Indus. Organization v. City of Miami, FL.*, 637 F.3d 1178 (11th Cir. 2011)("Municipality can be held liable under **§ 1983** when its employees cause constitutional injury as result of municipality's policy- or custom-based failure to adequately train or supervise its employees…. Inadequacy of police training may serve as basis for § 1983 liability only where failure to train amounts to deliberate indifference to rights of persons with whom police come into contact…. To establish municipality's deliberate indifference, plaintiff asserting failure to train or supervise claim in **§ 1983** suit must put forward some evidence that municipality was aware of need to train or supervise its employees in particular area…. Plaintiff asserting failure to train or supervise employees as basis for imposing liability against municipality under § 1983 may demonstrate notice by showing widespread pattern of prior abuse or even single earlier constitutional violation, but plaintiff must also demonstrate that constitutional violations were likely to recur without training…. In addition to notice of need to train employees, plaintiff asserting failure to train as basis for imposing liability against city under § 1983 must also establish that city made deliberate choice not to train its employees."

8. *Ferguson v. Veterans Admin.*, 723 F.2d 871 (11th Cir. 1984)("To prevail under Title VII, white female Veterans Administration employee, who alleged that employer's **failure to train** and **hire** for librarian's position violated Title VII, would have to show discrimination by her employer.")

9. *Mack v. S T Mobile Aerospace Engineering, Inc.*, 195 Fed.Appx. 829 (11th Cir. 2006)("Although coworker's statement that black employee was not promoted from apprentice to mechanic after one year of employment because he was black established prima face case of **failure to promote** based on race, employee failed to rebut employer's legitimate, nondiscriminatory

reason for failure to promote, that it mistakenly failed to perform his one-year evaluation and that, after mistake was discovered, employee was promoted and paid full back pay to account for missing evaluation, given absence of showing that coworker was involved in promotion decision, was employee's supervisor at time of evaluation, or based statement on knowledge of discrimination by any supervisor.")

10. *Doe ex. Rel Doe v. City of Demopolis*, 461 Fed.Appx. 915 (11th Cir. 2012) ("City's alleged **failure to train** police officer not to commit statutory rape did not show deliberate indifference to the rights of its inhabitants, and thus did not support **§ 1983** civil rights action brought against city by thirteen-year old victim who was statutorily raped by city police officer; city was entitled to rely on officer's common sense not to commit statutory rape.")

11. *Williams v. Limestone County, Ala.*, 198 Fed.Appx. 893 (11th Cir. 2006) ("Sheriff did not **demonstrate deliberate indifference** to serious medical needs of prisoner who suffered heart attack in jail, where there was no history or pattern of jail personnel's deliberate indifference that would render need for additional medical training obvious, contract with health provider gave sheriff every reason to assume that medical emergencies would be handled according to normal routine, and fact that providing personnel with additional training might have better addressed inmate's particular needs did not show deliberate indifference.")

12. *Belcher v. City of Foley, Ala.*, 30 F.3d 1390 (11th Cir. 1994)("**Failure to train** can amount to deliberate indifference, for purposes of imposing **§ 1983** liability on supervisory official, when need for more or different training is obvious, such as when there exists history of abuse by subordinates that might put supervisor on notice of need for corrective measures, and when failure to train is likely to result in violation of constitutional right.")

13. *Weiland v. Palm Beach County Sheriff's Office*, 792 F.3d 1313 (11th Cir. 2015)("A **§ 1983** plaintiff cannot rely upon the **doctrine of respondeat superior** to hold the government liable for an alleged civil rights violation, but must instead establish that the government unit has a policy or custom that caused the injury.")

U.S. Fifth Circuit Court of Appeals (Louisiana, Mississippi, Texas)

1. *Estate of Davis ex rel. McCully v. City of North Richland Hills*, 406 F.3d 375 (5th Cir. 2005)(Under 'doctrine of **qualified immunity**,' government officials performing discretionary functions generally are shielded from liability for civil damages insofar as their conduct does not violate clearly established statutory or constitutional rights of which reasonable person would have known.... Once raise, **§ 1983** plaintiff has the burden to rebut qualified immunity defense by establishing that official's allegedly wrongful conduct violated clearly established law.... Elements of § 1983 supervisory liability claim, based on failure to train or supervise, are that: (1) supervisor either failed to supervise or train subordinate official; (2) causal link exists between failure to train or supervise and violation of plaintiff's rights; and (3) failure to train or supervise amounts to deliberate indifference.... 'Deliberate indifference' element of § 1983 supervisory liability claim is stringent standard of fault, requiring proof that government actor disregarded known or obvious consequences of his or her action; official must both have been aware of facts from which inference could be drawn that substantial risk of serious harm existed, and he or she must also have drawn inference.... Actions and decisions by supervisory officials that are merely inept, erroneous, ineffective, or negligent do not amount to 'deliberate indifference,' such as would divest officials of qualified immunity from § 1983 liability.... To rely on narrow 'single incident exception' to requirement that there be pattern of relevant misconduct in order to deprive supervisor of qualified immunity from § 1983 liability on failure to train or supervise theory, plaintiff must prove that highly predictable consequence of failure to train would result in specific injury suffered, and that failure to train represented moving force behind constitutional violation.")

[9] Disability: Discrimination/ Harassment

In employment law, there is a cause of action called "disparate treatment-disability" or "hostile working environment- disability." Again, what the court wants to see is the entire story that underlies this case: basically, what happened? What is the time sequence of events? Who, what, when, where and how? All of this information needs to be included in the complaint in order to set forth a "cause of action." Although the federal "cause of action" need not include or articulate every single element listed within the "prima facie" case standard, the best course of action is to draft the federal "cause of action" so that each and every element of the "prima facie" case standard is included within the original complaint.

The Americans With Disabilities Act of 1990 ("ADA") is patterned after Title VII of the 1964 Civil Rights Act. The ADA is an important piece of labor legislation. It takes into account the important fact that even disabled workers may make a meaningful and significant contribution to the market place.

Under the ADA, employers are required to engage in an interactive dialogue with disabled workers in order to see if a reasonable accommodation can be made in order to allow the disabled person to work.

The disabled employee must be able to show that he or she can do the "essential functions" of a job, with a reasonable accommodation. The following list of cases provides a sample of the case law that has come out of the 5th and 11th U.S. Circuit Courts of Appeal.

Annotated Notes to §[10] Disability: Discrimination/Harassment

U.S. Eleventh Circuit Court of Appeals (Alabama, Florida, Georgia)

1. *Davis v. Florida Power & Light Co.*, 205 F.3d 1301 (11th Cir. 2000) ("To establish that employee is qualified individual with disability within meaning of ADA, employee must show either that he can **perform essential functions of his job** without accommodation, or, failing that, show that he can perform essential functions of his job with reasonable accommodation. Americans with Disabilities Act of 1990, § 101(8)."

2. *Holly v. Clairson Industries, LLC*, 492 F.3d 1247 (11th Cir. 2007)("To establish **prima facie case of discrimination under ADA**, plaintiff must show that: (1) he is disabled; (2) he is qualified individual; and (3)

he was subjected to unlawful discrimination because of his disability. Americans with Disabilities Act of 1990, § 2 et seq."

3. *D'Angelo v. ConAgra Foods, Inc.*, 422 F.3d 1220 (11th Cir. 2005)("To establish a prima facie case of employment discrimination under the **Americans with Disabilities Act** (ADA), a plaintiff must demonstrate that (1) he has a disability, (2) he is a qualified individual, which is to say, able to perform the essential functions of the employment position that he holds or seeks with or without reasonable accommodation, and (3) the defendant unlawfully discriminated against him because of the disability. Americans with Disabilities Act of 1990, § 102…"

4. *Lucas v. W.W. Grainger, Inc.*, 257 F.3d 1249 (11th Cir. 2001)("To establish a **prima facie case of discrimination** under the **ADA**, an employee must show that (1) he is disabled; (20 he was a qualified individual at the relevant time, meaning he could perform the essential functions of the job in question with or without reasonable accommodation; and (3) he was discriminated against because of his disability."

5. *Hilburn v. Murata Electronics North America, Inc.*, 181 F.3d 1220 (11th Cir. 1999)("Employee has burden of proving a prima facie case of **disability discrimination** by a preponderance of the evidence, which requires a demonstration that he or she (1) is disabled, (2) is a qualified individual, and (3) was subjected to unlawful discrimination because of his or her disability. Americans with Disabilities Act of 1990, § 102(a).")

6. *Cleveland v. Home Shopping Network, Inc.*, 369 F.3d 1189 (11th Cir. 2004) ("To establish a prima facie case of **ADA discrimination**, employee must show that: (1) she had a disability; (2) she was otherwise qualified to perform the job; and (3) she was discriminated against based upon the disability…. The McDonnell Douglas prima facie case method for establishing an employment discrimination claim was never intended to be rigid, mechanized, or ritualistic; it is merely a procedural device to facilitate an orderly focused evaluation of the evidence as it bears on the critical question of discrimination.")

7. *Greenberg v. BellSouth Telecommunications, Inc.*, 498 F.3d 1258 (11th Cir. 2007)("Claims of **disability discrimination** raised under the Florida

Civil Rights Act (FCRA) are analyzed under the same framework as the ADA.")

8. *Frazier-White v. Gee*, 818 F.3d 1249 (11th Cir. 2016)("To prevail on **disability discrimination** claim under the Americans with Disabilities Act (ADA) or Florida Civil Rights Act (FCRA), discharged employee was required to show that: (1) she was disabled, (2) she was a 'qualified individual' when she was terminated, and (3) she was discriminated against on account of her disability.")

9. *Shepard v. United Parcel Service, Inc.*, 470 Fed.Appx. 726 (11th Cir. 2012) ("Employee with chronic myeloid leukemia who was seeking to establish **prima facie case of disability discrimination** failed to provide sufficient evidence that he had a 'disability' under ADA when employer placed him on medical leave of absence; though he claimed his medical condition substantially limited major life activities of eating and sleeping, neither he nor his physician ever informed employer of those limitations while he was on medical leave of absence, employee also failed to establish that his condition substantially limited major life activity of working, and could not demonstrate that he had record of having impairment based solely on his prior medical leaves of absence and testimony that it was common knowledge at work he had leukemia, or that he was regarded as disabled.")

10. *Sicilia v. United Parcel Service, Inc.*, 279 Fed.Appx. 936 (11th Cir. 2008) ("To establish prima facie case of **disability discrimination** under the ADA, employee must show that (1) he has a disability, (2) he is a qualified person, and (3) his employer unlawfully discriminated against him because of his disability. Americans with Disabilities Act of 1990, § 102(a).")

11. *Farley v. Nationwide Mut. Ins. Co.*, 197 F.3d 1322 (11th Cir. 1999) ("Under the McDonnell Douglas framework, an **ADEA or ADA** plaintiff must first establish a prima facie case of discrimination, and the burden of production then shifts to the defendant who must articulate a legitimate non-discriminatory reason for the challenged employment decision; the plaintiff then bears the ultimate burden of persuasion that the defendant's proffered reason is a pretext for discrimination.")

12. *Terrell v. USAir*, 132 F.3d 621 (11th Cir. 1998)("To state prima facie case of **disability discrimination under ADA**, employee must show that: (1) he or she has disability; (2) with or without reasonable accommodations, he or she can perform essential functions of position he or she holds; and (3) he or she was discriminated against because of disability."

13. *Siudock v. Volusia County School Bd.*, 568 Fed.Appx. 659 (11th Cir. 2014) ("Former teacher could not perform essential function of his job with or without accommodations, and thus he was not qualified individual under **ADA**, precluding his claims against county school board for discrimination and failure to accommodate; even if board had accommodated teacher by allowing him to teach only gifted students, teacher still would have been unable to perform essential function of his job, as even gifted students would have disciplinary problems that could have caused teacher stress and exacerbated his diabetes, and, to extent that board did accommodate teacher, those accommodations were reasonable, even if they were not exact accommodations that teacher wanted.")

14. *Harrison v. Benchmark Electronics Huntsville, Inc.*, 593 F.3d 1206 (11th Cir. 2010)("Fact that temporary employee was not hired as a permanent employee, allegedly because of his responses to an allegedly unlawful medical inquiry into his reasons for taking barbiturates, was sufficient to establish that employee suffered damages as a result of the allegedly unlawful injury, as required for employee to establish prima facie case that employer violated the **ADA**'s bar against using medical examination or inquiries to discriminate.")

15. *Doe v. Dekalb County School Dist.*, 145 F.3d 1441 (11th Cir. 1998)("A person who is infected with human immunodeficiency virus (HIV) is 'disabled' for purposes of **Americans with Disabilities Act (ADA)**, even if he has not developed acquired immune deficiency syndrome (AIDS)."

16. *Gilliard v. Georgia Dept. of Corrections*, 500 Fed.Appx. 860 (11th Cir. 2012) ("Scintilla of evidence supporting allegation that employer breached the confidentiality of employee's medical records or made overly broad requests that caused her to release her entire medical record was insufficient to preclude summary judgment for employer on **ADA** confidentiality claims.")

U.S. Fifth Circuit Court of Appeals (Louisiana, Mississippi, Texas)

1. Frame v. City of Arlington, 657 F.3d 215 (5th Cir. 2011)("In an action under the ADA's Title II, which prohibits **disability discrimination** in the provision of public services, alleging that a city's newly built and altered sidewalks are inaccessible, a district court has discretion to craft an appropriate injunction based on the particular facts of the case, and thus will be able to ensure that the city's alleged violations are remedied in a reasonable manner.")

2. Rodriguez v. Eli Lilly and Co., 820 F.3d 759 (5th Cir. 2016)("To qualify as direct evidence of discrimination on the basis of **disability**, in violation of the ADA, workplace comments must be: (1) related to the protected class of persons of which the plaintiff of which the plaintiff is a member; (2) proximate in time to the terminations; (3) made by an individual with authority over the employment decisions at issue; and (4) related to the employment decision at issue. Americans with Disabilities Act of 1990, § 102, 42 U.S.C.A. § 12112.)"

3. Kemp v. Holder, 610 F.3d 231 (5th Cir. 2010)("To prevail on **Americans with Disabilities Act (ADA)** and Rehabilitation Act claims, a plaintiff must establish that (1) he is disabled within the meaning of the ADA, (2) he is qualified and able to perform the essential functions of his job, and (3) his employer fired him because of his disability. Rehabilitation Act of 1973, § 2 et seq., 29 U.S.C.A. § 701 et seq.; Americans with Disabilities Act of 1990, § 102(a), 42 U.S.C.A. § 12112(a).")

4. Neely v. PSEG Texas, Ltd. Partnership, 735 F.3d 242 (5th Cir. 2013)("Even under the ADA as amended by the **ADA Amendments Act (ADAAA)**, to prevail on a claim of disability discrimination under the ADA, a party must prove that (1) he has a disability; (2) he is qualified for the job; and (3) the covered entity made its adverse employment decision because of the party's disability....")

5. Daigle v. Liberty Life Ins. Co., 70 F.3d 394 (5th Cir. 1995)("Under McDonnell Douglas analysis, an employee claiming **disability** must first make out a prima facie case by showing that he or she suffers from a disability, he or she is qualified for the job, he or she was subject to adverse employment action, and he or she was replaced by a nondisabled person or was treated less favorably than nondisabled employees….")

6. *Pinkerton v. Spellings*, 529 F.3d 513 (5th Cir. 2008)("Same standard of causation that is applicable to discrimination claims under the **Americans with Disabilities Act (ADA)** also applies to disability discrimination claim under section of the Rehabilitation Act applicable to government employees…. To establish liability in employment discrimination action under the Americans with Disabilities Act (ADA), plaintiff must show that disability played a motivating role in adverse employment action, but need not establish that it was sole cause of discrimination; 'motivating factor' as opposed to 'sole causation' standard is appropriate standard of causation in causes of action under the ADA and, by extension, under provision of the Rehabilitation Act applicable to government employees.")

7. *Flowers v. Southern Regional Physician Services, Inc.*, 247 F.3d 229 (5th Cir. 2001)("In determining whether work environment is 'abusive' under **ADA**, reviewing court must consider entirety of evidence presented at trial, including frequency of discriminatory conduct, its severity, whether it is physically threatening or humiliating or mere offensive utterance, and whether it unreasonably interferes with employee's work performance.")

8. *Carmona v. Southwest Airlines Co.*, 604 F.3d 848 (5th Cir. 2010)("On an employee's claim of **disability discrimination** under the ADA, once an employer has produced sufficient evidence to support a nondiscriminatory explanation for its decision to terminate the employee, the employee may establish that he was the victim of intentional discrimination by showing that the employer's proffered explanation is unworthy of credence; it is permissible for the trier of fact to infer the ultimate fact of discrimination from the falsity of the employer's explanation.")

9 *Taylor v. Principal Financial Group, Inc.*, 93 F.3d 155 (5th Cir. 1996) ("In general, it is responsibility of **ADA** plaintiff to inform employer that accommodation is needed because of plaintiff's disability and once request has been made, the appropriate, reasonable accommodation is best determined through flexible, interactive process that involves both employer and plaintiff; in other words, it is plaintiff's initial request for

accommodation which triggers employer's obligation to participate in interactive process of determining one and once accommodation is properly requested, responsibility for fashioning reasonable accommodation is shared between employer and plaintiff.")

[10] Age Discrimination

In employment law, there is a cause of action called "disparate treatment- age discrimination." Again, what the court wants to see is the entire story that underlies this case: basically, what happened? What is the time sequence of events? Who, what, when, where and how? All of this information needs to be included in the complaint in order to set forth a "cause of action." Although the federal "cause of action" need not include or articulate every single element listed within the "prima facie" case standard, the best course of action is to draft the federal "cause of action" so that each and every element of the "prima facie" case standard is included within the original complaint.

The Age Discrimination in Employment Act (ADEA) is an amendment to the Fair Labor Standards Act (FLSA) and, therefore, does not provide the same remedies as Title VII of the 1964 Civil Rights Act and the Americans With Disabilities Act. Even though the U.S. Department of Labor enforces the FLSA, the U.S. Equal Employment Opportunity Commission enforces the ADEA, the ADA and Title VII. One of the key provision s of the ADEA is that it requires written releases and waivers for workers over the age of 40 who settle or waive various types of actions against employers. This provision requires that these employees have an opportunity to consult with an attorney; that they have 21 days to consider signing a written release, waiver or settlement of claims; and that they have 7 days to revoke after signing. The ADEA also protects employees who are over the age of 40 from unlawful discrimination, including harassment and wrongful termination or discriminatory lay-off. The difficulty with these cases is that they do require proof of "intent" which can be a daunting task. Therefore, the following list of cases is designed to help familiarize you with the various types of legal hurdles that litigants face with filing ADEA claims.

Annotated Notes to § [11] Age Discrimination

U.S. Eleventh Circuit Court of Appeals (Alabama, Florida, Georgia)

1. *Liebman v. Metropolitan Life Ins. Co.*, 808 F.3d 1294 (11th Cir. 2015) ("To establish a prima facie case of **retirement benefits** interference in violation of **ERISA**, an employee must show that he: (1) was entitled to ERISA protection; (2) was qualified for his position; and (3) was discharged under circumstances that give rise to an inference of discrimination.")

2. *Mora v. Jackson Memorial Foundation, Inc.*, 597 F.3d 1201 (11th Cir. 2010)("An **ADEA** plaintiff must show that age was the reason that the employer decided to act…. Because an ADEA plaintiff must establish 'but for' causality, no 'same decision' affirmative defense can exist; the employer either acted because of the plaintiff's age or it did not.")

3. *Kragor v. Takeda Pharmaceuticals America, Inc.*, 702 F.3d 1304 (11th Cir. 2012)("To make out a **prima facie case** of **age discrimination** under the ADEA, the plaintiff must show four things: (1) that she was a member of the protected group of persons between the ages of 40 and 70; (2) that she was subject to adverse employment action; (3) that a substantially younger person filled the position that she sought or from which she was discharged; and (4) that she was qualified to do the job for which she was rejected.")

4. *Hipp v. Liberty Nat. Life Ins. Co.*, 252 F.3d 1208 (11th Cir. 2001)("In lawsuit under the **Age Discrimination in Employment Act (ADEA)**, plaintiff who has not filed his own charge with the Equal Employment Opportunity Commission (EEOC) may piggyback onto another plaintiff's charge provided: (1) the relied upon charge, to which he is piggybacking, is not invalid, and (2) individual claims of filing and of non-filing plaintiff arise out of similar discriminatory treatment in same time frame.")

5. *Turlington v. Atlanta Gas Light Co.*, 135 F.3d 1428 (11th Cir. 1998) ("In **ADEA** case involving **discharge, demotion**, or **failure to hire**, plaintiff may establish prima facie case by showing: (1) that he was member of protected group of persons between ages of forty and seventy; (2) that he was subject to adverse employment action; (3) that substantially younger

person filled position that he sought or from which he was discharged; and (4) that he was qualified to do job for which he was rejected.")

6. *Chapman v. Al Transport*, 229 F.3d 1012 (11th Cir. 2000)("Under the burden-shifting framework for evaluating **ADEA claims** that are based upon circumstantial evidence of discrimination, the employee must first establish a prima facie case of discrimination.... On method an employee can use to establish a **prima facie case** for an **ADEA violation** is by sowing that he or she: (1) was a member of the protected age group; (2) was subjected to adverse employment action; (3) was qualified to do the job; and (4) was replaced by or otherwise lost a position to a younger individual.")

7. *Munoz v. Oceanside Resorts, Inc.*, 223 F.3d 1340 (11th Cir. 2000)("Elements necessary to establish a **prima facie case** of **age discrimination** under the **ADEA** supported by circumstantial evidence are: (1) the plaintiff was a member of the protected group of persons between the ages of forty and seventy; (2) that plaintiff was subject to adverse employment action; (3) that a substantially younger person filled the position from which he was discharged; and (4) that plaintiff was qualified to do the job from which he was discharged.")

8. *Jones v. BE&K Engineering Co.*, 146 Fed.Appx. 356 (11th Cir. 2005) ("Discharged employee failed to present evidence of employer's intent to **discriminate in discharging** him during employer's reduction in force, as required to establish prima facie case that his discharge violated **Age Discrimination in Employment Act (ADEA)**; evidence established that employer chose to discharge employee while retaining younger coworker because coworker's engineering degree made him more valuable for future needs of employer and demands of employer's clients.")

9. *Carter v. DecisionOne Corp. Through C.T. Corp. System*, 122 F.3d 997 (11th Cir. 1997)("Former employee presented sufficient evidence to support determination by jury that former employer's proffered reason for discharging employee, that is, her performance, was pretext for unlawful discrimination under **ADEA**, including statement by manager that it was preferable to have a 'nubile young woman' making sales calls, statement by employer's president that he had gotten rid of all the 'old sleazy people,'

and other evidence that older workers were replaced with younger ones and that younger sales representatives were treated better than employee.")

10. *Watkins v. Sverdrup Technology, Inc.*, 153 F.3d 1308 (11th Cir. 1998) ("Where employer produces evidence that it discharged **ADEA** plaintiff during a reduction in force (RIF), plaintiff establishes prima facie case by demonstrating (1) that he was in protected age group and was adversely affected by an employment decision, (2) that he was qualified for his current position for to assume another position at time of discharge, and (3) evidence by which fact finder reasonably could conclude that employer intended to discriminate on basis of age in reaching that decision.")

11. *Smith v. J. Smith Lanier & Co.*, 352 F.3d 1342 (11th Cir. 2003)("In **reduction in force (RIF)** case in which dismissed employee's position was eliminated in its entirety, employee establishes prima facie case of **age discrimination** by demonstrating: (1) that he/she was in protected age group and was adversely affected by employment decision; (2) that he/she was qualified for current position, or to assume another position, at time of discharge; and (3) evidence by which fact finder may reasonably conclude that employer intended to discriminate on basis of age in reaching employment decision.")

12. *Van Voorhis v. Hillsborough County Bd. Of County Com'rs*, 512 F.3d 1296 (11th Cir. 2008)("An **'adverse employment action'** is an ultimate employment decision, such as discharge or failure to hire, or other conduct that alters the employee's compensation, terms, conditions, or privileges of employment, deprives him or her of employment opportunities, or adversely affects his or her status as an employee.")

U.S. Fifth Circuit Court of Appeals (Louisiana, Mississippi, Texas)

1. *Rachid v. Jack In The Box, Inc.* 376 F.3d 305 (5th Cir. 2004)("To demonstrate **age discrimination** under ADEA, terminated employee must show that he was: (1) discharged; (2) qualified for position; (3) over 40 years old a t time of discharge; and (4) replaced by someone under 40, replaced by someone younger, or otherwise discharged because of age.")

2. *Russell v. McKinney Hosp. Venture*, 235 F.3d 219 (5th Cir. 2000)("A plaintiff's prima facie case under **Age Discrimination in Employment Act (ADEA)**, combined with sufficient evidence to find that the employer's asserted justification is false, may permit the trier of fact to conclude that the employee unlawfully discriminated.")

3. *West v. Nabors Drilling USA, Inc.*, 330 F.3d 379 (5th Cir. 2003)("To establish prima facie case of **age discrimination** in discharge case, employee must prove that: 1) he was discharged; 2) he was qualified for his position; 3) he was within protected class; and 4) he was replaced by someone outside protected class, someone younger, or was otherwise discharged because of his age.")

4. *Miller v. Raytheon Co.*, 716 F.3d 138 (5th Cir. 2013)("Under the burden-shifting framework set forth in McDonnell Douglas, the employee carries the initial burden of establishing a prima facie case of **age discrimination** under the ADEA and, if he succeeds, the burden shifts to the employer to provide a legitimate, nondiscriminatory reason for terminating employment; if the employer satisfies this burden, the burden shifts back to the employee to prove either that the employer's proffered reason was not true, but was instead a pretext for age discrimination, or that, even if the employer's reason is true, he was terminated because of his age.")

5. *Woodhouse v. Magnolia Hosp.*, 92 F.3d 248 (5th Cir. 1996)("Federal district court did not abuse its discretion in ordering employee, whose position as director of admissions within business office was eliminated during **reduction in force (RIF)** and who was not rehired for clinical nursing position, to be reinstated to the nursing position as remedy for age discrimination; employee requested that she be reinstated to nursing position and at time of trial, hospital had 11 such positions vacant, employee could not be reinstated to her director of admissions position because it no longer existed, and reinstatement was the preferred remedy.")

6. *Moss v. BMC Software, Inc.*, 610 F.3d 917 (5th Cir. 2010)("To establish an **ADEA claim**, a plaintiff relying on circumstantial evidence must put forth a prima facie case, at which point the burden shifts to the employer to provide a legitimate, non-discriminatory reason for the employment

decision, if the employer articulates a legitimate, non-discriminatory reason for the employment decision, the plaintiff must them be afforded an opportunity to rebut the employer's purported explanation, to show that the reason given is merely pretextual.")

7. *Machinchick v. PB Power, Inc.*, 398 F.3d 345 (5th Cir. 2005)("Employees producing only circumstantial evidence of discriminatory animus must negotiate McDonnell Douglas burden-shifting analysis, under which employee must first establish prima facie case of **age discrimination** by showing that (1) he was discharged, (2) he was qualified for position, (3) he was within protected class at time of discharge, and (4) he was either (i) replaced by someone outside protected class, (ii) replaced by someone younger, or (iii) otherwise discharged because of his age; once employee establishes prima facie case, burden of production shifts to employer to proffer legitimate nondiscriminatory reason for its employment action.")

8. *Armendariz v. Pinkerton Tobacco Co.*, 58 F.3d 144 (5th Cir. 1995)("Former employee failed to establish prima facie case of age discrimination in connection with his termination in **reduction in force (RIF)** or job elimination, as he failed to present evidence from which jury could have concluded that employer did not treat age as neutral factor in its decision; although former employee alleged that employer did not relocate him or rehire him for positions that subsequently became open in other territories because of his age, he did not allege or offer proof that there were openings at time he was terminated and employer produced evidence that it had long standing policy against relocating employees in former employee's position.")

[11] Lay-off/ Recall Rights/ Discrimination

In employment law, there is a cause of action called "discriminatory lay-off/ recall rights" Again, what the court wants to see is the entire story that underlies this case: basically, what happened? What is the time sequence of events? Who, what, when, where and how? All of this information needs to be included in the complaint in order to set forth a "cause of action." Although the federal "cause of action" need not include or articulate every single element listed within the "prima facie" case standard, the best course of action is to draft the federal "cause of action" so that each and every element of the "prima facie" case standard is included within the original complaint.

Closely tied to all of the federal and state labor and employment laws is the cause of action on discriminatory lay-off. This is because an employee might allege that he or she was wrongfully laid off or not called back to work for a number of reasons, such as union membership; whistleblower retaliation; race; sex; age; disability; national origin; religion; color; employee benefits such as retirement benefits, health insurance, etc. Therefore, you should keep in mind that a cause of action involving discriminatory lay-off and recall might encompass a broad range of important factors.

Annotated Notes to § [12] Lay-off/ Recall Rights/ Discrimination

U.S. Eleventh Circuit Court of Appeals (Alabama, Florida, Georgia)

1. Pettway v. American Cast Iron Pipe Co., 494 F.2d 211 (5th Cir. 1974)[11th Cir. Opinion]("'**Business necessity**' doctrine, under which employment practices which are nonintentionally discriminatory or neutral but perpetuate consequences of past discrimination may be permitted because of their overriding business necessity, places burden on defendant to justify such practice once discriminatory result is demonstrated.")

2. Watkins v. United Steel Workers of America, Local No. 2369, 516 F.2d 41 (5th Cir. 1975)[11th Cir. Opinion]("Even if 'last fired, first hired' provisions of negotiated **seniority system** were to be considered discriminatory, such system was insulated from being an unlawful employment practice on ground that it was a bona fide seniority system within exemption provision of Civil Rights Act of 1964 where the recall provision accorded white workers preference only over junior blacks on the basis of total employment…. Where each employee, regardless of race, is treated equally under **seniority system** which does not have the effect of 'locking in' past discrimination as to that employee, system is a bona fide one which is exempt from reaches of Civil Rights act of 1964.")

3. *E.E.O.C. v. Beverage Canners, Inc.*, 897 F.2d 1067 (11th Cir. 1990) ("Finding that employer discriminated against employees on basis of race, warranting injunctive relief, was sufficiently supported by evidence that plant manager and supervisor frequently made flagrant, revolting, and insulting racially derogatory remarks toward and in presence of blacks, and that company management had knowledge of such conduct.... Laid off black employee whose former job was filled by white applicant was discriminated against, though employer had no 'rehire' policy; overwhelming evidence of **racial hostility** by managers responsible for employment decisions constituted direct evidence of discriminatory intent in management decisions.")

4. *Miles v. M.N.C. Corp.*, 750 F.2d 867 (11th Cir. 1985)("Plaintiff in Title VII discriminatory discharge case must prove that he/she is member of protected class, was qualified for the position held, was discharged, and was replaced by person outside the protected class.... Once prima facie case of **employment discrimination** is proved under Title VII, burden shifts to employer to articulate legitimate, nondiscriminatory reason for its acts with regard to plaintiff, and burden on employer is one of production rather than persuasion.... If defendant employer in a Title VII discrimination case carries burden of production once a prima facie case is proved, presumption raised by the prima facie [six] is rebutted and employee must persuade the court that the reasons for not hiring plaintiff offered by the employer were pretextual.")

5. *James v. Stockham Valves & Fittings Co.*, 559 F.2d 310 (5th Cir. 1977) (11th Cir. Opinion)("In employment discrimination suit by black employees against employer, district court's finding that employer had at no time made initial job assignments either to departments or specific jobs on the basis of an employee's **race** was clearly erroneous.")

6. *Wallace v. Teledyne Continental Motors*, 138 Fed.Appx. 139 (11th Cir. 2005)("Worker could not show causal link between her layoff and filing of charge with Equal Employment Opportunity Commission (EEOC) supporting Title VII retaliation claim when employer's president ordered **layoffs** before EEOC charge was filed and worker was recalled after only 10 days.")

U.S. Fifth Circuit Court of Appeals (Louisiana, Mississippi, Texas)

1. Allen v. U.S. Steel Corp., 665 F.2d 689 (5th Cir. 1982)(In their original complaint, plaintiffs alleged that in violation of Title VII of the Civil Rights Act of 1964… and of the **Equal Pay Act of 1963**… defendant U.S. Steel discriminated against women in several ways, including its policies and practices concerning recruitment, hiring, initial job assignments, transfers, promotions, layoffs, recalls, wages and fringe benefits.")

2. Payne v. Travenol Laboratories Inc., 673 F.2d 798 (5th Cir. 1982)("In Title VII suit in which employer was found to have discriminated, decree had to be modified on remand with respect to provision that employees laid off and awaiting recall shall be recalled by **seniority date**, whether actual or constructive since under decree employee with normal seniority could fare better than class member with equal constructive seniority if employee with normal seniority had already been recalled after layoff while employee with constructive **seniority** still awaits recall, and since employee with normal seniority might also escape layoff altogether while class member with less normal seniority but equal constructive seniority is laid off.")

3. Watkins v. United Steel Workers of America, Local No. 2369, 516 F.2d 41 (5th Cir. 1975)(11th Cir. Opinion)("Black employees who had been laid off under negotiated **seniority system** with 'last hire, first fired' and 'last fired, first rehired' provisions and who never suffered discrimination at hands of the employer were in no better position to complain of recall system than were white workers who had been hired contemporaneously with them.")

[12] Retaliation/ Reprisal

In employment law, there is a cause of action called "retaliation" or "reprisal." Again, what the court wants to see is the entire story that underlies this case: basically, what happened? What is the time sequence of events? Who, what, when, where and how? All of this information needs to be included in the complaint in order to set forth a "cause of action."

Although the federal "cause of action" need not include or articulate every single element listed within the "prima facie" case standard, the best course of action is to draft the federal "cause of action" so that each and every element of the "prima facie" case standard is included within the original complaint.

Employees can have no legal or civil rights in the workplace if they are unable to file complaints and grievances. For this reason, the law against retaliation protects workers under a broad range of categories, including workers who are involved with labor organizing; reporting unhealthy or unsafe working conditions to a state or federal agency; serving in the military reserves; serving on jury duty; filing a charge of discrimination before the U.S. EEOC; or reporting sexual harassment to a senior manager in the workplace.

These examples listed in the Annotated Notes are called "protected activities" or "protected concerted activities." For this reason, retaliation claims are very important to the law of labor and employment.

Employees and employee advocates should always carefully consider whether there are any "protected activities" involved with their cases, and, if so, whether there has been retaliation for that "protected activity."

Annotated Notes to § [13] Retaliation/ Reprisal

U.S. Eleventh Circuit Court of Appeals (Alabama, Florida, Georgia)

1. *Pennington v. City of Huntsville*, 261 F.3d 1262 (11th Cir. 2001)("Employee alleging Title VII claim may not establish that an employer's proffered reason for adverse employment action is pretext for discrimination merely by questioning the wisdom of the employer's reason, as long as the reason is one that might motivate a reasonable employer…. Mixed-motive defense applies to retaliation claims under **§ 1983** and **Title VII**.")

2. *Crawford v. Carroll*, 529 F.3d 961 (11th Cir. 2008)("To make out prima facie case of **racial discrimination** under **Title VII** or in **§ 1983** equal protection claim, plaintiff must show that: (1) she belongs to protected class; (2) she was qualified to do job; (3) she was subjected to adverse employment

action; and (4) her employer treated similarly situated employees outside her class more favorably.")

3. *Harper v. Blockbuster Entertainment Corp.*, 139 F.3d 1385 (11th Cir. 1998)("For purposes of Title VII **retaliation** claim, plaintiff engages in 'statutorily protected activity' when he or she protests employer's conduct which is actually lawful, so long as he or she demonstrates good faith, reasonable belief that employer was engaged in unlawful employment practices.... In seeking to demonstrate that he or she protected employer's conduct based on good faith, reasonable belief that employer was engaged in unlawful employment practices, as required for Title VII retaliation claim, it is insufficient for plaintiff to allege his belief in this regard was honest and bona fide, but, rather, allegations and record must also indicate that belief, though perhaps mistaken, was objectively reasonable.")

4. *Williams v. Apalachee Center, Inc.*, 315 Fed.Appx. 798 (11th Cir. 2009) ("In order to constitute an adverse employment action for purposes of establishing a prima facie case under Title VII's **anti-retaliation** provision, the action must be materially adverse from the standpoint of a reasonable employee, such that it would dissuade a reasonable employee from making a discrimination charge.")

5. *Thomas v. Cooper Lighting, Inc.*, 506 F.3d 1361 (11th Cir. 2007)("The three-month lapse of time between the employee's complaints accusing her supervisor of **sexual harassment** and the termination of her employment did not constitute very close temporal proximity, so as to establish a causal connection between the harassment complaints and the termination, as required to establish a prima facie case of retaliation in violation of Title VII.")

6. *Wideman v. Wal-Mart Stores, Inc.*, 141 F.3d 1453 (11th Cir. 1998)("To establish causal relation element of prima facie case of **retaliation** under Title VII, plaintiff need only show that the protected activity and the adverse action are not wholly unrelated.")

7. *Underwood v. Department of Financial Services State of Florida*, 518 Fed. Appx. 637 (11th Cir. 2013)("To establish a prima facie case of **retaliation**, a plaintiff may show that he engaged in protected activity, he suffered a

materially adverse action, and a causal connection existed between the activity and the adverse action.")

8. *Merritt v. Dillard Paper Co.*, 120 F.3d 1181 (11th Cir. 1997)("Anti-**retaliation** provision of Title VII, which prohibits employers from taking action against employee who participates in another employee's Title VII proceeding, does not prohibit employer from imposing discipline, including termination, on any employee who sexually harasses or otherwise discriminates against other employees, so long as discipline is based on reason other than employee's participation in Title VII proceeding.")

9. *Little v. United Technologies, Carrier Transicold Div.*, 103 F.3d 956 (11th Cir. 1997)("Employee who opposed co-worker's racially offensive comment did not engage in statutorily protected activity so as to establish a prima facie case of **retaliation** under Title VII; co-worker's racially offensive comment alone was not attributable to employer and thus, employee's opposition to remark did not constitute opposition to unlawful employment practice.... Plaintiff who seeks to establish prima facie case of retaliation under the opposition clause of Title VII on the ground that he had good faith belief that employer was engaged in unlawful practices must not only show that he subjectively (that is, in good faith) believed that employer was engaged in unlawful employment practices, but also that his belief was objectively reasonable in light of the facts and record presented; it is not enough for plaintiff to allege that his belief in this regard was honest and bona fide for the allegations and record must also indicate that the belief, though perhaps mistaken, was objectively reasonable.")

10. *E.E.O.C. v. Total System Services, Inc.*, 221 F.3d 1171 (11th Cir. 2000) ("Provision in Title VII prohibiting employer from **retaliating** against employee because employee 'has made a charge, testified, assisted, or participated in any manner in an investigation, proceeding, or hearing under this subchapter' protects employee's involvement in proceedings and activities occurring in conjunction with or after the filing of formal charge with Equal Employment Opportunity Commission (EEOC) and does not protect employee's participation in employer's internal, in-house investigation, conducted apart from formal charge with EEOC.... Some employee must file charge with Equal Employment Opportunity

Commission (EEOC) or its designated representative or otherwise instigate proceedings under statute for employee's conduct to be protected under participation clause of Title VII's retaliation provision.")

11. *Anduze v. Florida Atlantic University*, 151 Fed.Appx. 875 (11th Cir. 2005)("African-American female employee of university did not engage in 'protected activity' within the meaning of the participation clause of Title VII, as required to establish prima facie Title VII **retaliation** claim, where employee had not yet filed her race discrimination charge with the Equal Employment Opportunity Commission (EEOC) at time the alleged adverse employment action was taken against employee.")

12. *Sullivan v. Natoinal R.R. Passenger Corp.*, 170 F.3d 1056 (11th Cir. 1999) ("**Retaliation** is a separate offense from discrimination under Title VII; employee need not prove underlying claim of discrimination for retaliation claim to succeed.")

13. *Shannon v. Bellsouth Telecommunications, Inc.*, 292 F.3d 712 (11th Cir. 2002)("'Adverse employment action' suffered by Title VII claimant does not refer only to ultimate employment decisions, such as decision to discharge employee; employer conduct falling short of ultimate employment decision may still be cognizable under Title VII if it reaches some threshold level of substantiality.... Reassignment of telephone company service technician to different geographical area did not constitute 'adverse employment action,' as required to support technician's Title VII **retaliation** claim, even though he claimed that new assignment made it more difficult for him to meet employer's performance standards.")

14. *Brown v. Alabama Dept. of Transp.*, 597 F.3d 1160 (11th Cir. 2010) ("The three elements of a prima facie case of **retaliation** under Title VII create a presumption that the adverse actin was the product of an intent to retaliate.... Once a Title VII plaintiff establishes a prima facie case of retaliation, the burden of production shifts to the defendant to rebut the presumption by articulating a legitimate, non-discriminatory reason for the adverse employment action, and if the defendant carries this burden of production, the presumption raised by the prima facie case is rebutted and drops from the case.")

15. *Harris v. Florida Agency for Health Care Admin.*, 611 Fed.Appx. 949 (11th Cir. 2015)("There was no causal connection between any of state employee's protected activities and his termination, and thus state agency did not **retaliate** against employee in violation of Title VII; employer's charge to Florida Commission on Human Relations and his complaint were filed more than one year before his termination.")

16. *Boyland v. Corrections Corp. of America*, 390 Fed.Appx. 973 (11th Cir. 2010)("Former employer's reason for terminating African-American corrections officer, that officer violated work policy and lied during the investigation, was not pretext for discrimination, as required for officer's **Title VII retaliation** action, even though other officers were not terminated for breaching policies; officer's breach of policy resulted in inmate having access to a gun and ammunition, which did not happen in breaches by other officers, and other officers did not lie in subsequent investigations.")

U.S. Fifth Circuit Court of Appeals (Louisiana, Mississippi, Texas)

1. *Septimus v. University of Houston*, 399 F.3d 601 (5th Cir. 2005)("Proper standard of proof on the causation element of a Title VII **retaliation** claims brought under a pretext theory; employee's ultimate burden is to prove that the employer's stated reason for the adverse action was merely a pretext for the real, retaliatory purpose.... Proper standard of proof on the causation element of a Title VII retaliation claim is that the adverse employment action taken against the employee would not have occurred 'but for' her protected activity.")

2. *McCoy v. City of Shreveport*, 492 F.3d 551 (5th Cir. 2007)("Under the framework for establishing a Title VII **retaliation** claim based upon circumstantial evidence, a Title VII plaintiff must establish that: (1) he participated in an activity protected by Title VII; (2) his employer took an adverse employment action against him; and (3) a causal connection exists between the protected activity and the adverse employment action.")

3. *Ackel v. National Communications, Inc.*, 339 F.3d 376 (5th Cir. 2003) ("In order to establish a prima facie claim of Title VII **retaliation**, an

employer must show: (1) that the employee engaged in activity protected by Title VII; (2) that an adverse employment action occurred, and (3) that a causal link existed between the protected activity and the adverse action.")

4 Long v. Eastfield College, 88 F.3d 300 (5th Cir. 1996)("In **retaliatory discharge** action under Title VII, college satisfied its burden to articulate legitimate, non-retaliatory reason for terminating employees who had filed hostile work environment complaints against their supervisors, where supervisors' termination recommendations asserted that employees had violated key replacement procedures and did not inform supervisors.")

§ 6.2 (m) National Labor Relations Act (Lay-off/ Recall Rights/ Discrimination)

The National Labor Relations Act of 1935 (NLRA) is the mother of federal labor and employment laws in the United States. Therefore, examples of workplace disputes and grievances that arise under the NLRA go as far back as the late 1930s and are quite extensive.

For this reason, there are plenty of examples of workplace retaliation and reprisal against unionized workers, and these examples may be used as examples in other types of federal actions, such as federal complaints that are based on sex, race, the Family and Medical Leave Act (FMLA), disability, age, or other basis. For this reason, non-unionized workers and their advocates should pay careful attention to laws that arise under the NLRA.

It is important to remember that the non-union members have many important rights under the NLRA. The NLRA was not enacted solely to regulate the unionized workplace or solely to protect union members. Therefore, non-union workers should also pay careful attention to this area of the law.

Annotated Notes to §[14] National Labor Relations Act (Lay-off/ Recall Rights/ Discrimination/ Unfair Labor Practices)

U.S. Eleventh Circuit Court of Appeals (Alabama, Florida, Georgia)

1. *N.L.R.B. v. U.S. Postal Service*, 526 F.3d 729 (11th Cir. 2008) ("Substantial evidence supported determination by National Labor Relations Board (NLRB) that supervisory Postal Service employee had unlawfully threatened to retaliate against Postal Service employee for filing **unfair practice charge** against him, based on evidence that, after learning that employee had filed such a charge, supervisor had telephoned employee to discuss charge, begun to yell at him for filing charge, and warned employee that he would be sorry and that he 'had better get a good attorney' because supervisor was going to sue; evidence showed that supervisor's statements were retaliatory in nature and were not made incident to any contemplated litigation, regardless of whether Petition Clause protection extended to unconsummated threats to sue.")

2. *N.L.R.B. v. McClain of Georgia, Inc.*, 138 F.3d 1418 (11th Cir. 1998)("To determine whether **anti-union animus** was motivating factor behind employer's decision to take adverse employment action, Wright Line test mandates three phases of proof, such that (1) General Counsel must first show by preponderance of evidence that protected activity was motivating factor in employer's decision to discharge employee, (2) such showing establishes statutory violation unless employer can show as affirmative defense that it would have discharged employee for legitimate reason regardless of protected activity, and (3) General Counsel may then offer evidence that employer's proffered 'legitimate' explanation is pre-textual, and thereby conclusively restore inference of unlawful motivation.")

3. *N.L.R.B. v. Contemporary Cars, Inc.*, 667 F.3d 1364 (11th Cir. 2012)("To determine whether a proposed group of employees constitutes a **separate 'craft unit**,' the National Labor Relations Board (NLRB) considers whether: (1) the employer assigns work according to need rather than on craft or jurisdictional lines, (2) the group participates in a formal training or apprenticeship program, (3) the group's work is functionally integrated with the work of excluded employees, (4) the group's duties overlap with the

duties of excluded employees, and (5) the group shares common interests with excluded employees, including wages, benefits, and cross-training.")

4. *Crew One Productions, Inc. v. N.L.R.B.*, 811 F.3d 1305 (11th Cir. 2016) ("In determining a worker's status under the National Labor Relations Act (NLRA) as **independent contractor** or **employee**, the **test for control** takes into account the degree of supervision, the entrepreneurial interests of the agent and any other relevant factors; it also distinguishes between control over the manner and means of the agent's performance and the details of the work, which is relevant, and mere economic control or control over the end result of the performance, which is not.")

5. *Cooper/ T. Smith, Inc. v. N.L.R.B.*, 177 F.3d 1259 (11th Cir. 1999) ("In proceedings before National Labor Relations Board's (NLRB), the burden of establishing the **supervisory status of an employee** on the party asserting such a status.... Three questions must be answered in the affirmative for an employee to be deemed a supervisor under National Labor Relations Act (NLRA): first, does the employee have authority to engage in 1 of the 12 listed activities; second, does the exercise of that authority require the use of independent judgment; third, does the employee hold the authority in the interest of the employer.... Docking pilots employed by stevedoring company were not 'supervisors' within the meaning of the National Labor Relations Act (NLRA), and were thus eligible for inclusion in bargaining unit; docking pilots did not use independent judgment when making informal evaluation of trainees' work, assigning tugboats, or communicating with captain during the docking process.")

6. *Kentov v. Sheep Metal Workers' Intern. Ass'n Local 15, AFL-CIO*, 418 F.3d 1259 (11th Cir. 2005)("In reviewing the grant of a **temporary injunctive relief** pending National Labor Relations Board (NLRB) resolution of certain unfair labor practice charges, court considers only: (1) whether the Board has shown reasonable cause to believe that a union has violated the National Labor Relations Act (NLRA) as alleged, and if so, (2) whether injunctive relief is 'just' and 'proper'.... Section of National Labor Relations Act (NLRA) prohibiting secondary boycotts aims to prohibit a union that has a labor dispute with one employer (the primary employer) from exerting pressure on another neutral employer (the secondary employer),

where the union's conduct is calculated to force the secondary employer to cease doing business with the primary employer.")

7. *Dowd v. International Longshoremen's Ass'n, AFL-CIO*, 975 F.2d 779 (11th Cir. 1992)("In addition to demonstrating reasonable cause to believe that unfair labor practice has occurred, National Labor Relations Board (NLRB) must show that equitable relief is just and proper under the circumstances, in order to obtain **an injunction under section of the NLRA** authorizing interim injunctive pending resolution of unfair labor practice charges by the NLRB.... Conclusion of district court considering petition for injunction under section NLRA that the National Labor Relations Board (NLRB) has presented a substantial and not frivolous legal theory is subject to plenary review on appeal.")

8. *N.L.R.B. v. Goya Foods of Florida*, 525 F.3d 1117 (11th Cir. 2008) ("Substantial evidence supported determinations by the National Labor Relations Board (NLRB) that the **discharge of three employees** was due to employees' **protected participation in labor union activity**, in violation of the National Labor Relations Act (NLRA); evidence showed that there was a pervasive anti-union animus leading up to the discharges, the discharged employees engaged in a brief and peaceful protest activity at the location of one of employer's customers shortly before their discharge, and the employer's justification for the terminations was weak.")

9. *Georgia Power Co. v. N.L.R.B.*, 427 F.3d 1354 (11th Cir. 2005)("**Courts have a narrow role when reviewing** National Labor Relations Board (**NLRB**) decisions: the rule which the NLRB adopts is judicially reviewable for consistency with the NLRA, and for rationality, but if it satisfies those criteria, the NLRB's application of the rule, if supported by substantial evidence on the record as a whole, must be enforced.")

10. *Forgers & Helpers, AFL-CIO v. N.L.R.B.*, 127 F.3d 1300 (11th Cir. 1997)("To establish violation of section of NLRA prohibiting employer from **discouraging membership in labor organization** through discrimination, charging party must prove that employer had knowledge of employees' union activities.... Employer's policy of refusing to consider applications containing information not requested on application form, as applied to applicants who wrote 'volunteer union organizer' on their

applications, did not violate section of NLRA prohibiting employer from discouraging membership in labor organization through discrimination; employer disqualified applicants who provided nonresponsive information regardless of whether such information was union-related, and employer invited all disqualified applicants to reapply."

11. *Lakeland Health Care Associates, LLC v. N.L.R.B.*, 696 F.3d 1332 (11th Cir. 2012)("To exercise independent judgment, for purposes of analysis of **whether an individual is a 'supervisor'** under National Labor Relations Act (*NLRA*), the individual must at minimum act, or effectively recommend action, free of the control of others and form an opinion or evaluation by discerning and comparing data. National Labor Relations Act, § 2(11)."

12. *Arlook for and on Behalf of N.L.R.B. v. S. Lichtenberg & Co. Inc.*, 952 F.2d 367 911th Cir. 1992)("District court should grant National Labor Relations Board's (NLRB) request for **injunctive relief** only when there is **reasonable cause to believe** that alleged **unfair labor practices** have occurred and requested injunctive relief is just and proper.... District court's role in determining whether there is reasonable cause to believe that labor violations have occurred warranting injunctive relief is limited to evaluating whether National Labor Relations Board's (NLRB) theories of law and fact are not insubstantial and frivolous and this evaluation has two components—legal question and factual threshold—and with respect to the legal question component, NLRB must present substantial, nonfrivolous, coherent legal theory of labor violation.")

13. *N.L.R.B. v. Dynatron/ Bondo Corp.*, 176 F.3d 1310 (11th Cir. 1999) ("Finding of National Labor Relations Board (NLRB), that employee terminated ostensibly for insubordination and using profane language was actually terminated because of **anti-union animus**, and that employer thus violated NLRA, was supported by substantial evidence, including evidence that employee received harsher treatment than other employees who committed similar offenses.")

14. *N.L.R.B. v. State of Fla., Dept. of Business Regulation, Div. of Pari-Mutuel Wagering*, 868 F.2d 391 (11th Cir. 1989)("District court properly granted **preliminary injunctive relief** to National Labor Relations

Board to enjoin enforcement of state court order requiring jai alai players to comply with state regulation and give 15 days notice before striking because state court order interfered with activity regulated by National Labor Relations Act.")

15. *Patel v. Quality Inn South*, 846 F.2d 700 (11th Cir. 1988) ("**Undocumented alien** was 'employee' entitled to protections of Fair Labor Standards Act; Immigration Reform and Control Act making it unlawful to hire illegal aliens and providing sanctions against employers who did so did not repeal or amend Fair Labor Standards Act.")

16. *Lobo v. Celebrity Cruises, Inc.*, 704 F.3d 882 (11th Cir. 2013)("**'Hybrid claim'** is type of claim in which employee simultaneously asserts (1) claim against employer pursuant to Labor Management Relations Act (LMRA) for **breach of collective bargaining agreement** (CBA), and (2) claim against union, which claim is implied under National Labor Relations Act (NLRA), for breach of union's duty of fair representation.")

17. *Stewart v. Spirit Airlines, Inc.*, 503 Fed.Appx. 814 (11th Cir. 2013) ("Pilot's allegations that he was subject to **anti-union animus** by airline's termination of him for recording his disciplinary hearing, in effort to initiate new custom or practice within airline of allowing employees to record fact-finding meetings prior to imposing discipline, did not state claim, under RLA provision prohibiting carriers from interfering with employee's efforts to join, organize, or assist in organizing union or exercise right to organize and bargain collectively, since pilot's effort to initiate new custom of allowing employees to record fact-finding meetings was not union-organizing activity.")

18. *N.L.R.B. v. Triple A Fire Protection, Inc.*, 136 F.3d 727 (11th Cir. 1998) ("Employer's repeated efforts to deal directly with employees outside normal channels of collective bargaining, by attempting to dissuade them from supporting union and creating incentives for them to abandon support for union, were per se violations of NLRA **s**ections prohibiting employer from interfering with exercise of rights guaranteed by NLRA and from refusing to bargain collectively with employee's representatives…. Employer's **refusal to negotiate** with union in fact as to any subject which is within scope of matters concerning which employer and union have statutory duty

to bargain collectively, and about which union seeks to negotiate, violates statute prohibiting employer from **refusing to bargain collectively** with representatives of employees, though employer has every desire to reach agreement with union upon over-all collective agreement and earnestly and in all good faith bargains to that end.")

19. *N.L.R.B. v. Austal USA, LLC*, 343 Fed.Appx. 448 (11th Cir. 2009) ("Substantial evidence supported decision of the National Labor Relations Board (NLRB) that employer had violated the National Labor Relations Act (NLRA) when it suspended pro-union employee prior to a union election, although employer argued that it **suspended employee** because of his work performance, where an administrative law judge (ALJ) made an adverse credibility finding against employer, based on its shifting rationale, and credited employee's testimony that employer put him in a position where he could not properly perform because of his **union activities**.")

20. *Florida Bd. Of Business Regulation Dept. of Business Regulation, Div. of Pari-Mutuel Wagering v. N.L.R.B.*, 686 F.2d 1362 (11th Cir. 1982)("Once National Labor Relations Board properly asserted its jurisdiction over labor dispute in state-regulated jai alai industry, Board's jurisdiction was exclusive with respect to actions arising under sections 8, 9, 10 of the National Labor Relations Act, including all charges of **unfair labor practices** by employers or labor organizations and all petitions for representation elections, and neither federal courts, excepted by way of review or on application by Board, nor state administrative agency, nor state courts might assume control over them.").

U.S. Fifth Circuit Court of Appeals (Louisiana, Mississippi, Texas)

1. *Watkins v. United Steel Workers of America, Local No. 2369*, 516 F.2d 41 (5th Cir. 1975)("Even if 'last hire, first fired' and **'last fired, first rehired'** provisions of negotiated seniority system were discriminatory, such system was exempt from being an unlawful employment practice where system was not the result of an intention to discriminate.... Express intent of provision of Civil Rights Act of 1964 that it shall not be an unlawful employment practice for employer to apply different conditions or privileges of employment pursuant to **bona fide seniority or merit**

system provided that such differences are not the result of an intention to discriminate was to preserve contractual rights of seniority as between whites and persons who had not suffered any effects of discrimination.")

2. *U.S. v. Hayes Intern. Corp.*, 456 F.2d 112 (5th Cir. 1972)("Any employment disadvantage presently operating against incumbent Negroes employed by particular employer due to past discriminatory practices violated Title VII of Civil Rights Act of 1964 and should be eliminated by giving Negroes opportunity to compete for openings in the 'white jobs' on basis of their **ability to perform and plant seniority** without regard to the seniority expectations of junior white employees.")

3. *Pettway v. American Cast Iron Pipe Co.*, 494 F.2d 211 (5th Cir. 1974) ("Where employer's **discriminatory testing requirements** for eligibility to supervisory positions of leadman and foreman were dropped before commencement of black employees' action under equal employment opportunity provisions of Civil Rights Act of 1964 and employer represented that black employees were thereafter qualified and being considered for such positions, case would be remanded for taking of evidence on issue whether selection of such supervisory personnel on basis of subjective judgment of all-white superintendents was operating independently of testing to discriminate against black employees.")

§ 6.03 FEDERAL EMPLOYMENT LAW

PRIMA FACIE CASE STANDARDS

(Discovery/ Trial/ Evidentiary Stage)

§ 6.03 Federal Prima Facie Case Standards

As previously stated, the "prima facie" case is a legal standard which courts use to determine if there is sufficient evidence to move forward to an evidentiary hearing or trial. The standard is typically applied whenever a party files a motion for summary judgment, at the close of pre-trial discovery; or a motion for a directed verdict, at the close of opening statements at the beginning or during the middle or end of a trial proceeding. There are certain basic legal elements for each cause of action. These legal elements require proof. In other words, there must be some evidence to show each element within a prima-facie case standard, in order for a case to move forward. As a practical matter, most lawyers will plead both the "cause of action" and the "prima facie case" standard together, thus ensuring that a complaint has the best chance of withstanding a motion to dismiss, motion for summary judgment, and, later at trial, a motion for directed verdict. Below, I have provided the most common prima facie case standards that are used in the federal law of employment.

****

[1] Failure To Promote

To establish a prima facie case for race discrimination, the following elements must be proved:

1. The employee is a member of a particular race (i.e., a protected group);
2. The employee was qualified and applied for a promotion;
3. The employee was rejected despite his qualifications; and,
4. Other equally or less qualified employees who were not members of the protected class were promoted.[129]

HUMAN RESOURCES MANAGEMENT

Annotated Notes to § [1] Race Discrimination

Wilson v. B/E Aerospace, Inc., 376 F.3d 1079 1089 (11th Cir. 2004)

Williams-Boldware v. Denton Cnty. Tex, 741 F.3d 635, 643 (5th Cir. 2013)

[2] Race Discrimination

To establish a prima facie case for race discrimination, the following elements must be proved:

5. The employee is a member of a particular race (i.e., a protected group);
6. The employee was subjected to an adverse employment action;

7. The employer treated similarly-situated employees outside of the employee's particular race (i.e., classification) more favorably;
8. The employee was qualified to do or perform the job.

Annotated Notes to § [2] Race Discrimination

Holifield v. Remo, 115 F.3d 1555 (11th Cir. 1997)

[3] Color Discrimination

To establish a prima facie case for color discrimination, the following elements must be proved:

1. The employee has a particular skin color or skin complexion to which others find objectionable (i.e., a protected group);

2. The employee was subjected to an adverse employment action;
3. The employer treated similarly-situated employees who do not have the same skin color or skin complexion as the employee's (i.e., classification) more favorably;
4. The employee was qualified to do or perform the job.

Annotated Notes to § [3] Color Discrimination

Bryant v. Bell Atlantic Maryland, Inc., 288 F.3d 124 (4th Cir. 2002).

Richardson v. HRHH Gaming Senior Mezz, LLC, 99 F.Supp.3d 1267 (D.Nev. 2015).

****

[4] National Origin Discrimination

To establish a prima facie case for national origin discrimination, the following elements must be proved:

1. The employee is of a particular nationality or national origin (i.e., a protected group);
2. The employee was subjected to an adverse employment action;
3. The employer treated similarly-situated employees who do not share the same nationality or national origin (i.e., classification) more favorably;
4. The employee was qualified to do or perform the job.

Annotated Notes to § [4] National Origin Discrimination

Espinoza v. Farah Mfg. Co., Inc., 414 U.S. 86 (1973)

****

[5] Sex Discrimination

To establish a prima facie case for sex discrimination, the following elements must be proved:

1. The employee has a particular sex or gender (i.e., a protected group);
2. The employee was subjected to an adverse employment action;
3. The employer treated similarly-situated employees who were of the opposite sex or gender (i.e., classification) more favorably;
4. The employee was qualified to do or perform the job.

Annotated Notes to § [5] Sex Discrimination

Jones v. Frank, 973 F.2d 673 (8th Cir. 1992).

Wilson v. B/E Aerospace, Inc., 376 F.3d 1079 (11th Cir. 2004)

****

[6] Religious Discrimination

To establish a prima facie case for religious discrimination, the following elements must be proved:

1. The employee has a particular religion or is a member of particular religious group (i.e., a protected group);
2. The employee was subjected to an adverse employment action;
3. The employer treated similarly-situated employees who did not share the same religion as the employee, or who were not members of the same religious group as the employee (i.e., classification), more favorably;
4. The employee was qualified to do or perform the job.

Annotated Notes to § [6] Religious Discrimination

Tepper v. Potter, 505 F.3d 508 (6th Cir. 2007)

EEOC v. United Health Programs of America, Inc., 213 F.Supp.3d 377 (N.Y.E.D. 2016).

****

[7] Hostile Work Environment (Under Title VII)

To establish a prima facie case for harassment or hostile work environment, the following elements must be proved:

1. The employee belongs to a particular protected group (e.g., race, sex, color, ethnic origin, religion, age, disability, or membership in a labor union);
2. The employee was subjected to unwelcome harassment;
3. The harassment was based upon the employee's protected group status (e.g., race, sex, color, ethnic origin, religion, age, disability, or membership in a labor union);
4. The harassment was sufficiently severe or pervasive to alter the terms and conditions of the employee's employment, and to create a discriminatorily abusive working environment; and
5. A basis for holding the employer liable.

Annotated Notes to § [7] Hostile Working Environment

Henson v. City of Dundee, 682 F.2d 897 (11th Cir. 1982).

****

[8] Failure to Train

To establish a prima facie case for failure to train an employee because of his protected status (i.e., race, sex, color, ethnic origin, religion, age, disability, or membership in a labor union), the following elements must be proved:

1. The employee is a member of a protected class (race, sex, color, ethnic origin, religion, age, disability, or membership in a labor union);
2. The employee satisfactorily performed the duties required in his position;
3. The employer had a policy of providing on-the-job training; and
4. The employee was not provided training under circumstances giving rise to an inference of discrimination.

Annotated Notes to §[8] Failure to Train

Lopez v. *Metropolitan Life Insurance Co.*, 930 F.2d 157 (2nd Cir. 1990)

****

[9] Failure to Promote/Hire

To establish a prima facie case for failure to promote or hire, the following elements must be proved:

1. The employee/applicant is a member of a protected group (i.e., race, sex, color, ethnic origin, religion, age, disability, or membership in a labor union);
2. The employee/applicant applied and was qualified for a job for which the employer was seeking applicants;
3. Despite the employee's/applicant's qualifications, he or she was rejected; and

4. After the employee's/applicant's rejection, the position remained open and the employer continued to seek applicants from persons of the employee's/applicant's qualifications.

Annotated Notes to § [9] Failure to Promote

McDonnell Douglass Corp. v. Green, 411 U.S. 792 (1973)

****

[10] Disability Discrimination

To establish a prima facie case for disability discrimination, the following elements must be proved:

1. The employee has a disability (i.e., the legal definition of "disability" as is defined in Section 902 of Americans With Disabilities Act Amendments Act of 2008);
2. The employee was subjected to an adverse employment action;
3. The employer treated similarly-situated employees who did not have the same disability as the employee (i.e., classification) more favorably;
4. The employee was qualified to do or perform the job.

Annotated Notes to § [10] Disability Discrimination

E.E.O.C. v. LHT Group, Inc., 773 F.3d 688 (5th Cir. 2014)

Burton v. Freescale Semiconductor, Inc., 798 F.3d 222 (5th Cir. 2015)

****

[11] Disability -- Failure to Accommodate

To establish a prima facie case for failure to accommodate a disability, the following elements must be proved:

1. The employee has a disability (i.e., the legal definition of "disability" as is defined in Section 902 of Americans With Disabilities Act Amendments Act of 2008);
2. The employee requested the employer to make a reasonable accommodation for the employee's disability;
3. The employer refused provide the reasonable accommodation; and
4. The employee was qualified to do the job and capable of performing the job with a reasonable accommodation to his or her disability.

Annotated Notes to § [11] Disability- Failure to Accommodate

E.E.O.C. v. LHT Group, Inc., 773 F.3d 688 (5th Cir. 2014)

Burton v. Freescale Semiconductor, Inc., 798 F.3d 222 (5th Cir. 2015)

****

[12] Age Discrimination

To establish a prima facie case for age discrimination, the following elements must be proved:

1. The employee is age 40 years old or older;
2. The employee was subjected to an adverse employment action;
3. The employer treated similarly-situated employees who were either younger than 40 years old, or substantially younger than the employee, more favorably;
4. The employee was qualified to do or perform the job.

Annotated Notes to § [12] Age Discrimination

Gross v. FBL Financial Services, Inc., 557 U.S. 167 (2009)

O'Connor v. Consolidated Coin Caterers Corp., 517 U.S. 308 (1996)

****

[13] Discriminatory Lay-Off

To establish a prima facie case for lay-off discrimination, the following elements must be proved:

1. The employee is a member of a protected class (i.e., race, sex, color, ethnic origin, religion, age, disability, or membership in a labor union);
2. The employee was performing according to his employer's legitimate expectations;
3. The employee was terminated; and
4. Other similarly-situated employees who were not in the same protected class were treated more favorably.[130]

Annotated Notes to § [13] Discriminatory Lay-Off

Sakellar v. Lockheed Missiles and Space Co., 765 F.2d 1453 (9th Cir. 1985).

****

[14] Discriminatory Recall Rights

To establish a prima facie case for "job recall" discrimination, the following elements must be proved:

---

[130] See, e.g., *Oxman v. WLS-TV*, 846 F.2d 448 (7th Cir. 1988).

1. The employee is a member of a protected class (i.e., race, sex, color, ethnic origin, religion, age, disability, or membership in a labor union);
2. At the time of the reduction in force, the employee applied for but did not receive another position;
3. Other similarly-situated employees who were not in the same protected class did receive that position;
4. The employee was qualified for that position.

Annotated Notes to § [14] Discriminatory Recall Rights

Sakellar v. Lockheed Missiles and Space Co., 765 F.2d 1453 (9th Cir. 1985).

****

[15] Retaliation

To establish a prima facie case for "retaliation" discrimination, the following elements must be proved:

1. The employee opposed illegal conduct or engaged in protected activity (e.g., filing a charge of discrimination at the U.S. Equal Employment Opportunity Commission or participating as a witness in an investigation or court proceeding);
2. The employee suffered an adverse employment action; and
3. There is a causal connection between the opposition or protected activity and the
4. adverse employment action.

Annotated Notes to § [15] Retaliation

Burlington Northern and Santa Fe Ry. Co. v. White, 548 U.S. 53 (2006)

Clark County School Dist. v. Breeden, 532 U.S. 268 (2001)

[16] Reprisal Under Sec. 8(3)(a) of National Labor Relations Act

To establish a prima facie case for "reprisal" under the National Labor Relations Act, the following elements must be proved:

1. The employee engaged in protected activity under Section 7 of the National Labor Relations Act[131];
2. The employee suffered an adverse employment action; and
3. There is a causal connection between the opposition or protected activity and the adverse employment action.[132]

Annotated Notes to § [16] Reprisal Under Sec. 8(3)(a) of the National Labor Relations Act

Medeco Sec. Locks, Inc. v. N.L.R.B., 142 F.3d 733 (4th Cir. 1998)

Tacky Backing Co. v. N.R.R.B., 254 F.3d 114 (D.C. Cir. 2001)

---

[131] Sec. 7 of the NLRA states, "Employees shall have the right to self-organization, to form, join, or assist labor organizations, to bargain collectively through representatives of their own choosing, and to engage in other concerted activities for the purpose of collective bargaining or other mutual aid or protection, and shall also have the right to refrain from any or all such activities except to the extent that such right may be affected by an agreement requiring membership in a labor organization as a condition of employment as authorized in section 8(a)(3) [section 158(a)(3) of this title]."

[132] The General Counsel of the National Labor Relations Board enforces Section 8(3)(a) of the NLRA. The General Counsel must "make a prima facie showing sufficient to support the inference that (the employer's opposition to) protected conduct was a 'motivating factor' in the employee's (discharge) decision. Once this is established, the burden will shift to the employer to demonstrate that the same action would have taken place even in the absence of the protected conduct." *Wright Line*, 251 N.L.R.B. 1083 (1980), enforced, 662 F.2d 899 (1st Cir. 1981), cert. denied, 455 U.S. 989 (1982).

Feist v. Louisiana, Dept. of Justice, Office of Atty. Gen., 730 F.3d 450 (5th Cir. 2013)

§ 6.04 Human Resources and Strategic Risk Management

Over the past few decades, the human resources profession has evolved an administrative and clerical function into a senior managerial position that functions as the "business" partner to senior-level managers. This strategic human resources function has become more complex and requires a greater level of strategic-management skill-sets. One of the major skill-sets now required from human resources leaders is that of employee relations and litigation risk management. Today, more than ever before, human resources professionals must be able to recognize potential violations of a multitude of state and federal antidiscrimination laws; and they must be able to take proactive steps to prevent such violations, or to resolve the sort of workplace conflict that can ripen into lawsuits. Human resources professionals must also know their way around the local offices of the National Labor Relations Board, the U.S. Equal Employment Opportunity Commission, the U.S. Department of Labor, and the state and local fair employment practices agencies. They must know how to effectively respond to charges of discrimination and carefully evaluate the merit of various charges and allegations. In addition, where the working environment is also governed by a collective bargaining agreement ("labor agreement"), the human resources professional should retain a working knowledge of how labor agreements incorporate these same federal and state antidiscrimination laws into the language of the labor agreement. These antidiscrimination issues may be set forth as labor grievances under a labor agreement.

Therefore, human resources professionals must take inventory of the nature of complaints and grievances that are being lodged from within the workforce, and they must assist both workers and supervisors with finding methods to resolve workplace problems. Sometimes this may require restructuring jobs, teams, and the flow of work (e.g., techno-structural changes such as total quality management (TQM) and Six-Sigma implementations). Sometimes this may mean establishing a "high performance" organization (HI PO), which gives lower-level workers more input into the decision-making aspects of the work. Sometimes this might mean restructuring the compensation packages, in order give workers a greater share of the profits. Sometimes this may mean revisiting the organization's values, culture and ethics policies. Sometimes this might mean building a brand new "conflict resolution" management program. Sometimes, this might mean implementing a cultural diversity program.

§ 6.05 Conclusion

This chapter is designed to provide lay readers with a comprehensive overview of federal anti-discrimination laws, as they may be applied under a collective bargaining agreement ("labor agreement"); in a labor union grievance proceeding; in a labor arbitration proceeding; and in state or federal court litigation. These laws are more frequently litigated in federal or state court, but labor union advocates should beware that in most union grievances, these laws also apply to grievance proceedings, through the express language of the labor agreement. For this reasons, this chapter also helps labor advocates and employees to better understand the nature and legal components of various federal anti-discrimination laws. Employees, union stewards, union officials, employee advocates, front-line managers, supervisors, and senior level managers should be able to better recognize the sort of fact patterns which a judge or an arbitrator will look for to determine if a violation of the law has occurred. Each federal anti-discrimination law has multiple forms of causes of action—hostile working environment, retaliation, discriminatory termination, failure to train, failure to promote, disparate impact, etc. And each cause of action has its own unique legal elements. It is important for employees to have a basic understanding of what these legal elements are; otherwise, they will not know whether a violation of important workplace rights has occurred. In addition, employers must also understand what these legal elements are, in order to properly train their supervisors in how to prevent workplace discrimination from taking place.

Chapter Six Bibliography

Books:

Ford, Roderick O. *Understanding Employment Law*. Tampa, FL: Xlibris Pub., 2017.

References:

45A American Jurisprudence (Second), Job Discrimination §§ 1-771.

45B American Jurisprudence (Second), Job Discrimination §§ 772-1887.

45C American Jurisprudence (Second), Job Discrimination §§ 1888-2726.

Cases:

See Attached Law Digest, Chapter Six.

Chapter Seven

UNION'S DUTY OF FAIR REPRESENTATION

§ 7.01 Introduction 245

§ 7.02 Historical Development- Steele v. Louisville & N.R. Co.(1944)....... 248

§ 7.03 U.S. Supreme Court- Further Developments 250

§ 7.04 U.S. Eleventh Circuit (Alabama, Florida and Georgia) 251

§ 7.05 U.S. Fifth Circuit (Louisiana, Mississippi, and Texas) 254

§ 7.06 Other U.S. Circuits—Further Developments............................ 256

§ 7.07 Human Resources and Strategic Risk Management 258

§ 7.08 Conclusion 258

§ 7.01 Introduction

In this final chapter, we end this treatise on American labor law as we began it, that is to say, by focusing on labor's fundamental Bill of Rights, insofar as those rights are manifested in a labor union's duty to provide fair representation to individual American workers. This duty to provide fair representation should remind union officials and labor advocates that the primary objective of federal labor legislation is to promote the morale, welfare, and interests of individual American workers. For this reason, American labor unions owe an important fundamental "duty of fair representation" to these individual American workers. This duty of fair representation essentially epitomizes labor's Bill of Rights, because labor unions must deal justly and fairly with every employee whom they represent. The idea that the labor union must deal justly with each and every individual union member comes from a variety of sources. In general, working environments where there is a strong union presence, the collective bargaining agreement ("labor agreement") governs most of the terms, conditions, and privileges of employment. The labor agreement is a general labor contract between the employer and the union. The *primary beneficiaries* of this contract are the individual employees who are within the bargaining unit for whom the labor agreement was negotiated and ratified. And since the employees within the bargaining unit are the "beneficiaries," the labor union is the "trustee," which means that the labor union has a "fiduciary duty" toward the employees-beneficiaries (i.e., the employees within the bargaining unit). This fiduciary duty includes the duty to fairly represent these employees at the negotiating or *formation phase* of the labor agreement (i.e., during the period when the union and employer are negotiating to create a new labor agreement)[133] and the *administrative phase* of the CBA (i.e., during the three-year period after the labor agreement has been ratified).[134]

In general, a labor union must act with due diligence and it must protect the best interests of all of the employees within the bargaining unit. This includes fairly representing each union member during the negotiation phase of the collective bargaining agreement and adequately representing individual union members whenever they file grievances and appeals of disciplinary actions. Whenever, if ever, a labor union fails to

---

[133] See, e.g., Chapter Four, "Negotiating the Collective Bargaining Agreement."

[134] See, e.g., Chapter Five, "Administration of the Collective Bargaining Agreement."

discharge this solemn obligation, then it breaches its statutory duty of fair representation that is imposed under the National Labor Relations Act and the Taft-Hartley Act of 1947:

> The duty of fair representation arises from a union's legal status as the sole and exclusive bargaining representative of employees' interests with their employer.... The duty of fair representation is not the equivalent of the duty of reasonable care under common law; it is a procedural right (duty of good faith representation of membership) and not a general duty of due care.... Even if a union's action is authorized under its constitution, it may still breach the duty of fair representation. A labor union's duty of fair representation traditionally runs only to members of the collective-bargaining unit; a union's statutory duty of fair representation does not extend to those persons who are not members of the pertinent bargaining unit....[135]

> Exclusive representation is a necessary prerequisite to a labor union's statutory duty to represent fairly. The duty of fair representation requires a union to serve the interests of all its members without hostility or discrimination, to exercise its discretion with good faith and honesty, and to avoid any arbitrary conduct. This duty to fairly represent members extends both to the negotiation of a collective-bargaining agreement and the administration of that same agreement.... The duty of fair representation is breached only when actions are arbitrary, discriminatory, or in bad faith.[136]

> For purposes of its duty of fair representation, a union's conduct is arbitrary only when it is irrational, which means without a rational basis or explanation. This standard allows a wide range of reasonableness that gives the union room to make discretionary

---

[135] 48 Am Jur Second, Labor and Labor Relations § 1080.

[136] Ibid, § 79.

decisions and choices, even if those judgments are ultimately found to be wrong.

Arbitrary conduct is demonstrated if in light of the factual and legal landscape at the time of the union's actions, the union's behavior is so far outside a wide range of reasonableness as to be irrational. If a union's judgment is in question, the plaintiff may prevail only if the conduct was discriminatory or in bad faith; arbitrariness alone would not be enough. Only when the challenged conduct is procedural or ministerial would arbitrariness become controlling.

Simple negligence, ineffectiveness, or a mistake of judgment is not enough. The union must have acted in reckless disregard of the employee's rights. Finally, the union only breaches its duty of fair representation when its conduct prejudice a strong interest of the employee. A union may breach its duty by conducting an arbitration of a grievance in a perfunctory, apathetic, indifferent, and cursory way. An act of omission may be so egregious and unfair as to be arbitrary if the individual interest at stake is strong and the union's failure to perform a ministerial act completely extinguishes the employee's right to pursue the claim.[137]

An employee whose rights have been violated by a labor organization's failure to provide fair representation may sue both the labor union and the employer for "breach of contract [i.e., the Collective Bargaining Agreement]" pursuant to Section 301 of the Taft-Hartley Act of 1947. If the labor union breaches its duty of fair representation, and an "innocent" employer is deemed jointly liable for the employee's damages, that "innocent" employer can recover its share of damages directly from the at-fault labor union.[138]

In addition, Title VII of the Civil Rights Act of 1964 imposes various obligations upon labor unions, the breach of which may also lead to civil liability.[139] Thus, Title VII also imposes upon labor unions the statutory duty of fair representation as well:

---

[137] 48A Am Jur Second, Labor and Labor Relations §1274.

[138] Ibid, § 1282.

[139] 45B Am Jur Second, Job Discrimination §§ 1048-1053.

To establish a prima facie Title VII claim against a union for breach of its duty of fair representation, the plaintiff must show that:

- The *employer* violated the collective bargaining agreement with respect to the plaintiff;
- The *union* permitted the violation to go unrepaired, thereby breaching the union's duty of fair representation; and
- There was some indication that the union's actions were motivated by a discriminatory animus.[140]

In other words, under Title VII, the employee must prove that the union breached its duty of fair representation *because of* his or her race, color, sex, religion, or national origin, etc. Presumably, similar claims may be made under the Age Discrimination in Employment Act (ADEA) and the Americans with Disabilities Act (ADA).

§ 7.02 Historical Development- Steele v. Louisville & N.R. Co.(1944)

Importantly, a labor union's "duty of fair representation" is a judicial creation which grew out of pre-Civil Rights era efforts by African American workers during the 1940s, as memorialized in the landmark case of *Steele v. Louisville & N.R. Co.*[141] These African American workers were non-union members, but they were members of the same "bargaining unit" that included white workers. Unfortunately, during the early 1940s, the A.F. of L. craft unions typically refused to admit African Americans into their craft unions, even though they worked in the same crafts as similarly-situated white employees who were allowed to join these unions. In *Steele v. Louisville & N.R. Co.*, an A.F. of L. craft union negotiated a labor agreement that expressly barred African American workers from attaining promotions into certain positions. These African American workers received representation from the National Association for the Advancement of Colored People (NAACP), which retained the legal

---

[140] Ibid., §1048.

[141] *Steele v. Louisville & N.R. Co.*, 323 U.S. 192, 65 S. Ct. 226, 89 L. Ed. 173 (1944).

counsel of Charles Hamilton Houston, Dean of the Howard University Law School, to represent these workers. The NAACP litigated this case in the Alabama lower courts. At the trial-court and intermediate appellate court-levels, the A.F. of L. won persuasive court decisions, which upheld its right to discriminate against African American workers who worked the same bargaining units as similarly-situated white workers. Unfortunately, the Alabama Supreme Court upheld these lower courts' decisions, and the NAACP appealed the case to the United States Supreme Court. The U. S. Supreme Court agreed to review the Alabama Supreme Court's decision, upon a *writ of certiorari*, and the case was styled *Steele v. Louisville & N.R. Co.* (1944).[142]

In *Steele*, the U.S. Supreme Court overturned the Alabama Supreme Court. The U.S. Supreme Court in *Steele* held that a trade-union, that is duly elected to represent a bargaining unit, could not discriminate against the employees who worked within that bargaining unit, regardless of whether those employees were members of the labor union. What troubled the Supreme Court was that the black employees (non-union members) who worked within the same bargaining unit as the white employees (union members), were being expressly diminished, disadvantaged, and discriminated against during the labor union's contract negotiations with the employer. The Supreme Court made it quite clear that the labor union's obligations extended to all employees who worked within the same bargaining unit, regardless of whether or not these employees were active union members or not. In addition, the Supreme Court also held that a labor union could not discriminate between employees within the same bargaining unit, on the basis of their race. In other words, the *Steele* Court held that racial discrimination inherently violates a labor union's duty of fair representation.

For this reason, the Supreme Court's holding in *Steele* is the first federal court ruling to overturn racial discrimination in the terms, conditions, and privileges of employment. Today, a labor union's common law duty to not discriminate against bargaining unit members on the basis of race is not only enforceable under federal labor laws, such as the Railway Labor Act and the National Labor Relations Act, but it may also be enforced under both state and federal anti-discrimination laws, such as Title VII of the 1964 Civil Rights Act.

---

[142] Ibid.

§ 7.03 U.S. Supreme Court- Further Developments

After the *Steele* decision, the duty of fair representation took on a much different and broader connotation within American labor and employment jurisprudence. Today, in the post-Civil Rights era (1970 to present), "racial discrimination" claims are almost always handled and resolved outside of the labor arenas through state and federal anti-discrimination agencies such as the U.S. Equal Employment Opportunity Commission. A labor union's duty of fair representation, which primarily involve race discrimination, is typically handled and resolved as a Title VII and Section 1981 case, which is adjudicated in the U.S. Equal Employment Opportunity Commission and (or) state or federal court. However, a labor union's duty of fair representation, which does not involve racial discrimination—but instead involves other forms of "breaches"—are normally handled as an "unfair labor practice" claim before the National Labor Relations Board, or as a "breach of contract" claim pursuant to Section 301 of the Taft-Hartley Act of 1947. Since there are essentially different forms of this "duty of fair representation," employees, union officials, and attorneys need to understand which form is more appropriate for their claims, particularly because various administrative forums (e.g., the NLRB, EEOC, etc.) have different statutes of limitations (filing deadline) periods.

In the case of *Vaca v. Sipes*,[143] the United States Supreme Court ruled that individual union members may elect to sue both the labor union and the employer, or only the labor union, for breach of the collective bargaining agreement. That is to say, when the union takes steps that violate a particular term of the labor agreement and also impairs an employee's terms, conditions, or privileges of employment, then that particular employee may sue the labor union directly in court, under Section 301 of the Taft-Hartley Act. The *Vaca c*ourt stated that an "[e]mployee may seek judicial enforcement of his contractual rights where union has sole power under collective bargaining contract to invoke higher stages of grievance procedure and employee has been prevented from exhausting contractual remedies by union's wrongful refusal to process the grievance.... Wrongfully discharged employee may bring action against his employer in face of defense based on failure to exhaust contractual remedies, provided employee can prove that union as bargaining agent,

---

[143] *Vaca v. Sipes*, 386 U.S. 171, 87 S.Ct. 903 (1967).

breached its duty of fair representation in handling of employee's grievance, even assuming that breach of duty by union is an unfair labor practice."

Importantly, the U.S. Supreme Court clearly delineated between union actions that are adverse to employees, but which are nevertheless permissible, and union actions which breach the duty of fair representation. In the case of *Marquez v. Screen Actors Guild, Inc.*,[144] Court held that a union breaches its duty of fair representation only if it fails "to exercise its discretion with complete good faith and honesty, and to avoid arbitrary conduct.... Union breaches the duty of fair representation when its conduct toward a member of the bargaining unit is arbitrary, discriminatory, or in bad faith.... For purposes of its duty of fair representation, union's conduct can be classified as 'arbitrary' only when it is irrational; when it is without a rational basis or explanation...."[145] The labor practitioner should therefore pay careful attention to the words "arbitrary, discriminatory, or in bad faith," since these are the legally operative words which govern cases involving the breach of the duty of fair representation.

Lastly, whenever a union breaches its duty of fair representation under a collective bargaining agreement, an employee has two options. He or she may sue both the employer and the union, since both parties are responsible for properly administering the collective bargaining agreement; or he or she may sue only the union, in which case the union may interplead the employer into the action, as necessary. See, e.g., *Breininger v. Sheet Metal Workers Intern. Ass'n Local Union No. 6*,[146] holding that a "[c]laim against union that union breached its duty of fair representation does not require that employee bring concomitant claim against employer that employer breached collective-bargaining agreement."

§ 7.04 U.S. Eleventh Circuit (Alabama, Florida and Georgia)

For practitioners in Alabama, Florida and Georgia, the U.S. Eleventh Circuit Court of Appeals has created a very high burden for union members

---

[144] *Marquez v. Screen Actors Guild, Inc.*, 525 U.S. 33, 119 S.Ct. 292 (1998).

[145] Id.

[146] *Breininger v. Sheet Metal Workers Intern. Ass'n Local Union No. 6*, 493 U.S. 67, 110 S.Ct. 424 (1989).

to overcome in order to prove that the union breached its duty of fair representation. But this high burden is in line with established Supreme Court jurisprudence and is fairly uniformly reflected across other federal circuits.

In the case of *Parker v. Connors Steel Co.*[147], the court ruled that the law differentiates between (a) negotiating a collective bargaining agreement and (b) administering a collective bargaining agreement, saying "[n]ature of duty of fair representation which union owes its members is determined by considering context in which duty is asserted, and thus, duty of fair representation in context of negotiations may be determined by different standard than is duty owed in processing of grievances or ratification of concession agreements...." With respect to the duty of fair representation involving negotiating a collective bargaining agreement, the *Parker* court held that "[v]iolation of union's duty of fair representation in context of negotiations with company is established if union's conduct in negotiations is arbitrary, irrational, or undertaken in bad faith...." In other words, the labor union must do something that is on the verge of criminal activity, such as bribery; or the labor union must do something that is obviously discriminatory, such as expressly discriminating against a group of employees because of race (see, e.g. *Steele v. Louisville & N.R. Co*, supra), in order to violate the duty of fair representation with respect to collective bargaining. The *Parker* court went on to conclude that a "[c]ompany's duty to bargain in good faith with an employer does not require it to enter collective bargaining agreement that it finds unacceptable."

Again, as previously mentioned, employees, union officials and attorneys should pay careful attention to the form or type of "breach of duty of fair representation" claim that they will be filing. Some of these claims should go through the U.S. Equal Employment Opportunity Commission, which enforces different statutes of limitations (deadlines) periods. However, most "breach of duty of fair representation" claims will be governed by the National Labor Relations Act or the Taft-Hartley Act of 1947. These federal statutes generally require that ULP chargers or lawsuits must be filed within six-months from the date of the discriminatory act. See, e.g., *Erkins v. United Steelworkers of America, AFL-CIO-CLC*,[148] holding that "[i]n suit for breach of collective bargaining agreement, state contract

---

[147] *Parker v. Connors Steel Co.*, 855 F.2d 1510 (11th Cir. 1988).

[148] *Erkins v. United Steelworkers of America, AFL-CIO-CLC*, 723 F.2d 837 (11th Cir. 1984).

law provides applicable limitations period.... Union members' class action against union for its alleged breach of duty of fair representation was subject to six-month statute of limitations established in National Labor Relations Act, and thus, as members admitted that they discovered facts constituting evidence of alleged fraud and breach of duty more than six months prior to bringing of suit, action was time barred.")

Most breach of duty of fair representation claims stem from allegations by union members that the union did not fairly represent them in their grievance hearings. In order to successfully prosecute such a claim, the employee must have very strong evidence that the union acted with flagrant disregard to his or her rights under the grievance processes and procedures. For example, in *Harris v. Schwerman Trucking Co.*[149], the court held that a labor union will be given the benefit of the doubt in most circumstances; its good-faith judgments as to how to tactically approach a grievance hearing will not be second-guessed by the courts or the NLRB; it is, furthermore, "allowed considerable latitude in its representation of employees; the grievance and arbitration process is not conducted in a judicial forum and union representatives are not held to strict standards of trial advocacy and neither negligence on part of union nor a mistake in judgment is sufficient to support a claim that union acted in an arbitrary and perfunctory manner."[150]

As an example of the wide latitude given to unions in the conduct of their duty to fairly represent employees, see the case of *Higdon v. United Steelworkers of America, AFL-CIO-CLC*,[151] where the court explained:

> Union did not breach its duty of fair representation by failing to investigate argument between employee and customer since employee was discharged for insubordination and failure to follow instructions to submit a report concerning the incident, and not for his role in the argument.... Union did not breach its duty of fair representation simply by allegedly failing to give grievant employee notice of, and opportunity to attend, a segment of his grievance process.... Negligence does not constitute a breach of duty of fair representation.... Evidence did not support employee's

---

[149] *Harris v. Schwerman Trucking Co.*, 668 F.2d 1204 (11th Cir. 1982).

[150] Ibid

[151] *Higdon v. United Steelworkers of America, AFL-CIO-CLC*, 706 F.2d 1561 (11th Cir. 1983).

allegation that union acted discriminatorily or in bad faith while handling his grievance in which it chose not to proceed to final step of arbitration."[152]

§ 7.05 U.S. Fifth Circuit (Louisiana, Mississippi, and Texas)

The U.S. Fifth Circuit has adopted a definition of the union's duty of fair representation that reflects the U.S. Supreme Court's holding in *Vaca v. Sipes*, supra. See, e.g., *Grovner v. Georgia-Pacific Corp.*,[153] holding that "[t]o prevail on claim that union breached its duty of fair representation, discharged employee must demonstrate that union's conduct was arbitrary, discriminatory or in bad faith or that union discharged its duties in a perfunctory manner."

The wide latitude which the U.S. Eleventh Circuit gives to unions in discharging their duty of fair representation has also been recognized in the U.S. Fifth Circuit. See, e.g., the case of *Turner v. Air Transport Dispatchers' Ass'n*,[154] where the court explained that the union's duty of fair representation "does not confer an absolute right on an employee to have his complaint carried through all stages of the grievance procedure."[155] Further, the *Turner* court held that when a union discharges its duty to fair representation, it maintains a "nonarbitrary discretionary power to settle, abandon, or fail to file a grievance, even if it can be later demonstrated that the employee's claim was meritorious."[156] However, at a minimum, the union must take certain preliminary steps in order discharge its duty of fair representation when representing an employee, such as the duty to fairly "investigate and to ascertain the merit of employee's grievances."[157] This duty to investigate means that the union must fairly gather together all of the relevant facts pertaining to a grievance.[158] The failure to properly

---

[152] Ibid.

[153] *Grovner v. Georgia-Pacific Corp.*, 625 F.2d 1289 (5th Cir. 1980).

[154] *Turner v. Air Transport Dispatchers' Ass'n*, 468 F.2d 297 (5th Cir. 1972).

[155] Ibid.

[156] Ibid.

[157] Ibid.

[158] Ibid.

investigate a grievance is certainly a "text-book" example of a breach of the union's duty of fair representation.[159]

However, after a labor union discharges its obligation to collect the facts, it is not obligated to adopt the aggrieved employee's interpretation of those facts. Nor is it required to agree with aggrieved employee's position; the mere failure to agree with the employee as to the possible outcome of a grievance does not constitute a breach of the duty of fair representation.[160] Similarly, the court in *Freeman v. O'Neal Steel, Inc.*,[161] held that "[i]t is within union's discretion to discontinue grievance procedure prior to selection of an arbitrator," meaning that the union is not obligated to adopt the viewpoints of the aggrieved union member and may discontinue the grievance whenever it deems discontinuance to be prudent."[162]

As previously mentioned, post-Civil Rights era (1970 to present) "racial discrimination" claims are almost always handled and resolved outside of the labor arenas, such as the National Labor Relations Board, and through state and federal anti-discrimination agencies such as the U.S. Equal Employment Opportunity Commission. Since there are essentially different forms of the "duty of fair representation," employers, union officials, and attorneys need to understand which form is more appropriate for their claims, particularly because various administrative or court forums have different statutes of limitations (filing deadlines) periods. In the Fifth Circuit, the court has specifically addressed this issue in the case of *Guerra v. Manchester Terminal Corp.*,[163] the court explained that an aggrieved employee who files a union grievance pursuant to a collective bargaining agreement, or an unfair labor practice charge before the National Labor Relations Board, may still simultaneously purse a civil rights claim, pursuant to Title VII of the 1964 Civil Rights Act, before the U.S. Equal Employment Opportunity Commission.[164] In *Guerra*, the court stated: "[a] plaintiff does not lose his rights to an adjudication regarding causes of action created by

---

[159] Ibid., but see, also, *Freeman v. O'Neal Steel, Inc.*, 609 F.2d 1123 (5th Cir. 1980)(holding that a union's discretion "is not boundless and is confined by duty to investigate grievance and determine its merit.").

[160] Ibid.

[161] *Freeman v. O'Neal Steel, Inc.*, 609 F.2d 1123 (5th Cir. 1980).

[162] Ibid.

[163] *Guerra v. Manchester Terminal Corp.*, 498 F.2d 641 (5th Cir. 1974).

[164] Ibid.

Title VII of the Civil Rights Act of 1964 or the Civil Rights Act of 1866 simply because the conduct of which he complains also is an unfair labor practice.... Employment discrimination may be prosecuted simultaneously in the courts and before the National Labor Relations Board. National Labor Relations Act, § 8 as amended...."[165]

§ 7.06 Other U.S. Circuits—Further Developments

Finally, I would encourage attorneys to borrow from other federal circuit courts when defining the union's duty of fair representation, because oftentimes these other circuits have given more clarity to the same definitions and terms which the U.S. Supreme Court has officially embraced.

For example, the U.S. Sixth Circuit (Kentucky, Tennessee, Michigan), has addressed the definition of "duty of fair representation" by distinguishing it from terms such as "fraud" and "bad faith." In the case of *Farmer v. ARA Services, Inc.*,[166] the court held that "bad faith or fraud" need not be proven in order to establish that a union did not discharge its duty of fair representation.[167] Instead, the only evidence that is needed to prove "breach" is evidence showing that the union's actions were "otherwise arbitrary or perfunctory" and "something more than negligence."

The U.S. Seventh Circuit (Illinois, Indiana, Wisconsin) has addressed the issue of the union's breach of the duty of fair representation which violated Title VII of the 1964 Civil Rights Act, in the case of *Babrocky v.*

---

[165] Ibid.

[166] *Farmer v. ARA Services, Inc.*, 660 F.2d 1096 (6th Cir. 1981).

[167] Ibid.

Jewel Food Co.[168]; and also violated 42 U.S.C. § 1981, in the case of *Waters v. Wisconsin Steel Works of Intern Harvester Co.*[169]

The U.S. Eight Circuit (Arkansas, Iowa) has addressed the issue of whether a labor union's breach of its duty of fair representation also violated Title VII in the case of *Donnell v. General Motors Corp.*[170] And, similarly, the U.S. Tenth Circuit (Colorado, Kansas, Oklahoma, New Mexico) has addressed the same issue in the case of *York v. American Tel. & Tel. Co.*[171]

---

[168] *Babrocky v. Jewel Food Co.*, 773 F.2d 857 (7th Cir. 1985)("Establishing a prima facie Title VII claim against a union based on a breach of duty of fair representation requires union members to show that employer violated collective bargaining agreement with respect to union members, that union permitted the breach to go unrepaired, thus breaching its own duty of fair representation, and some indication that union's actions were motivated by discriminatory animus.... Allegations that union joined in employer's maintenance of sex-segregated job category through its operation of its hiring hall and its acquiescence in instituting the 1:4 ratio of male meat cutters to female meat wrappers which employer allegedly relied on to justify laying off only women were sufficient to establish a prima facie case of Title VII discrimination against union.")

[169] *Waters v. Wisconsin Steel Works of Intern Harvester Co.*, 502 F.2d 1309 (7th Cir. 1974) ("Worker complaining that his right to enter into employment contract with company on same basis as whites was impaired by joint action of the union and company had standing to sue under 1866 civil rights statute though he was nonmember of union.... In fashioning substantive body of law under 1866 civil rights statute, courts should, in effort to avoid undesirable substantive law conflicts, look to principles of law created under equal employment opportunity legislation for direction.")

[170] *Donnell v. General Motors Corp.*, 576 F.2d 1292 98th Cir. 1978)("In Title VII employment discrimination action brought on ground that employer and union had discriminated against plaintiff with respect to entry into skilled trades' training programs established by employer and union, plaintiff established prima facie case of racial discrimination on basis that educational requirements for the programs had a disparate impact on black employees at employer's plant.")

[171] *York v. American Tel. & Tel. Co.*, 95 F.3d 948 (10th Cir. 1996)("To establish a prima facie Title VII claim against union for breach of its duty of fair representation, plaintiff must show that: employer violated collective bargaining agreement with respect to plaintiff; union permitted violation to go unrepaired, thereby breaching union's duty of fair representation, and there was some indication that union's actions were motivated by discriminatory animus.... Union's statutory duty of fair representation does not oblige it to take action on every grievance brought by every member.")

§ 7.07 Human Resources and Strategic Risk Management

Under the Section 301 of the Taft-Hartley Act of 1947, an employee may sue both a labor union and an employer for breach of the collective bargaining agreement, whenever, if ever, the said labor union breaches its duty of fair representation. Importantly, human resources professionals need to understand the nature of this hybrid lawsuit; i.e., that an employer can be held *jointly liable* together with a labor union, even though the employer was not responsible for the labor union's reckless and arbitrary negligence. Furthermore, although human resources professionals generally have no duty to advise union officials, they should work closely with union officials to ensure that grievance procedures are conducted fairly and in accordance with the terms and procedures within the operative collective bargaining agreement.

Human resource professionals who work in a unionized environment should also thoroughly understand the collective bargaining agreement ("labor agreement"); the function of any operative grievance procedures within the labor agreement; the overlap between these grievance procedures and unfair labor practices charges before the National Labor Relations Board; and nature of other administrative charges of discrimination in federal agencies such as the U.S. Equal Employment Opportunity Commission, the U.S. Department of Labor, and the Occupational Safety and Health Administration. These federal agencies will often bear down upon the employer's human resources official and defense attorneys for the turn-over of important documents and to provide very detailed and specific responses to employee's charges of discrimination. Therefore, human resources professionals must be able to adequately investigate and address a variety of administrative charges within a variety of federal agencies that enforce various labor and employment laws.

§ 7.08 Conclusion

In a unionized workplace, the collective bargaining agreement is one of the most important legal documents within the organization. It exists primarily to benefit workers within the bargaining unit. For this reason, labor unions must ensure that they fairly and adequately represent these workers in order that all workers within the bargaining unit receive fair treatment and all of the benefits of labor agreement. The failure to adequately represent these workers could result in a "breach of contract" claim, whereby both the labor union and the employer could be held liable for damages to the aggrieved workers. In addition, grievances under a collective bargaining agreement may also include allegations that also implicate other state or federal laws, such as Title VII of the 1964 Civil Rights Act. Thus, most, if not all, of the issues contained in a union grievance could also be re-litigated in another forum, such as an unemployment compensation board, the U.S. Equal Employment Opportunity Commission, or the National Labor Relations Board. For this reason, human resources professionals in unionized working environments need to have versatile skill-sets that require the ability to manage labor-management relations.

Chapter Seven References

Books:

Ford, Roderick O. *Understanding Employment Law*. Tampa, FL: Xlibris Pub., 2017.

Gelhaus, Robert J. and James Oldham. *Labor Law*. Chicago, IL: The BarBri Group, 2002.

Gormon, Richard A. and Matthew W. Finkin. *Basic Text on Labor Law: Unionization and Collective Bargaining*. St. Paul, MN: West Publishing Co., 2004.

References:

45B Am Jur Second, Job Discrimination §§ 1048-1053.

48 Am Jur Second, Labor and Labor Relations §§ 1080-1090.

48A Am Jur Second, Labor and Labor Relations §§ 1273-1276.

51A Corpus Juris Secundum, Labor Relations §§ 734-773.

Case Law:

U.S. Supreme Court

Steele v. Louisville & N.R. Co., 323 U.S. 192, 65 S. Ct. 226, 89 L. Ed. 173 (1944)

Vaca v. Sipes, 386 U.S. 171, 87 S.Ct. 903 (1967)

Breininger v. Sheet Metal Workers Intern. Ass'n Local Union No. 6, 493 U.S. 67, 110 S.Ct. 424 (1989)

Marquez v. Screen Actors Guild, Inc., 525 U.S. 33, 119 S.Ct. 292 (1998)

U.S. Eleventh Circuit Court of Appeals (Alabama, Florida, Georgia)

Parker v. Connors Steel Co., 855 F.2d 1510 (11th Cir. 1988)

Erkins v. United Steelworkers of America, AFL-CIO-CLC, 723 F.2d 837 (11th Cir. 1984)

Harris v. Schwerman Trucking Co., 668 F.2d 1204 (11th Cir. 1982)

Higdon v. United Steelworkers of America, AFL-CIO-CLC, 706 F.2d 1561 (11th Cir. 1983)

U.S. Fifth Circuit Court of Appeals (Louisiana, Mississippi, Texas)

Turner v. Air Transport Dispatchers' Ass'n, 468 F.2d 297 (5th Cir. 1972)

Freeman v. O'Neal Steel, Inc., 609 F.2d 1123 (5th Cir. 1980)

Grovner v. Georgia-Pacific Corp., 625 F.2d 1289 (5th Cir. 1980)

Guerra v. Manchester Terminal Corp., 498 F.2d 641 (5th Cir. 1974)

U.S. Sixth Circuit Court of Appeals (Kentucky, Tennessee, Michigan)

Farmer v. ARA Services, Inc., 660 F.2d 1096 (6th Cir. 1981)

U.S. Seventh Circuit Court of Appeals (Illinois, Indiana, Wisconsin)

Babrocky v. Jewel Food Co., 773 F.2d 857 (7th Cir. 1985)

Waters v. Wisconsin Steel Works of Intern Harvester Co., 502 F.2d 1309 (7th Cir. 1974)

U.S. Eight Circuit Court of Appeals (Arkansas, Iowa)

Donnell v. General Motors Corp., 576 F.2d 1292 98th Cir. 1978)

U.S. Tenth Circuit Court of Appeals (Colorado, Kansas, Oklahoma, New Mexico)

York v. American Tel. & Tel. Co., 95 F.3d 948 (10th Cir. 1996)

Appendix A

DIRECTORY OF H.R. AND EMPLOYMENT LAW TRAINING CENTERS

For More Information:

Human Resources Certification and Employment Law Training Centers

American Law Institute (U.S.)
4025 Chestnut Street
Philadelphia, PA 19104

Chartered Institute of Personnel and Development (UK)
151 The Broadway
London SW19 1JQ

Cornell University (U.S.)
School of Industrial and Labor Relations
309 Ives Hall
Ithaca, New York 14853

Human Resources Certification Institute (U.S.)
1725 Duke Street
Suite 700
Alexandria, VA 22314

Human Resources Professional Association (Canada)
150 Bloor Street West,
Suite 200,
Toronto, Ontario, M5S 2X9

National Employment Lawyers Association (U.S.)
Employee Rights Advocates
2201 Broadway, Suite 310
Oakland, California 94612

Michigan State University (U.S.)
School of Human Resources and Labor Relations
S. Kedzie Hall
East Lansing, MI 48824

Society for Human Resources Management (U.S.)
1800 Duke Street
Suite 100
Alexandria, VA 22314

Appendix B

LABOR LAW DIGEST

LABOR LAW DIGEST
Table of Contents

Chapter One	269
Chapter Two	271
Chapter Three	276
Chapter Four	279
Chapter Five	285
Chapter Six	288
Chapter Seven	350

CHAPTER ONE (LABOR'S BILL OF RIGHTS: THE LANDRUM-GRIFFIN ACT OF 1959)

Case Law:

U.S. Supreme Court

Calhoun v. Harvey, 379 U.S. 134 (1964)("Labor-Management Reporting and Disclosure Act title, setting standards for eligibility and qualifications of candidates and officials and permitting individual members to file complaint with Secretary of Labor challenging validity of any election because of violations of such title, sets up exclusive method for protecting rights guaranteed thereby and disputes relating to eligibility of candidates for office are to be resolved by administrative and judicial procedure set out in that title... Complaint, alleging that union constitution and bylaws which permitted only self-nomination and restricted eligibility for office deprived union members of fair opportunity to nominate, alleged dispute to be resolved by administrative and judicial procedures set out in Title IV of Labor-Management Reporting and Disclosure Act and was insufficient to invoke jurisdiction of District Court under Title I. Labor-Management Reporting and Disclosure Act of 1959, §§ 101 et seq.")

United States v. Brown, 381 U.S. 437 (1965)("Term 'member of the Communist Party,' in statute making it crime for member to serve as officer or employee of labor union, was not merely convenient permissible shorthand term for list of characteristics of persons likely to incite political strikes, but was prohibited empirical judgment of particular group of men. Labor-Management Reporting and Disclosure Act of 1959, § 504....")

Wirtz v. Local Union No. 125, Laborers' International Union of North America AFL-CIO, 389 U.S. 477 (1968)("Where union member's protest challenged only runoff election of union officers and did not challenge general election but Secretary of Labor's investigation of protest revealed that the same unlawful conduct had probably occurred at earlier election, Secretary could challenge alleged violations as to both elections and was not limited to challenging runoff election. Labor-Management Reporting and Disclosure Act of 1959, §§ 401(e)....")

Trbovich v. UMW, 404 U.S. 528 (1972)("Provision of

Labor-Management Reporting and Disclosure Act of 1959 making suit by Secretary of Labor the 'exclusive' post-selection remedy for violation of Title IV prohibits union members from initiating a private suit to set aside an election. Labor-Management Reporting and Disclosure Act of 1959, §§ 402(b)".).

Hall v. Cole, 412 U.S. 1 (1973) ("Successful action by union member under LMRD Act, challenging his expulsion as violation to right of free speech, granted substantial service to union and its members by dispelling 'chill' on rights of others and contributing to preservation of union democracy, and court had power to shift costs of litigation to benefited class by awarding plaintiff attorneys' fees. Labor-Management Reporting and Disclosure Act of 1959, §§ 101(a)(1-5)....")

Local 3489, United Steel Workers v. Usery, 429 U.S. 305 (1977)("In enacting Labor-Management Reporting and Disclosure Act provisions as to elections, Congress was not concerned only with corrupt union leadership but with goal of free and democratic union elections as preventive measure to curb possibility of abuse by benevolent as well as malevolent entrenched leadership.... Union office eligibility rule was to be judged not by burden it imposed on individual candidate to qualify but by its effect on free and democratic processes of union government; procedures that unduly restrict free choice among candidates are forbidden without regard to their success or failure in maintaining corrupt leadership. Labor-Management Reporting and Disclosure Act of 1959, § 401(e)....")

Reed v. United Transportation Union, 488 U.S. 319 (1989)("Claims under section of LMRD Act prohibiting union from interfering with members' right to free speech as to union matters are governed by state general or residual personal injury statute of limitation.... Though section of LMRD Act prohibiting union from union member's free speech rights as to union matters creates personal rights, union member vindicates those rights also serves public goals, in that he necessarily renders a substantial service to his union as institution and to all of its members, contributing to improvement or preservation of democracy within the union. Labor-Management Reporting and Disclosure Act of 1959, § 101(a)(2)....")

CHAPTER TWO (LOCK-OUTS, STRIKES, PICKETING, BOYCOTTS)

Case Law:

U.S. Supreme Court

NLRB v. MacKay Radio & Telegraph Co., 304 U.S. 333 (1938) ("Where a strike was called because it was deemed 'advisable in view of the unsatisfactory state of the negotiations' for execution of a contract touching wages and terms and conditions of employment, there was an existing 'labor dispute' within National Labor Relations Act, notwithstanding there was no evidence that employer had been guilty of any unfair labor practice prior to the strike, since it was unnecessary for National Labor Relations Board to find what was in fact the state of negotiations when strike was called, or in so many words that labor dispute as defined by the act existed.... The wisdom of employees, their justification or lack of it, in attributing to employer an unreasonable or arbitrary attitude in connection with negotiations for execution of a contract touching wages and terms and conditions of employment cannot determine whether, when employees struck, they did so as a consequence of, or in connection with, a current 'labor dispute' within National Labor Relations Act.... If employees strike in connection with a current labor dispute, their action is not to be construed as a renunciation of employment relation, but they remain 'employees' for the remedial purposes specified in NLRA.... Under NLRA an employer is not bound to discharge those who were hired to fill places of strikers upon their election to resume their employment in order to create placed for them, and hence assurance by employer to those who accepted employment during strike, that if they so desired their places might be permanent, was not an 'unfair labor practice,' nor was it such to reinstate only so many of strikers as there were vacant places to be filled.")

Thornhill v. Alabama, 310 U.S. 88 (1940)("The freedom of speech and of the press which are secured by the First Amendment against abridgment by the United States are among the fundamental personal rights and liberties which are secured to all persons by the Fourteenth Amendment against abridgment by a state...the existence of a penal statute which sweeps within its ambit activities that in ordinary circumstances constitute an exercise of freedom of speech or of the press, and which readily lends itself to harsh and discriminatory enforcement by local prosecuting official against particular groups deemed to merit their displeasure, results in a continuous and pervasive restraint on all freedom of discussion that might reasonably be regarded as within its purview…. Where the range of activities proscribed by Alabama statute, whether characterized as picketing or loitering or otherwise, embraced nearly practicable, effective means whereby those interested, including the employees directly affected might enlighten the public of the nature and causes of a labor dispute, the danger of injury to an industrial concern is neither so serious nor so imminent as to justify such sweeping proscription of freedom of discussion.")

NLRB V. Fruit & Vegetable Packers & Warehousemen Local 760, 377 U.S. 58 (1964)("When consumer picketing is employed to persuade customers not to buy the struck product, such picketing does not constitute an unfair labor practice even if site of the appeal is expanded to include the premises of a secondary employer, but, if consumer picketing is employed to persuade customers not to trade at all with the secondary employer, the union does more than merely follow the struck product, and commits an unfair labor practice through creating a separate dispute with the secondary with the secondary employer…. A proscribed secondary boycott would not be established merely because union picketing confined to persuading customers to cease buying product of the primary employer was effective to reduce secondary employer's sales of product of primary employer, even if that led or might have led to secondary employer's dropping of the product as a poor seller.")

American Ship Building Co. v. NLRB, 380 U.S. 300 (1965)("The Supreme Court granted certiorari to resolve an asserted conflict among the circuits upon question whether an employer commits an unfair labor practice when he temporarily lays off or 'locks out' his employees during a labor dispute to bring economic pressure in support of his bargaining position…. Employer's use of temporary layoff of employees solely as a means to bring economic pressure to bear in support of employer's bargaining position, after an impasse had been reached, was not inconsistent with right to bargain collectively or with right to strike so that employer did not commit an unfair labor practice by such layoff.")

Textile Workers Union of America v. Darlington Manufacturing Co., 380 U.S. 263 (1965)("The United States Supreme Court granted certiorari to consider important questions under NLRA, relating to employer's right to close part or all of business.... So far as NLRA is concern, employer has absolute right to terminate his entire business for any reason he pleases, including antiunion motives, but such right does not include ability to close part of a business no matter what the reason... The bona fide complete liquidation of a business, yielding no future benefit for employer in labor relations, is not the type of discrimination prohibited by statute even if motivated more by spite against union than by business reasons.... In case of discriminatory partial closing of one plant which is part of a larger enterprise, as in case of 'runaway shop' and 'temporary closing' cases, NLRB may order reinstatement of discharged employees in other parts of the business.")

Trans World Airlines v. Flight Attendants, 489 U.S. 426 (1989) ("After strike ended, airline employer was not required by the NLRA or by the federal common law developed under the Act to displace flight attendants who worked during the strike in order to reinstate striking flight attendants with greater seniority.... After strike ended, airline employer was not required by the Railway Labor Act to displace flight attendants who worked during the strike in order to reinstate striking flight attendants with greater seniority; crossover policy, which created incentive for flight attendants either not to join or to abandon the strike, was an exercise of peaceful economic power which the airline was legally free to deploy once the Act's private dispute resolution mechanisms had been exhausted, and nothing in the collective bargaining agreement or any poststrike agreement between airline and union prohibited the crossover policy.")

U.S. Circuit Courts

Department & Specialty Store Employees' Union, Local 1265 v. Brown, 284 F.2d 619 (9th Cir. 1960), cert. denied, 366 U.S. 934 (1961) ("Under statute making certain types of recognitional picketing by labor organizations an unfair labor practice and authorizing National Labor Relations Board to secure injunction and call an expedited election, all that is required even as a preliminary to seeking injunction is that the Board have reasonable cause to believe that there has been a violation of Act.... Fact that picketing by union may have been informational and advisory to extent of being permissible under statute making it an unfair labor practice for labor organizations to engage in certain types of recognitional picketing was of no significance where picketing also had as one of its objects the forcing and requiring of employer to recognize it as a bargaining agent of employer's nonunion employees.")

Inter-Collegiate Press v. NLRB, 486 F.2d 837 (8th Cir. 1973)("Employer's hiring of temporary employees during lawful bargaining lockout was not 'inherently destructive' of employee's rights and was not violation of the NLRA, in view of fact that employer's conduct did not jeopardize union's position as bargaining agent and union did not suffer any diminution in its capacity to effectively represent employees in the bargaining unit.")

International Paper Co. v. NLRB, 115 F.3d 1045 (D.C. Cir. 1997) ("Employer did not commit unfair labor practice by implementing permanent subcontract for maintenance work during lawful lockout; contract was not inherently destructive of employee rights, and permitted employer to save $7.2 million per year over cost of continuing maintenance in house…. Employer did not commit unfair labor practice by failing to produce, to union, certain pages of cost study on its proposed permanent subcontract for maintenance work, where content of those pages was cumulative of information already produced.")

Great Western Broadcasting Corp., v. NLRB, 356 F.2d 434 (9th Cir.) ("Although radio station was engaged in advertising services as well as tangible articles, union activities to force others to cease advertising with station with which union had labor dispute was within the publicity proviso of statute excepting from the illegal secondary boycott provision publicity for purpose of truthfully advising public that a product or products are produced by employer with whom labor organization has a primary dispute and are distributed by another employer…. Publicity proviso of illegal secondary boycott statute is to be given as broad an application as the statutory prohibition against union activities to force another to cease using, selling or handling products of another particular person or to cease doing business with such person.")

National Labor Relations Board

International Woodworkers, Local Union 303, 144 NLRB 912 (1963) ("The complaint alleges that on various occasions subsequent to September 1962, Respondent, International Woodworkers of America, Local Union 3-3, AFL-CIO, had engaged in unfair labor practices within the meaning of Section 8(b)(1)(A) of the Act by various acts, including mass picketing, blocking access to the plant, damaging cars of nonstrikers, and inflicting physical injury upon nonstrikers with hot coffee and otherwise....CONCLUSION OF LAW... By restraining and coercing employees of Western Wirebound Box Co. in the exercise of the rights guaranteed by Section 7 of the Act, Respondent had engaged in unfair labor practices within the meaning of Section 8(b)(1)(A) of the Act.")

Johns-Manville Products Corp., 223 NLRB 1317 (1976)("By the discriminatory replacement of its entire complement of unit employees on April 8, 1974, Respondent in effect withdrew recognition of and undermined the objective and effectiveness of the Union as the duly elected collective-bargaining representative of its unit employees, in violation of Section 8(a)(5) of the Act.")

CHAPTER THREE (PROTECTED CONCERTED ACTIVITY)

Part A. It has long been settled that when an individual employee has been authorized to speak on behalf of another employee or employees, the individual's action is deemed concerted.[172]

Walter Brucker & Co., 273 N.L.R.B. 1306 (1984)("We agree with the judge that Wright's discussion with his fellow employees at lunch on 6 November about the applicable wage rate for performing corrective punch list work at the project was an effort to initiate and promote concerted action. As the judge noted, when Wright spoke to the Respondent and later to the Authority, he voiced a complaint about wages that Culbreath and he both shared. Wright was clearly acting 'on the authority of other employees.' Because the record shows that Culbreath refrained from making his own wage complaint, relying instead on Wright to resolve the matter.")

---

[172] Kenneth T. Lopatka, *NLRA Rights in the Nonunion Workplace* (Arlington, VA: BNA Books, 2010), p. 102

Cone Bros. Contracting Co., 125 N.L.R.B. 843 (1959)("The only issue here is whether the Company discriminatorily discharged Exum by reason of his union affiliation or because he engaged in concerted activities with other employees.... By discriminating in regard to the hire and tenure of employment of Gerald W. Exum, the Company has engaged in and is engaging in unfair labor practices within the meaning of Section 8(a)(3) and (1) of the Act.")

Smith Victory Co., 90 N.L.R.B. 2089 (1950)("By discriminating in regard to the hire of employment of Florence McMaster because she engaged in concerted activities with and on behalf of other employees for the purpose of collective bargaining and other mutual aid and protection, Respondent interfered with, coerced, and restrained its employees in the exercise of rights guaranteed by Section 7 of the Act, and Respondent has thereby engaged and is engaging in unfair labor practices within the meaning of Section 8(a)(3) of the Act.")

Part B. All that seems to be necessary to infer authorization is that more than one employee exhibit a concern about a particular aspect of their employment and decide that they want

it changed. When a single employee articulates that protest on behalf of the group, he or she will be found to have been implicitly authorized by his or her coworkers and thus to be acting concertedly.[173]

Eastex, Inc. v. NLRB, 437 U.S. 556 (1978)("National Labor Relations Act's definition of 'employee' was intended to protect employees when they engage in otherwise proper concerted activities in support of employees of employers other than their own, and it has long been held that 'mutual aid and protection' encompasses such activity.... Employees do not lose their protection under the 'mutual aid or protection' clause of the National Labor Relations Act when they seek to improve terms and conditions of employment or otherwise improve their lot as employees through channels outside the immediate employee-employer relationship National Labor Relations Act, §§ 2(3).")

Barnsider, Inc., 195 N.L.R.B. 754 (1972)("By discharging James P. Walsh on April 27, 1971, because of his concerted activities in protesting certain policies of the Respondent relating to working conditions, the Respondent engaged in unfair labor practices within the meaning of Section 8(a)(1) of the Act.... By failing and refusing on April 29, 1971, and thereafter until May 6, 1971, to honor the unconditional request of its employees named in footnote 1, above, to return to work, thereby locking out and discriminating against said employees because they had engaged in concerted activities for the purpose of collective bargaining and other mutual aid and protection, the Respondent engaged in unfair labor practices within the meaning of Section 8(a)(1) and (3) of the Act.")

Hugh H. Wilson Corp., 171 N.L.R.B. 1040 (1968)("By interfering with, restraining, or coercing its employees in the exercise of rights guaranteed in Section 7 of the Act, Respondent has engaged in and is engaging in unfair labor practices within the meaning of Section 8(a)(1) of the Act.... Said unfair labor practices affect commerce within the meaning of Section 2(6) and (7) of the Act.")

Guernsey-Muskingum Elec. Co-op., 124 N.L.R.B. 618 (1959)("By discharging James Richard (Dick) Boyer, thus discriminating in regard to his hire and tenure of employment because he had engaged in protected concerted activities for the purposes of collective bargaining or other mutual aid and protection, the

---

[173] Ibid.

Respondent had engaged in and is engaging in unfair labor practices within the meaning of Section 8(a)(3) and (1) of the Act.... By interfering with, restraining, and coercing its employees in the exercise of the rights guaranteed in Section 7 of the Act, the Respondent has committed unfair labor practices within the meaning of Section 8(a)(1) of the Act.")

CHAPTER FOUR (COLLECTIVE BARGAINING)

U.S. Supreme Court

J.I. Case Co. v. NLRB, 321 U.S. 332 (1944)("Individual contracts between employer and employees, regardless of circumstances justifying their execution and regardless of their terms, may not be used by employer to defeat or delay procedure prescribed by National Labor Relations Act looking to collective bargaining, nor to exclude a contracting employee from a duty ascertained bargaining unit, nor to forestall bargaining or to limit terms of collective agreement.")

Order of Railroad Telegraphers v. Railway Express Agency, Inc., 321 U.S. 342 (1944)("'Collective bargaining', though not defined in Railway Labor Act, generally has been considered to absorb and give statutory approval to philosophy of bargaining as worked out in the labor movement in United States, and to include right of representatives of employees' units to be consulted and to bargain upon the exceptional as well as the routine rates, rules, and working conditions.")

Brooks v. NLRB, 348 U.S. 96 (1954)("If employer has doubts about his duty to continue bargaining on ground that employees have deserted their certified union, it is his responsibility to petition National Labor Relations Board for relief, while continuing to bargain in good faith at least until Board has given some indication that his claim has merit.")

NLRB v. Truitt Manufacturing Co., 351 U.S. 149 (1956)("Under circumstances of the case, record on certiorari, including evidence that employer refused to furnish financial information while claiming economic inability to pay increased wages, supported National Labor Relations Board's finding of employer's refusal to bargain in good faith.")

John Wiley & Sons, Inc. v. Livingston, 376 U.S. 543 (1964) ("Corporate employer was required to arbitrate with union under collective bargaining agreement between union and another corporation which had merged with and disappeared into corporate employer, where business entity had remained the same, there was wholesale transfer of the merged employer's employees to corporate employer's plant without difficulty and union had made its position known well before merger and never had departed from it.")

NLRB v. Gissel Packing Co., 395 U.S. 575 (1969)("Union is not limited to **NRLB** election to obtain recognition as exclusive bargaining representative of unorganized employees and can establish majority status by possession of cards signed by majority of employees authorizing union to represent them…. Employer has duty to bargain whenever union representative presents convincing evidence of support of majority of employees.")

H.K. Porter Co. v. NLRB, 397 U.S. 99 (1970)("**NLRB** has power under **NLRA** to require employers and employees to negotiate, but is without power to compel company or union to agree to any substantive contractual provision of collective-bargaining agreement.")

NLRB v. Burns International Security Services, Inc., 406 U.S. 272 (1972)("Where an employer remains the same, a certification of bargaining unit by the **NLRB** carries with it an almost conclusive presumption that the majority representative status of the union continues for reasonable time, usually one year; after this period, there is rebuttable presumption of majority representation…. If there is change of employers and almost complete turnover of employees, certification of bargaining representative by National Labor Relations Board may not bar challenge if the successor employer is not bound by the collective bargaining contract, particularly if the new employees are represented by another union or if the old unit is ruled an accretion to another unit.")

Golden State Bottling Co. v. NLRB, 414 U.S. 168 (1973)("**NLRB** order requiring a bona fide successor to reinstate with backpay an employee illegally discharged by predecessor because of union activities, but not requiring the successor to cease and desist, struck an equitable balance among the competing interests of the successor, the public, and the employee, taking into consideration the avoidance of labor strife, prevention of a deterrent effect of the exercise of rights guaranteed to employees, and protection for the victimized employee, together with the relatively minimal cost to the bona fide successor.")

Emporium Capwell Co. v. Western Addition Community Organization, 420 U.S. 50 (1975)("Intendent of collective bargaining agreement provision allowing individual employee or group of employees to present grievances to employer without intervention of bargaining representative as long as the adjustment is not inconsistent with terms of agreement was to permit employees to present grievances and to authorize employer to entertain them without opening itself to liability for dealing directly with employees, but NLRA did not protect this right by making it an unfair labor practice for employer to refuse to entertain such a presentation and did not authorize resort to economic coercion on such employer's refusal.")

Nolde Bros., Inc. v. Local No. 358, Bakery & Confectionary Workers Union, 430 U.S. 243 (1977)("Where union exercised its right to terminate collective bargaining agreement which provided for severance pay for employees and required arbitration of any 'grievance' arising between parties, and employer thereafter closed its plant, issue whether employees were entitled to severance pay after plant's closure was one arising under collective bargaining agreement and was subject to arbitration even though it arose only after agreement had been terminated.")

Detroit Edison Co. v. NLRB, 440 U.S. 301 (1979)("Employer did not commit unfair labor practice when it refused to disclose, without written consent from individual employees, aptitude test scores linked with employee names, in light of sensitive nature of testing information, minimal burden placed on union, and absence of evidence that employer had fabricated concern for employee confidentially only to frustrate union in discharge of its responsibilities.")

NLRB v. Bildisco & Bildisco, 465 U.S. 513 (1984)("A collective bargaining agreement subject to the NLRA is an 'executory contract' subject to rejection by a debtor in possession.... A bankruptcy court should permit rejection of a collective-bargaining agreement by a debtor in possession if the debtor can show that the collective-bargaining agreement burdens the estate, and that after careful scrutiny, the equities in favor of rejecting the labor contract; however, before acting on petition to modify or reject a collective-bargaining agreement, bankruptcy court should be persuaded that reasonable efforts to negotiate a voluntary modification have been made and are not likely to produce a prompt and satisfactory solution.")

Fall River Dyeing & Finishing Corp. v. NLRB, 482 U.S. 27 (1987) ("'Successor' employer's obligation to bargain with union representing its predecessor's employees is not limited to situation where union in question only recently was certified before transition in employers; when union certified for more than one year has rebuttable presumption of majority status, that status continues despite change in employers, and new employer has obligation to bargain with union so long as new employer is in fact successor of old employer and majority of its employees were employed by its predecessor.")

National Labor Relations Board

Mar-Jac Poultry Co., 136 N.L.R.B. 785 (1962)("In the case before us the employer has bargained with the certified union for only 6 months. It has, largely through its refusal to bargain, taken from the Union a substantial part of the period when Unions are generally at their greatest strength—the 1-year period immediately following the certification. Thus to permit the Employer now to obtain an election would be to allow it to take advantage of its own failure to carry out its statutory obligation, contrary to the very reasons for the establishment of the rule that a certification requires bargaining for at least 1 year. We shall, therefore, in this case and in future cases revealing similar inequities, grant the Union a period of at least 1 year of actual bargaining from the date of the settlement agreement.").

Perfect Service Gas Co., 146 N.L.R.B. 1686 (1964)("The Refusal to Bargain... I find no violation with respect to the two specific issues cited by General Counsel as violative of Section 8(a)(5), namely, the refusal to incorporate the profit-sharing and hospitalization plans into the contract.")

Gopher Aviation, Inc., 160 N.L.R.B. 1698 (1966)("The Respondent unreasonably delayed commencing negotiations…. The Respondent also unduly protracted the negotiations after they commenced in January 1965.")

American Sink Top & Cabinet Co., 242 N.L.R.B. 408 (1979)(NLRB affirmed "complaint [which] alleges in substance that, on February 3, 1978, Respondent encouraged and induced its employees to sign a petition seeking the Union's decertification as their bargaining representative, thereby violating Section 8(a)(1); and that one of its agents interrogated an employee about the Union on April 11, 1978, further violating Section 8(a)(1). The complaint also alleges that, in July 1978, Respondent unilaterally eliminated the grievance procedure established by a recently expired bargaining contract between it and the Union, thereby violating Section 8(a)(5) and (1).

Columbus Products, 259 N.L.R.B. 220 (1981)("Respondent does not have to provide the Union with information it does not need to process a grievance through arbitration…. Therefore, it is my view as the Union has access to all of the information it needs to process the grievance through arbitration it is not incumbent upon Respondent to disclose the names of witnesses which it specifically has indicated it does not intend to call in the arbitration proceedings.")

Colgate-Palmolive Co., 261 N.L.R.B. 90 (1982)("The well-established proposition that an employer's obligation under the Act to furnish a collective-bargaining agent with requested information is limited only to the extent that the information requested must be potentially relevant to the Union's performance of its responsibilities on behalf of unit employees.")

Borden Chemical Co., 261 N.L.R.B. 64 (1982)("The statutory duty of employers to provide relevant information, requested by the collective-bargaining representatives of their employees, has long been recognized.... Therein, this Board noted that interchanged concepts-coupled with the communication of facts peculiarly within the knowledge of either party—constitutes the essence of the bargaining process. Thus, the general obligation of concerned employers to provide requested information, which a collective-bargaining representative may require for the proper performance of its duties, can no longer be questioned.")

Gourmet Foods, Inc., 270 N.L.R.B. 1105 (1984)("Here, as we have seen, Respondent's purpose in pursuing its discipline against the 27 members was clear and straightforward—to retaliate against those members who refused to join Respondent in its unprotected strike in violation of the collective-bargaining agreement.")

Service Electric Co., 281 N.L.R.B. 633 (1986)("In sum, though the Union had given notice that the strike was ended, between August 12 and September 30 none of the strikers offered to return to work, the Union never explained why none of them were offering to return, and there is no evidence that any of them, either personally or through their representative, had abandoned interest in continued employment with Respondent. But for the hiring of replacements, the continued withholding by the strikers of their services would have continued to interfere with Respondent's production to the same degree after August 12 as had been the fact during the almost 14-month period prior to that date—a period during which the General Counsel concedes that a strike had been occurring and one during which there had been no difference in the conduct of the striking employees... Inasmuch as the General Counsel concedes that there was no bargaining obligation for replacements' employment terms during the strike and since

I conclude that a preponderance of the evidence does not support the conclusion that the strike had been terminated solely by virtue of the Union's August 12 letter, it follows that there is no basis for concluding that Respondent had violated the Act by refusing, after August 12, the Union's demand that employment terms for replacements be restored to the levels prevailing prior to commencement of the strike on June 14, 1982.")

Alwin Manufacturing Co., 326 NLRB No. 63 (1998)[holding in *Alwin Mfg. Co., Inc. v. N.L.R.B.*, 192 F.3d 133 ("Evidence supported National Labor Relations Board's (NLRB) finding that employer's unilateral, and unlawful, implementation of production standards was a motivating factor for strike, thus supporting finding that strike was unfair labor practices strike, so that company violated NLRA by replacing striking workers and otherwise treating them as economic strikers; production standards, initially implemented prior to expiration of union contract, were one of the core issues in negotiations, and striking worker told local newspaper that one reason for the strike was that employer was discharging workers for failing to meet performance standards.")

CHAPTER FIVE (ADMINISTRATION OF THE COLLECTIVE BARGAINING AGREEMENT)

U.S. Supreme Court

Vaca v. Sipes, 386 U.S. 171 (1967) (In general, a union breaches its duty of fair representation whenever, if ever, its conduct is "arbitrary, discriminatory, or in bad faith.")

NLRB v. Weingarten, Inc., 420 U.S. 251 (1975)(The United States Supreme Court has held that a union member is required to have a union official present if the said union member is questioned by a supervisor or manager, with the objective of determining whether a rule violation has occurred, whereby the said union member might be disciplined.).

Hines v. Anchor Motor Freight, Inc., 424 U.S. 554 (1976)(If the union 'arbitrarily' refuses to press an employee's grievance under the procedures outlined in the agreement, or otherwise fails to represent her fairly, the employee may then bring suit against the employer to enforce the collective bargaining agreement—on the theory that, as a member of the bargaining unit, she is a third-party beneficiary of the agreement…— individual employee could sue because union had 'arbitrarily' failed to take the case to arbitration.)

United Paperworkers International Union v. Misco, 484 U.S. 29 (1987) (Great deference is to be given to labor arbitration decisions. Federal appellate courts must refrain from reexamining the merits of labor arbitration decisions.)

American Labor Arbitration Reports

Douglas *Aircraft Co., Inc.*, 1 LA 350 (June 30, 1945)("Issues: I Discharge of Ode Luckett… which union claimed was unjust and asks reinstatement without loss of seniority and payment for fine lost….II Discharge of Kenneth Gardner… which union claimed was unjust and ask reinstatement without loss of seniority and payment…." Summary of Awards: Reinstatement of both Luckett and Garner, with full seniority).

Douglas Aircraft Co., Inc., 3 LA 598 (June 7, 1946)(Issue "— Discharge for repeated violations of plan rule…. Award. John V. Manning shall be reinstated as an employee of the Douglas Aircraft Company, Inc., with full seniority as of March 1, 1946, the date of his discharge, and shall be paid for time lost in the period between March

18 and March 28, 1946, less any monies earned or received from California state unemployment insurance during that period.").

Joy MFG Co., 6 LA 430 (July 31, 1946)("It ruled that the subject employee was improperly discharged, that he shall 'be reinstated without 'loss of seniority; and that he shall be reimbursed for all monies lost as a result of the discharge.");

United States Spring & Bumper Co., 5 LA 109 (October 4, 1946) ("Employees who were discharged for alleged participation in dice •game in violation of rule forbidding gambling on premises should be reinstated with back pay and restoration of all employment rights. Employees should. however, receive written reprimand which shall be entered into their personnel records. Discharge penalty was too severe under circumstances since (I) there is no evidence that all employees who were discharged actually participated in gambling, (2) other participants were not disciplined, (3) rule had not previously been enforced, (4) there is no substantial evidence that employees were familiar with plant rule though it was posted and is part of employee manual, (5) discharge was not known to be penalty for violation of ride, (6) employees were not warned before discharge, and (7) employees were skilled workers with considerable seniority who never received previous warning for violation of any plant rule.")

Chrysler Corp., 5 LA 420 (October 17, 1946)("Employees who obeyed spirit of recently announced company rule against abuse of washup period privilege but technically violated one detail of rule may not be punished for such violation where evidence indicates that violation was result of their not having been adequately informed of details of rule.")

Norwich Pharmacal Co., 5 LA 536 (December 10, 1946)("Employer may hot levy discipline: Against an employee for committing aMact which is not wrong per se and which has been previously condoned unless it has been made known to the employees in unequivocal language ...that such shall be regarded as contrary to company rules");

WLEU Broadcasting Co., 7 LA 150 (March 6, 1947)("Under contract which permits employer to discharge for just cause but requires employer to give employees reasonable warning before discharge, discharge is excessive penalty for first rule violation or first insubordinate act of an employee since discharge is not normally imposed for first offense of such character and contract reference to "warning" clearly implies that offenses should be followed by Warning or by disciplinary measure, which is less severe than discharge. Appropriate penalty for employee who was first offender on both counts is two-week suspension.")

Alan Wood Steel Co., 3 LA 557 (June 15, 1947)("Five-day layoff should not have been imposed where employee, although he repeatedly violated plant rule, had never been warned or reprimanded: therefore and (2) repeated breach of same rule by other employees had established a practice which employees may have been justified in believing proper inasmuch as employer had in past failed to enforce rule. Employee is awarded back pay for time off.")

Allis-Chalmers MFG Co., 8 LA 177 (June 24, 1947)("Employee who was given disciplinary layoff for violating plant rule prohibiting employees from selecting. their own work materials without foreman's permission was disciplined without "cause" in violation of contract, despite fact that employee picked wrong material by mistake and caused spoilage, since employer condoned violation of rule over long period of time and never warned employee against selection of his own work materials. Employer may not condone practice for long time and impose discipline only when some loss results to company.")

Enterprise Wire Co. and Enterprise Independent Union (46 LA 359, 1966) ("Daugherty's seven tests are as follows:

- Was the employee forewarned of the consequences of his or her actions?
- Are the employer's rules reasonably related to business efficiency and performance the employer might reasonably expect from the employee?
- Was an effort made before discipline or discharge to determine whether the employee was guilty as charged?
- Was the investigation conducted fairly and objectively?
- Did the employer obtain substantial evidence of the employee's guilt?
- Were the rules applied fairly and without discrimination?
- Was the degree of discipline reasonably related to the seriousness of the employee's offense and the employee's past record?

CHAPTER SIX (THE CBA AND FEDERAL ANTIDISCRIMINATION LAWS)

Failure to Promote

U.S. Eleventh Circuit Court of Appeals (Alabama, Florida, Georgia)

Wilson v. B/E Aerospace, Inc, 376 F.3d 1079 (11th Cir. 2004)("Under the McDonnell Douglas framework, to prevail on a Title VII failure to promote claim, an employee may establish a prima facie case of sex discrimination by showing that: (1) she is a member of a protected class, (2) she was qualified and applied for the promotion, (3) she was rejected despite her qualifications, and (4) other equally or less qualified employees who were not members of the protected class were promoted.")

Combs v. Plantation Patterns, 106 F.3d 1519 (11th Cir. 1997) ("To establish prima facie case of discriminatory failure to promote, plaintiff must prove that he is a member of protected class, that he was qualified for and applied for promotion, that he was rejected, and that other equally or less qualified employees who were not members of protected class were promoted....

By meeting its burden of producing legitimate reasons for its decision to promote another candidate rather than black employee to welding supervisor position, former employer successfully eliminated presumption of discrimination that initially accomplished black employee's prima facie case under Title VII, where employer proffered evidence in support of three legitimate, nondiscriminatory reasons for its promotion decision, including other candidate's superior welding experience and superior supervisory experience, and recommendations of supervisors.")

Denney v. City of Albany, 247 F.3d 1172 (11th Cir. 2001)("Under the rubric of McDonnell Douglas, to establish a prima facie case of discriminatory failure to promote, Title VII plaintiff must prove: (1) that plaintiff is a member of a protected class, (2) that plaintiff was qualified for and applied for the promotion, (3) that plaintiff was rejected, and (4) that other equally or less qualified employees who were not members of the protected class were promoted."

Stuart v. Jefferson County Dept. of Human Resources, 152 Fed.Appx. 798 (11th Cir. 2005)("Employee failed to establish that employer's reason for not selecting him for a promotional position, that the female chosen for the position had more experience for the position, was a pretext for gender discrimination under Title VII; he failed to offer any evidence that he was more qualified than the female."

Walker v. Mortham, 158 F.3d 1177 (11th Cir. 1998)("In order to establish prima facie case of discrimination under Title VII using the McDonnell Douglas framework, an employee or job applicant need not identify the successful applicant for his or her coveted position, but need only establish that such applicant is not within her protected class.")

Brown v. Alabama Dept. of Transp. 597 F.3d 1160 (11th Cir. 2010) ("The plaintiff bears the burden of establishing a prima facie case of discrimination in Title VII cases that are supported by circumstantial evidence.... In the failure-to-promote context, a prima facie Title VII case consists of showing these elements: (1) that the plaintiff belongs to a protected class; (2) that she applied for and was qualified for a promotion; (3) that she was rejected despite her qualifications; and (4) that other equally or less-qualified employees outside her class were promoted.")

Price v. M & H Valve Co., 177 Fed.Appx. 1 (11th Cir. 2006) ("Employee establishes prima facie case of discriminatory failure to promote by showing that (1) he is a member of a protected class, (2) he was qualified and applied for the promotion, (3) he was rejected despite his qualifications, and (4) other equally or less qualified employees who were not members of the protected class were promoted."

Vessels v. Atlanta Independent School System, 408 F.3d 763 (11th Cir. 2005) ("Where an employer does not formally announce a position, but rather uses informal and subjective procedures to identify a candidate, a plaintiff, in order to establish a prima facie case of discrimination under McDonnell Douglas framework, need not show that he applied for the position, only that the employer had some reason to consider him for the post.... To demonstrate that he was qualified for the position, a Title VII plaintiff seeking to establish prima facie failure to promote claim need only show that he or she satisfied an employer's objectively verifiable qualifications; employer may then introduce its subjective evaluations of the plaintiff at the later stages of the *McDonnell Douglas* framework.")

Williams v. Waste Management, Inc., 411 Fed.Appx. 226 (11th Cir. 2011)("African-American employee's failure to apply for open position precluded recovery on his failure to promote claim, given absence of any evidence that employer had engaged in systematic discrimination that had successfully deterred job applications from members of minority groups.... Two-month gap between African-American employee's complaints about racially derogatory comments and employer's failure to promote him was not enough to establish a prima face case of retaliation under Title VII or § 1981.")

Connor v. Lafarge North America, Inc., 343 Fed.Appx. 537 (11th Cir. 2009)("Employer's legitimate, nondiscriminatory reason for failure to promote African-American employee, that he performed poorly in interviews for that position, specifically in portions of interview dealing with crucial areas of leadership, decision-making, safety, and computer skills, was not pretext for race discrimination in violation of Title VII, although person hired for position did not have listed qualifications for 'minimum of 2 years cement plant or terminal operating experience' and 'supervisory experience' and employee did; employer declared all internal candidates qualified by virtue of their being internal candidates and based promotion decision on interviews alone, there was no evidence that employer had ever filled supervisory positions using any method other than exclusive reliance on interviews, and employee admitted that 4 of 5 panel members did not harbor racial animus toward him.")

Summerlin v. M & H Valve Co., 167 Fed.Appx. 93 (11th Cir. 2006) ("African-American male employee [did] not need to show that he was more qualified than the non-minority individual who received the promotion, in order to establish prima facie claim for racial failure-to-promote discrimination under Title VII.... Employer's proffered legitimate reason for promoting non-minority individual rather than African-American male employee to supervisory position, that the non-minority individual was more qualified and had more experience, was not pretext for race discrimination, as required to prove a Title VII racial failure-to-promote discrimination claim; non-minority individual had over 10 years experience, in contrast to employer's two months of experience, and non-minority individual had three years of supervisory experience in the business, and employee's only supervisory experience was outside of the business.")

U.S. Fifth Circuit Court of Appeals (Louisiana, Mississippi, Texas)

Davis v. Dallas Area Rapid Transit, 383 F.3d 309 (5th Cir. 2004)("Prima facie case of discrimination in

Title VII failure-to-promote case requires showing that: (1) employee is member of protected class; (2) he sought and was qualified for position; (3) he was rejected for position; and (4) employer continued to seek, or promoted, applicants with plaintiff's qualifications.")

Shackelford v. Deloitte & Touche, LLP, 190 F.3d 398 (5th Cir. 1999) ("A prima facie case is established under Title VII once the employee has proved that he or she: (1) is a member of a protected class; (2) was qualified for his or her position; (3) was subjected to an adverse employment action; and 4) was replaced by someone outside the protected class.")

Trevino v. Celanese Corp., 701 F.2d 397 (5th Cir. 1983)("Discriminatory failure to promote represents an actionable, continuing violation of Title VII.... For purposes of Title VII employment discrimination, an employee may be promoted, or denied promotion, from one to another nominally independent entity provided the two entities' activities, operations, ownership or management are sufficiently interrelated, and whether transfer from one work force to another constitutes a 'promotion' or a 'hiring' depends on the facts of each case.")

Race Discrimination

U.S. Eleventh Circuit Court of Appeals (Alabama, Florida, Georgia)

Equal Employment Opportunity Commission v. Catastrophe Management Solutions, 2016 WL 7210059 (11th Cir. 2016)("To prevail on disparate treatment claim, Title VII plaintiff must demonstrate that employer intentionally discriminated against her on basis of protected characteristic.... Disparate impact claim under Title VII does not require proof of discriminatory intent, but rather targets employment practice that has actual, though not necessarily deliberate, adverse impact on protected groups..... Title VII plaintiff can prove disparate treatment by direct evidence that workplace policy, practice, or decision relies expressly on protected characteristic, or by circumstantial evidence.... Meaning of word 'race' in Title VII is, like any other question of statutory interpretation, question of law for court.... When words are not defined in statute, they are interpreted as taking their ordinary, contemporary, common meaning.")

Crawford v. Carroll, 529 F.3d 961 (11th Cir. 2008)("To make out prima facie case of racial discrimination under Title VII or in § 1983 equal protection claim, plaintiff must show that: (1) she belongs to protected class; (2) she was qualified to do job; (3) she was subjected to adverse employment action; and (4) her employer treated similarly situated employees outside her class more favorably.... Prima facie case of retaliation under Title VII requires showing that: (1) employee engaged in activity protected under Title VII: (2) she suffered adverse employment action; and (3) there was causal connection between protected activity and adverse employment action.... In order to satisfy 'adverse employment action' element of Title VII discrimination action, employee must show either ultimate employment decision, i.e. termination, failure to hire, or demotion, or, for conduct falling short of ultimate employment decision, serious and material change in terms, conditions or privileges of employment.... Poor performance evaluation that directly results in denial of pay raise of any significance clearly affects employee's compensation and thus constitutes adverse employment action under Title VII.")

In re Birmingham Reverse Discrimination Employment Litigation, 20 F.3d 1525 (11th Cir. 1994) ("Employers may develop affirmative action plans designed to further Title VII's purpose of eliminating effects of discrimination in workplace.... In determining whether affirmative action plan was implemented consistent with Title VII's purpose and without unduly infringing interests of nonblacks, Court of Appeals was required to first determine whether employer's consideration of race of promotional candidates was justified by manifest racial imbalance that reflected underrepresentation of blacks in traditionally segregated job categories, and, if such justification was present when plan was developed, to determine whether plan itself provided proper remedy for that imbalance.... For purposes of challenge under Title VII to affirmative action plan, when job requires no special expertise, determining whether market imbalance exists that would justify race-conscious decision making by employer involves comparison of percentage of minority employees in that job with percentage of minorities in general labor market; however, when job requires special skills or training, appropriate comparison is to those in labor market who possess that special skill or training... For trial court to conclude that remedial action under Title VII is warranted, there must be sufficient evidence to allow it to make factual determination that employer had strong basis in evidence for its conclusion that remedial action was necessary.... Before city may settle Title VII litigation by consent decree, it is necessary that trial court make some finding that city engaged in past discrimination, in order to allow for proper judicial review of city's use of race in its affirmative action plan.")

Equal Employment Opportunity Commission v. Catastrophe Management Solutions, 2016 WL 7210059 (11th Cir. 2016)("To prevail on disparate treatment claim, Title VII plaintiff must demonstrate that employer intentionally discriminated against her on basis of protected characteristic.... Disparate impact claim under Title VII does not require proof of discriminatory intent, but rather targets employment practice that has actual, though not necessarily deliberate, adverse impact on protected groups.... Title VII plaintiff can prove disparate treatment by direct evidence that workplace policy, practice, or decision relies expressly on protected characteristic, or by circumstantial evidence.... One way to figure out meaning of word that is not defined in statute is by looking at dictionaries in existence around time of enactment.")

Standard v. A.B.E.L. Services, Inc., 161 F.3d 1318 (11th Cir. 1998) ("To establish a prima facie case of retaliation under the ADA, employee must show (1) that he engaged in statutorily protected activity, (2) that he suffered an adverse employment action, and (3) a causal link between the protected activity and the adverse action.... To engage in protected activity for purposes of ADA retaliation claim, it is sufficient that an employee have a good faith, objectively reasonable belief that his activity is protected by the statute.... Employee's requests for accommodation of his back injury did not constitute statutorily protected activity, for purposes of ADA retaliation claim, absent showing that he had good faith, objectively reasonable belief that he was disabled under the ADA at time he made the requests.... In determining whether an injury substantially limits a major life activity, so as to constitute disability under ADA, court considers (1) the nature and severity of the impairment, (2) the duration or expected duration of the impairment, and (3) the permanent or long term impact, or the expected permanent or long term impact of or resulting from the impairment.... To make out a prima facie case of age discrimination for a reduction-in-force termination, former employee must prove that (1) he was a member of the age group protected by the ADEA at the time of his termination, (2) he was qualified at the time of his termination, and (3) there is evidence from which a reasonable fact finder could conclude that the employer intended to discriminate on the basis of age in making the decision.... To establish a case under Title VII, a plaintiff may use three different kinds of evidence of discriminatory intent: direct evidence, circumstantial evidence or statistical evidence; the analytical framework and burden of production varies depending on the method of proof chosen.... Under McDonnell Douglass burden-shifting framework for establishing employment discrimination claims, once plaintiff establishes prima facie case of discrimination, the employer must offer legitimate, nondiscriminatory reasons for the employment action to rebut the presumption of discrimination; if the employer successfully rebuts the presumption, the burden shifts back to the plaintiff to discredit the proffered nondiscriminatory reasons by showing that they are pretextual.... Former employee who was discharged as part of reduction-in-force could establish a prima facie case of discrimination under Title VII by (1) showing that he was a member of protected group and was adversely affected by an employment decision, (2) proving that he was qualified for his own position or to assume another position at the time of the discharge, and (3) producing sufficient evidence from which a rational fact finder could conclude that his employer intended to discriminate against him in making the discharge decision.... Title VII plaintiff may show that employer's proffered reasons for challenged employment decision are pretext (1) by showing that the legitimate nondiscriminatory reasons should not be believed, or (2) by showing that, in light of all the evidence, discriminatory reasons more likely motivated the decision than the proffered reasons.... To directly attack employer's proffered nondiscriminatory reasons for employment decision, Title VII plaintiff must demonstrate such weaknesses, implausibilities, inconsistencies, incoherencies or contradictions in the employer's proffered legitimate reasons for its action that a reasonable fact finder could find all of those reasons unworthy of credence.... To establish prima facie case of discriminatory failure to promote, plaintiff in § 1981 case must show that (1) he was in a protected group, (2) he was not given the promotion, (3) he was qualified for the position and (4) someone outside of the protected group was given the position.")

Smith v. CH2M Hill Inc., 521 Fed.Appx. 773 (11th Cir. 2013) ("Employee's allegations were sufficient to state plausible claim for race discrimination under Title VII; employee alleged that he was black, that he had experience and was qualified for his work, that his termination was substantially motivated by race, that he was replaced by non-African-American person, and that less-qualified non-African-American persons in his job classification retained their employment when he was discharged, that he was pressured by city officials to selectively enforce applicable codes in racially discriminatory manner, in effect enforcing some codes against black citizen under circumstances substantially similar to a situation in which he had been directed not to enforce those codes against white citizen, and that, after he objected to discriminatory enforcement, city demanded that employers remove him from his job and employers complied and terminated him with full knowledge of discriminatory motive.")

Paye v. Secretary of Defense, 157 Fed.Appx. 234 (11th Cir. 2005)("Asian-American former employee had to offer evidence on summary judgment about race of her replacement, if any, evidence about any other Asian-American employees and whether they also were subject to discriminatory actions, or evidence about any employees who were not fired after failing to meet performance improvement plan (PIP) requirements, in order to establish prima facie case of race discrimination under Title VII against Department of Defense, as employer, under test that required her to show that someone outside her protected class was treated differently than she was or under her theory that she should have been required to show only that she was replaced by someone outside her class.")

Hill v. Emory University, 346 Fed.Appx. 390 (11th Cir. 2009) ("Employee failed to show that private university employer's stated reasons for terminating him, that the funds from which employee was paid were running budget deficits and the program that employee was hired to develop was handled primarily by an outside vendor, where pretext for race discrimination, as required to prevail in § 1918 termination claim.... Employee of private university employer failed to establish prima facie claim of wage discrimination on account of race, as would support Title VII claim; although coworkers who were not members of racial minority received salary increases, and employee did not, the coworkers were not similarly situated to employee, since they presented the employer with evidence of a competing job offer, while employee did not.... Employee of private university was not subjected to severe and pervasive harassment as required to establish Title VII hostile work environment claim; although employee alleged that his workgroup was referenced to a counseling session, that employee was demoted, that his requests for supporting office staff were denied, one of his hiring decision was denied, that his request to attend educational conference was denied, that his request to reclassify himself was denied, that employee was never assigned any direct reports, that he was never assigned any office space, that he was not awarded pay raises comparable to his coworkers, and that employer failed to reabsorb him after his job was terminated or provide him with a list of available job openings, such actions were not so severe or pervasive as to alter the terms and conditions of employment.")

Vessels v. Atlanta Independent School System, 408 F.3d 763 (11th Cir. 2005) ("Where an employer does not formally announce a position, but rather uses informal and subjective procedures to identify a candidate, a plaintiff, in order to establish a prima facie case of discrimination under McDonnell Douglas framework, need not show that he applied for the position, only that the employer had some reason to consider him for the post.... To demonstrate that he was qualified for the positon, a Title VII plaintiff seeking to establish prima facie failure to promote claim need only show that he or she satisfied an employer's objectively verifiable qualifications; employer may then introduce its subjective evaluations of the plaintiff at the later stages of the McDonnell Douglas framework.... Where an employee seeks to prove through qualifications alone that race-neutral reasons for failure to promote were pretextual, the difference in qualifications must be so glaring that no reasonable impartial person could have chosen the candidate selected for the promotion in question over the employee; however, where the qualifications disparity is not the sole basis for arguing pretext, the disparity need not be so dramatic to support an inference of pretext.")

Holifield v. Reno, 115 F.3d 1555 (11th Cir. 1997)("Employer presented legitimate, non-discriminatory reason for transferring and later terminating black doctor, as required to rebut doctor's prima facie case of race discrimination in violation of Title VII, by showing that evaluations indicated schism between doctor and his colleagues, supervisors, and support staff, and that reviewers recommended doctor be removed for delaying treatment and evaluation of patients, displaying unprofessional behavior toward staff and physicians, and causing conflict within department and with administration.... Black doctor's unsubstantiated assertion that his supervisors began documenting untrue assessment of his performance to terminate him because of his race was insufficient to show that employer's articulated reason for transfer and termination was pretext for race discrimination in violation of Title VII.... Peer review, performance appraisals, and testimony of supervisors, colleagues, and medical staff showing that work for which black doctor was responsible was not performed properly was fatal to doctor's claim he was transferred and terminated in violation of Title VII, in retaliation for filing equal employment opportunity complaint and expressing concerns about racism to his supervisor.")

U.S. Fifth Circuit Court of Appeals (Louisiana, Mississippi, Texas)

McCoy v. City of Shreveport, 492 F.3d 551 (5th Cir. 2007) ("Assuming a Title VII plaintiff has exhausted his administrative remedies, he may prove a claim of intentional discrimination or retaliation either by direct or circumstantial evidence.... Under the framework for establishing a Title VII discrimination claim based upon circumstantial evidence, the plaintiff must first establish a prima facie case of discrimination, which requires a showing that the plaintiff: (1) is a member of a protected group; (2) was qualified for the position at issue; (3) was discharged or suffered some adverse employment action by the employer; and (4) was replaced by someone outside his protected group or was treated less favorably than other similarly situated employees outside the protected group.... Under the framework for establishing a Title VII retaliation claim based upon circumstantial evidence, a Title VII plaintiff must establish that: (1) he participated in an activity protected by Title VII; (2) his employer took an adverse employment action against him; and (3) a causal connection exists between the protected activity and the adverse employment action.... If a Title VII plaintiff makes a prima facie showing, the burden then shifts to the employer to articulate a legitimate, nondiscriminatory or nonretaliatory reason for its employment action.... In a

Title VII action, the employer's burden of articulating a legitimate, nondiscriminatory or nonretaliatory reason for its employment action is only one of production, not persuasion, and involves no credibility assessment.... If the employer meets its burden of production by articulating a legitimate, nondiscriminatory or nonretaliatory reason for its employment action, the Title VII plaintiff then bears the ultimate burden of proving that the employer's proffered reason is not true but instead is a pretext for the real discriminatory or retaliatory purpose.... To carry the burden of proving that an employer's proffered reason is not true but instead is a pretext for the real discriminatory or retaliatory purpose, a Title VII plaintiff must rebut each nondiscriminatory or nonretaliatory reason articulated by the employer.... In determining whether an employer's actions toward a Title VII plaintiff constitute a constructive discharge, the Court of Appeals examines the following relevant factors: (1) demotion; (2) reduction in salary; (3) reduction in job responsibilities; (4) reassignment to menial or degrading work; (5) badgering, harassment, or humiliation by the employer calculated to encourage the employee's resignation; or (6) offers of early retirement that would make the employee worse off whether the offer were accepted or not.... The inquiry into whether an employer's actions toward a Title VII plaintiff constitute a constructive discharge is an objective one, 'reasonable employee,' test under which the Court of Appeals ask whether a reasonable person in the plaintiff's shoes would have felt compelled to resign.")

Okoye v. University of Texas Houston Health Science Center, 245 F.3d 507 (5th Cir. 2001)("In order to survive summary judgment in Title VII case, former employee was required to raise a genuine issue as to a material fact that employer discriminated against her, and to do so, was required to satisfy burden shifting test annunciated in *McDonnell Douglas Corp.*"

Simmons-Myers v. Caesars Entertainment Corp., 515 Fed.Appx. 269 (5th Cir. 2013)("Termination of white employee was not racial discrimination that would violate § 1981, where employee's position was completely eliminated, all co-workers in same position, all of whom, other than employee, were black, were all fired, and employee was not replaced.")

Laxton v. Gap Inc., 333 F.3d 572 (5th Cir. 2003)("In Title VII employment discrimination action, evidence demonstrating that employer's explanation for adverse employment action is false or unworthy of credence taken together with employee's prima facie case is likely to support inference of discrimination even without further evidence of defendant's true motive.... Employee's prima facie case of discrimination under Title VII combined with showing of pretext in employer's proffered nondiscriminatory reason for adverse employment action is insufficient to establish discrimination only when: (1) record conclusively reveals some other, nondiscriminatory reason for employer's decision, or (2) plaintiff creates only weak issue of fact as to whether employer's reason was untrue, and there is abundant and uncontroverted evidence that no discrimination occurred.")

Byers v. Dallas Morning News, Inc., 209 F.3d 419 (5th Cir. 2000)("In order to establish prima facie case of discriminatory discharge based on race in violation of Title VII, employee must establish: (1) that he/she is member of protected group; (2) that he/she was qualified for the position held; (3) that he/she was discharged from position; and (4) that he/she was replaced by someone outside of the protected group.... White newspaper employee who was discharged from management position shortly after his supervisor was replaced by another employee, who happened to be black, did not establish prima facie case of reverse racial discrimination in violation of Title VII, where each of the two employees who took over his duties was also white, and employee failed to produce any evidence that supervisor acted with discriminatory intent, but relied solely on his subjective belief that supervisor had discriminated against him because he was white.")

Color Discrimination ("Colorism")

U.S. Eleventh Circuit Court of Appeals (Alabama, Florida, Georgia)

Word v. AT & T, 576 Fed.Appx. 908 (11th Cir. 2014)("Employer's terminating African American employee for five consecutive unexcused absences after employee had been previously suspended was not pretext for retaliation for employee's filing administrative discrimination charge, as would violate Title VII and § 1981; employee was not only employee to advance to next level of discipline after only one occurrence, occurrence was five consecutive absences, employer's attendance guidelines did not dictate number of occurrences as sole measuring stick for determining discipline, and employee did not fill out paperwork to request vacation…. Two Caucasian and two lighter-skinned African American co-workers who were reinstated after termination and subsequently discharged as second time after multiple absences or tardies were not similarly situated to African American employee terminated after one occurrence that followed reinstatement, as required for employee's Title VII and § 1983 race and color discrimination claims; employee's occurrence was being absent for five consecutive days, which was more total time missed than co-workers'.")

Walker v. Secretary of the Treasury, Internal Revenue Service, 713 F.Supp. 403 (U.S. N.D. Ga. 1989)("Allegation by black former employee that she was discharged by black supervisor because she was a light-skinned black person, while supervisor was a dark-skinned black person, stated a cause of action for discrimination under Title VII…. In the employment context, § 1981 is not available to federal employees; Title VII establishes the exclusive remedy for federal employment discrimination…. Actions of federal officials under color of federal law rather than state law are not subject to suit under § 1983.")

U.S. Fifth Circuit Court of Appeals (Louisiana, Mississippi, Texas)

Khalfani v. Balfour Beatty Communities, LLC, 595 Fed.Appx. 363 (5th Cir. 2014)("We analyze this case pursuant to our Title VII jurisprudence. In general, that analysis follows in three parts: (1) the employee-plaintiff must make a prima facie case of unlawful retaliation or race/color discrimination, (2) the burden of production shifts to the employer-defendant, who must articulate a legitimate, non-discriminatory reason for the challenged action, and (3) if it does, the plaintiff can show that the defendant's stated reason is pretextual.")

Other U.S. Circuit Courts of Appeal and Lower-level District Courts

Bryant v. Bell Atlantic Maryland, Inc., 288 F.3d 124 (4th Cir. 2002)(4th Cir. 2002)("Color discrimination in violation of Title VII arises when the particular hue of the employee's skin is the cause of the discrimination, such as in the case where a dark-colored African-American individual is discriminated against in favor of a light-colored African-American individual…. ")

Williams v. Wendler, 530 F.3d 584 (7th Cir. 2008)("The university authorities were not choosing between black and white in punishing the hazers, but between black and black, which is like choosing between white and white. There can, it is true, be 'racial' discrimination within the same race, broadly defined, because 'race' is a fuzzy term.... Title VI, like Title VII, forbids discrimination on the basis of color as well as on the basis of race; since light-skinned blacks sometimes discriminate against dark-skinned blacks, and vice versa, and either form of discrimination is literally 'color discrimination.'... ").

Cooper v. Jackson-Madison County General Hospital District, 742 F.Supp. 2d 941 (U.S. W.D. Tenn. 2010)("Although the terms race and color were not defined by Congress in Title VII, the two terms are not synonymous; 'color' refers to pigmentation, complexion, or skin shade or tone, and 'color discrimination' occurs when a person is discriminated against based on the lightness, darkness, or other color characteristic of the person.

Richardson v. HRHH Gaming Senior Mezz, LLC, 99 F.Supp.3d 1267 (U.S. D.Nev. 2015)(Color discrimination and race discrimination are similar but they are not the same. Therefore, an individual may not rely upon his "race" EEOC charge of discrimination to bring a "color" discrimination complaint in federal court. "The Cooper court, relying in part on an EEOC compliance manual, explained the difference between race and color discrimination, stating that color discrimination 'arises when the particular hue of the plaintiff's skin is the cause of the discrimination, such as in the case where a dark-colored African-American individual is discriminated against in favor of a light-colored African-American individual.'")

National Origin Discrimination

U.S. Supreme Court

Espinoza v. Farah Mfg. Co., 414 U.S. 86 (1973)(NOTE: citation taken from Zascha Blanco Abbott, "Equal Employment Opportunity Laws: Substantive Claims, Defenses and Related Matters"© 15th Florida Bar Labor and Employment Law Annual Update and Certification Review, Vol. II (2015)("Although non-citizens may be subject to discrimination based on their national origin, discrimination on the basis of citizenship is not per se national origin discrimination. After Espinoza, the EEOC revised its guidelines concerning national origin. The revised guidelines state that Title VII is violated if an employer's citizenship requirement has the purpose or effect of discrimination against persons of a particular national origin. 29 C.F.R. § 1606.5.")

U.S. Eleventh Circuit Court of Appeals (Alabama, Florida, Georgia)

Jianxin Fong v. Sch. Bd., 2014 U.S. App. LEXIS 21224 * 6-7 (11th Cir. 2014) (NOTE: citation taken from Zascha Blanco Abbott, "Equal Employment Opportunity Laws: Substantive Claims, Defenses and Related Matters"© 15th Florida Bar Labor and Employment Law Annual Update and Certification Review, Vol. II (2015)("Discrimination based on an employee's accent can be national origin discrimination. However, an employee's heavy accent or difficulty with spoken English can be a legitimate basis for adverse employment action where effective communication skills are reasonably related to job performance.")

Albert-Aluya v. Burlington Coat Factory Warehouse Corp., 470 Fed. Appx. 847 (11th Cir. 2012)("Nigerian-born employee established prima facie case that she was wrongfully terminated because of her national origin in violation of Title VII; her supervisor often made derogatory comments to her about her African ethnicity and accent and employee testified that at meeting where she was told of firing, regional manager stated that termination was because of her 'thick African accent' and 'being too brash with people' and regional human resource generalist criticized her for 'failing to speak more like an American.'")

Abbes v. Embraer Services, Inc., 195 Fed.Appx. 898 (11th Cir. 2006)("Terminated employee, a Canadian and Tunisian citizen, failed to present a prima facie case of national origin discrimination under Title VII; employee presented no evidence that employer treated similarly situated engineers outside of his protected class more favorably than him.... Terminated employee... failed to prove that any alleged harassment was so severe that if altered the terms and conditions of his employment, as required to prove claim of national origin harassment under Title VII; even if the acts employee complained of qualified as unwelcome harassment, he presented no evidence that employer's management took these actions because of his Tunisian background.")

Alvarez v. Royal Atlantic Developers, Inc., 610 F.3d 1253 (11th Cir. 2010) ("Cuban American employee's testimony that other employees told her they heard discriminatory remarks about Cubans was inadmissible hearsay, which could not be used to defeat summary judgment on her Title VII national-origin discrimination claim, where employee did not offer any affidavits or deposition testimony from these other employees.... Although employer planned to fire employee by the time employee sent letter to employer's chief executive officer (CEO) asserting that employer's chief financial officer (CFO) was planning to fire employee and a co-worker because they were of Cuban origin, the letter did cause employee to be fired the day after she e-mailed it, which was sooner than she otherwise would have been, and thus employee suffered an adverse action, as element of her Title VII retaliation claim.... Employer's proffered reason for firing employee sooner than it was planning to, that letter she sent to employer's chief executive officer (CEO) after decision to terminate had been made, which letter asserted that employer's chief financial officer (CFO) was planning to fire employee and a co-worker because they were of Cuban origin, demonstrated that employee was unhappy working for the company and thus it would be 'awkward and counterproductive' to keep her around, was not a legitimate, non-retaliatory reason under Title VII to fire employee.")

Aristyld v. City of Lauderhill, 543 Fed.Appx. 905 (11th Cir. 2013) ("City employee failed to identify any similarly situated individual outside of his protected class who was treated more favorably, as required to establish prima facie case of discriminatory failure-to-promote on the basis of his national origin.... City employee failed to show that city's proffered legitimate, nondiscriminatory reasons for his termination, that is, multiple complaints about the conditions in the bathrooms and park recreation areas he was required to clean, were pretextual, as would support his retaliatory hostile work environment claim under Title VII.")

Standard v. A.B.E.L. Services, Inc., 161 F.3d 1318 (11th Cir. 1998)("Alleged statements of management members that company's president wanted only Hispanics to be hired and that one of the reasons why Caucasian employee was not considered for certain promotion was because he was not Hispanic did not constitute direct evidence of race or national origin discrimination with regard to employee's termination; such management members did not make decision to terminate employee, and statements referred to hiring practices for department other than employee's…. [and] did not constitute direct evidence of race or national origin discrimination with regard to employee's termination; any direct link between the statement and discriminatory intent against employee was broken when employee was hired on the management member's recommendation, and employee had not worked in production department.")

Enwonwu v. Fulton-Dekalb Hosp. Authority, 286 Fed.Appx. 586 (11th Cir. 2008)("Black female former employee of Nigerian national origin had to establish that policy of county employer of requiring all help desk employees to work in data center was serious and material change in terms, conditions, or privileges of her employment and that transfer from help desk office to data center involved reduction in pay, prestige, or responsibility to show that she suffered adverse employment action when employer required her to work in data center when other employees had been allowed to work in office, on her Title VII claim that policy to work in data center had been applied disparately…. Terms and conditions of employment of black female employee of Nigerian national origin had not been altered, and discriminatorily abusive working environment had not been created, in violation of Title VII, on supervisor's statement that 'people not like [that employee], have tried [to complain] but that the point is you have to do what [the other supervisor] says,' even if statement was based upon protected characteristic.")

Tippie v. Spacelabs Medical, Inc., 180 Fed.Appx. 51 (11th Cir. 2006) ("Female, American employee failed to prove by a preponderance of evidence that failure to promote her was based on discriminatory animus for her national origin or gender, in violation of Title VII; employee was unable to show her qualifications were so much better than those of candidate who was not American or female that no reasonable person could have chosen candidate for the position, and employer's reasons for selecting candidate were consistent throughout the entire hiring process.")

Cazeau v. Wells Fargo Bank, N.A., 614 Fed.Appx. 972 (11th Cir. 2015) ("Employee, a male of Haitian origin who worked as bank teller, failed to demonstrate that employer's proffered reasons for not promoting him to service manager were pretext for discrimination based on national origin in violation of Title VII; employer cited, as bases for its actions, other applicant's superior qualification, as well as internal company policy limiting eligibility to employees who had been in their current position for at least 12 months unless that requirement was waived by a manager or by human resources, and though employee, who had been in his lead teller position for 12 months, contended that he had received permission from his supervisor and store manager to apply for the service manager position, there was no evidence to rebut recruiter's testimony that he had not been contacted by a manager giving employee permission to apply, nor did employee offer evidence to rebut employer's contention that other applicant was more qualified.")

U.S. Fifth Circuit Court of Appeals (Louisiana, Mississippi, Texas)

E.E.O.C. v. WC&M Enterprises, Inc., 496 F.3d 393 (5th Cir. 2007) ("Party may be able to establish Title VII discrimination claim based on national origin, even though the party committing the alleged discriminatory acts does not correctly identify the first party's actual country of origin.... To state hostile work environment claim under Title VII, plaintiff must show: (1) that victim belongs to protected group; (2) that victim was subjected to unwelcome harassment; (3) that this harassment was based on protected characteristic; (4) that harassment affected a term, condition or privilege of employment; and (5) that victim's employer knew or should have known of harassment and failed to take prompt remedial action.... To determine whether victim's work environment was objectively offensive, as required for employer to be liable on 'hostile work environment' theory under Title VII, courts consider totality of circumstances, including: (1) frequency of discriminatory conduct; (2) its severity; (3) whether it is physically threatening or humiliating, or merely an offensive utterance; and (4) whether it interferes with employee's work performance; however, no single factor is determinative."

Pickens v. Shell Technoliogy Ventures, 118 Fed.Appx. 842 (5th Cir. 2004)("Multinational employer's proffered reason for terminating American employee was not pretext for discrimination based on national origin; director, who was American, exclusively made decision to terminate employee, and fact that Scottish executive who had made anti-American comments, e-mailed director recommending that employee be fired, did not reflect that executive leverage or control over director's decisionmaking, as required to impute his discriminatory attitude to director.")

Sex Discrimination

U.S. Supreme Court

Price Waterhouse v. Hopkins, 490 U.S. 228, 235 (1989))(NOTE: citation taken from Zascha Blanco Abbott, "Equal Employment Opportunity Laws: Substantive Claims, Defenses and Related Matters"© 15th Florida Bar Labor and Employment Law Annual Update and Certification Review, Vol. II (2015)("Title VII's prohibition against gender discrimination includes discrimination based on sexual stereotypes, such as an expectation that women should dress in a certain way, or should not be aggressive or use profanity.... Recently, 'sex stereotyping' has provided the basis for a number of claims involving employees who are undergoing reassignment, either with or without surgery.")

U.S. Eleventh Circuit Court of Appeals (Alabama, Florida, Georgia)

Jeffries v. Harris County Community Action Ass'n, 615 F.2d 1025 (11th Cir. 1980)("Where claims of race discrimination, sex discrimination, and discrimination based on both race and sex were properly raised in the pleadings and at trial and former employee contended that district court erred in its consideration of each of her claims of discrimination in promotion, all the claims were properly before the reviewing court.")

Willingham v. Macon Tel. Pub. Co., 507 F.2d 1084 (5th Cir. 1975)[binding 11th Cir. opinion]("Inclusion of 'sex plus' discrimination within the proscription of the Civil Rights Act has legitimate legislative and judicial underpinning.... Distinctions in employment practices between men and women on the basis of something other than immutable characteristics or legally protected rights do not inhibit employment opportunities in violation of the Civil Rights Act.")

Glenn v. Brumby, 663 F.3d 1312 *(11th Cir. 2011)*(NOTE: citation taken from Zascha Blanco Abbott, "Equal Employment Opportunity Laws: Substantive Claims, Defenses and Related Matters"© 15th Florida Bar Labor and Employment Law Annual Update and Certification Review, Vol. II (2015)("In December 2011... the Eleventh Circuit held that a public employer's firing of a male employee, who was transitioning to female, because of the transition was a constitutional violation (equal protection). The court noted that a person is transgender 'precisely because of the perception that his or her behavior transgresses gender stereotypes.'... Therefore, discrimination against transsexuals or transgendered people was necessarily unlawful sex discrimination.... Although the decision was reached on constitutional grounds, it also applies to Title VII. See also *Barnes v. City of Cincinnati*, 401 F.3d 729 (6th Cir. 2005); *Smith v. City of Salem*, 378 F.3d 566 (6th Cir. 2004)(suspension of male transsexual firefighter based on failure to conform to sex stereotypes violated Title VII and equal protection). However, an employer must be aware that the person is transgendered, or perceived him as such. *Hunter v. UPS, Inc.*, 697 F.3d 697 (8th Cir. 2012).")

Toney v. Montgomery Jobs Corps, 211 Fed.Appx. 816 (11th Cir. 2006) ("Supervisor's statements to black male employee that she was a strong independent black woman and male employee could not handle it merely suggested that she may have fired male employee because of his sex but was not direct evidence that firing was discriminatory.... Black male former employee failed to establish that he was similarly situated to female employees whom he identified as receiving favorable treatment, and thus, he failed to establish a prima face case of sex discrimination; although former employee pointed to evidence of several instances where females were only reprimanded for engaging in a similar practice that violated workplace policy, that evidence ignored three other instances of misconduct that he was involved in or accused of that female employees were not.")

Weeks v. Southern Bell Tel. & Tel. Co., 408 F.2d 228 (5th Cir. 1969)[binding 11th Cir. opinion] ("Telephone and telegraph company which denied switchman's job because applicant was a woman had burden of proof to demonstrate that such position fit within the 'bona fide occupational qualification' exception to Civil Rights Act prohibiting discrimination in employment on account of sex.")

Diaz v. Pan Am. World Airways, Inc., 442 F.2d 385 (5th Cir. 1971) [binding 11th Cir. opinion]("Being a female was not a bona fide occupational qualification for job of flight cabin attendant and employer's refusal to hire males solely because of their sex constituted violation of 1964 Civil Rights Act.")

Miranda v. B & B Cash Grocery Store, Inc., 975 F.2d 1518 (11th Cir. 1992)("Employee's failure to establish prima facie case under Equal Pay Act does not preclude employee from bringing claim for sex-based wage discrimination under Civil Rights Act.")

Langley v. State Farm Fire & Cas. Co., 644 F.2d 1124 (5th Cir. 1981)[binding 11th Cir. opinion] ("To establish a violation for sex discrimination under Title VII of the Civil Rights Act of 1964, a plaintiff must initially prove that challenged policy has a discriminatory effect on women by establishing that the policy, although neutral on its face, imposes on female employees a substantial burden that men need not suffer; if this prima facie case is established, then burden shifts to employer to justify a challenged practice and, if employer meets this burden, plaintiff, to recover, must then show that employer could use alternative practices to accomplish same purpose without discriminatory effects.")

Hardin v. Stychcomb, 691 F.2d 1364 (11th Cir. 1982)("In action alleging employment discrimination in sheriff's department based on sex, defendants failed to prove that it was essential to functioning of sheriff's department that all new deputy sheriffs be initially assigned to county jail and also failed to prove that they could not rearrange job responsibility so that female deputies assigned to male section of jail would not have to perform duties that impinged upon inmate privacy rights; thus, bona fide occupational qualification exception to Title VII did not justify defendants' arbitrary practice of funneling deputy sheriffs into positions reserved almost exclusively for males.")

E.E.O.C. v. Joe's Stone Crab, Inc., 220 F.3d 1263 (11th Cir. 2000)("In sex discrimination case against restaurant, finding of disparate treatment would require no more than a finding that women were intentionally treated differently by restaurant because of or on account of their gender, and, if restaurant deliberately and systematically excluded women from food server positions based on a sexual stereotype which simply associated 'fine-dining ambience' with all-male food service, it then could be found liable under Title VII for intentional discrimination regardless of whether it also was motivated by ill-will or malice toward women.")

Causey v. Ford Motor Co., 516 F.2d 416 (5th Cir. 1975)[binding 11th Cir. opinion]("Plaintiff had burden of establishing a prima face case of discrimination in civil rights employment discrimination case; once prima facie case was established, burden to articulate some legitimate, nondiscriminatory reasons for action shifted to defendants; upon rebuttal evidence being offered, ultimate burden of persuasion by preponderance of evidence that discrimination had taken place fell upon plaintiff.")

Orr v. Frank R. MacNeill & Son, Inc., 511 F.2d 166 (5th Cir. 1975) [binding 11th Cir. opinion]("In equal employment opportunity case, evidence that employer paid female worker's male successor almost same salary as she had been receiving although he was less experienced was not probative of sex discrimination in absence of evidence that successor's work was not done as well.... Evidence as a whole, in equal employment opportunity case, failed to sustain district court's determination that job of plaintiff female worker was 'substantially equal' to other jobs, performed by men, or that there had been any discrimination by reason of sex.")

Womack v. Runyon, 147 F.3d 1298 (11th Cir. 1998)("Male employee could not maintain sex discrimination claim based on contention that he was denied promotion due to favoritism shown to supervisor's alleged paramour, who was selected for the position; preferential treatment based on consensual relationship between supervisor and female employee did not constitute cognizable sex discrimination cause of action under Title VII.")

U.S. Fifth Circuit Court of Appeals (Louisiana, Mississippi, Texas)

E.E.O.C. v. Boh Bros. Const. Co., L.L.C., 731 F.3d 444 (5th Cir. 2013) ("Under Title VII, an employer's liability for workplace harassment depends on the status of the harasser: if the harassing employee is the victim's co-worker, the employer is liable only if it was negligent in controlling working conditions; if the harasser is a 'supervisor,' and the harassment culminates in a tangible employment action, the employer is strictly liable; and if the harasser is a 'supervisor,' and no tangible employment action is taken, the employer may escape liability by establishing, as an affirmative defense, that the employer exercised reasonable care to prevent and correct any harassing behavior and that the victim unreasonably failed to take advantage of the preventive or corrective opportunities that the employer provided.... An employer can satisfy the first prong of the Ellerth/Faragher defense to Title VII claims of vicarious liability for sexual harassment carried out by supervisors in their employ, that the employer exercised reasonable care to prevent and correct promptly any sexually harassing behavior, by implementing suitable institutional policies and educational programs regarding sexual harassment.") See, also, Zascha Blanco Abbott, "Equal Employment Opportunity Laws: Substantive Claims, Defenses and Related Matters"© 15th Florida Bar Labor and Employment Law Annual Update and Certification Review, Vol. II (2015)("In *EEOC v. Boh Bros. Const. Co.*, 731 F.3d 444 (5th Cir. 2013), the Fifth Circuit examined whether gender stereotyping could support a same sex sexual harassment claim where the plaintiff alleged he was harassed by his male supervisor on a construction crew not for not being 'manly' enough. Reasoning that 'because of sex' includes failure to conform to gender stereotypes, the court focused on the harasser's subjective perception of his victim to conclude that a jury properly found same sex sexual harassment. Whether the plaintiff was or was not actually 'manly' was beside the point.")

Smith v. Liberty Mut. Ins. Co., 569 F.2d 325 (5th Cir. 1978) ("Congress, by its proscription of sex discrimination in Title VII of Civil Rights Act of 1964, intended only to guarantee equal job opportunities for males and females.... Evidence supported trial court's finding that black job applicant was not refused employment because of his race, and that refusal was, instead, grounded on permissible basis that applicant appeared effeminate.")

Willingham v. Macon Tel. Pub. Co., 507 F.2d 1084 (5th Cir. 1975) ("Employer's grooming code, requiring different hair lengths for male and female employees, constituted discrimination on the basis of grooming standards, not on the basis of sex, and was thus outside the proscription of the Civil Rights Act.")

Jefferies v. Harris County Community Action Ass'n, 615 F.2d 1025 (5th Cir. 1980)("Where claims of race discrimination, sex discrimination, and discrimination based on both race and sex were properly raised in the pleadings and at trial and former employee contended that district court erred in its consideration of each of her claims of discrimination in promotion, all the claims were properly before the reviewing court.")

Plemer v. Parsons-Gilbane, 713 F.2d 1127 (5th Cir. 1983)("Where female former employee's evidence, apart from statistics showing that women were generally on the bottom rung of pay ladder, made a prima facie case under the Equal Pay Act and Title VII by demonstrating that she was paid less than her male successor for identical position, the statistics were relevant and should have been considered in determining whether asserted justifications for the pay differential was pretextual.")

Religion Discrimination

U.S. Eleventh Circuit Court of Appeals (Alabama, Florida, Georgia)

Morrissette-Brown v. Mobile Infirmary Medical Center, 506 F.3d 1317 (11th Cir. 2007)("An employee asserting religious discrimination under Title VII must first establish a prima facie case of religious discrimination by presenting evidence sufficient to prove that (1) he had a bona fide religious belief that conflicted with an employment requirement, (2) he informed his employer of his belief, and (3) he was discharged for failing for failing to comply with the conflicting employment required.")

Beadle v. Hillsborough County Sheriff's Dept., 29 F.3d 589 (11th Cir. 1994)("For purposes of section of Title VII provision prohibiting employer from discriminating against employee on basis of religion unless employer demonstrates that he is unable to reasonably accommodate employee's religious beliefs without 'undue hardship' on conduct of business, phrase 'undue hardship' refers to any act that would require an employer to bear great than a de minimis cost in accounting employee's beliefs.")

Dixon v. The Hallmark Companies, Inc., 627 F.3d 849 (11th Cir. 2010) ("To prevail on Title VII claim of failure to accommodate religious beliefs, plaintiffs must establish that (1) they held a bona fide religious belief that conflicted with an employment requirement; (2) they informed employer or that belief; and (3) they were discharged for failing to comply with the conflicting employment requirement.")

Lubestsky v. Applied Card Systems, Inc., 296 F.3d 1301 (11th Cir. 2002) ("Decision-maker who ordered rescission of employment offer did not know that applicant was Orthodox Jew, and applicant thus failed to establish prima facie Title VII case, where recruiter testified she never told decision-maker about plaintiff's religion, decision-maker testified he didn't know applicant was Orthodox Jew, and decision-maker testified he ordered rescission based on his recollection of applicant's personality and demeanor during previous encounter.")

Mack Muhammad v. Cagle's Inc., 379 Fed.Appx. 801 (11th Cir. 2010)("Former employee failed to establish prima facie case of religious discrimination in violation of Title VII where former employee did not show that he was qualified for superintendent position from which he was terminated or show that similarly situated employees who were not Muslim were treated more favorably or that he was replaced by non-Muslim employee.")

Postell v. Green County Hosp. Authority, 265 Fed.Appx. 856 (11th Cir. 2008)("Employee alleging religious discrimination against employer in violation of Title VII was required to show that she was terminated or permanently removed from work schedule, constructively discharged, or suffered any other adverse employment action in contrast with similarly situated employees.... Hospital's failure to return employee to schedule, after her complaints of discrimination, did not constitute a materially adverse employment action, as required to establish a prima facie case of retaliation in violation of Title VII.")

Beadle v. City of Tampa, 42 F.3d 633 (11th Cir. 1995)("Once employer demonstrates that it reasonably accommodated employee's religious needs, statutory inquiry in connection with religious discrimination claim ends.")

Richardson v. Dougherty County, Ga., 185 Fed.Appx. 785 (11th Cir. 2006)("Seven Day Adventist deputy did not present evidence that employees outside of his protected class were treated more favorably than him, as was required to establish a prima facie case of religious discrimination, based on disparate treatment; other deputies accused of sexual misconduct, all of whom were outside of deputy's protected class, were, like him, given the option of resigning or termination.")

Walden v. Centers for Disease Control and Prevention, 669 F.3d 1277 (11th Cir. 2012)("In religious accommodation cases, court applies a burden-shifting framework akin to that articulated in *McDonnell Douglas*; under that framework, the plaintiff must first establish a prima facie claim by presenting evidence sufficient to prove that (1) she had a bona fide religious belief that conflicted with an employment requirement, (2) she informed her employer of her belief, and (3) she was discharged for failing to comply with the conflicting employment requirement.")

Jordan v. Conway, 441 Fed.Appx. 761 (11th Cir. 2011)("Georgia deputy sheriff who was terminated after appearing at his ex-wife's church after having been told by pastor on previous occasions not to return, despite having been acquitted of criminal trespass charge, failed to establish prima facie case of religious discrimination under Title VII based on circumstantial evidence; no one from sheriff's department ordered him to stay away from the church until after incident in question, so he could not have been terminated for failing to comply with sheriff's department requirement that he avoid the church.")

Bush v. Regis Corp. 257 Fed. Appx. 219 (11th Cir. 2007) ("Employer offered employee, who was a Jehovah's Witness, a reasonable accommodation other religious beliefs, thus defeating her discrimination claim under Title VII, despite her claim that a Sunday shift prevented her from doing field service with her family, which constituted a bona fide religious belief; field service was not required to be performed on Sundays, but rather, that was the day the employee and her family wished to perform field service.")

Dixon v. Palm Beach County Parks and Recreation Dept., 343 Fed. Appx. 500 (11th Cir. 2009)("County parks and recreation department's conduct in giving African-American Christian employee a written record of counseling, initially denying employee's requests for Sundays off, and transferring him from the bicycle patrol unit were not 'adverse employment actions,' as required to establish prima facie discrimination claims, and retaliation claim under Title VII; the employee's actions did not result in a serious and material change in the terms, conditions, and privileges of employment.")

Cooper v. General Dynamics, Convair Aerospace Division, Ft. Worth Operation, 533 F.2d 163 (5th Cir. 1976) [11th Cir. Opinion]("Civil Rights Act requirement that employer tolerate all religious conduct except that which cannot be reconciled with business-like operations extended to beliefs of certain employees that any support of a labor union, including payment of dues under agency shop provisions, is a godless act and inconsistent with the commandment to love one's neighbor, i.e., the employer, and that support of the union places a person's soul in jeopardy; Act mandates that all reasonable accommodations of employees' beliefs be considered, including permitting continuation of regular work assignment while not paying union dues or equivalent.")

U.S. Fifth Circuit Court of Appeals (Louisiana, Mississippi, Texas)

Equal Employment Opportunity Commission v. Mississippi College, 626 F.2d 477 (5th Cir. 1980)("Only the relationship between a church and its minister is exempt from coverage of Title VII; relationship between a religious educational institution and its faculty is not exempt from such coverage.")

Mousa v. Capital Area Human Services Dist., 463 Fed.Appx. 253 (5th Cir. 2012)("State employer's reasons for terminating employment of internal auditor who was of Egyptian ethnicity, that he had failed to make progress during probationary period on his single work assignment and had continuously complained about almost every aspect of his job and the workplace, were legitimate and non-discriminatory, rather than pretext for racial discrimination in violation of Title VII.")

Dediol v. Best Chevrolet, Inc., 655 F.3d 435 (5th Cir. 2011)("To establish a prima facie case of harassment based on religion under Title VII, a plaintiff must produce evidence that (1) he belongs to a protected class; (2) he was subject to unwelcome harassment; (3) the harassment was based on religion; (4) the harassment affected a term, condition, or privilege of employment; and (5) the employer knew or should have known of the harassment and failed to take prompt remedial action.")

Cooper v. General Dynamics, Convair Aerospace Division, Ft. Worth Operation, 533 F.2d 163 (5th Cir. 1976)("All forms and aspects of an employee's religion, however eccentric, and not merely Sabbath observance, are protected under the Civil Rights Act except those which cannot be, in practice and with honest effort, reconciled with a business-like operation…. Under provision of Civil Rights Act requiring union and employer to tolerate religious practices unless doing so would create an undue hardship, court must consider hardship imposed on the union as well as on the employer.")

Aryain v. Wal-Mart Stores Texas LP, 534 F.3d 473 (5th Cir. 2008) ("A retaliation claim under Title VII may rest on an action that a reasonable employee would have found to be materially adverse, which in this context means it well might have dissuaded a reasonable worker from making or supporting a charge of discrimination…. Alleged poor treatment of employee by her supervisors did not rise to level of material adversity required to establish *prima facie* case of retaliation under Title VII, but instead, treatment fell into category of petty slights, minor annoyances, and simple lack of good manners regularly encountered in workplace; alleged poor treatment included transferring employee to infant department, requiring employee to break down clothing racks on hot day, undesirable break schedule, looking at employee angrily, and making employee wait outside manager's office for a long time.")

Weber v. Roadway Exp., Inc., 199 F.3d 270 (5th Cir. 2000)("To establish a prima facie case of religious discrimination under Title VII, an employee must establish that he or she had a bona fide religious belief that conflicted with an employment requirement, informed the employer of the belief, and was discharged for failing to comply with the conflicting employment requirement.... Employer did not violate Title VII when it failed to accommodate truck driver's religious beliefs which required him to refrain from making overnight runs with a female partner, inasmuch as 'skipping over' truck driver when scheduling such runs might adversely affect other drivers, and thus would impose undue hardship, notwithstanding that affected drivers had no contract entitling them to a particular run or job preference.")

Butler v. MBNA Technology, Inc., 111 Fed.Appx. 230 (5th Cir. 2004) ("Single alleged incident in which coworker posted picture and quote was neither pervasive nor severe, as was required to establish hostile work environment claim under Title VII; essence of alleged harassment was employee's disapproval of quotation that she felt took a tenet of her religion out of context, there was no evidence that coworker intended the posting to serve as a commentary on the Muslim religion, and, when employee complained that picture offended her, employer's personnel department promptly investigated and had picture removed.")

Daniels v. City of Alrington, Tex., 246 F.3d 500 (5th Cir. 2001)("Police officer terminated for wearing cross pin on his uniform, in violation of police department policy which prohibited wearing pins on uniform unless approved by police chief, could not establish religious discrimination claim under Title VII; officer failed to respond to police chief's reasonable offers of accommodation, which included allowing officer to wear cross ring or bracelet instead of pin.")

Tagore v. U.S., 735 F.3d 324 (5th Cir. 2013)("Title VII does not require religious accommodations that impose more than de minimis costs on an employer.")

Turpen v. Missouri-Kansas-Texas R.Co., 736 F.2d 1022 (5th Cir. 1984)("Religious discrimination prohibition of Title VII does not require an employer to bypass duly elected bargaining representatives to negotiate directly with individual employees to determine whether the employee would be willing to swap work days with an employee whose work schedule called for him to work on his Sabbath.")

Nobach v. Woodland Village Nursing Center, Inc., 799 F.3d 374

(5th Cir. 2015)("When evaluating causation in a Title VII case, the question is not what the employer knew about the employee's religious beliefs, nor is the question whether the employer knew that there would be a conflict between the employee's religious belief and some job duty; instead, the critical question is what motivated the employer's employment decision.")

Hostile Working Environment/ Harassment

U.S. Eleventh Circuit Court of Appeals (Alabama, Florida, Georgia)

Miller v. Kenworth of Dothan, Inc., 277 F.3d 1269 (11th Cir. 2002) ("A hostile work environment claim under Title VII is established upon proof that the workplace is permeated with discriminatory intimidation, ridicule, and insult, that is sufficiently severe or pervasive to alter the conditions of the victim's employment and create an abusive working environment…. To establish a hostile work environment claim under Title VII, an employee must show: (1) that he belongs to a protected group; (2) the he has been subject to unwelcome harassment; (3) that the harassment must have been based on a protected characteristic of the employee, such as national origin; (4) that the harassment was sufficiently severe or pervasive to alter the terms and conditions of employment and create a discriminatory abusive working environment; and (5) that the employer is responsible for such environment under either a theory of vicarious or of direct liability.")

Gowski v. Peake, 682 F.3d 1299 (11th Cir. 2012)("To establish a hostile work environment claim under Title VII, a plaintiff must show that the workplace is permeated with discriminatory intimidation, ridicule, and insult, that is sufficiently severe or pervasive to alter the conditions of the victim's employment and create an abusive working environment…. To be actionable in a retaliatory hostile work environment claim under Title VII, an employer's behavior must result in both an environment that a reasonable person would find hostile or abusive and an environment that the victim subjectively perceives to be abusive.")

Reeves v. C.H. Robinson Worldwide, Inc., 594 F.3d 798 (11th Cir. 2010)("To prove a hostile work environment under Title VII, a plaintiff must show that her employer discriminated because of her membership in a protected group, and that the offensive conduct was either severe or pervasive enough to alter the terms or conditions of employment.... Title VII is not a civility code, and not all profane or sexual language or conduct will constitute discrimination in the terms and conditions of employment.")

Adams v. Austal, U.S.A., L.L.C., 754 F.3 1240 (11th Cir. 2014)("An employee alleging a Title VII hostile work environment claim must prove five elements if he bases his harassment claim on race: (1) that he is a member of a protected class; (2) that he was subjected to unwelcome racial harassment; (3) that the harassment was based on his race; (4) that the harassment was severe or pervasive enough to alter the terms and conditions of his employment and create a discriminatorily abusive working environment; and (5) that the employer is responsible for the environment under a theory of either vicarious or direct liability.")

Jones v. UPS Ground Freight, 683 F.3d 1283 (11th Cir. 2012)("An employer is liable to an employee for racially hostile work environment under both Title VII and § 1981 if employee proves that: (1) he belongs to protected group, (2) he was subjected to unwelcome harassment, (3) harassment was based on his membership in protected group, (4) it was severe or pervasive enough to alter terms and conditions of employment and create hostile or abusive working environment, and (5) employer is responsible for that environment under theory of either vicarious or direct liability.")

Mendoza v. Borden, Inc., 195 F.3d 1238 (11th Cir. 1999)("To establish hostile-environment sexual-harassment claim under Title VII based on harassment by a supervisor, employee must show: (1) that he or she belongs to a protected group; (2) that employee has been subject to unwelcome sexual harassment, such as sexual advances, requests for sexual favors, and other conduct of a sexual nature; (3) that harassment was based on the sex of the employee; (4) that harassment was sufficiently severe or pervasive to alter terms and conditions of employment and create a discriminatorily abusive working environment; and (5) a basis for holding employer liable.")

Chambless v. Louisiana-Pacific Corp., 481 F.3d 1345 (11th Cir. 2007)("A Title VII hostile work environment claim depends on a series of separate acts that collectively constitute one unlawful employment practice.... The entire time period of the alleged hostile work environment may be considered by a court for the purposes of determining liability, if an act relating to the claim occurred within the limitations period.")

McCann v. Tillman, 526 F.3d 1370 (11th Cir. 2008)("To establish a prima facie showing of retaliation under Title VII, the plaintiff must show (1) that she engaged in statutorily protected expression; (2) that she suffered an adverse employment action; and (3) that there is some causal relation between the two events.... To establish a hostile work environment claim under Title VII, an employee must show: (1) that she belongs to a protected group; (2) that she has been subject to unwelcome harassment; (3) that the harassment must have been based on a protected characteristic of the employee; (4) that the harassment was sufficiently severe or pervasive to alter the terms and conditions of employment and create a discriminatorily abusive working environment; and (5) that the employer is responsible for such environment under either theory of vicarious or of direct liability.")

Perry v. Rogers, 627 Fed.Appx. 823 (11th Cir. 2015)("African-American agent of state alcoholic beverage control board established prima facie case of retaliation under Title VII through evidence that agent's placement under supervision of another employee the month after she filed discrimination complaint, and his subsequent close monitoring of her, constituted materially adverse action that was causally related to her protected activity.")

McKitt v. Alabama Alcoholic Beverage Control Bd., 571 Fed.Appx. 867 (11th Cir. 2014)("State employer's alleged disparate treatment of employee was not objectively severe or pervasive, and thus employer did not create racially hostile work environment in violation of Title VII, where alleged harassment was not physically threatening or frequent, and employee only heard one overtly racially derogatory remark over the course of 19 years of employment.")

Bryant v. Jones, 575 F.3d 1281 (11th Cir. 2009)("[Qualified Immunity under § 1983]: To prove that government official is not entitled to qualified immunity, § 1983 plaintiff must first show that official violated a constitutional right and then demonstrate that the constitutional right was clearly established at the time of the alleged wrongful act; if court, after viewing all evidence in light most favorable to plaintiff and drawing all inferences in his favor, determines that plaintiff has satisfied these two requirements, then defendant may not obtain qualified immunity.")

Freeman v. City of Riverdale, 330 Fed.Appx. 863 (11th Cir. 2009) ("Former city employee did not make prima facie case of hostile work environment under Title VII, discrete acts of alleged race discrimination that occurred more than 180 days prior to filing of charge with Equal Employment Opportunity Commission (EEOC) had to be charged separately and could not be considered, and in any case, 11 incidents involving use of racially derogatory language over period of 13 years were too sporadic and isolated, and therefore, did not demonstrate that discrimination was so severe or pervasive as to create hostile work environment.")

Smith v. Naples Community Hosp., Inc., 433 Fed.Appx. 797 (11th Cir. 2011)("Alleged instances involving female hospital employee's male supervisor, in which he allegedly acted in manner that was aggressive, angry, and physically threatening, were not sufficiently severe to alter conditions of employee's employment and create hostile work environment, thus precluding employee's hostile work environment claim based on gender under Title VII and Florida Civil Rights Act (FCRA).")

Hulsey v. Pride Restaurants, LLC, 367 F.3d 1238 (11th Cir. 2004)("An employer is liable under Title VII if it, even unknowingly, permits a supervisor to take a tangible employment action against an employee because she refused to give in to his sexual overtures; liability exists regardless of whether the employee took advantage of any employer-provided system for reporting harassment.")

Barrow v. Georgia Pacific Corp., 144 Fed.Appx. 54 (11th Cir. 2005) ("Employee failed to establish that alleged racial harassment, including symbols and slurs, was sufficiently severe or pervasive to alter his working conditions, as required to prevail on hostile work environment claims under § 1981; he presented evidence of isolated, sporadic instances of racial harassment over his more than 14 years of employment.")

Dar Dar v. Associated Outdoor Club, Inc., 201 Fed.Appx. 718 (11th Cir. 2006)("In determining whether female employee's claims that male co-worker had asked her whether she had even seen 'built-in butt' depicted in magazine ad, and that another male co-worker had told her he had seen an individual's 'whale of a dick' while in men's restroom, were sufficiently severe and pervasive to create hostile working environment, trial court was required to consider incidents as a whole under totality of circumstances, and not in isolation.")

Walton v. Johnson & Johnson Services, Inc., 347 F.3d 1272 (11th Cir. 2003)("Under 'aided by agency' theory, employer is subject to vicarious liability to victimized employee under Title VII for actionable hostile environment created by supervisor with immediate or successively higher authority over employee.... To succeed on Title VII sexual harassment claim based on *constructive discharge*, employee must show that her working conditions were so difficult that reasonable person would have felt compelled to resign, standard is higher than that for proving hostile work environment.")

Kelly v. Dun & Bradstreet, Inc., 557 Fed.Appx. 896 (11th Cir. 2014)("Employee alleged in Equal Employment Opportunity Commission (EEOC) charge that he suffered a hostile work environment, and thus, provided sufficient facts for the EEOC to investigate the claim.")

U.S. Fifth Circuit Court of Appeals (Louisiana, Mississippi, Texas)

Huckabay v. Moore, 142 F.3d 233 (5th Cir. 1998)(Hostile working environment. "In determining whether 'continuing violation' exists under Title VII, inquiry may involve several factors, including (1) subject matter, (2) frequency, and (3) perhaps most importantly, degree of permanence; these factors inquire whether alleged acts involve same type of discrimination, tending to connect them in continuing violation, whether alleged acts are recurring or are more in nature of isolated assignment or employment decision, and whether act has degree of permanence which should trigger employee's awareness of and duty to assert his or her expected without being dependent on continuing intent to discriminate.")

Sheperd v. Comptroller of Public Accounts of State of Texas, 168 F.3d 871 (5th Cir. 1999)("There are five elements necessary to set forth a sexually hostile work environment claim under Title VII: (1) that the employee belongs to a protected class, (2) that the employee was subject to unwelcome sexual harassment, (3) that the harassment was based on sex, (4) that the harassment affected a term, condition or privilege of employment, and (5) that the employer knew or should have known of the harassment and failed to take prompt remedial action.")

Hernandez v. Yellow Transp., Inc., 670 F.3d 644 (5th Cir. 2012)("Harassment 'affects a term, condition, or privilege of employment,' as required to support hostile work environment claim under Title VII, if it is sufficiently severe or pervasive to alter conditions of victim's employment and create an abusive working environment.... In deciding whether workplace harassment is sufficiently severe or pervasive to alter conditions of victim's employment, and to support hostile work environment claim, courts consider: frequency of the discriminatory conduct; its severity; whether it is physically threatening or humiliating, or a mere offensive utterance; and whether it unreasonably interferes with employee's work performance.")

Brooks v. Firestone Polymers, LLC, 640 Fed.Appx. 393 (5th Cir. 2016) ("Alleged incident in which African-American employee was asked not to use a restroom, which he perceived as a racially discriminatory request, did not support hostile work environment claim under § 1981, where employee used the restroom anyway, did not report the incident despite being asked about it by management, and stated that he viewed it as settled and that it did not recur.... Alleged incident in which employer's video monitors showed offensive images was not sufficiently severe or pervasive to create a hostile work environment under § 1981; alleged incident was isolated and, upon learning of the displays, management took prompt remedial action that ended the display of the images.... Alleged incidents in which racial slurs were used, 'black faces' were drawn in bathroom stalls in the workplace, and manager commented that as long as he was in charge of a certain unit, 'there would be no blacks in the control room' were not sufficiently severe or pervasive to create a hostile work environment under § 1981; while alleged incidents were reprehensible, they established only isolated incidents and offhand remarks, did not involve physical threats, were not apparently addressed to African-American employee, and did not appear to have interfered with his work.... Alleged incident in which African-American employee found a miniature hangman's noose placed inside his hard hat at work did not create a hostile work environment that was actionable under § 1981; employee did not show how incident affected the terms and conditions of his employment, it appeared to have been an isolated incident, and there was no indication that employer knew or should have known about the incident.")

E.E.O.C. v. WC&M Enterprises, Inc., 496 F.3d 393 (5th Cir. 2007) ("Title VII is violated, on 'hostile work environment' theory, when workplace is permeated with discriminatory intimidation, ridicule and insult that is sufficiently severe or pervasive to alter conditions of victim's employment and create abusive working environment.")

Harvill v. Westward Communications, L.L.C., 433 F.3d 428 (5th Cir. 2005)("In determining whether a work environment is hostile or abusive within the meaning of Title VII, courts look at the totality of the circumstances including the frequency of the discriminatory conduct, its severity, whether it is physically threatening or humiliating, or a mere offensive utterance, and whether it unreasonably interferes with an employee's work performance.... To be actionable as sexual harassment under Title VII, based on a hostile work environment, the challenged conduct must be both objectively offensive, meaning that a reasonable person would find it hostile and abusive, and subjectively offensive, meaning that the victim perceived it to be so.")

Lauderdale v. Texas Dept. of Criminal Justice, Institutional Div., 512 F.3d 157 (5th Cir. 2007)("Where the claim of harassment is against a supervisor, there are four elements of a Title VII hostile working environment claim: (1) that the employee belongs to a protected class, (2) that the employee was subject to unwelcome sexual harassment, (3) that the harassment was based on sex, and (4) that the harassment affected a 'term, condition, or privilege' of employment.")

Farpella-Crosby v. Horizon Health Care, 97 F.3d 803 (5th Cir. 1996)("To be actionable, conduct being challenged in hostile work environment sexual harassment claim must create environment that reasonable person would find hostile or abusive.... Mere utterance of epithet which engenders offensive feelings in employee is not alone sufficient to support Title VII liability.")

Hockman v. Westward Communictions, LLC, 407 F.3d 317 (5th Cir. 2004) ("Male coworker's alleged harassment of female employee, in purportedly making offhand remark to her about another female employee's body and asking her to come into work early so that they could be alone together, in allegedly once slapping her 'behind' with newspaper and once attempting to kiss her, in once speaking to her as she washed her hands through open door of restroom, and in brushing up against her breasts and backside on multiple occasions, was not so severe and pervasive as to 'affect term, condition, or privilege of employment,' as required to support her hostile-work-environment claim; incidents were generally isolated and non-serious in nature or, in case of 'brushings,' originally perceived as being accidental and not sufficiently severe to support hostile-work-environment claim.")

Ramsey v. Henderson, 286 F.3d 264 (5th Cir. 2002)("In determining whether workplace constitutes hostile work environment, for purpose of Title VII claim, court considers: frequency of discriminatory conduct; its severity; whether it is physically threatening or humiliating, or mere offensive utterance; and whether it unreasonably interferes with employee's work performance.")

Weller v. Citation Oil & Gas Corp., 84 F.3d 191 (5th Cir. 1996)("Title VII is only meant to bar conduct that is so severe and pervasive that it destroys protected class member's opportunity to succeed in the workplace.")

Failure To Train

U.S. Eleventh Circuit Court of Appeals (Alabama, Florida, Georgia)

Gold v. City of Miami, 151 F.3d 1346 (11th Cir. 1998)("Allegation of failure to train or supervise can be basis for municipal liability under § 1983 only where municipality inadequately trains or supervises its employees, this failure to train or supervise is a city policy, and that policy causes employees to violate citizen's constitutional rights.... Since municipality rarely will have express written or oral policy of inadequately training or supervising its employees, § 1983 plaintiff may prove city policy by showing that municipality's failure to train evidenced a 'deliberate indifference' to rights of its inhabitants, and, to establish a 'deliberate or conscious choice' or such 'deliberate indifference,' plaintiff must present some evidence that municipality knew of need to train and/or supervise in particular area and the municipality made deliberate choice not to take any action. 42 U.S.C.A. § 1983")

Price v. M & M Valve Co., 177 Fed.Appx. 1 (11th Cir. 2006) ("Employee establishes prima face case of discriminatory failure to promote by showing that (1) he is a member of a protected class, (2) he was qualified and applied for the promotion, (3) he was rejected despite his qualifications, and (4) other equally or less qualified employees who were not members of the protected class were promoted.... Before employee may pursue Title VII discrimination claim, he first must exhaust his administrative remedies by filing timely charge of discrimination with Equal Employment Opportunity Commission (EEOC); to be timely within a nondefendant state, such as Alabama, charge must be filed within 180 days of the last discriminatory act.... To extent he was relying on Title VII, African-American employee failed to timely exhaust his administrative remedies before bringing claims of discriminatory failure to promote, as he did not file Equal Employment Opportunity Commission (EEOC) charge until 184 days after one employee's promotion to supervisory position and more than 20 months after another's promotion.")

Grech v. Clayton County, Ga., 335 F.3d 1326 (11th Cir. 2003)("County's liability under § 1983 may not be based on doctrine of respondeat superior.... County is liable under § 1983 only when county's official policy causes constitutional violation.... Plaintiff may establish that county's official policy caused constitutional violation, as required to hold county liable under § 1983, by identifying either (1) officially promulgated county policy, or (2) unofficial custom or practice of county shown through repeated acts of final policymaker for county.... Plaintiff alleging that county's official policy caused constitutional violation, as required to hold county liable under §1983, (1) must show that county has authority and responsibility over governmental function in issue, and (2) must identify those officials who speak with final policymaking authority for county concerning act alleged to have caused particular constitutional violation in issue.... County sheriff was not county policymaker for his law enforcement conduct and policies regarding warrant information on state computer systems of training and supervision of his employees in that regard, as require to hold county liable under § 1983 for alleged false arrest and violation of due process arising from arrest of arrestee on expired bench warrant which had not been withdrawn from computer systems.")

Holder v. Nicholson, 287 Fed. Appx. 784 (11th Cir. 2008) ("Federal employee's termination was separate act from other prior allegedly discriminatory and retaliatory actions against her, such as purported assault by co-worker and failure to promote, and thus employee was required to contact EEO counselor within 45 days of her firing in order to preserve her claims under Title VII and ADEA. Age Discrimination in Employment Act of 1967.")

DaCosta v. Birmingham Water Works & Sewer Bd., 256 Fed.Appx. 283 (11th Cir. 2007)("Employer's reason for failing to promote Indian employee, that he had not completed classes and certification tests necessary for the positions involved and outlined in company policy, was legitimate non-discriminatory reason for employment decision, for purposes of employee's discrimination action against employer alleging violations of Title VII and §§ 1981 and 1983....")

Sewell v. Town of Lake Hamilton, 117 F.3d 488 (11th Cir. 1997)("To hold municipality liable under § 1983 for failure to train and supervise police officer, it is not enough to show that situation will arise and that taking wrong course in that situation will result in injuries to citizens; rather, there must be likelihood that failure to train or supervise will result in officer making wrong decision.... Where proper response is obvious to all without training or supervision, then failure to train or supervise is generally not 'so likely' to produce wrong decision as to support inference of deliberate indifference by city policymakers to need to train or supervise; thus, failure to train or supervise in such circumstances will not lead to municipal liability under § 1983.")

American Federation of Labor and Congress of Indus. Organization v. City of Miami, FL., 637 F.3d 1178 (11th Cir. 2011)("Municipality can be held liable under § 1983 when its employees cause constitutional injury as result of municipality's policy- or custom-based failure to adequately train or supervise its employees.... Inadequacy of police training may serve as basis for § 1983 liability only where failure to train amounts to deliberate indifference to rights of persons with whom police come into contact.... To establish municipality's deliberate indifference, plaintiff asserting failure to train or supervise claim in § 1983 suit must put forward some evidence that municipality was aware of need to train or supervise its employees in particular area.... Plaintiff asserting failure to train or supervise employees as basis for imposing liability against municipality under § 1983 may demonstrate notice by showing widespread pattern of prior abuse or even single earlier constitutional violation, but plaintiff must also demonstrate that constitutional violations were likely to recur without training.... In addition to notice of need to train employees, plaintiff asserting failure to train as basis for imposing liability against city under § 1983 must also establish that city made deliberate choice not to train its employees."

Ferguson v. Veterans Admin., 723 F.2d 871 (11th Cir. 1984)("To prevail under Title VII, white female Veterans Administration employee, who alleged that employer's failure to train and hire for librarian's position violated Title VII, would have to show discrimination by her employer.")

Mack v. S T Mobile Aerospace Engineering, Inc., 195 Fed.Appx. 829 (11th Cir. 2006)("Although coworker's statement that black employee was not promoted from apprentice to mechanic after one year of employment because he was black established prima face case of failure to promote based on race, employee failed to rebut employer's legitimate, nondiscriminatory reason for failure to promote, that it mistakenlyfailed to perform his one-year evaluation and that, after mistake was discovered, employee was promoted and paid full back pay to account for missing evaluation, given absence of showing that coworker was involved in promotion decision, was employee's supervisor at time of evaluation, or based statement on knowledge of discrimination by any supervisor.")

Doe ex. Rel Doe v. City of Demopolis, 461 Fed.Appx. 915 (11th Cir. 2012) ("City's alleged failure to train police officer not to commit statutory rape did not show deliberate indifference to the rights of its inhabitants, and thus did not support § 1983 civil rights action brought against city by thirteen-year old victim who was statutorily raped by city police officer; city was entitled to rely on officer's common sense not to commit statutory rape.")

Williams v. Limestone County, Ala., 198 Fed.Appx. 893 (11th Cir. 2006)("Sheriff did not demonstrate deliberate indifference to serious medical needs of prisoner who suffered heart attack in jail, where there was no history or pattern of jail personnel's deliberate indifference that would render need for additional medical training obvious, contract with health provider gave sheriff every reason to assume that medical emergencies would be handled according to normal routine, and fact that providing personnel with additional training might have better addressed inmate's particular needs did not show deliberate indifference.")

Belcher v. City of Foley, Ala., 30 F.3d 1390 (11th Cir. 1994)("Failure to train can amount to deliberate indifference, for purposes of imposing § 1983 liability on supervisory official, when need for more or different training is obvious, such as when there exists history of abuse by subordinates that might put supervisor on notice of need for corrective measures, and when failure to train is likely to result in violation of constitutional right.")

Weiland v. Palm Beach County Sheriff's Office, 792 F.3d 1313 (11th Cir. 2015)("A § 1983 plaintiff cannot rely upon the doctrine of respondeat superior to hold the government liable for an alleged civil rights violation, but must instead establish that the government unit has a policy or custom that caused the injury.")

U.S. Fifth Circuit Court of Appeals (Louisiana, Mississippi, Texas)

Disability: Discrimination/Harassment

U.S. Eleventh Circuit Court of Appeals (Alabama, Florida, Georgia)

Davis v. Florida Power & Light Co., 205 F.3d 1301 (11th Cir. 2000)("To establish that employee is qualified individual with disability within meaning of ADA, employee must show either that he can perform essential functions of his job without accommodation, or, failing that, show that he can perform essential functions of his job with reasonable accommodation. Americans with Disabilities Act of 1990, § 101(8)."

Holly v. Clairson Industries, LLC, 492 F.3d 1247 (11th Cir. 2007) ("To establish prima facie case of discrimination under ADA, plaintiff must show that: (1) he is disabled; (2) he is qualified individual; and (3) he was subjected to unlawful discrimination because of his disability. Americans with Disabilities Act of 1990, § 2 et seq."

D'Angelo v. ConAgra Foods, Inc., 422 F.3d 1220 (11th Cir. 2005)("To establish a prima facie case of employment discrimination under the Americans with Disabilities Act (ADA), a plaintiff must demonstrate that (1) he has a disability, (2) he is a qualified individual, which is to say, able to perform the essential functions of the employment position that he holds or seeks with or without reasonable accommodation, and (3) the defendant unlawfully discriminated against him because of the disability. Americans with Disabilities Act of 1990, § 102..."

Lucas v. W.W. Grainger, Inc., 257 F.3d 1249 (11th Cir. 2001)("To establish a prima facie case of discrimination under the ADA, an employee must show that (1) he is disabled; (20 he was a qualified individual at the relevant time, meaning he could perform the essential functions of the job in question with or without reasonable accommodation; and (3) he was discriminated against because of his disability."

Hilburn v. Murata Electronics North America, Inc., 181 F.3d 1220 (11th Cir. 1999)("Employee has burden of proving a prima facie case of disability discrimination by a preponderance of the evidence, which requires a demonstration that he or she (1) is disabled, (2) is a qualified individual, and (3) was subjected to unlawful discrimination because of his or her disability. Americans with Disabilities Act of 1990, § 102(a).")

Cleveland v. Home Shopping Network, Inc., 369 F.3d 1189 (11th Cir. 2004)("To establish a prima facie case of ADA discrimination, employee must show that: (1) she had a disability; (2) she was otherwise qualified to perform the job; and (3) she was discriminated against based upon the disability.... The McDonnell Douglas prima facie case method for establishing an employment discrimination claim was never intended to be rigid, mechanized, or ritualistic; it is merely a procedural device to facilitate an orderly focused evaluation of the evidence as it bears on the critical question of discrimination.")

Greenberg v. BellSouth Telecommunications, Inc., 498 F.3d 1258 (11th Cir. 2007)("Claims of disability discrimination raised under the Florida Civil Rights Act (FCRA) are analyzed under the same framework as the ADA.")

Frazier-White v. Gee, 818 F.3d 1249 (11th Cir. 2016)("To prevail on disability discrimination claim under the Americans with Disabilities Act (ADA) or Florida Civil Rights Act (FCRA), discharged employee was required to show that: (1) she was disabled, (2) she was a 'qualified individual' when she was terminated, and (3) she was discriminated against on account of her disability.")

Shepard v. United Parcel Service, Inc., 470 Fed.Appx. 726 (11th Cir. 2012)("Employee with chronic myeloid leukemia who was seeking to establish prima facie case of disability discrimination failed to provide sufficient evidence that he had a 'disability' under ADA when employer placed him on medical leave of absence; though he claimed his medical condition substantially limited major life activities of eating and sleeping, neither he nor his physician ever informed employer of those limitations while he was on medical leave of absence, employee also failed to establish that his condition substantially limited major life activity of working, and could not demonstrate that he had record of having impairment based solely on his prior medical leaves of absence and testimony that it was common knowledge at work he had leukemia, or that he was regarded as disabled.")

Sicilia v. United Parcel Service, Inc., 279 Fed.Appx. 936 (11th Cir. 2008)("To establish prima facie case of disability discrimination under the ADA, employee must show that (1) he has a disability, (2) he is a qualified person, and (3) his employer unlawfully discriminated against him because of his disability. Americans with Disabilities Act of 1990, § 102(a).")

Farley v. Nationwide Mut. Ins. Co., 197 F.3d 1322 (11th Cir. 1999) ("Under the McDonnell Douglas framework, an ADEA or ADA plaintiff must first establish a prima facie case of discrimination, and the burden of production then shifts to the defendant who must articulate a legitimate non-discriminatory reason for the challenged employment decision; the plaintiff then bears the ultimate burden of persuasion that the defendant's proffered reason is a pretext for discrimination.")

Terrell v. USAir, 132 F.3d 621 (11th Cir. 1998)("To state prima facie case of disability discrimination under ADA, employee must show that: (1) he or she has disability; (2) with or without reasonable accommodations, he or she can perform essential functions of position he or she holds; and (3) he or she was discriminated against because of disability."

Siudock v. Volusia County School Bd., 568 Fed.Appx. 659 (11th Cir. 2014)("Former teacher could not perform essential function of his job with or without accommodations, and thus he was not qualified individual under ADA, precluding his claims against county school board for discrimination and failure to accommodate; even if board had accommodated teacher by allowing him to teach only gifted students, teacher still would have been unable to perform essential function of his job, as even gifted students would have disciplinary problems that could have caused teacher stress and exacerbated his diabetes, and, to extent that board did accommodate teacher, those accommodations were reasonable, even if they were not exact accommodations that teacher wanted.")

Harrison v. Benchmark Electronics Huntsville, Inc., 593 F.3d 1206 (11th Cir. 2010)("Fact that temporary employee was not hired as a permanent employee, allegedly because of his responses to an allegedly unlawful medical inquiry into his reasons for taking barbiturates, was sufficient to establish that employee suffered damages as a result of the allegedly unlawful injury, as required for employee to establish prima facie case that employer violated the ADA's bar against using medical examination or inquiries to discriminate.")

Doe v. Dekalb County School Dist., 145 F.3d 1441 (11th Cir. 1998)("A person who is infected with human immunodeficiency virus (HIV) is 'disabled' for purposes of Americans with Disabilities Act (ADA), even if he has not developed acquired immune deficiency syndrome (AIDS)."

Gilliard v. Georgia Dept. of Corrections, 500 Fed.Appx. 860 (11th Cir. 2012)("Scintilla of evidence supporting allegation that employer breached the confidentiality of employee's medical records or made overly broad requests that caused her to release her entire medical record was insufficient to preclude summary judgment for employer on ADA confidentiality claims.")

U.S. Fifth Circuit Court of Appeals (Louisiana, Mississippi, Texas)

Frame v. City of Arlington, 657 F.3d 215 (5th Cir. 2011)("In an action under the ADA's Title II, which prohibits disability discrimination in the provision of public services, alleging that a city's newly built and altered sidewalks are inaccessible, a district court has discretion to craft an appropriate injunction based on the particular facts of the case, and thus will be able to ensure that the city's alleged violations are remedied in a reasonable manner.")

Rodriguez v. Eli Lilly and Co., 820 F.3d 759 (5th Cir. 2016)("To qualify as direct evidence of discrimination on the basis of disability, in violation of the ADA, workplace comments must be: (1) related to the protected class of persons of which the plaintiff of which the plaintiff is a member; (2) proximate in time to the terminations; (3) made by an individual with authority over the employment decisions at issue; and (4) related to the employment decision at issue. Americans with Disabilities Act of 1990, § 102, 42 U.S.C.A. § 12112.)"

Kemp v. Holder, 610 F.3d 231 (5th Cir. 2010)("To prevail on Americans with Disabilities Act (ADA) and Rehabilitation Act claims, a plaintiff must establish that (1) he is disabled within the meaning of the ADA, (2) he is qualified and able to perform the essential functions of his job, and (3) his employer fired him because of his disability. Rehabilitation Act of 1973, § 2 et seq., 29 U.S.C.A. § 701 et seq.; Americans with Disabilities Act of 1990, § 102(a), 42 U.S.C.A. § 12112(a).")

Neely v. PSEG Texas, Ltd. Partnership, 735 F.3d 242 (5th Cir. 2013)("Even under the ADA as amended by the ADA Amendments Act (ADAAA), to prevail on a claim of disability discrimination under the ADA, a party must prove that (1) he has a disability; (2) he is qualified for the job; and (3) the covered entity made its adverse employment decision because of the party's disability....")

Daigle v. Liberty Life Ins. Co., 70 F.3d 394 (5th Cir. 1995)("Under McDonnell Douglas analysis, an employee claiming disability must first make out a prima facie case by showing that he or she suffers from a disability, he or she is qualified for the job, he or she was subject to adverse employment action, and he or she was replaced by a nondisabled person or was treated less favorably than nondisabled employees....")

Pinkerton v. Spellings, 529 F.3d 513 (5th Cir. 2008)("Same standard of causation that is applicable to discrimination claims under the Americans with Disabilities Act (ADA) also applies to disability discrimination claim under section of the Rehabilitation Act applicable to government employees.... To establish liability in employment discrimination action under the Americans with Disabilities Act (ADA), plaintiff must show that disability played a motivating role in adverse employment action, but need not establish that it was sole cause of discrimination; 'motivating factor' as opposed to 'sole causation' standard is appropriate standard of causation in causes of action under the ADA and, by extension, under provision of the Rehabilitation Act applicable to government employees.")

Flowers v. Southern Regional Physician Services, Inc., 247 F.3d 229 (5th Cir. 2001)("In determining whether work environment is 'abusive' under ADA, reviewing court must consider entirety of evidence presented at trial, including frequency of discriminatory conduct, its severity, whether it is physically threatening or humiliating or mere offensive utterance, and whether it unreasonably interferes with employee's work performance.")

Carmona v. Southwest Airlines Co., 604 F.3d 848 (5th Cir. 2010)("On an employee's claim of disability discrimination under the ADA, once an employer has produced sufficient evidence to support a nondiscriminatory explanation for its decision to terminate the employee, the employee may establish that he was the victim of intentional discrimination by showing that the employer's proffered explanation is unworthy of credence; it is permissible for the trier of fact to infer the ultimate fact of discrimination from the falsity of the employer's explanation.")

Taylor v. Principal Financial Group, Inc., 93 F.3d 155 (5th Cir. 1996) ("In general, it is responsibility of ADA plaintiff to inform employer that accommodation is needed because of plaintiff's disability and once request has been made, the appropriate, reasonable accommodation is best determined through flexible, interactive process that involves both employer and plaintiff; in other words, it is plaintiff's initial request for accommodation which triggers employer's obligation to participate in interactive process of determining one and once accommodation is properly requested, responsibility for fashioning reasonable accommodation is shared between employer and plaintiff.")

Age Discrimination

U.S. Eleventh Circuit Court of Appeals (Alabama, Florida, Georgia)

Liebman v. Metropolitan Life Ins. Co., 808 F.3d 1294 (11th Cir. 2015) ("To establish a prima facie case of retirement benefits interference in violation of ERISA, an employee must show that he: (1) was entitled to ERISA protection; (2) was qualified for his position; and (3) was discharged under circumstances that give rise to an inference of discrimination.")

Mora v. Jackson Memorial Foundation, Inc., 597 F.3d 1201 (11th Cir. 2010)("An ADEA plaintiff must show that age was the reason that the employer decided to act.... Because an ADEA plaintiff must establish 'but for' causality, no 'same decision' affirmative defense can exist; the employer either acted because of the plaintiff's age or it did not.")

Kragor v. Takeda Pharmaceuticals America, Inc., 702 F.3d 1304 (11th Cir. 2012)("To make out a prima facie case of age discrimination under the ADEA, the plaintiff must show four things: (1) that she was a member of the protected group of persons between the ages of 40 and 70; (2) that she was subject to adverse employment action; (3) that a substantially younger person filled the position that she sought or from which she was discharged; and (4) that she was qualified to do the job for which she was rejected.")

Hipp v. Liberty Nat. Life Ins. Co., 252 F.3d 1208 (11th Cir. 2001)("In lawsuit under the Age Discrimination in Employment Act (ADEA), plaintiff who has not filed his own charge with the Equal Employment Opportunity Commission (EEOC) may piggyback onto another plaintiff's charge provided: (1) the relied upon charge, to which he is piggybacking, is not invalid, and (2) individual claims of filing and of non-filing plaintiff arise out of similar discriminatory treatment in same time frame.")

Turlington v. Atlanta Gas Light Co., 135 F.3d 1428 (11th Cir. 1998)("In ADEA case involving discharge, demotion, or failure to hire, plaintiff may establish prima facie case by showing: (1) that he was member of protected group of persons between ages of forty and seventy; (2) that he was subject to adverse employment action; (3) that substantially younger person filled position that he sought or from which he was discharged; and (4) that he was qualified to do job for which he was rejected.")

Chapman v. Al Transport, 229 F.3d 1012 (11th Cir. 2000)("Under the burden-shifting framework for evaluating ADEA claims that are based upon circumstantial evidence of discrimination, the employee must first establish a prima facie case of discrimination.... On method an employee can use to establish a prima facie case for an ADEA violation is by sowing that he or she: (1) was a member of the protected age group; (2) was subjected to adverse employment action; (3) was qualified to do the job; and (4) was replaced by or otherwise lost a position to a younger individual.")

Munoz v. Oceanside Resorts, Inc., 223 F.3d 1340 (11th Cir. 2000)("Elements necessary to establish a prima facie case of age discrimination under the ADEA supported by circumstantial evidence are: (1) the plaintiff was a member of the protected group of persons between the ages of forty and seventy; (2) that plaintiff was subject to adverse employment action; (3) that a substantially younger person filled the position from which he was discharged; and (4) that plaintiff was qualified to do the job from which he was discharged.")

Jones v. BE&K Engineering Co., 146 Fed.Appx. 356 (11th Cir. 2005) ("Discharged employee failed to present evidence of employer's intent to discriminate in discharging him during employer's reduction in force, as required to establish prima facie case that his discharge violated Age Discrimination in Employment Act (ADEA); evidence established that employer chose to discharge employee while retaining younger coworker because coworker's engineering degree made him more valuable for future needs of employer and demands of employer's clients.")

Carter v. DecisionOne Corp. Through C.T. Corp. System, 122 F.3d 997 (11th Cir. 1997)("Former employee presented sufficient evidence to support determination by jury that former employer's proffered reason for discharging employee, that is, her performance, was pretext for unlawful discrimination under ADEA, including statement by manager that it was preferable to have a 'nubile young woman' making sales calls, statement by employer's president that he had gotten rid of all the 'old sleazy people,' and other evidence that older workers were replaced with younger ones and that younger sales representatives were treated better than employee.")

Watkins v. Sverdrup Technology, Inc., 153 F.3d 1308 (11th Cir. 1998)

("Where employer produces evidence that it discharged ADEA plaintiff during a reduction in force (RIF), plaintiff establishes prima facie case by demonstrating (1) that he was in protected age group and was adversely affected by an employment decision, (2) that he was qualified for his current position for to assume another position at time of discharge, and (3) evidence by which fact finder reasonably could conclude that employer intended to discriminate on basis of age in reaching that decision.")

Smith v. J. Smith Lanier & Co., 352 F.3d 1342 (11th Cir. 2003) ("In reduction in force (RIF) case in which dismissed employee's position was eliminated in its entirety, employee establishes prima facie case of age discrimination by demonstrating: (1) that he/she was in protected age group and was adversely affected by employment decision; (2) that he/she was qualified for current position, or to assume another position, at time of discharge; and (3) evidence by which fact finder may reasonably conclude that employer intended to discriminate on basis of age in reaching employment decision.")

Van Voorhis v. Hillsborough County Bd. Of County Com'rs, 512 F.3d 1296 (11th Cir. 2008)("An 'adverse employment action' is an ultimate employment decision, such as discharge or failure to hire, or other conduct that alters the employee's compensation, terms, conditions, or privileges of employment, deprives him or her of employment opportunities, or adversely affects his or her status as an employee.")

U.S. Fifth Circuit Court of Appeals (Louisiana, Mississippi, Texas)

Rachid v. Jack In The Box, Inc. 376 F.3d 305 (5th Cir. 2004)("To demonstrate age discrimination under ADEA, terminated employee must show that he was: (1) discharged; (2) qualified for position; (3) over 40 years old a t time of discharge; and (4) replaced by someone under 40, replaced by someone younger, or otherwise discharged because of age.")

Russell v. McKinney Hosp. Venture, 235 F.3d 219 (5th Cir. 2000)("A plaintiff's prima facie case under Age Discrimination in Employment Act (ADEA), combined with sufficient evidence to find that the employer's asserted justification is false, may permit the trier of fact to conclude that the employee unlawfully discriminated.")

West v. Nabors Drilling USA, Inc., 330 F.3d 379 (5th Cir. 2003) ("To establish prima facie case of age discrimination in discharge case, employee must prove that: 1) he was discharged; 2) he was qualified for his position; 3) he was within protected class; and 4) he was replaced by someone outside protected class, someone younger, or was otherwise discharged because of his age.")

Miller v. Raytheon Co., 716 F.3d 138 (5th Cir. 2013)("Under the burden-shifting framework set forth in McDonnell Douglas, the employee carries the initial burden of establishing a prima facie case of age discrimination under the ADEA and, if he succeeds, the burden shifts to the employer to provide a legitimate, nondiscriminatory reason for terminating employment; if the employer satisfies this burden, the burden shifts back to the employee to prove either that the employer's proffered reason was not true, but was instead a pretext for age discrimination, or that, even if the employer's reason is true, he was terminated because of his age.")

Woodhouse v. Magnolia Hosp., 92 F.3d 248 (5th Cir. 1996)("Federal district court did not abuse its discretion in ordering employee, whose position as director of admissions within business office was eliminated during reduction in force (RIF) and who was not rehired for clinical nursing position, to be reinstated to the nursing position as remedy for age discrimination; employee requested that she be reinstated to nursing position and at time of trial, hospital had 11 such positions vacant, employee could not be reinstated to her director of admissions position because it no longer existed, and reinstatement was the preferred remedy.")

Moss v. BMC Software, Inc., 610 F.3d 917 (5th Cir. 2010)("To establish an ADEA claim, a plaintiff relying on circumstantial evidence must put forth a prima facie case, at which point the burden shifts to the employer to provide a legitimate, non-discriminatory reason for the employment decision, if the employer articulates a legitimate, non-discriminatory reason for the employment decision, the plaintiff must them be afforded an opportunity to rebut the employer's purported explanation, to show that the reason given is merely pretextual.")

Machinchick v. PB Power, Inc., 398 F.3d 345 (5th Cir. 2005)("Employees producing only circumstantial evidence of discriminatory animus must negotiate McDonnell Douglas burden-shifting analysis, under which employee must first establish prima facie case of age discrimination by showing that (1) he was discharged, (2) he was qualified for position, (3) he was within protected class at time of discharge, and (4) he was either

(i) replaced by someone outside protected class, (ii) replaced by someone younger, or (iii) otherwise discharged because of his age; once employee establishes prima facie case, burden of production shifts to employer to proffer legitimate nondiscriminatory reason for its employment action.")

Armendariz v. Pinkerton Tobacco Co., 58 F.3d 144 (5th Cir. 1995) ("Former employee failed to establish prima facie case of age discrimination in connection with his termination in reduction in force (RIF) or job elimination, as he failed to present evidence from which jury could have concluded that employer did not treat age as neutral factor in its decision; although former employee alleged that employer did not relocate him or rehire him for positions that subsequently became open in other territories because of his age, he did not allege or offer proof that there were openings at time he was terminated and employer produced evidence that it had long standing policy against relocating employees in former employee's position.")

Lay-off/ Recall Rights/ Discrimination

U.S. Eleventh Circuit Court of Appeals (Alabama, Florida, Georgia)

Pettway v. American Cast Iron Pipe Co., 494 F.2d 211 (5th Cir. 1974)[11th Cir. Opinion]("'Business necessity' doctrine, under which employment practices which are nonintentionally discriminatory or neutral but perpetuate consequences of past discrimination may be permitted because of their overriding business necessity, places burden on defendant to justify such practice once discriminatory result is demonstrated.")

Watkins v. United Steel Workers of America, Local No. 2369, 516 F.2d 41 (5th Cir. 1975)[11th Cir. Opinion] ("Even if 'last fired, first hired' provisions of negotiated seniority system were to be considered discriminatory, such system was insulated from being an unlawful employment practice on ground that it was a bona fide seniority system within exemption provision of Civil Rights Act of 1964 where the recall provision accorded white workers preference only over junior blacks on the basis of total employment.... Where each employee, regardless of race, is treated equally under seniority system which does not have the effect of 'locking in' past discrimination as to that employee, system is a bona fide one which is exempt from reaches of Civil Rights act of 1964.")

E.E.O.C. v. Beverage Canners, Inc., 897 F.2d 1067 (11th Cir. 1990)("Finding that employer discriminated against employees on basis of race, warranting injunctive relief, was sufficiently supported by evidence that plant manager and supervisor frequently made flagrant, revolting, and insulting racially derogatory remarks toward and in presence of blacks, and that company management had knowledge of such conduct.... Laid off black employee whose former job was filled by white applicant was discriminated against, though employer had no 'rehire' policy; overwhelming evidence of racial hostility by managers responsible for employment decisions constituted direct evidence of discriminatory intent in management decisions.")

Miles v. M.N.C. Corp., 750 F.2d 867 (11th Cir. 1985)("Plaintiff in Title VII discriminatory discharge case must prove that he/she is member of protected class, was qualified for the position held, was discharged, and was replaced by person outside the protected class.... Once prima facie case of employment discrimination is proved under Title VII, burden shifts to employer to articulate legitimate, nondiscriminatory reason for its acts with regard to plaintiff, and burden on employer is one of production rather than persuasion.... If defendant employer in a Title VII discrimination case carries burden of production once a prima facie case is proved, presumption raised by the prima facie [six] is rebutted and employee must persuade the court that the reasons for not hiring plaintiff offered by the employer were pretextual.")

James v. Stockham Valves & Fittings Co., 559 F.2d 310 (5th Cir. 1977)(11th Cir. Opinion)("In employment discrimination suit by black employees against employer, district court's finding that employer had at no time made initial job assignments either to departments or specific jobs on the basis of an employee's race was clearly erroneous.")

Wallace v. Teledyne Continental Motors, 138 Fed.Appx. 139 (11th Cir. 2005)("Worker could not show causal link between her layoff and filing of charge with Equal Employment Opportunity Commission (EEOC) supporting Title VII retaliation claim when employer's president ordered layoffs before EEOC charge was filed and worker was recalled after only 10 days.")

U.S. Fifth Circuit Court of Appeals (Louisiana, Mississippi, Texas)

Allen v. U.S. Steel Corp., 665 F.2d 689 (5th Cir. 1982)(In their original complaint, plaintiffs alleged that in violation of Title VII of the Civil Rights Act of 1964… and of the Equal Pay Act of 1963… defendant U.S. Steel discriminated against women in several ways, including its policies and practices concerning recruitment, hiring, initial job assignments, transfers, promotions, layoffs, recalls, wages and fringe benefits.")

Payne v. Travenol Laboratories Inc., 673 F.2d 798 (5th Cir. 1982)("In Title VII suit in which employer was found to have discriminated, decree had to be modified on remand with respect to provision that employees laid off and awaiting recall shall be recalled by seniority date, whether actual or constructive since under decree employee with normal seniority could fare better than class member with equal constructive seniority if employee with normal seniority had already been recalled after layoff while employee with constructive seniority still awaits recall, and since employee with normal seniority might also escape layoff altogether while class member with less normal seniority but equal constructive seniority is laid off.")

Watkins v. United Steel Workers of America, Local No. 2369, 516 F.2d 41 (5th Cir. 1975)(11th Cir. Opinion)("Black employees who had been laid off under negotiated seniority system with 'last hire, first fired' and 'last fired, first rehired' provisions and who never suffered discrimination at hands of the employer were in no better position to complain of recall system than were white workers who had been hired contemporaneously with them.")

Retaliation/ Reprisal

U.S. Eleventh Circuit Court of Appeals (Alabama, Florida, Georgia)

Pennington v. City of Huntsville, 261 F.3d 1262 (11th Cir. 2001) ("Employee alleging Title VII claim may not establish that an employer's proffered reason for adverse employment action is pretext for discrimination merely by questioning the wisdom of the employer's reason, as long as the reason is one that might motivate a reasonable employer.… Mixed-motive defense applies to retaliation claims under § 1983 and Title VII.")

Crawford v. Carroll, 529 F.3d 961 (11th Cir. 2008)("To make out prima facie case of racial discrimination under Title VII or in § 1983 equal protection claim, plaintiff must show that: (1) she belongs to protected class; (2) she was qualified to do job; (3) she was subjected to adverse employment action; and (4) her employer treated similarly situated employees outside her class more favorably.")

Harper v. Blockbuster Entertainment Corp., 139 F.3d 1385 (11th Cir. 1998)("For purposes of Title VII retaliation claim, plaintiff engages in 'statutorily protected activity' when he or she protests employer's conduct which is actually lawful, so long as he or she demonstrates good faith, reasonable belief that employer was engaged in unlawful employment practices.... In seeking to demonstrate that he or she protected employer's conduct based on good faith, reasonable belief that employer was engaged in unlawful employment practices, as required for Title VII retaliation claim, it is insufficient for plaintiff to allege his belief in this regard was honest and bona fide, but, rather, allegations and record must also indicate that belief, though perhaps mistaken, was objectively reasonable.")

Williams v. Apalachee Center, Inc., 315 Fed.Appx. 798 (11th Cir. 2009)("In order to constitute an adverse employment action for purposes of establishing a prima facie case under Title VII's anti-retaliation provision, the action must be materially adverse from the standpoint of a reasonable employee, such that it would dissuade a reasonable employee from making a discrimination charge.")

Thomas v. Cooper Lighting, Inc., 506 F.3d 1361 (11th Cir. 2007) ("The three-month lapse of time between the employee's complaints accusing her supervisor of sexual harassment and the termination of her employment did not constitute very close temporal proximity, so as to establish a causal connection between the harassment complaints and the termination, as required to establish a prima facie case of retaliation in violation of Title VII.")

Wideman v. Wal-Mart Stores, Inc., 141 F.3d 1453 (11th Cir. 1998)("To establish causal relation element of prima facie case of retaliation under Title VII, plaintiff need only show that the protected activity and the adverse action are not wholly unrelated.")

Underwood v. Department of Financial Services State of Florida, 518 Fed.Appx. 637 (11th Cir. 2013) ("To establish a prima facie case of retaliation, a plaintiff may show that he engaged in protected activity, he suffered a materially adverse action, and a causal connection existed between the activity and the adverse action.")

Merritt v. Dillard Paper Co., 120 F.3d 1181 (11th Cir. 1997)("Anti-retaliation provision of Title VII, which prohibits employers from taking action against employee who participates in another employee's Title VII proceeding, does not prohibit employer from imposing discipline, including termination, on any employee who sexually harasses or otherwise discriminates against other employees, so long as discipline is based on reason other than employee's participation in Title VII proceeding.")

Little v. United Technologies, Carrier Transicold Div., 103 F.3d 956 (11th Cir. 1997)("Employee who opposed co-worker's racially offensive comment did not engage in statutorily protected activity so as to establish a prima facie case of retaliation under Title VII; co-worker's racially offensive comment alone was not attributable to employer and thus, employee's opposition to remark did not constitute opposition to unlawful employment practice.... Plaintiff who seeks to establish prima facie case of retaliation under the opposition clause of Title VII on the ground that he had good faith belief that employer was engaged in unlawful practices must not only show that he subjectively (that is, in good faith) believed that employer was engaged in unlawful employment practices, but also that his belief was objectively reasonable in light of the facts and record presented; it is not enough for plaintiff to allege that his belief in this regard was honest and bona fide for the allegations and record must also indicate that the belief, though perhaps mistaken, was objectively reasonable.")

E.E.O.C. v. Total System Services, Inc., 221 F.3d 1171 (11th Cir. 2000) ("Provision in Title VII prohibiting employer from retaliating against employee because employee 'has made a charge, testified, assisted, or participated in any manner in an investigation, proceeding, or hearing under this subchapter' protects employee's involvement in proceedings and activities occurring in conjunction with or after the filing of formal charge with Equal Employment Opportunity Commission (EEOC) and does not protect employee's participation in employer's internal, in-house investigation, conducted apart from formal charge with EEOC.... Some employee must file charge with Equal Employment Opportunity Commission (EEOC) or its designated representative or otherwise instigate proceedings under statute for employee's conduct to be protected under participation clause of Title VII's retaliation provision.")

Anduze v. Florida Atlantic University, 151 Fed.Appx. 875 (11th Cir. 2005)("African-American female employee of university did not engage in 'protected activity' within the meaning of the participation clause of Title VII, as required to establish prima facie Title VII retaliation claim, where employee had not yet filed her race discrimination charge with the Equal Employment Opportunity Commission (EEOC) at time the alleged adverse employment action was taken against employee.")

Sullivan v. Natoinal R.R. Passenger Corp., 170 F.3d 1056 (11th Cir. 1999) ("Retaliation is a separate offense from discrimination under Title VII; employee need not prove underlying claim of discrimination for retaliation claim to succeed.")

Shannon v. Bellsouth Telecommunications, Inc., 292 F.3d 712 (11th Cir. 2002)("'Adverse employment action' suffered by Title VII claimant does not refer only to ultimate employment decisions, such as decision to discharge employee; employer conduct falling short of ultimate employment decision may still be cognizable under Title VII if it reaches some threshold level of substantiality.... Reassignment of telephone company service technician to different geographical area did not constitute 'adverse employment action,' as required to support technician's Title VII retaliation claim, even though he claimed that new assignment made it more difficult for him to meet employer's performance standards.")

Dixon v. The Hallmark Companies, Inc., 627 F.3d 849 (11th Cir. 2010) ("To prevail on Title VII claim of failure to accommodate religious beliefs, plaintiff must establish that: (1) they held a bona fide religious belief that conflicted with an employment requirement; (2) they informed employer of that belief; and (3) they were discharged for failing to comply with the conflicting employment requirement.")

Brown v. Alabama Dept. of Transp., 597 F.3d 1160 (11th Cir. 2010)("The three elements of a prima facie case of retaliation under Title VII create a presumption that the adverse actin was the product of an intent to retaliate.... Once a Title VII plaintiff establishes a prima facie case of retaliation, the burden of production shifts to the defendant to rebut the presumption by articulating a legitimate, non-discriminatory reason for the adverse employment action, and if the defendant carries this burden of production, the presumption raised by the prima facie case is rebutted and drops from the case.")

Harris v. Florida Agency for Health Care Admin., 611 Fed.Appx. 949 (11th Cir. 2015)("There was no causal connection between any of state employee's protected activities and his termination, and thus state agency did not retaliate against employee in violation of Title VII; employer's charge to Florida Commission on Human Relations and his complaint were filed more than one year before his termination.")

Boyland v. Corrections Corp. of America, 390 Fed.Appx. 973 (11th Cir. 2010)("Former employer's reason for terminating African-American corrections officer, that officer violated work policy and lied during the investigation, was not pretext for discrimination, as required for officer's Title VII retaliation action, even though other officers were not terminated for breaching policies; officer's breach of policy resulted in inmate having access to a gun and ammunition, which did not happen in breaches by other officers, and other officers did not lie in subsequent investigations.")

U.S. Fifth Circuit Court of Appeals (Louisiana, Mississippi, Texas)

Septimus v. University of Houston, 399 F.3d 601 (5th Cir. 2005)("Proper standard of proof on the causation element of a Title VII retaliation claims brought under a pretext theory; employee's ultimate burden is to prove that the employer's stated reason for the adverse action was merely a pretext for the real, retaliatory purpose.... Proper standard of proof on the causation element of a Title VII retaliation claim is that the adverse employment action taken against the employee would not have occurred 'but for' her protected activity.")

McCoy v. City of Shreveport, 492 F.3d 551 (5th Cir. 2007)("Under the framework for establishing a Title VII retaliation claim based upon circumstantial evidence, a Title VII plaintiff must establish that: (1) he participated in an activity protected by Title VII; (2) his employer took an adverse employment action against him; and (3) a causal connection exists between the protected activity and the adverse employment action.")

Ackel v. National Communications, Inc., 339 F.3d 376 (5th Cir. 2003) ("In order to establish a prima facie claim of Title VII retaliation, an employer must show: (1) that the employee engaged in activity protected by Title VII; (2) that an adverse employment action occurred, and (3) that a causal link existed between the protected activity and the adverse action.")

Long v. Eastfield College, 88 F.3d 300 (5th Cir. 1996)("In retaliatory discharge action under Title VII, college satisfied its burden to articulate legitimate, non-retaliatory reason for terminating employees who had filed hostile work environment complaints against their supervisors, where supervisors' termination recommendations asserted that employees had violated key replacement procedures and did not inform supervisors.")

National Labor Relations Act (Lay-off/ Recall Rights/ Discrimination)

U.S. Eleventh Circuit Court of Appeals (Alabama, Florida, Georgia)

N.L.R.B. v. U.S. Postal Service, 526 F.3d 729 (11th Cir. 2008) ("Substantial evidence supported determination by National Labor Relations Board (NLRB) that supervisory Postal Service employee had unlawfully threatened to retaliate against Postal Service employee for filing unfair practice charge against him, based on evidence that, after learning that employee had filed such a charge, supervisor had telephoned employee to discuss charge, begun to yell at him for filing charge, and warned employee that he would be sorry and that he 'had better get a good attorney' because supervisor was going to sue; evidence showed that supervisor's statements were retaliatory in nature and were not made incident to any contemplated litigation, regardless of whether Petition Clause protection extended to unconsummated threats to sue.")

N.L.R.B. v. McClain of Georgia, Inc., 138 F.3d 1418 (11th Cir. 1998) ("To determine whether anti-union animus was motivating factor behind employer's decision to take adverse employment action, Wright Line test mandates three phases of proof, such that (1) General Counsel must first show by preponderance of evidence that protected activity was motivating factor in employer's decision to discharge employee, (2) such showing establishes statutory violation unless employer can show as affirmative defense that it would have discharged employee for legitimate reason regardless of protected activity, and (3) General Counsel may then offer evidence that employer's proffered 'legitimate' explanation is pretextual, and thereby conclusively restore inference of unlawful motivation.")

N.L.R.B. v. Contemporary Cars, Inc., 667 F.3d 1364 (11th Cir. 2012) ("To determine whether a proposed group of employees constitutes a separate 'craft unit,' the National Labor Relations Board (NLRB) considers whether: (1) the employer assigns work according to need rather than on craft or jurisdictional lines, (2) the group participates in a formal training or apprenticeship program, (3) the group's work is functionally integrated with the work of excluded employees, (4) the group's duties overlap with the duties of excluded employees, and (5) the group shares common interests with excluded employees, including wages, benefits, and cross-training.")

Crew One Productions, Inc. v. N.L.R.B., 811 F.3d 1305 (11th Cir. 2016)("In determining a worker's status under the National Labor Relations Act (NLRA) as independent contractor or employee, the test for control takes into account the degree of supervision, the entrepreneurial interests of the agent and any other relevant factors; it also distinguishes between control over the manner and means of the agent's performance and the details of the work, which is relevant, and mere economic control or control over the end result of the performance, which is not.")

Cooper/ T. Smith, Inc. v. N.L.R.B., 177 F.3d 1259 (11th Cir. 1999) ("In proceedings before National Labor Relations Board's (NLRB), the burden of establishing the supervisory status of an employee on the party asserting such a status…. Three questions must be answered in the affirmative for an employee to be deemed a supervisor under National Labor Relations Act (NLRA): first, does the employee have authority to engage in 1 of the 12 listed activities; second, does the exercise of that authority require the use of independent judgment; third, does the employee hold the authority in the interest of the employer…. Docking pilots employed by stevedoring company were not 'supervisors' within the meaning of the National Labor Relations Act (NLRA), and were thus eligible for inclusion in bargaining unit; docking pilots did not use independent judgment when making informal evaluation of trainees' work, assigning tugboats, or communicating with captain during the docking process.")

Kentov v. Sheep Metal Workers' Intern. Ass'n Local 15, AFL-CIO, 418 F.3d 1259 (11th Cir. 2005)("In reviewing the grant of a temporary injunctive relief pending National Labor Relations Board (NLRB) resolution of certain unfair labor practice charges, court considers only: (1) whether the Board has shown reasonable cause to believe that a union has violated the National Labor Relations Act (NLRA) as alleged, and if so, (2) whether injunctive relief is 'just' and 'proper'…. Section of National Labor Relations Act (NLRA) prohibiting secondary boycotts aims to prohibit a union that has a labor dispute with one employer (the primary employer) from exerting pressure on another neutral employer (the secondary employer), where the union's conduct is calculated to force the secondary employer to cease doing business with the primary employer.")

Dowd v. International Longshoremen's Ass'n, AFL-CIO, 975 F.2d 779 (11th Cir. 1992)("In addition to demonstrating reasonable cause to believe that unfair labor practice has occurred, National Labor Relations Board (NLRB) must show that equitable relief is just and proper under the circumstances, in order to obtain an injunction under section of the NLRA authorizing interim injunctive pending resolution of unfair labor practice charges by the NLRB.... Conclusion of district court considering petition for injunction under section NLRA that the National Labor Relations Board (NLRB) has presented a substantial and not frivolous legal theory is subject to plenary review on appeal.")

N.L.R.B. v. Goya Foods of Florida, 525 F.3d 1117 (11th Cir. 2008)("Substantial evidence supported determinations by the National Labor Relations Board (NLRB) that the discharge of three employees was due to employees' protected participation in labor union activity, in violation of the National Labor Relations Act (NLRA); evidence showed that there was a pervasive anti-union animus leading up to the discharges, the discharged employees engaged in a brief and peaceful protest activity at the location of one of employer's customers shortly before their discharge, and the employer's justification for the terminations was weak.")

Georgia Power Co. v. N.L.R.B., 427 F.3d 1354 (11th Cir. 2005) ("Courts have a narrow role when reviewing National Labor Relations Board (NLRB) decisions: the rule which the NLRB adopts is judicially reviewable for consistency with the NLRA, and for rationality, but if it satisfies those criteria, the NLRB's application of the rule, if supported by substantial evidence on the record as a whole, must be enforced.")

International Broth. Of Boilermakers, Iron Ship Builders, Blacksmiths, Forgers & Helpers, AFL-CIO v. N.L.R.B., 127 F.3d 1300 (11th Cir. 1997)("To establish violation of section of NLRA prohibiting employer from discouraging membership in labor organization through discrimination, charging party must prove that employer had knowledge of employees' union activities.... Employer's policy of refusing to consider applications containing information not requested on application form, as applied to applicants who wrote 'volunteer union organizer' on their applications, did not violate section of NLRA prohibiting employer from discouraging membership in labor organization through discrimination; employer disqualified applicants who provided nonresponsive information regardless of whether such information was union-related, and employer invited all disqualified applicants to reapply."

Lakeland Health Care Associates, LLC v. N.L.R.B., 696 F.3d 1332 (11th Cir. 2012)("To exercise independent judgment, for purposes of analysis of whether an individual is a 'supervisor' under National Labor Relations Act (NLRA), the individual must at minimum act, or effectively recommend action, free of the control of others and form an opinion or evaluation by discerning and comparing data. National Labor Relations Act, § 2(11)."

Arlook for and on Behalf of N.L.R.B. v. S. Lichtenberg & Co. Inc., 952 F.2d 367 911th Cir. 1992)("District court should grant National Labor Relations Board's (NLRB) request for injunctive relief only when there is reasonable cause to believe that alleged unfair labor practices have occurred and requested injunctive relief is just and proper.... District court's role in determining whether there is reasonable cause to believe that labor violations have occurred warranting injunctive relief is limited to evaluating whether National Labor Relations Board's (NLRB) theories of law and fact are not insubstantial and frivolous and this evaluation has two components—legal question and factual threshold—and with respect to the legal question component, NLRB must present substantial, nonfrivolous, coherent legal theory of labor violation.")

N.L.R.B. v. Dynatron/ Bondo Corp., 176 F.3d 1310 (11th Cir. 1999)("Finding of National Labor Relations Board (NLRB), that employee terminated ostensibly for insubordination and using profane language was actually terminated because of anti-union animus, and that employer thus violated NLRA, was supported by substantial evidence, including evidence that employee received harsher treatment than other employees who committed similar offenses.")

N.L.R.B. v. State of Fla., Dept. of Business Regulation, Div. of Pari-Mutuel Wagering, 868 F.2d 391 (11th Cir. 1989)("District court properly granted preliminary injunctive relief to National Labor Relations Board to enjoin enforcement of state court order requiring jai alai players to comply with state regulation and give 15 days notice before striking because state court order interfered with activity regulated by National Labor Relations Act.")

Patel v. Quality Inn South, 846 F.2d 700 (11th Cir. 1988)("Undocumented alien was 'employee' entitled to protections of Fair Labor Standards Act; Immigration Reform and Control Act making it unlawful to hire illegal aliens and providing sanctions against employers who did so did not repeal or amend Fair Labor Standards Act.")

Lobo v. Celebrity Cruises, Inc., 704 F.3d 882 (11th Cir. 2013)("'Hybrid claim' is type of claim in which employee simultaneously asserts (1) claim against employer pursuant to Labor Management Relations Act (LMRA) for breach of collective bargaining agreement (CBA), and (2) claim against union, which claim is implied under National Labor Relations Act (NLRA), for breach of union's duty of fair representation.")

Stewart v. Spirit Airlines, Inc., 503 Fed.Appx. 814 (11th Cir. 2013) ("Pilot's allegations that he was subject to anti-union animus by airline's termination of him for recording his disciplinary hearing, in effort to initiate new custom or practice within airline of allowing employees to record fact-finding meetings prior to imposing discipline, did not state claim, under RLA provision prohibiting carriers from interfering with employee's efforts to join, organize, or assist in organizing union or exercise right to organize and bargain collectively, since pilot's effort to initiate new custom of allowing employees to record fact-finding meetings was not union-organizing activity.")

N.L.R.B. v. Triple A Fire Protection, Inc., 136 F.3d 727 (11th Cir. 1998) ("Employer's repeated efforts to deal directly with employees outside normal channels of collective bargaining, by attempting to dissuade them from supporting union and creating incentives for them to abandon support for union, were per se violations of NLRA sections prohibiting employer from interfering with exercise of rights guaranteed by NLRA and from refusing to bargain collectively with employee's representatives.... Employer's refusal to negotiate with union in fact as to any subject which is within scope of matters concerning which employer and union have statutory duty to bargain collectively, and about which union seeks to negotiate, violates statute prohibiting employer from refusing to bargain collectively with representatives of employees, though employer has every desire to reach agreement with union upon over-all collective agreement and earnestly and in all good faith bargains to that end.")

N.L.R.B. v. Austal USA, LLC, 343 Fed.Appx. 448 (11th Cir. 2009)

("Substantial evidence supported decision of the National Labor Relations Board (NLRB) that employer had violated the National Labor Relations Act (NLRA) when it suspended pro-union employee prior to a union election, although employer argued that it suspended employee because of his work performance, where an administrative law judge (ALJ) made an adverse credibility finding against employer, based on its shifting rationale, and credited employee's testimony that employer put him in a position where he could not properly perform because of his union activities.")

Florida Bd. Of Business Regulation Dept. of Business Regulation, Div. of Pari-Mutuel Wagering v. N.L.R.B., 686 F.2d 1362 (11th Cir. 1982)("Once National Labor Relations Board properly asserted its jurisdiction over labor dispute in state-regulated jai alai industry, Board's jurisdiction was exclusive with respect to actions arising under sections 8, 9, 10 of the National Labor Relations Act, including all charges of unfair labor practices by employers or labor organizations and all petitions for representation elections, and neither federal courts, excepted by way of review or on application by Board, nor state administrative agency, nor state courts might assume control over them.").

U.S. Fifth Circuit Court of Appeals (Louisiana, Mississippi, Texas)

Watkins v. United Steel Workers of America, Local No. 2369, 516 F.2d 41 (5th Cir. 1975)("Even if 'last hire, first fired' and 'last fired, first rehired' provisions of negotiated seniority system were discriminatory, such system was exempt from being an unlawful employment practice where system was not the result of an intention to discriminate…. Express intent of provision of Civil Rights Act of 1964 that it shall not be an unlawful employment practice for employer to apply different conditions or privileges of employment pursuant to bona fide seniority or merit system provided that such differences are not the result of an intention to discriminate was to preserve contractual rights of seniority as between whites and persons who had not suffered any effects of discrimination.")

U.S. v. Hayes Intern. Corp., 456 F.2d 112 (5th Cir. 1972)("Any employment disadvantage presently operating against incumbent Negroes employed by particular employer due to past discriminatory practices violated Title VII of Civil Rights Act of 1964 and should be eliminated by giving Negroes opportunity to compete for openings in the 'white jobs' on basis of their ability to perform and plant seniority without regard to the seniority expectations of junior white employees.")

Pettway v. American Cast Iron Pipe Co., 494 F.2d 211 (5th Cir. 1974) ("Where employer's discriminatory testing requirements for eligibility to supervisory positions of leadman and foreman were dropped before commencement of black employees' action under equal employment opportunity provisions of Civil Rights Act of 1964 and employer represented that black employees were thereafter qualified and being considered for such positions, case would be remanded for taking of evidence on issue whether selection of such supervisory personnel on basis of subjective judgment of all-white superintendents was operating independently of testing to discriminate against black employees.")

CHAPTER SEVEN (UNION DUTY OF FAIR REPRESENTATION)

U.S. Supreme Court

Steele v. Louisville & N.R. Co., 323 U.S. 192, 65 S. Ct. 226, 89 L. Ed. 173 (1944)(A trade-union chosen as bargaining representative under Railway Labor Act which discriminates on the ground of race against members of a craft or class represented by it, irrespective of whether they are members of the union, may be enjoined and union members may also be enjoined from taking the benefit of such discriminatory action, and the railroad is not bound by or entitled to take the benefit of a contract which the bargaining representative is prohibited by statute from making.")

Vaca v. Sipes, 386 U.S. 171, 87 S.Ct. 903 (1967)("Employee may seek judicial enforcement of his contractual rights where union has sole power under collective bargaining contract to invoke higher stages of grievance procedure and employee has been prevented from exhausting contractual remedies by union's wrongful refusal to process the grievance…. Wrongfully discharged employee may bring action against his employer in face of defense based on failure to exhaust contractual remedies, provided employee can prove that union as bargaining agent, breached its duty of fair representation in handling of employee's grievance, even assuming that breach of duty by union is an unfair labor practice.")

Breininger v. Sheet Metal Workers Intern. Ass'n Local Union No. 6, 493 U.S. 67, 110 S.Ct. 424 (1989)("Claim against union that union breached its duty of fair representation does not require that employee bring concomitant claim against employer that employer breached collective-bargaining agreement.")

Marquez v. Screen Actors Guild, Inc., 525 U.S. 33, 119 S.Ct. 292 (1998)("Duty of fair representation requires a union to serve the interests of all members without hostility or discrimination toward any, to exercise its discretion with complete good faith and honesty, and to avoid arbitrary conduct…. Union breaches the duty of fair representation when its conduct toward a member of the bargaining unit is arbitrary, discriminatory, or in bad faith…. For purposes of its duty of fair representation, union's conduct can be classified as 'arbitrary' only when it is irrational; when it is without a rational basis or explanation….")

U.S. Eleventh Circuit Court of Appeals (Alabama, Florida, Georgia)

Parker v. Connors Steel Co., 855 F.2d 1510 (11th Cir. 1988)("Nature of duty of fair representation which union owes its members is determined by considering context in which duty is asserted, and thus, duty of fair representation in context of negotiations may be determined by different standard than is duty owed in processing of grievances or ratification of concession agreements.... Violation of union's duty of fair representation in context of negotiations with company is established if union's conduct in negotiations is arbitrary, irrational, or undertaken in bad faith.... Company's duty to bargain in good faith with union does not require it to enter collective bargaining agreement that it finds unacceptable.")

Erkins v. United Steelworkers of America, AFL-CIO-CLC, 723 F.2d 837 (11th Cir. 1984)("In suit for breach of collective bargaining agreement, state contract law provides applicable limitations period.... Union members' class action against union for its alleged breach of duty of fair representation was subject to six-month statute of limitations established in National Labor Relations Act, and thus, as members admitted that they discovered facts constituting evidence of alleged fraud and breach of duty more than six months prior to bringing of suit, action was time barred.")

Harris v. Schwerman Trucking Co., 668 F.2d 1204 (11th Cir. 1982) ("In order to establish that a union has breached its duty of fair representation it must be shown that union's handling of a grievance was either arbitrary, discriminatory, or in bad faith.... Union is allowed considerable latitude in its representation of employees; the grievance and arbitration process is not conducted in a judicial forum and union representatives are not held to strict standards of trial advocacy and neither negligence on part of union nor a mistake in judgment is sufficient to support a claim that union acted in an arbitrary and perfunctory manner.")

Higdon v. United Steelworkers of America, AFL-CIO-CLC, 706 F.2d 1561 (11th Cir. 1983)("Union did not breach its duty of fair representation by failing to investigate argument between employee and customer since employee was discharged for insubordination and failure to follow instructions to submit a report concerning the incident, and not for his role in the argument.... Union did not breach its duty of fair representation simply by allegedly failing to give grievant employee notice of, and opportunity to attend, a segment of his grievance process.... Negligence does not constitute a breach of duty of fair representation.... Evidence did not support employee's allegation that union acted discriminatorily or in bad faith while handling his grievance in which it chose not to proceed to final step of arbitration.")

U.S. Fifth Circuit Court of Appeals (Louisiana, Mississippi, Texas)

Turner v. Air Transport Dispatchers' Ass'n, 468 F.2d 297 (5th Cir. 1972) (Union's duty of fair representation does not confer an absolute right on an employee to have his complaint carried through all stages of the grievance procedure; employee is subject to union's nonarbitrary discretionary power to settle, abandon, or fail to file a grievance, even if it can be later demonstrated that the employee's claim was meritorious.... Union's duty of fair representation includes an obligation to investigate and to ascertain the merit of employee's grievances, but further investigation is unnecessary when it appears that the only difference between employee and employer concerns interpretation of collective bargaining agreement and not dispute over facts.")

Freeman v. O'Neal Steel, Inc., 609 F.2d 1123 (5th Cir. 1980)("It is within union's discretion to discontinue grievance procedure prior to selection of an arbitrator, but such discretion is not boundless and is confined by duty to investigate grievance and determine its merit.")

Grovner v. Georgia-Pacific Corp., 625 F.2d 1289 (5th Cir. 1980)("To prevail on claim that union breached its duty of fair representation, discharged employee must demonstrate that union's conduct was arbitrary, discriminatory or in bad faith or that union discharged its duties in a perfunctory manner.")

Guerra v. Manchester Terminal Corp., 498 F.2d 641 (5th Cir. 1974) ("A plaintiff does not lose his rights to an adjudication regarding causes of action created by Title VII of the Civil Rights Act of 1964 or the Civil Rights Act of 1866 simply because the conduct of which he complains also is an unfair labor practice.... Employment discrimination may be prosecuted simultaneously in the courts and before the National Labor Relations Board. National Labor Relations Act, § 8 as amended....")

U.S. Sixth Circuit Court of Appeals (Kentucky, Tennessee, Michigan)

Farmer v. ARA Services, Inc., 660 F.2d 1096 (6th Cir. 1981)("Bad faith or fraud is not necessary element of charge of unfair representation if union's conduct is otherwise arbitrary or perfunctory.... Arbitrary perfunctory union conduct which exhibits something more than negligence is breach of duty of fair representation.")

U.S. Seventh Circuit Court of Appeals (Illinois, Indiana, Wisconsin)

Babrocky v. Jewel Food Co., 773 F.2d 857 (7th Cir. 1985)(Establishing a prima facie Title VII claim against a union based on a breach of duty of fair representation requires union members to show that employer violated collective bargaining agreement with respect to union members, that union permitted the breach to go unrepaired, thus breaching its own duty of fair representation, and some indication that union's actions were motivated by discriminatory animus.... Allegations that union joined in employer's maintenance of sex-segregated job category through its operation of its hiring hall and its acquiescence in instituting the 1:4 ratio of male meat cutters to female meat wrappers which employer allegedly relied on to justify laying off only women were sufficient to establish a prima facie case of Title VII discrimination against union.")

Waters v. Wisconsin Steel Works of Intern Harvester Co., 502 F.2d 1309 (7th Cir. 1974)("Worker complaining that his right to enter into employment contract with company on same basis as whites was impaired by joint action of the union and company had standing to sue under 1866 civil rights statute though he was nonmember of union.... In fashioning substantive body of law under 1866 civil rights statute, courts should, in effort to avoid undesirable substantive law conflicts, look to principles of law created under equal employment opportunity legislation for direction.")

U.S. Eight Circuit Court of Appeals (Arkansas, Iowa)

Donnell v. General Motors Corp., 576 F.2d 1292 98th Cir. 1978) ("In Title VII employment discrimination action brought on ground that employer and union had discriminated against plaintiff with respect to entry into skilled trades' training programs established by employer and union, plaintiff established prima facie case of racial discrimination on basis that educational requirements for the programs had a disparate impact on black employees at employer's plant.")

U.S. Tenth Circuit Court of Appeals (Colorado, Kansas, Oklahoma, New Mexico)

York v. American Tel. & Tel. Co., 95 F.3d 948 (10th Cir. 1996)("To establish a prima facie Title VII claim against union for breach of its duty of fair representation, plaintiff must show that: employer violated collective bargaining agreement with respect to plaintiff; union permitted violation to go unrepaired, thereby breaching union's duty of fair representation, and there was some indication that union's actions were motivated by discriminatory animus…. Union's statutory duty of fair representation does not oblige it to take action on every grievance brought by every member."

www.ingramcontent.com/pod-product-compliance
Lightning Source LLC
Chambersburg PA
CBHW020625220526
45464CB00001B/25